OLD TESTAMENT
THEOLOGY

T0339351

OLD TESTAMENT THEOLOGY

READING THE HEBREW BIBLE AS CHRISTIAN SCRIPTURE

R. W. L. Moberly

Baker Academic

a division of Baker Publishing Group
Grand Rapids, Michigan

© 2013 by R. W. L. Moberly

Published by Baker Academic
a division of Baker Publishing Group
P.O. Box 6287, Grand Rapids, MI 49516-6287
www.bakeracademic.com

Paperback edition published 2015
ISBN 978-0-8010-9772-0

Printed in the United States of America

The Library of Congress has cataloged the hardcover edition as follows:
Moberly, R. W. L.
    Old Testament theology : reading the Hebrew Bible as Christian scripture /
R. W. L. Moberly.
        pages cm
    Includes bibliographical references and index.
    ISBN 978-0-8010-4885-2 (cloth)
    1. Bible. Old Testament—Theology. I. Title.
BS1192.5.M64 2013
230′.0411—dc23   2013017369

To Jon Levenson,
wise biblical interpreter and interfaith interlocutor

Contents

Preface

In this book I discuss some of the scriptural content that I have thought about, prayed about, given addresses about, and taught for the last twenty years or so. I have written some earlier and shorter versions of the subject matter of each chapter, though each chapter here is a genuinely new discussion. Those who know me may recognize some of the songs that I sing. I hope that the book's content, like a good wine, may have acquired some depth and flavor through the long period of its being aged and matured in the mental cellar.

The book is also a sequel and complement to my work *The Theology of the Book of Genesis* (Cambridge: Cambridge University Press, 2009). Both there and here I try to model a way of doing Old Testament theology that is built around a dialectic between ancient text and contemporary questions, within a Christian frame of reference that is alert to other frames of reference. In the earlier book the readings of the biblical text are restricted to Genesis; here they range (selectively) across the canon of Hebrew scripture; also the readings here are fuller and more detailed than was possible in the earlier book.

Although I had made a start on the book earlier, most of it was written in the spring and summer of 2012, while I was on regular research leave. I am grateful to my colleagues for taking over many of my responsibilities so as to give me space and time to write. As usual, I did not travel on my research leave but remained in the congenial context of Abbey House, with books and friends (and a wonderful view of the cathedral) readily accessible.

I am, as always, deeply grateful to friends who have read drafts of the material and suggested improvements. My wife, Jenny, meticulously read everything and helped improve my clarity of thought and expression. David Day warned me when I was in danger of becoming too heavy for the non-specialist reader. Richard Briggs gave me some "aha!" moments for improving my argument. Anthony Bash ruthlessly weeded out some of my irritating and redundant English idioms of which I had ceased to be aware. Patrick Morrow gave me some wonderful insights from the rabbis and helped fine-tune some of what I'm trying to say. Even if I did not incorporate all their wisdom, I hope they will all find that the text has improved since they read it. As ever, though, only I can be blamed for my decisions and delinquencies. I am grateful also to Jon Parker, who as my research assistant for some of the time made access to some of the bibliography much easier. (If only I too could be as computer literate as my research students.)

I have much appreciated the publishing process with Baker Academic. Jim Kinney has been a congenial colleague at conferences for many years, and I am happy to show concrete appreciation for his wining and dining me! He has also valuably contributed to the shape of this book. Brian Bolger has been a helpful and responsive editor, a pleasure to work with. Finally, I am grateful for the local help of my friend Douglas Earl for his compilation of the indexes.

Abbreviations

Old Testament

Gen.	Genesis	Song	Song of Songs
Exod.	Exodus	Isa.	Isaiah
Lev.	Leviticus	Jer.	Jeremiah
Num.	Numbers	Lam.	Lamentations
Deut.	Deuteronomy	Ezek.	Ezekiel
Josh.	Joshua	Dan.	Daniel
Judg.	Judges	Hosea	Hosea
Ruth	Ruth	Joel	Joel
1–2 Sam.	1–2 Samuel	Amos	Amos
1–2 Kings	1–2 Kings	Obad.	Obadiah
1–2 Chron.	1–2 Chronicles	Jon.	Jonah
Ezra	Ezra	Mic.	Micah
Neh.	Nehemiah	Nah.	Nahum
Esth.	Esther	Hab.	Habakkuk
Job	Job	Zeph.	Zephaniah
Ps./Pss.	Psalm/Psalms	Hag.	Haggai
Prov.	Proverbs	Zech.	Zechariah
Eccles.	Ecclesiastes	Mal.	Malachi

New Testament

Matt.	Matthew	1–2 Cor.	1–2 Corinthians
Mark	Mark	Gal.	Galatians
Luke	Luke	Eph.	Ephesians
John	John	Phil.	Philippians
Acts	Acts	Col.	Colossians
Rom.	Romans	1–2 Thess.	1–2 Thessalonians

1–2 Tim.	1–2 Timothy	1–2 Pet.	1–2 Peter
Titus	Titus	1–3 John	1–3 John
Philem.	Philemon	Jude	Jude
Heb.	Hebrews	Rev.	Revelation
James	James		

General

//	parallel to	*BHK*	*Biblia Hebraica*, ed. Rudolf Kittel (Stuttgart: Württembergische Bibelanstalt, 1937)
§/§§	section/s		
AB	Anchor Bible		
ABD	*The Anchor Bible Dictionary*, 6 vols., ed. David Noel Freedman et al. (New York: Doubleday, 1992)	*BHQ*	*Biblia Hebraica Quinta*, ed. A. Schenker et al. (Stuttgart: Deutsche Bibelgesellschaft, 2007–)
ABS	Archaeology and Biblical Studies	*BHS*	*Biblia Hebraica Stuttgartensia*, ed. K. Elliger and W. Rudolph (Stuttgart: Deutsche Bibelgesellschaft, 1967/77)
ACCS	Ancient Christian Commentary on Scripture: Old Testament [series], general ed., Thomas C. Oden (Downers Grove, IL: InterVarsity, 2001–)		
		BibInt	*Biblical Interpretation*
		BibS(N)	Biblische Studien (Neukirchen, 1951–)
AD	anno Domini	BJS	Brown Judaic Studies
ad loc.	*ad locum*, at the place discussed	BLS	Bible and Literature Series
		BO	Berit Olam
		BS	Biblical Seminar
AG	Analecta Gorgiana	*BTB*	*Biblical Theology Bulletin*
ANET	*Ancient Near Eastern Texts Relating to the Old Testament*, ed. James B. Pritchard, 3rd ed. (Princeton, NJ: Princeton University Press, 1969)	*BZ*	*Biblische Zeitschrift*
		BZAW	Beihefte zur Zeitschrift für die alttestamentliche Wissenschaft
		CBQ	*Catholic Biblical Quarterly*
		CBSC	Cambridge Bible for Schools and Colleges
ASOR	American Schools of Oriental Research	*CD*	Karl Barth, *Church Dogmatics*, trans. G. W. Bromiley et al., 13 vols. (Edinburgh: T&T Clark, 1936–77); from German, *Die kirchliche Dogmatik* (Zurich: Theologischer Verlag Zurich, 1932–67)
AT	author's translation		
AV	Authorized Version (= KJV)		
b.	Babylonian Talmud		
BBRS	Bulletin for Biblical Research Supplements		
BC	before Christ		
BDB	*A Hebrew and English Lexicon of the Old Testament*, ed. Francis Brown, S. R. Driver, and Charles A. Briggs (Oxford: Clarendon, 1907)	CEB	Common English Bible
		cf.	*confer*, compare
		chap./chaps.	chapter/chapters
		CSCD	Cambridge Studies in Christian Doctrine

CSsR	Congregatio Sanctissimi Redemptoris, Congregation of the Most Holy Redeemer		and Takamitsu Muraoka, 2 vols., Subsidia biblica 14/I–II (Rome: Pontifical Biblical Institute, 1991)
CWS	Classics of Western Spirituality	JPSBC	Jewish Publication Society Bible Commentary
DCH	*The Dictionary of Classical Hebrew*, 8 vols., ed. David J. A. Clines (Sheffield: Sheffield Academic / Phoenix Press, 1993–2011)	JSNTSS	Journal for the Study of the New Testament: Supplement Series
DH	Deuteronomistic History/ Historian	JSOT	*Journal for the Study of the Old Testament*
ECC	Eerdmans Critical Commentary	JSOTSS	Journal for the Study of the Old Testament: Supplement Series
ed./eds.	editor/s, edited by, edition	JSR	*Journal of Scriptural Reasoning*, http://etext.lib.virginia .edu/journals/ssr/
e.g.	*exempli gratia*, for example		
esp.	especially		
ESV	English Standard Version	JTI	*Journal of Theological Interpretation*
ET	English translation		
etc.	*et cetera*, and the rest	JTIS	Journal of Theological Interpretation Supplements
FAT	Forschungen zum Alten Testament	KD	Karl Barth, *Die kirchliche Dogmatik*. See CD
FOTC	Fathers of the Church		
Gk.	Greek	LBT	Library of Biblical Theology
GKC	*Gesenius' Hebrew Grammar*, ed. E. Kautzsch and A. E. Cowley (Oxford: Clarendon, 1910)	LCL	Loeb Classical Library
		LHBOTS	Library of Hebrew Bible / Old Testament Studies (formerly Journal for the Study of the Old Testament: Supplement Series)
HBM	Hebrew Bible Monographs		
Heb.	Hebrew		
HTR	*Harvard Theological Review*	lit.	literally
HTS	Harvard Theological Studies	LNTS	Library of New Testament Studies
IBCTP	Interpretation: A Bible Commentary for Teaching and Preaching	LXX	Septuagint
		mg.	margin/al
ICC	International Critical Commentary	MT	Masoretic Text
		n/n.	note
i.e.	*id est*, that is	NCB	New Century Bible
intro.	introduction, introduced by	NICOT	New International Commentary on the Old Testament
ISBL	Indiana Studies in Biblical Literature		
		NIV	New International Version (2011)
ITL	The International Theological Library		
		NIVAC	NIV Application Commentary
JB	The Jerusalem Bible		
JBL	*Journal of Biblical Literature*	NJPS	New Jewish Publication Society Translation
JM	*A Grammar of Biblical Hebrew*, by Paul Joüon	NKJV	New King James Version

NRSV	New Revised Standard Version	SBT	Studies in Biblical Theology
NRSVA	New Revised Standard Version, Anglicised	SC	Sources chrétiennes
		SHBC	Smyth & Helwys Bible Commentary
NSCE	New Studies in Christian Ethics	SFSHJ	South Florida Studies in the History of Judaism
NT	New Testament	SJ	Society of Jesus (Jesuit)
OBO	Orbis biblicus et orientalis	SNT	Supplements to Novum Testamentum
OBS	Oxford Bible Series		
OBT	Overtures to Biblical Theology	SOTBT	Studies in Old Testament Biblical Theology
OCD	Discalced Carmelite Order	STAC	Studien und Texte zu Antike und Christentum
OT	Old Testament		
OTG	Old Testament Guides	STI	Studies in Theological Interpretation
OTL	Old Testament Library		
OTT	Old Testament Theology	*TynBul*	*Tyndale Bulletin*
P	Priestly source (of the Pentateuch)	*TDOT*	*Theological Dictionary of the Old Testament*, ed. G. Johannes Botterweck, Helmer Ringgren, and Heinz-Josef Fabry, 15 vols. (Grand Rapids and Cambridge, UK: Eerdmans, 1974–2006; ET from German of 1970–95)
4QSam^a	4QSamuel^a, a Dead Sea Scroll from Qumran Cave 4		
REB	Revised English Bible		
RelSRev	*Religious Studies Review*		
repr.	reprinted (by/of)		
RES	*Répertoire d'épigraphie sémitique*, ed. Jean-Baptiste Chabot and Charles Clermont-Ganneau et al. (Paris: Imprimerie nationale, 1900–1968)	TOTC	Tyndale Old Testament Commentaries
		trans.	translator, translated by
		UCOP	University of Cambridge Oriental Publications
RSV	Revised Standard Version	v./vv.	verse/verses
RV	Revised Version	vol./vols.	volume/volumes
SAC	Studies in Antiquity and Christianity	*VT*	*Vetus Testamentum*
		VTS	Vetus Testamentum: Supplement Series
SBL	Society of Biblical Literature		
SBLDS	Society of Biblical Literature Dissertation Series	WBC	Word Biblical Commentary
		ZAW	*Zeitschrift für die alttestamentliche Wissenschaft*
SBLSS	Society of Biblical Literature Symposium Series		
SBONTNET	Sacred Books of the Old and New Testaments: A New English Translation		

Introduction

In this book I am trying to do two things, corresponding to the two parts of the book's title. In terms of the main title, *Old Testament Theology*, I am contributing to a familiar genre of biblical scholarship, while at the same time modifying it in a way that seems to me appropriate at a time when biblical scholarship is open to new possibilities. Most contributions to Old Testament theology aim to be more or less comprehensive, in some way covering the Old Testament as a whole. Here I am selective and consider only a few passages. However, I hope that these passages are *representative* of Israel's scriptures and allow many of its characteristic and leading concerns to emerge. Indeed, most of the standard topics that one would expect to find in an Old Testament theology—God, monotheism, idolatry, election, covenant, torah, prophecy, psalms, wisdom—do appear in the pages that follow, despite some notable absences, such as creation or sacrifice.

In terms of the subtitle, *Reading the Hebrew Bible as Christian Scripture*, I want to give prime place to issues of hermeneutics. On the one hand I take with full seriousness the fact that Israel's scriptures were written in Hebrew and collected, collated, and used before Christianity appeared in history (hence the wording *Hebrew Bible*). On the other hand, I take with equal seriousness the fact that these documents have been, and still are, received and privileged by Christians in such a way as to function authoritatively for Christian faith (hence *Christian Scripture*). The difficult question of how best to hold these two perspectives together has, in one way or another, been central to much modern biblical scholarship. Within their own frame of reference, a growing number of Jewish biblical scholars also face these questions as they seek to combine ancient historical perspectives on their foundational documents with viewpoints from rabbinic and post-rabbinic reception, and also to probe the

1

relationship between Scripture and halakah. The current scholarly context is made more complex by the growing number of scholars who, because of their particular interests, may be uninterested in—or who, because of their ideological anxieties, may be actively resistant to—continuing reception of Israel's scriptures as either privileged or authoritative. Whatever the biblical scholar's perspective, however, hermeneutical decisions are inescapable (hence *Reading . . . as*).

The Role of Hermeneutics

The importance of basic hermeneutical decisions, focused in the notion of *reading as*, is nicely spelled out by Richard Briggs:

> Rather than talking bluntly about what "scripture is" . . . we might better learn to speak of "scripture as" whenever we want to offer judgments or criteria regarding the responsible interpretation of scripture. . . . The shift from "is" to "as" represents, in my judgment, one of the most fundamental hermeneutical contributions to reflection on the nature of human interpretation of the world and texts around us. . . . Garrett Green, in one of the most sustained theological treatments of the matter, offers the notion that it is the shift from Kant's "copula of judgement" ("is") to the "copula of imagination" ("as"). . . . The postmodern mood, at least arguably, blurs the huge significance of "as/is" into a vague sense of everything being open to ideological and political spin, which is not untrue as far as it goes, but is rather an occasional social consequence of what is going on and not the fundamental point at stake.[1]

With specific reference to biblical interpretation, one insight that has emerged with particular clarity in recent years is that there are a variety of legitimate perspectives and questions that may be brought to the study of the biblical text, and these can require differing modes of study. As I once put it: "How we use the Bible depends on why we use the Bible. In practice, many of the disagreements about how are, in effect, disagreements about why, and failure to recognize this leads to endless confusion."[2] A concern to read the

1. Richard S. Briggs, "Biblical Hermeneutics and Scriptural Responsibility," in *The Future of Biblical Interpretation: Responsible Plurality in Biblical Hermeneutics*, ed. Stanley E. Porter and Matthew R. Malcolm (Milton Keynes: Paternoster, 2013), 36–52. The work of Garrett Green, to which reference is made, is his *Imagining God: Theology and the Religious Imagination* (San Francisco: Harper & Row, 1989), 70–74, esp. 73.
2. R. W. L. Moberly, *The Old Testament of the Old Testament*, OBT (Minneapolis: Fortress, 1992; repr., Eugene, OR: Wipf & Stock, 2001), 2. In the first clause I have changed italics to roman type.

Hebrew Bible as Christian Scripture will undoubtedly not be shared by all biblical scholars—though there is always the hope that any mode of biblical study, if well carried out, will still be illuminating to others whose own preferred mode of study is different.

One consequence of my focus on reading the Hebrew Bible as Christian Scripture is that I offer extended reflection on the nature of the varying interpretive decisions that can be made with reference to the particular texts I am studying, in the hope that this will clarify what is, and is not, involved in the proposed reading strategy. Since this present study is selective and representative, further work along the lines proposed here would naturally round out and nuance the general approach. Interestingly, a not-dissimilar recent proposal for a dialogical biblical theology—in which there is interplay between biblical text, historic appropriations, and contemporary theological concerns—comes from a Jewish scholar, Benjamin Sommer.[3] I hope that my approach to reading the Hebrew Bible as Christian Scripture, far from closing down dialogue between Christians and Jews, will contribute to making the dialogue more interesting and worthwhile and help improve the quality of our disagreements as well as agreements.

Of course, theoretical discussion as to the nature of hermeneutics, and about perspectives and strategies for reading, can be extensive. I have made some contribution to such discussions elsewhere and do not propose to add to them here.[4] In any case, my sense of the way biblical scholarship works is that no amount of impressive-sounding discussion of hermeneutical theory or of particular approaches will make much impact until people can see how the proposals work in practice and how they genuinely enable a better grasp of

---

3. Benjamin D. Sommer, "Dialogical Biblical Theology: A Jewish Approach to Reading Scripture Theologically," in *Biblical Theology: Introducing the Conversation*, by Leo G. Perdue, Robert Morgan, and Benjamin D. Sommer, LBT (Nashville: Abingdon, 2009), 1–53. An earlier landmark essay is by Jon Levenson, "Theological Consensus or Historicist Evasion? Jews and Christians in Biblical Studies," in his *The Hebrew Bible, the Old Testament, and Historical Criticism* (Louisville: Westminster John Knox, 1993), 82–105.

4. For example, see my *The Bible, Theology, and Faith*, CSCD (Cambridge: Cambridge University Press, 2000), 1–44; "How May We Speak of God? A Reconsideration of the Nature of Biblical Theology," *TynBul* 53/2 (2002): 177–202; "How Can We Know the Truth? A Study of John 7:14–18," in *The Art of Reading Scripture*, ed. Ellen F. Davis and Richard B. Hays (Grand Rapids: Eerdmans, 2003), 239–57; "Biblical Criticism and Religious Belief," *JTI* 2/1 (2008): 71–100; *The Theology of the Book of Genesis*, OTT (Cambridge: Cambridge University Press, 2009), 1–20; "'Interpret the Bible Like Any Other Book?' Requiem for an Axiom," *JTI* 4/1 (2010): 91–110; "What Is Theological Commentary? An Old Testament Perspective," in *Theological Commentary: Evangelical Perspectives*, ed. R. Michael Allen (London and New York: T&T Clark, 2011), 172–86; "Theological Interpretation, Presuppositions, and the Role of the Church: Bultmann and Augustine Revisited," *JTI* 6/1 (2012): 1–22; "Biblical Hermeneutics and Ecclesial Responsibility," in Porter and Malcolm, eds., *Future of Biblical Interpretation*, 105–25.

particular biblical texts. If there is no such recognition, the learned theoretical discussion will simply gather dust. So my aim in this book is to "get on with it" and offer readings of the Hebrew text of Israel's scriptures that will, I hope, demonstrate the fruitfulness of the overall approach being advocated. I will, however, return briefly to hermeneutical issues in the epilogue by way of reflection on the readings offered.[5]

I think there can be little doubt that, in the nineteenth and twentieth centuries, a distancing of Old Testament study from classic Christian understandings and priorities, and the plausible locating of biblical texts in their likely ancient contexts of origin, had for the most part an enormous positive impact on people's ability to read the familiar texts freshly and with deeper understanding of some of their dimensions. Such fruitfulness constituted a major justification for the mode of study. Unfortunately, the continuation of such study has not always remained as fruitful: it has given rise to its own scholasticisms, with no shortage of specialist scholarly wrangles. My concern here is to retain awareness of the enduring philological and historical insights that have emerged and to recontextualize them within a frame of reference that puts different questions to the texts. My hope is that this attempt to reintegrate Old Testament study with classic Christian understandings and priorities may in its own way have an impact on people's ability to read the biblical texts freshly and to acquire a deeper understanding of some of their dimensions. The "aha!" factor, when one comes to "see" something significant in a text, is always an aspiration for work in the humanities—though it depends not only on the author but also on the reader. If, however, readers who are unpersuaded by my interpretations undertake to offer better interpretations of the biblical passages in question, that also would be a welcome outcome.

Memorandum to the Reader

Each of the eight chapters represents a study of a particular text and/or issue, which can be read on its own. However, the chapters are probably best read sequentially so that a cumulative hearing of significant voices in Old Testament theology, together with a better understanding of the hermeneutical proposals, can then emerge. The sequence of chapters loosely follows the sequence of the Jewish canon: Law, Prophets, Writings.

5. Unfortunately, issues relating to historic Christian appropriation of Israel's scriptures via the Septuagint lie beyond the scope of this study other than in occasional footnote discussions of text and interpretation.

In each chapter there are passages in a smaller font that serve three distinct purposes. Some of them give detailed discussion, often of a philological nature, in support of a contention in the main argument. Some of them constitute an excursus, a discussion of an issue related to the main argument but not essential to it. Some of them give an example of a contemporary issue that illustrates what is being said about the content of the biblical text. A reader who just wants to follow the main argument could omit these smaller-font passages since the argument resumes after these excursions at the point where it was before them. However, I hope that most readers will find the content of these smaller-font passages worthwhile.

When referring to God, I consistently capitalize pronouns and possessives ("He," "His"). This is partly because such capitalization is an ancient reverential practice, which I consider to be valuable (even if unfashionable). It is comparable to the reverential use of "the LORD" or "YHWH" so as not to use a vocalized form of the name of Israel's God ("Yahweh"), an ancient Jewish practice widely observed by Christian translators of Israel's scriptures, which I also follow. However, the capitalization is also because of the contentious contemporary issue of gendered language in relation to God. God is beyond gender, yet religious language must use analogical language drawn from life in the world. As I use the capitalized "He," I seek to stand in continuity with the Old Testament's own use of the masculine pronoun, while recognizing that God is not masculine in human terms. Although the Old Testament does not develop the point that God transcends gender, the combined absence of a consort for YHWH and rejection of the notion of feminine deities in the canonical texts, whatever may have been going on in Israelite religion on the ground, suggests that the classic understanding of God's transcendence of gender is rooted (tacitly? incipiently?) in those Hebrew texts that have been received as authoritative by Jews and Christians.

I do not presuppose a knowledge of Hebrew on the part of the reader, though I hope that the periodic discussions of Hebrew usage, in transliteration, may encourage the Hebrew-less reader to start learning. My chosen general-purpose system of transliteration is user-friendly: I indicate long vowels and vowel letters with a macron (ā), very short vowels with a breve (ĕ), and minimize diacritical marks (e.g., *shūv* rather than *šûb*, to indicate that the Hebrew word for "turn/repent" is pronounced *shoov*). Those who know Hebrew do not need extra diacritics (even if they may quite properly prefer them), while those who do not know Hebrew may find them puzzling. The one exception is the use of *ḥ* to indicate a hard "h," as in Loch Ness.

Although I work from the Hebrew text of Israel's scriptures in *Biblia Hebraica Stuttgartensia*, I cite the biblical text in the English translation provided by the NRSV (except as noted). Where I think the translation is problematic, I signal that by dotted underlining in my citation (e.g., m̤a̤i̤d̤e̤n̤s̤), explain what I consider preferable, and say why. However, I only pick out problematic text-critical and philological issues when it makes a difference to my argument: I do not want to clutter the text and footnotes or allow the wood to be obscured by the trees.

1

A Love Supreme

Where is a good place to begin if one wishes to hear the primary and most resonant voices of the Hebrew Bible? There are many possible starting points. One could certainly do worse than begin at the beginning with Genesis 1, since this majestic account of God's creative work, together with its depiction of humanity as made "in the image of God," introduces and frames all that follows in the canonical collection and continues to have enormous resonance. Nonetheless I propose that one can fruitfully start elsewhere, with one particular passage whose foundational and focal nature can readily be demonstrated—Deuteronomy 6:4–9, widely known by its Jewish name (derived from its first word in the Hebrew), the Shema.[1]

Introduction to the Shema

In the Shema, Moses, who is the speaking voice throughout Deuteronomy, says:

> [4]Hear, O Israel: The LORD is our God, the LORD alone.[a] [5]You shall love the LORD your God with all your heart, and with all your soul, and with all your might.

In this chapter I develop three of my earlier studies: "Toward an Interpretation of the Shema," in *Theological Exegesis: Essays in Honor of Brevard S. Childs*, ed. Christopher R. Seitz and Kathryn Greene-McCreight (Grand Rapids: Eerdmans, 1999), 124–44; "How Appropriate Is 'Monotheism' as a Category for Biblical Interpretation?" in *Early Jewish and Christian Monotheism*, ed. Loren T. Stuckenbruck and Wendy E. S. North, JSNTSS 263 (London and New York: T&T Clark, 2004), 216–34; and "Pentateuch" in *The New Interpreter's Dictionary of the Bible: Me–R*, vol. 4, ed. Katharine Doob Sakenfeld (Nashville: Abingdon, 2009), 436–37.

1. "The Shema" is really shorthand for the name of the historic Jewish practice of daily prayer, the *Qěrī'at-Shěma'*, which is classically composed of Deut. 6:4–9; 11:13–21; and Num. 15:37–41, together with certain blessings (somewhat abbreviated in some recent Jewish practice).

⁶Keep these words that I am commanding you today in your heart. ⁷Recite them to your children and talk about them when you are at home and when you are away, when you lie down and when you rise. ⁸Bind them as a sign on your hand, fix them as an emblem on your forehead, ⁹and write them on the doorposts of your house and on your gates.

ᵃ Or, the LORD our God is one LORD; or, the LORD our God, the LORD is one; or, the LORD is our God, the LORD is one.

The primary importance of this paragraph is indicated in three interrelated ways. First and most broadly, its history of reception and use is enormous. Down the centuries countless Jews have recited these words morning and night (following the rabbinic construal of v. 7b), and many have used these words as their dying words, not least when they have been killed for being Jews. It is within this Jewish context that Jesus stands when he singles out 6:4–5 as the commandment that is "first of all," that is, of supreme importance (Mark 12:28–30).

Second, the contextualization of these words within Deuteronomy means that they appear in the Old Testament's most systematic account of the relationship between YHWH and Israel, whose perspectives inform substantial parts of the histories and the prophetic literature. Moreover, within Deuteronomy itself, these words are the keynote of Moses's exposition of the covenant between YHWH and Israel. They are the first thing Moses says after being appointed as prophet/mediator between YHWH and Israel, which happens after YHWH's direct address to Israel in the Ten Commandments is felt by Israel to be overwhelming (Deut. 5:22–33). The Shema follows a prefatory "Now this is the commandment . . . that the LORD your God charged me to teach you" (6:1).

Third, there is the straightforward implication of the wording of 6:4–9 in itself. First, YHWH, and YHWH alone, is presented as the appropriate recipient of Israel's undivided allegiance (vv. 4–5). Then "these words" that Moses commands are of such importance that they are to be kept in mind, taught to the next generation, discussed constantly, displayed upon one's person, and inscribed upon the entrances to both private and public spaces (vv. 6–9). It is hard to imagine greater emphasis than this being laid upon the significance of the Shema. Thus the history of its use and also its weighty contextual location are fully appropriate to the content of the Shema in itself.

One of the almost inescapable drawbacks of the regular use, or common knowledge, of famous biblical passages is that people can, through routine, become dulled as to the often-astonishing implications of the material. So it is worth trying to highlight the enormity of what the Shema says.

For some years my son and I have been regular supporters of one of the leading football (i.e., soccer) clubs in the North East of England, Sunderland

AFC. The junior supporters' club, of which he was a member while under sixteen, is called 24–7, the common contemporary idiom for "all the time." The club magazine is called *A Love Supreme*. I confess that I note these names with a certain wry amusement and do not take them seriously; nor, I imagine, do numerous other Sunderland supporters (despite the passion with which many in the North East follow football), for we know what it is to live in a culture of linguistic inflation. And yet the idea of a love supreme that is for all the time is exactly that of which the Shema speaks; it is something that millions down the ages have taken with full seriousness. That is the content to which any worthwhile discussion must try to do justice.

Toward Establishing a Context for Interpreting the Shema

All attempts to discuss the Shema face two basic problems: translation and contextualization. Initially, therefore, it will be appropriate briefly to outline both these problems and the characteristic interpretations of the text to which they give rise.

The Problem of Translation

After the initial, and straightforward, invocation "Hear, O Israel," there is more than one way of rendering the words that follow. Most modern translations, like the NRSV (cited above), offer in a margin/footnote at least three renderings other than that in the main text—though the various options tend to reduce to two main alternatives, in both of which it is clear that the final word *'eḥād* is in some way being predicated of Israel's God.

The difficulty of translation arises from two factors. One is the fact that the Hebrew text is a noun clause consisting of four words with no verb: *yhwh 'ĕlōhēnū yhwh 'eḥād*. It is regular Hebrew idiom to dispense with the verb if the clause in question is a subject-predicate clause in which the implied verb is some form of the verb "to be" ("A is B"). So almost all translators assume, surely rightly, that 6:4 presents such a subject-predicate clause. The problem is that it is not fully clear what is the subject and what is the predicate, a difficulty not helped by the fact that in Hebrew word order the predicate may either precede or follow the subject. All the translation variants arise from differing decisions as to subject and predicate. Nonetheless, despite differences, almost all interpreters agree that the final term, *'eḥād*, is in some way being predicated of Israel's deity.[2]

The other difficulty is the sense to be ascribed to the final word, *'eḥād*. Should it have its common numerical sense, "one," or does the context require it to have a different sense, such as "alone"?[3]

2. The sole apparent use of the wording of Deut. 6:4 elsewhere in the OT, in Zech. 14:9—"And the LORD will become king over all the earth; on that day the LORD will be one [*'eḥād*] and his name one [*'eḥād*]"—clearly takes "one" as the substantive predicate but does not clarify its precise sense.

3. Hebrew more readily expresses "alone" with *bādād* than with *'eḥād*, as in Deut. 32:12, *yhwh bādād yanḥennū* ("YHWH alone led him" [AT]).

Views differ as to which of these senses should be chosen.[4] Historically, the rendering "one" has predominated. For example, the LXX renders *'eḥād* by *heis* (one): *kyrios ho theos hēmōn kyrios heis estin.* Elsewhere it expresses "You are God/Lord alone" with *monos* (alone): *sy ei ho theos/kyrios monos* (Ps. 85:10 [86:10 ET]; 4 Regnorum 19:15 [2 Kings 19:15]).

Of the two main alternatives, one is "The LORD is our God, the LORD alone."[5] The other is "The LORD our God, the LORD is one." The apparent difference in meaning is that the sense of the former concerns *the relationship between YHWH and Israel.* The point is that their relationship is to be exclusive, which is a primary and recurrent concern in Deuteronomy; in such a formulation, however, it is compatible with recognition of a plurality of deities ("whatever other deities there may be, Israel must adhere to YHWH alone"). In the latter rendering the text is saying something about *YHWH Himself.* The point is that He is "one"; whatever precisely that may mean, it has regularly been taken to be a *locus classicus* for biblical monotheism[6]—and correspondingly, the denial of the existence of any other deity.[7] Thus the difference between the translations is apparently weighty.

The Problem of Contextualization (1): Living Tradition as Context for Interpretation

The basic problem of understanding that is focused in translation is compounded by another basic problem: what is considered to be the appropriate context for interpreting the passage? To try to clarify some of the issues at stake, I will outline three differing approaches.

One of the fundamental rules that we learn in biblical studies, as in the humanities generally, is "Interpret a text in its context." This simple-sounding principle, however, obscures the difficulty that there is more than one context for most significant texts, especially biblical texts.[8] In the case of the Shema in particular, the question "Which context?" is both weighty and contested.

4. I have discussed the translation more fully in my "'Yahweh Is One': The Translation of the Shema," in *Studies in the Pentateuch*, ed. J. A. Emerton, VTS 61 (Leiden: Brill, 1990), 209–15; repr. in my *From Eden to Golgotha: Essays in Biblical Theology*, SFSHJ 52 (Atlanta: Scholars Press, 1992), 75–81. A good recent discussion of translation is by Lucien-Jean Bord and David Hamidovic, "Écoute Israël (Deut. VI 4)," *VT* 52/1 (2002):13–29.

5. Thus major contemporary translations such as the NRSV and NJPS. The CEB varies the form but not the sense: "Our God is the LORD! Only the LORD!"

6. This traditional translation and interpretation is still advocated by, e.g., Robert Alter: "The statement stands, then, as it has been traditionally construed, as a ringing declaration of monotheism" (*The Five Books of Moses* [New York and London: W. W. Norton, 2004], 912).

7. The issues for monotheism posed by these two renderings in the OT will be discussed toward the end of this chapter.

8. See further chap. 5 below, "Isaiah and Jesus."

For much of Jewish and Christian history, a common working assumption has been that the biblical canon as a whole, within the life and worship of an observant/believing community, provides the context for any particular verse; moreover, this context can include theological understandings and formulations that have arisen in post-biblical discussions. There is a long history of theological and philosophical reflection on what is entailed by God's being "one" and on the nature of the "love" that should be directed to Him.

For Jews, unsurprisingly, the wording of the Shema has acquired its own existence in life and liturgy. It is, as Gunther Plaut puts it, "an example of original text and later tradition coalescing and impinging upon each other to a remarkable degree." Plaut goes on to speak of the Shema as richly meaningful:

> The *Shema* thus came to be like a precious gem, in that the light of faith made its words sparkle with rich brilliance of varied colors. Negatively, it underscored the Jew's opposition to polytheism and pagan ethics, to the dualism of the Zoroastrians, the pantheism of the Greeks, and the trinitarianism of the Christians. Positively, the One God was seen to imply one humanity and therefore demanded the brotherhood of all; it spoke of the world as the stage for the ethical life and linked monotheism and morality. It meant that God undergirded all laws for nature and for mankind; hence heaven and earth as well as human history were His domain. . . . These principles were seen by generations of Jews as rays shining forth from the *Shema*, as from a diamond set into a crown of faith and proven true and enduring in human history.[9]

Time-honored issues (Jewish resistance to polytheism, pantheism, or trinitarianism) and contemporary concerns (affirmation of monotheism and morality) come together in this jewel of great and enduring value.

Somewhat comparably, Michael Fishbane concludes the introductory chapter to his recent *Jewish Theology* thus:

> When we think of Jewish theology and its various components, we are put in mind of its most central statement of principle. This is stated in scripture and has been repeatedly interpreted over the ages. [Citation of Deut. 6:4–9 follows.]
>
> Such is the theological charge: to affirm God in one's life, through mind and heart and deed, through teaching and interpretation everywhere; and to cultivate a mindfulness of this duty through signs and symbols, so that one will always be reminded of the sanctity of the body and its actions—in the home (as the domain of one's family and future generations) and in the city (as the domain of society and the sphere of interpersonal values). A modern Jewish

9. W. Gunther Plaut, *The Torah: A Modern Commentary* (New York: Union of American Hebrew Congregations: 1981), 1365, 1369–70.

theology will do this in its own distinctive way, resonant with our contemporary sensibilities and mind-set.[10]

The Shema still functions today as a fundamental articulation of the responsibilities of Jewish life and thought.

In a Christian frame of reference, one cannot find sentiments comparable to those of Plaut or Fishbane. Historic Christian use of the Shema has been both less in extent and more complexly refracted than Jewish use; and perhaps most important, the Shema has not featured in the practices of everyday Christian life. Christian use has predominantly had two concerns: on the one hand, the oneness of God in 6:4, and on the other hand, love for God in verse 5.

For example, in Christian theology there has regularly been a felt need to show that the affirmation of God as "one" is compatible with a trinitarian understanding of God—or even, that it underwrites it. Jaroslav Pelikan, for example, considers that for the Cappadocian fathers in the fourth century AD, the "monotheism" of Deuteronomy 6:4 was "the bulwark of the Nicene dogma of the Trinity," and "the orthodox dogma of the Trinity . . . [was] the only way to vindicate the Shema, in the face of the Christian worship of Christ as divine."[11]

In his famous work *The Trinity*, Hilary of Poitiers, a contemporary of the Cappadocians, discusses this passage in relation to Arian denial of the deity of Jesus. Hilary reads Deuteronomy 6:4 as mediated by the New Testament, not least by the language and thought of 1 Corinthians 8:6 ("For us there is one God, the Father, from whom are all things, . . . and one Lord, Jesus Christ, through whom are all things"—a passage that indeed appears to be an explicitly Christian reformulating of the Shema in such a way as to include Jesus).[12] He sees these passages together as directly bearing upon the Arian controversy. In this way he well exemplifies living and contemporary ecclesial faith as one prime context for interpretation:

> This is their [the Arians'] central doctrine: "We know that there is only one God, for Moses has declared: 'Hear, O Israel, the Lord thy God is one.'" Has anyone dared to raise any doubts about this doctrine? Has any one of those who believe in God been heard to teach anything else except that there is one God, from whom are all things, one power without birth, and this one power

10. Michael Fishbane, *Sacred Attunement: A Jewish Theology* (Chicago and London: Chicago University Press, 2008), 45.

11. Jaroslav Pelikan, *Christianity and Classical Culture* (New Haven and London: Yale University Press, 1993), 29, 94.

12. See, e.g., N. T. Wright, "Monotheism, Christology and Ethics: 1 Corinthians 8," in his *The Climax of the Covenant* (Edinburgh: T&T Clark, 1991), 120–36.

without a beginning? [Thus Hilary initially affirms belief in these words as fully orthodox.] But, we cannot deny that the Son of God is God simply because there is only one God. Moses, or, rather, God through Moses, ordered that this first commandment, to believe in the one God, should be given to the people both in Egypt and in the desert who were addicted to idolatry and to the worship of the pretended deities. [Hilary sees the purpose of the words as to inhibit idolatry, not to preclude belief in the divinity of the Son.] This decree was right and fitting, for there is one God from whom are all things. Let us see whether the same Moses also acknowledges the divinity of Him through whom are all things. [Hilary continues to read Deut. 6:4 via the terminology of 1 Cor. 8:6.] For, since God is one, nothing is taken away from the Father because the Son is also God. [Hilary argues that God's being "one" does not preclude Jesus as Son from being included in that oneness, and he thinks that he can find attestation to plurality within the one God elsewhere within the writings of Moses.][13]

Indeed, Pelikan himself sees Deuteronomy 6:4 as the foundation of Christian creedal faith: "Behind and beneath all the primitive creeds of the apostolic and sub-apostolic era there stands the primal creed and confession of the Christian church, The Shema: 'Hear, O Israel: The LORD our God is one LORD.'"[14]

More recently, with regard to 6:5, Alan Jacobs has nicely summed up the Christian significance of Jesus's construal of our text:

When asked by a scribe to name the greatest of the commandments, Jesus complied by citing two injunctions, one from Deuteronomy (6:5) and one from Leviticus (19:18): "You shall love the Lord your God with all your heart, and with all your soul, and with all your mind. This is the great and first commandment. And a second is like it, You shall love your neighbor as yourself" ([Matt.] 22:37–40 RSV). But he then goes on to make the greater, and more startling, claim that upon these two commandments "depend all the law and the prophets." That the one identified by the Christian Church as incarnate Love speaks these words compels our closest attention to them. To say that "all the law and the prophets"

---

13. Hilary of Poitiers, *The Trinity* 4.15; in Hilary, *The Trinity*, trans. Stephen McKenna, CSsR, in FOTC 25 (New York: FOTC, 1954), 103–4. When commenting on Deut. 6:4 in the sixteenth century, John Calvin commends the fact that "the orthodox Fathers aptly used this passage against the Arians; because since Christ is everywhere called God, He is undoubtedly the same Jehovah who declares Himself to be the One God" (vol. 1 of [4] *Commentaries on the Four Last Books of Moses: Arranged in the Form of a Harmony*, trans. Charles William Bingham, in *Calvin's Commentaries* [Edinburgh: Calvin Translation Society, 1852–55; repr., Grand Rapids: Baker Books, 2005], 420).

14. Jaroslav Pelikan, ed., *Credo: Historical and Theological Guide to Creeds and Confessions of Faith in the Christian Tradition*, vol. 4 of *Creeds and Confessions of Faith in the Christian Tradition*, ed. Jaroslav Pelikan and Valerie Hotchkiss (New Haven: Yale University Press, 2003), 374.

"depend" upon these two commandments—or this twofold commandment—is to say that the multitude of ordinances and exhortations in the Old Testament presuppose the love that Jesus enjoins. No one can meet the demands of the Law who does not achieve such love.[15]

Thus the concerns of the Shema, at least in part, are important within Christian faith—but as framed by the New Testament and recontextualized within a Christian frame of reference.

The Problem of Contextualization (2): Point of Origin as Context for Interpretation

Modern biblical scholarship has characteristically set aside historic theological, philosophical, and existential debates in relation to continuing Jewish and Christian use of the biblical text; instead it has argued (or assumed) that the primary context for interpretation should be the ancient historical context of origin. Given the predominant consensus that the late seventh century BC is the period in which Deuteronomy, or at least an early version of the book, should be located, the concern becomes to articulate a late monarchic context that makes sense of Deuteronomy's declaration about YHWH. This generally goes in one (or both) of two main directions.

On the one hand, archaeological and epigraphic discoveries make it possible to envisage a context in which there were several local deities—Yhwh of Teman, Yhwh of Samaria—who apparently needed, in the view of the Deuteronomists, to be recognized to be in fact one and the same;[16] thus the concern of the text becomes the unity (in effect a "unification") of YHWH. As Feldmeier and Spieckermann put it: "One can easily recognize the intention of the emphasis on the unity of YHWH in the Šema' [Shema] after the destruction of the northern kingdom. . . . A YHWH of Samaria no longer competes with a YHWH of Jerusalem. Rather, one YHWH acts everywhere."[17] The point of this can be seen in religio-political terms, "to create the unity of the people

15. Alan Jacobs, *A Theology of Reading: The Hermeneutics of Love* (Boulder, CO: Westview, 2001), 9.

16. For the text of the ninth/eighth-century inscriptions from Kuntillet ʿAjrûd, in which these divine designations occur, see Rainer Albertz, *A History of Israelite Religion in the Old Testament Period*, trans. John Bowden (German, 1992; ET, London: SCM, 1994), 1:86.

17. Reinhard Feldmeier and Hermann Spieckermann, *God of the Living: A Biblical Theology*, trans. Mark E. Biddle (Waco: Baylor University Press, 2011), 98; cf. Gerhard von Rad's observation that one way of reading the Shema is as "a confession of the oneness of Yahweh in face of the multiplicity of divergent traditions and sanctuaries of Yahweh" (*Deuteronomy*, trans. Dorothea Barton, OTL [German, 1964; ET, London: SCM, 1966], 63).

out of the unity of God. . . . The one God unifies the former, predominantly hostile, fraternal nations into one nation of brothers."[18]

On the other hand, it is possible to read the Shema as in some way programmatic for Josiah's reform, which usually involves making a close connection between 6:4 and the regulation about the place of worship in 12:1–14, the first of the specific requirements in Deuteronomy's legal code. Thus, for example, Rainer Albertz depicts 6:4 as "the reform slogan which was hammered home to the population time and again in public pronouncements,"[19] and Norman Gottwald comparably articulates an agenda for the slogan: "The sonorous, almost mesmerizing, liturgical style of Deuteronomy and DH interpretive passages sets forth a solemn coherent message about the indivisible unity of *one God* for *one people* in *one land* observing *one cult*."[20] Feldmeier and Spieckermann similarly observe: "The one YHWH has one cultic site—naturally in the city of Jerusalem. . . . The one place of worship corresponds to the singularity of God with respect to the indivisibility of God's presence in the one, new Israel."[21]

Such scenarios are indeed imaginable and plausible, and they appeal especially to interpreters who want to envisage the socio-political dimensions and resonances of biblical language in its context of origin. Yet they have drawbacks. One drawback, often obscured by the confident manner of formulation, is the strongly conjectural nature of such scenarios: however plausible they seem, these apparently solid bricks are comprised of only a few straws.

On the one hand, for example, we simply do not know how people at the time envisaged the implications of phrases such as "Yhwh of Teman/Samaria," and it would be entirely possible to read such phrases as indicating nothing other than some special local presence or manifestation of a single deity (perhaps at a memorable moment in the past, and/or in relation to the identity of a particular shrine), who was recognized to transcend these locations and to be present elsewhere also.

In an Egyptian-Hittite treaty of about 1280 BC, divine witnesses are invoked, including "the Re, the lord of the sky" and "the Re of the town of Arinna" and also "Seth, the lord of the sky," "Seth of Hatti," "Seth of the town of Arinna" (and Seth of various other locations).[22] Since Re was the sun, it is unlikely that the plural designations imply more than one Re or any "unification" of Re. In more recent history Roman Catholics have not thought that the singular identity of the Virgin Mary is imperiled by her particular association with certain locations: Notre Dame de Chartres, Notre Dame de Lourdes, and so forth.

18. Feldmeier and Spieckermann, *God of the Living*, 98.
19. Albertz, *Israelite Religion*, 206.
20. Norman K. Gottwald, *The Hebrew Bible: A Socio-Literary Introduction* (Philadelphia: Fortress, 1985), 390.
21. Feldmeier and Spieckermann, *God of the Living*, 100.
22. See *ANET*, 199–201, esp. 201.

On the other hand, Deuteronomy presents no evidence for constantly repeated "public pronouncements" (other than in the Shema's own instructions to recite, ponder, teach, and display its wording), and it has no repeated use of the numeral "one." Where one might most expect it, and where the conjecture of a slogan for religious reform almost requires it, as in the legislation for the place of sacrificial worship in 12:1–14, the text does not speak of worship at "one place" (*māqōm 'eḥād*), but rather of worship at "the place that YHWH will choose" (12:5, 11, 14). Relatedly, Israel is not "one people" (*'am/gōy 'eḥād*) but "a holy people . . . [whom] YHWH has chosen out of all the peoples on earth to be his people" (7:6 AT; cf. 10:14–15; 14:2).

Interestingly, there is a well-known text, in Josephus's *Jewish Antiquities* (written in the late first century AD), that does indeed repeat "one" in a somewhat formulaic or catchword way. In the course of summarizing Moses's laws for Israel's constitution, Josephus depicts them as making this requirement: "Let there be one holy city in that place in the land of Canaan, . . . and let there be one temple therein, and one altar of stones. . . . In no other city let there be either altar or temple, for God is one and the Hebrew race is one."[23]

Josephus does not linger to spell out precisely why one temple is entailed by one deity and people, which is unfortunate since the logic is hardly self-evident. Probably the best conjecture is that it relates to the requirement for Israel to converge on Jerusalem for major festivals ("Three times a year all your males shall appear before the LORD your God at the place that he will choose" [Deut. 16:16]) and also to go there for other significant religious undertakings, such as the offering of sacrifice or the celebratory feast of the tithe (12:1–14; 14:22–27), on the grounds that such coming together of the people before God at one particular temple symbolically represents and enables the national unity of Israel before their God; synagogues, when they developed, were places for local gathering. The understanding that pilgrimage to a foundational site relates closely to unity and identity is reflected comparably in the Islamic requirement that every Muslim, at least once in life when circumstances allow, should make pilgrimage to Mecca—the hajj.

It may well be that unifying pilgrimage in some form is what Deuteronomy envisages, and that this gave rise to Jewish practices of pilgrimage to Jerusalem, which in turn were a precedent for Islamic practices. Nonetheless, the biblical text does not speak of "one God, one people, one temple." This does not mean that Deuteronomy was not associated with Josiah's reform. It

---

23. Josephus, *Jewish Antiquities* 4:200–201; in *Josephus*, ed. and trans. H. St. J. Thackeray, LCL 242 (Cambridge, MA: Harvard University Press, 1967), 4:571–73.

simply recognizes that there is no reform slogan in the biblical text. We know less about the context of origin than we would like.

The Problem of Contextualization (3): The World of the Text as Context for Interpretation

The basic issue is how the notion of "context" should be construed. As it stands, Deuteronomy says nothing about Josiah's (or any other comparable) reform and presents the Shema entirely in terms of the logic and implications of the covenant between YHWH and Israel as expounded by Moses. I have no desire to challenge the scholarly consensus that Deuteronomy is a post-Moses composition, probably from the seventh century (or, as a persistent minority opinion has maintained, from the sixth century, or possibly even later); instead I seek rather to clarify the different perspectives by which it is meaningful to read the text. In the first place, one should distinguish between "the world within the text" (Moses's addressing Israel in Moab, as Israel is about to cross the Jordan into the promised land) and "the world behind the text" (a possible reform movement in seventh-century Judah, or some other comparable scenario). These different perspectives, or "contexts," should be carefully distinguished and not prematurely conflated. Certainly the way in which one reads the world within the text can and should be appropriately informed and nuanced by one's best guesses as to the likely world behind the text. Yet to collapse the former into the latter is not to take seriously the dynamics of the text;[24] it also risks reducing the mode of its expression (at least among suspiciously-inclined interpreters) into little more than a covert, and quite likely manipulative, form of religiously inspired political maneuvering.

The opposite problem, of course, is that some interpreters, usually those of a conservative/traditional disposition who suspect that a seventh-century date impugns the integrity or authenticity of the text, collapse the world behind the text into the world within the text, such that no, or minimal, difference is allowed to be recognized between the two; the text must be read as the words of the historical Moses.

Although interpreters whose interest lies primarily, or solely, in a history of Israelite/Judahite religion may reasonably be interested in the world of the text in relation to the world behind the text, it does not follow that all readers

---

24. One might compare reading Gen. 1 in terms of the world within the text (the creation of the world by God, its being the object of His delight, and humanity made in the image of God) and reading it in terms of the putative world behind the text (its composition reflecting the concerns of certain Judahites in Babylonian exile). For a fuller discussion of the significance of this distinction, see my *The Theology of the Book of Genesis*, OTT (Cambridge: Cambridge University Press, 2009), 42–57.

of Israel's scriptures should share that interest—as has become clear from the widespread recognition in recent years of legitimate diversity of interest and perspective in readers' approaches to the biblical text. Moreover, in addition to the perspectives of the world within the text and the world behind the text, there is the further perspective of "the world in front of the text," which is a continuing people of Israel that understands itself to be addressed by the text. This in-front-of-the-text world is realized in those diverse communities of Jews and Christians who see their identity as standing in continuity with that of biblical Israel and are open to being shaped in certain ways by the text received as authoritative. Those whose interest lies in the enduring significance of the biblical text as Jewish and Christian scripture may legitimately maintain a primary focus on the world within the text in relation to the world in front of the text. For the fundamental assumption embodied in canonical preservation and reception is that the language and concerns of the text—God and Israel, divine call and human response, faithfulness and unfaithfulness, a choice between life and death (Deut. 30:15–20)—have continuing resonance and application. However much the text may arise out of certain conflicted situations in the ancient world, it has a meaning and a value that is not restricted to its time of origin but rather is enduring, as attested by "a great cloud of witnesses" down through the centuries.

In what follows I will offer a reading of the Shema whose primary concern is the relationship between the world within and the world in front of the text, though I will keep an eye also on the world behind the text insofar as it helps nuance the reading.

A Reading of the Shema

A Reading of Deuteronomy 6:4–5

The best way to start must be to attempt to offer a persuasive reading of the key term in Deuteronomy 6:4, which is in some way predicated of YHWH: "one" ('ehād).

The immediate contextual clue is that the meaning of "one" ('ehād) should be such as to make appropriate the response of unreserved love that is specified in 6:5. Idiomatically, I suggest that the Hebrew verb at the beginning of 6:5 (vĕ'āhavtā) should be rendered "so you should love YHWH your God."

The nature of the connection between verse 4 and verse 5 is not always brought out in translations. The common Hebrew conjunction at the beginning of 6:5, vav, is sometimes entirely omitted (as in NRSV, NJPS, CEB) or simply translated "and" (as in RSV, REB). However, the text contains a common Deuteronomic idiom—a vav (wāw) consecutive perfect (vĕqātal) in the second person—whose force is to draw an inference as to what should be done on the basis of what has just been said: "so you shall/should/must . . ." Here are three examples: Deuteronomy 8:5 articulates what Israel is to understand on the basis of Yhwh's testing and provision while they were in the wilderness (8:2–4) with *vĕyādaʿtā*, "so you should know/take to heart that as a man disciplines his son, so Yhwh your God disciplines you" (AT). In 10:19 the appropriate response to knowing that Yhwh is a God who does justice and "loves the sojourner" (10:18) is *vaʾăhavtem*, "so you must love the sojourner" (AT). In 30:19b Moses spells out the appropriate response to the life-and-death challenge that has been set before Israel (30:15–19a) with *ūbāḥartā*, "so you must choose life" (AT).[25]

If unreserved love is the appropriate response to, and consequence of, the declaration that Yhwh is *ʾeḥād*, then *ʾeḥād* should have a sense that is commensurate with this.

Within the Old Testament one passage stands out above others in the resonance between its usage of *ʾeḥād* and that of the Shema. In one of the extended sequences in the Song of Songs in which the male lover eulogizes his beloved (6:4–10), the lover envisages himself in quasi-Solomonic mode as having a vast harem at his disposal (6:8–10):[26]

> [8]There are sixty queens and eighty concubines,
>   and maidens[27] without number.
> [9]My dove, my perfect one, is the only one [*ʾaḥat*],
>   the darling [*ʾaḥat*] of her mother,
>   flawless to her that bore her.
> The maidens saw her and called her happy;
>   the queens and concubines also, and they praised her:[28]

25. Samuel Rolles Driver, when discussing the *vav* (*wāw*) consecutive with the perfect, observes: "In fact, the *wāw* possesses really in this connexion a demonstrative significance, being equivalent to *then* or *so*" (*A Treatise on the Use of the Tenses in Hebrew and Some Other Syntactical Questions*, ed. W. Randall Garr, 3rd ed. [Oxford: Clarendon, 1892; repr., Grand Rapids: Eerdmans, 1998], 117). See also discussion of the idiom in *JM* §119e; and *GKC* §112aa, ff.

26. The mode is quasi-Solomonic since the narrative of Kings ascribes to Solomon himself an even larger harem than that in the Song: "seven hundred princesses and three hundred concubines" (1 Kings 11:3).

27. Since "maiden" in English historically signifies a woman who is unmarried and/or a virgin, it is not a good rendering of *ʾalmāh* in this context, and "young women" would be preferable. The distinction within the text is probably between social classes: royalty (queens), nobility, i.e., those with appropriate status to be secondary wives ("concubines"), and young peasant women from the villages. The wondrously beautiful Abishag from the village of Shunem should probably be envisaged as one such peasant woman (1 Kings 1:1–4). Given her exceptional beauty, it is perhaps unsurprising that Abishag, despite her particular context in relation to the elderly David, should have on occasion been imaginatively identified with the beloved woman of the Song. This seems to be the implication of the Syriac reading of 1 Kings 1:3, *Shilomit* (see BHS, ad loc.), which appears to identify Abishag with (or else perhaps make her an ancestor of) the beloved woman who is "the Shulammite" in Song 6:13 (7:1 MT).

28. I understand the words of 6:10 to represent the praise uttered by those mentioned in 6:9b. To clarify this, I have therefore changed the NRSV's full stop at the end of 6:9 to a colon.

[10]"Who is this that looks forth like the dawn,
    fair as the moon, bright as the sun,
    terrible as an army with banners?"

The impressive range of choice that the lover has (v. 8) is, in effect, irrelevant for the simple reason that there is only one woman who really matters to him. If he has her, what need for others? For she is *'aḥat* (the feminine of *'eḥād*), which here clearly has the sense of "the one and only," "unique" (v. 9). She is special, unlike any other. As the lover considers his beloved, not only is she the "one and only" to him, her lover, but also she is the "one and only" to her mother. Indeed, so exceptional is she that all the potential competitors for the man's affections do not resent her but rather acknowledge her supreme radiance as that of which one cannot but be in awe (vv. 9b–10).

The man's words express the particularizing logic of love (unlike, arguably, the logic of lust). Although in the envisaged scenario there are in fact many women available, his words are personal and relational. It is the reality of one singling out another in such a way as, "forsaking all others," to focus solely on her. This reality the woman also reciprocates when she indicates that, even in a huge crowd, her eyes are only on him since he is "more conspicuous than ten thousand" (5:10 AT).[29]

In Song 6:9 the meaning of *'eḥād* is clear and unambiguous, and this meaning is related to the logic of love. Since *'eḥād* in Deuteronomy 6:4 is also related to the logic of love, it makes good sense to ascribe the same meaning to *'eḥād* in each context. If YHWH our God is "the one and only," then Israel's unreserved love is indeed the appropriate response.

On this reading the argument that 6:4 is *either* about an exclusive relationship between YHWH and Israel (with other gods recognized) *or* about the nature of YHWH as "one" (with other gods denied) is misleading and offers a false alternative. If YHWH is "one" in the sense of "the one and only," then it means that He is such that the people of Israel must be exclusive in their faithfulness and allegiance to Him. This construal does not deny the possible reality, in some sense, of "other gods"; indeed, such a denial would be odd in the context of Deuteronomy, given its repeated warnings against going after "other gods."[30] Nonetheless, the point is that, whatever "other gods" there may be, such "other gods" should be of no existential interest to Israel, but rather are to be displaced, rejected, and disregarded, since Israel's focus is to be on YHWH alone.

    29. Compare *dōdī lī wa'ānī lō*, "My beloved is mine and I am his" (2:16; cf.6:3; 7:10 [11 MT]), which is expressive in its simplicity.
    30. In the immediate aftermath of the Shema, there are warnings against "other gods" in Deut. 6:14; 7:4; 8:19; 11:16, 28.

Israel's response of love to "the one and only" is spelled out in 6:5. It is difficult to know how far to analyze the individual words since the rhetorical force lies in the whole: Israel's love should be total. However, the specific terms pose some further challenges of both translation and interpretation.

In Hebrew idiom "heart" (*lēvāv*) regularly refers to the seat of thought,[31] and so it depicts thinking rather than feeling; there is thus a case for rendering it as "mind." "Soul," though a time-honored and often-still-retained rendering of Hebrew *nephesh*, is likely to mislead. For a common meaning of "soul" in English is the spiritual or immaterial part of humans, distinct from the body, which may perhaps survive death. Such a sense is far removed from the Old Testament's own frame of reference. Other Deuteronomic use of *nephesh* depicts it as the seat of emotion and desire,[32] which would be best captured in English either by "heart" or by "being."[33] It is a common Deuteronomic idiom to link *lēvāv* with *nephesh* to depict a full response to YHWH (10:12; 30:2, 10). The present passage is unusually emphatic in adding a third element, *mě'ōd*, traditionally and no doubt correctly rendered "might/strength"; *mě'ōd* is usually an adverb yet is uniquely used as a noun here and in one related passage that depicts King Josiah in the context of his reform as, in effect, a paradigm of what our text envisages: "Before him there was no king like him, who turned to the LORD with all his mind [*lēvāv*], with all his being [*nephesh*], and with all his might [*mě'ōd*], according to all the law of Moses" (2 Kings 23:25 AT). Rabbinic tradition took *mě'ōd* to mean "money/possessions." This is surely a fine example of a meaning that is unlikely to have been held by the author of Deuteronomy yet is a good construal of the text. For it felicitously captures one of the major ways in which people can have impact within their life setting and thereby realizes the thrust of the biblical text.

Christians are most familiar with the requirement to love God via its New Testament rendering in Mark's account, whose wording has also been much used liturgically: "You shall love the Lord your God with all your heart, and with all your soul, and with all your mind, and with all your strength" (12:30). Here it appears that the initial term (*lēvāv*, heart) has received a double rendering, both "heart" and "mind," perhaps to try to capture its full implications, in a context where the idiomatic sense of the heart as the seat of thought may have been less clear. As such it would be a good example of the need to change in order to remain the same.[34]

The key word in 6:5 is "love." Although this is an uncontroversial rendering of the common Hebrew verb *'āhēv*, we need to probe a little to discover what

31. For example, Ps. 14:1, "The fool says in his heart, 'There is no God'"; or Isa. 10:7, "his [Assyria's] mind [*lēvāv*] does not so think" (AT).

32. For example, Deut. 12:20, "When . . . you say, 'Let me eat meat,' for you desire [lit., your *nephesh* desires] to eat meat, then you may eat meat as much as you desire [lit., in all the desire of your *nephesh*]" (AT); or Deut. 24:15, where an Israelite is to pay the wage to a poor laborer with no delay, "for he is poor, and he sets his heart [lit., bears his *nephesh*] upon it" (AT); cf. 1 Sam. 18:1, which depicts Jonathan's strong attachment to David: "And Jonathan's heart [*nephesh*] was bound to the heart [*nephesh*] of David, and Jonathan loved him as himself [lit., as his *nephesh*]" (AT).

33. Admittedly, "soul" in the idiom "the life and soul of the party" is perhaps not a bad approximation to this sense of *nephesh*; but it still would be a poor translation. The translational problems here illustrate well the difficulty of rendering the anthropic idioms of one culture into idioms of another.

34. The puzzling variations in the wording of Deut. 6:5 in the three Synoptic Gospels are interestingly discussed by Paul Foster, "Why Did Matthew Get the *Shema* Wrong? A Study of Matthew 22:37," *JBL* 122/2 (2003): 309–33.

it does, and what it does not, entail. In contemporary parlance the verb "love" almost inescapably entails strong feelings. How far should an understanding of "love" as "feel strongly attracted and/or attached to" be found in the biblical text? I offer three perspectives.

First, if Moses is prescribing love, can feelings be prescribed? It all depends on how they are envisaged. Jeffrey Tigay says, "The idea of commanding a feeling is not foreign to the Torah, which assumes that people can cultivate proper attitudes." As an example of this, he cites "You shall not hate your kinsfolk in your heart; . . . you shall not bear a grudge against your countrymen" (Lev. 19:17–18 AT).[35] Alternatively, Moshe Weinfeld says, "Characteristic of Deuteronomy is love which can be commanded, i.e., loyalty."[36] Perhaps the central point is that Hebrew verbs depicting mental and emotional states typically envisage actions commensurate with the state—thus to "remember" (zākar) includes acting upon a particular awareness, to "hear" (shāma') includes acting upon what one hears through obeying, and to "love" ('āhēv) includes actions that express one's orientation toward another.[37]

Second, Moses in the Shema is addressing Israel as a people in the context of outlining the covenant between YHWH and Israel. This corporate, covenantal context makes the language of Deuteronomy comparable to that of certain ancient Near Eastern treaties. Such treaties between a victorious overlord and a vassal country can specify that a vassal should "love" its overlord, where the primary sense is clearly that of obedient allegiance rather than loving feelings.[38]

This and other much-discussed parallels of terminology (and of form) in ancient treaties need to be used with some care in interpreting Deuteronomy. In the context of treaties between conqueror and conquered, the sense of "love" is likely to focus maximally on conduct and minimally on intention or motivation, other than fear of reprisal. This can readily engender cynicism about such "love," for it is not difficult to become doubtful as to whether such obedient compliance is really a positive and desirable quality

35. Jeffrey Tigay, *The JPS Torah Commentary: Deuteronomy* (Philadelphia and Jerusalem: Jewish Publication Society, 1996), 76.

36. Moshe Weinfeld, *Deuteronomy and the Deuteronomic School* (Oxford: Clarendon, 1972), 333.

37. Thus in the Decalogue we read, "those who love me and keep my commandments" (Deut. 5:10); and subsequently "love" is linked with other verbs of responsive life practices, when Moses articulates what YHWH requires of Israel: "to fear the LORD your God, to walk in all his ways, to love him, to serve the LORD your God with all your heart and with all your soul, and to keep the commandments of the LORD your God" (10:12–13). There is a comparable understanding also in the NT, where Jesus says: "If you love me, you will keep my commandments" (John 14:15).

38. See William L. Moran, "The Ancient Near Eastern Background of the Love of God in Deuteronomy," *CBQ* 25 (1963): 77–87.

for human beings; perhaps it would be better to restrict mere compliance to animals and encourage humans to think of freely chosen cooperation. Deuteronomy's concern is for a thoroughgoing internalization and appropriation of obedient action toward Yhwh, so that action and intention fully cohere, and so do practice and thought. If a human overlord sought such a response from people, it would tend toward a repressive totalitarianism, where people were expected to internalize their oppression. The exception would be when rulers rightly engage the hearts and minds of their people, but then the response can be *given* rather than exacted or manipulated. Because Yhwh has delivered Israel from oppression in Egypt and offers a way that leads to blessing and life, Israel can give Him obedient and unreserved allegiance, and this can be genuinely life-enhancing.

Third, although the Shema is addressed to Israel as a people, there is a long history of its appropriation by individuals (within the context of their belonging to God's people). Here one should still retain a primary sense of "love" as allegiance, rather than focusing on its emotional dimensions. This is not just for philological reasons, but also for psychological and pastoral reasons. For there are many whose spiritual life may be low on "emotion," because of personality and/or experience, without any diminution of authenticity.

Ruth Burrows, for example, has written many searching books on the spiritual life out of her experience as a Carmelite nun. On the one hand she says:

> Perhaps we should ask ourselves if we are not too taken up with our own initiatives and activities . . . and fail somewhat in attention to the first commandment, that we must love God with our whole heart, soul, mind and strength. Unless the first commandment dominates our life and motivates our concerns, then there is a danger of our just beating the air.[39]

Yet on the other hand she also says:

> I know many people who say simply and sincerely that they love God and their lives prove that this is not mere sentiment. For myself, I have never been able to say it. It has seemed presumptuous for me to do so. . . . Most certainly, I have wanted to love him and it has been and is my belief, my hope and my confidence that, when his work in me is complete, I will love him because I will love with the heart of Christ. It is hard, at least for me, to detach the word "love" from feeling and in my case feelings of love, generally speaking, have been absent. Still I maintain that trust includes everything and is infinitely pleasing to God.[40]

39. Ruth Burrows, OCD, *Love Unknown* (London and New York: Continuum, 2011), 115–16.
40. Ibid., 143–44.

Although at first sight what she says about loving God may appear inconsistent, the point is that she understands unreserved love of God to be primarily about trust and obedience in relation to what she terms "objective realities," and only marginally about feelings. As such she surely stands in deep continuity with the priorities of the biblical text.

By way of concluding this discussion of Deuteronomy 6:4–5, it might be appropriate to suggest a new translation that changes somewhat the Hebrew idiom in the interests of a fresh expression of its meaning: "Hear, O Israel: YHWH our God, YHWH is the one and only. So you should love YHWH your God with all your thinking, with all your longing, and with all your striving."

A Reading of Deuteronomy 6:6–9

The Shema continues:

> [6]Keep these words that I am commanding you today in your heart. [7]Recite them to your children and talk about them when you are at home and when you are away, when you lie down and when you rise. [8]Bind them as a sign on your hand, fix them as an emblem on your forehead, [9]and write them on the doorposts of your house and on your gates.

What are "these words" that are to be kept, recited, talked about, bound, fixed, and written?[41] Because "these words" are what Moses is "commanding you today," it is sometimes felt appropriate to see a wide referent here—perhaps the Ten Words/Commandments, or perhaps the content of Deuteronomy as a whole. However, since "these" is a context-specific term,[42] it surely makes best sense to take the referent of "these" as the immediately preceding content of verses 4–5, in whole or in part. Probably the decisive factor is how one interprets verses 8–9, since the pondering, teaching, and discussing of verses 6–7 could be taken equally well with a broad or a narrow referent. Insofar as one envisages specific practices of writing "these words" so that they are visible on one's person and on the entrances to private and public buildings,[43] it must surely be a short, easily written, and easily read text that is envisaged.[44] This rules

41. The verbs in vv. 7–9 have a third-person-plural suffix ("them") as the pronominal object, for which "these words" in v. 6 must be the antecedent.
42. "These words" in Deut. 1:1 clearly introduces the content of the book that follows, while "these words" in 5:22 comparably specifies the immediately preceding Ten Words/Commandments.
43. In Deut. 6:9 "house" represents private/domestic space, while "gates" represents the entrance to a town and thus public space.
44. See T. Veijola, "Höre Israel! Der Sinn und Hintergrund von Deuteronomium VI 4–9," VT 42 (1992): 528–41, esp. 537–40.

out the Ten Words/Commandments, never mind the book of Deuteronomy as a whole. It leaves verses 4–5, especially if it is solely the affirmation that "YHWH our God, YHWH is the one and only" or even just "YHWH is the one and only" (four or two words respectively in Hebrew), as eminently eligible for display.

Discussion of verses 8–9 tends to be hampered both by too ready a recourse to a dichotomy of reading the text either "literally" or "metaphorically" and by too ready a recourse to traditional Jewish practice as an example of the former. Christian commentators have tended simply to assume that the language of these verses is metaphorical.[45] There is, however, nothing in context to suggest that something other than specific practices is envisaged.[46] Furthermore, there are sufficient analogous practices from the wider world of ancient Israel to make it likely that specific practices are envisaged here.[47]

The rabbinic interpretation that adult males should wear tefillin/phylacteries at times of prayer, and that containers with texts should be affixed to door-posts, is not a *literal* reading—the text says nothing about donning something specifically at prayer times, or about affixing containers—but a *serious* reading, which attempts to realize in an appropriate way something of what the text envisages in life contexts other than that in which Deuteronomy originated. In itself verse 8 most likely envisages writing "these words" on bands: on wristbands, to be a constant reminder of their allegiance to their bearers, and on headbands (or perhaps on an emblem on headgear),[48] to display the allegiance of the bearers to others. Similarly, verse 9 most likely envisages the actual writing and display of "these words" on the entrances to both private

45. Gerhard von Rad observes: "It is not clear what significance is attached to the tokens which serve as reminders and so forth. Probably we still have to do here with a figurative mode of expression, which was then later understood literally and led to the use of the so-called phylacteries" (*Deuteronomy*, 64). Or, as John Thompson more bluntly puts it: "What was given originally as a metaphor became for later Jews a literal injunction" (*Deuteronomy*, TOTC [London: Inter-Varsity, 1974], 123).

46. The commonly cited Exod. 13:9, 16, where prescriptions for unleavened bread and the redemption of the firstborn are followed by "It shall serve as a sign on your hand and as an emblem/memorial on your forehead" (AT)—where the terminology is almost identical to that in Deut. 6:8—is not a good analogy, because in context its sense cannot be other than metaphorical, a figurative way of expressing the commemorative function of the practices in question. The figurative idiom in Exodus is probably dependent on the specific practice in Deuteronomy.

47. See Othmar Keel, "Zeichen der Verbundenheit: Zur Vorgeschichte und Bedeutung der Forderungen von Deuteronomium 6,8f. und Par.," in *Mélanges Dominique Barthélemy*, by D. Barthélemy, P. Casetti, O. Keel, and A. Schenker, OBO 38 (Fribourg: Éditions universitaires; Göttingen: Vandenhoeck & Ruprecht, 1981), 159–240.

48. The precise sense of Hebrew *tōtāphōt* is unclear and must be inferred contextually; cf. the specification that the high priest should have the inscription "Holy to YHWH" attached to his turban (Exod. 28:36–38 AT).

and public buildings, and such writing might well be on the lintel overhead rather than the upright. These are *symbolic* acts, expressing Israel's identity and allegiance in public ways. The rabbinic practices are likewise symbolic acts of allegiance that, even if not envisaged in the text, remain consonant with the text's concern.

Thus Deuteronomy 6:6–9 underlines the all-important nature of the preceding words as a summary of what is at the heart of the covenant between YHWH and Israel. The fact that YHWH is the one and only for Israel does not just call for a response of unreserved love and allegiance but also requires concrete practices and symbols as part of regular daily life. In general "these words" are to be kept in mind constantly (v. 6). More specifically, they are to be passed on to the next generation (children are to be inducted into Israel's identity and allegiance from their earliest years) and are to be a regular subject for conversation (v. 7). Although the idiom of "at home and away, . . . when you lie down and when you rise" may be primarily a way of saying "at all times," the rabbinic requirement of specific recitation when one goes to bed and when one gets up has been valuable. It represents the recognition that specific practices give content and focus to a general awareness.[49] The display of allegiance to YHWH on one's person, in a way that will remind both self and others, means that in a world of contested allegiances Israel is required to be up front and courageous about its allegiance (v. 8). The marking of places where one lives, both domestic and civic, with this allegiance (so that one becomes aware of it at the point of transition into those places), likewise means that Israel's allegiance is never privatized but rather is integral to all the space that Israel inhabits (v. 9).

Curiously, Richard Dawkins strongly emphasizes that the practice of bringing up children to have religious beliefs is iniquitous and best labeled "indoctrination."[50] Characteristic is this lament: "I think we should all wince when we hear a small child being labeled as belonging to some particular religion or another. Small children are too young to decide their views on the origins of the cosmos, of life and of morals. The very sound of the phrase 'Christian child' or 'Muslim child' should grate like fingernails on a blackboard."[51] Dawkins appears to combine an excessively intellectualized conception of religious faith with a distinctly underdeveloped sense of the social nature of religious knowledge, identity, and practice. In any case, it is hardly unreasonable for adults to seek to form children in patterns of thinking and living that they believe to be good—as Dawkins himself has no doubt done.

49. It is a recurrent problem that general religious affirmations easily become empty of real content. One can say, "My time and money belong to God," when in fact they may remain at one's disposal in a way that might not differ from how they would be if they did not belong to God. The requirement to dedicate a seventh of time and a tenth of money to God can give teeth to the general affirmation.

50. Richard Dawkins, *The God Delusion* (London: Bantam, 2006), 254–64, 311–40.

51. Ibid., 318.

Some Complexities in Christian Appropriation of the Shema

In the preceding section I have offered a basic reading of Deuteronomy 6:4–9. In order to develop this reading in relation to Christian understanding, I will look further at three of the many issues it raises: I will begin with hermeneutics and the nature of Old Testament interpretation, then I will turn to monotheism and idolatry.

Hermeneutical Considerations (1): What Should Christians Write and Display, and Why?

Initially I return to my opening observation that Christians have primarily been interested in Deuteronomy 6:4–5. This can be developed by comparing characteristic Christian and Jewish approaches to 6:6–9, the instructions to recite, teach, and display the foundational words that YHWH is the one and only.

Within a Jewish frame of reference, it is notable that the first tractate of the Mishnah, *Berakot* ("Benedictions/Blessings"), begins with the question "From what time in the evening may the *Shemaʿ* be recited?"[52] The text continues with discussion of the implications of the biblical instructions and the varying construals that have been offered. Whatever the disagreements over the observance of the Shema, the premise of *Berakot*, which underlies and would have been shared by all the differing voices cited, is that the Shema must be heeded and observed. The instructions of verses 6–9 have been important for Jews, essentially because so many have felt, and still feel, under obligation to do, in one way or other, what the text specifies. Correspondingly, contemporary Jewish commentaries on Deuteronomy tend to give substantial space to the question of what kind of practice is envisaged by these instructions, and to canvass historic Jewish debates thereon.[53]

One can contrast Joseph Lienhard's valuable recent compilation of Christian commentators on Deuteronomy in antiquity (commentators later than, but not far removed in time from, the Mishnah).[54] The relevant section on the Shema is headed "6:4–9, The Great Commandment"; that is, the Old Testament text is characterized with the terminology of Jesus (as appropriate to a Christian frame of reference). More strikingly, however, the editor gives, under the heading of "6:4–9," an English translation of only verses 4 and 5. All the commentators

---

52. *The Mishnah*, trans. Herbert Danby (Oxford: Clarendon, 1933), 2.

53. See, e.g., the substantial excursuses devoted to the Shema and its observance in Tigay, *The JPS Torah Commentary: Deuteronomy*, 438–44.

54. Joseph T. Lienhard, SJ, ed., with Ronnie J. Rombs, under Thomas C. Oden, general ed., *Ancient Christian Commentary on Scripture: Old Testament*, vol. 3, *Exodus, Leviticus, Numbers, Deuteronomy* (Downers Grove, IL: InterVarsity, 2001), esp. 282–85.

who are then cited discuss verse 4, in relation to the nature of God, and verse
5, in relation to the love of God. That constitutes the whole section. In other
words, 6:6–9 appears to be entirely absent in early Christian commentators;
this is material on which they apparently had nothing to say, at least in the judgment of the editor. Why? It is difficult to resist the surmise that this is because
ancient Christians considered themselves under no obligation to do what these
verses say—unlike 6:4–5, which they did feel obliged to understand and practice.
Comparably, contemporary Christian commentaries on Deuteronomy tend to
devote most of their space and interest to 6:4–5, then do relatively little with
6:6–9, though something of historic Jewish practice in relation to verses 8–9 is
usually noted. One might contrast this with the extensive space that Christian
scholars tend to devote to the eucharistic words of Jesus in commentaries on the
Gospels and on 1 Corinthians 11:23–26. This emphasis is presumably related
to the Christian sense of pressure, in this context, in some way to do that of
which the text speaks. In its own small way, the study of Deuteronomy 6:6–9
illustrates something of the social nature of interest and knowledge.

Characteristic Christian approaches to the Shema are deeply formed by
instincts and assumptions derived from the New Testament—rightly and inevitably so. On the one hand, it is surely a desire to follow Jesus's linkage of
love of God with love of neighbor (which the Gospels also show to be already
an accepted Jewish understanding)[55] that has generally caused the instructions
about recitation and display to recede from sight. For once one speaks of loving
God and loving neighbor, then one is likely, again following the lead of Jesus, to
see this as a fundamental hermeneutical key to understanding Israel's scriptures
and also the life of faith more generally. In a certain sense it would be odd to
return to the wording of Deuteronomy 6 once the words of primary importance
in 6:4–5 have been taken in a different direction through recontextualization.

On the other hand, the logic of faith in Jesus has led to Christians having *alternative*, and in certain ways *equivalent*, practices to those envisaged
in Deuteronomy 6:6–9. The all-important words to be recited on a regular
basis, not least to frame the day through use in the morning and the evening,
become the words of the Lord's Prayer, the model prayer that Jesus taught to
his disciples. The symbol that is to be displayed as a marker of identity and
allegiance becomes the cross, the prime symbolic shorthand expression of
Christian faith. Christians often wear a cross around the neck or in a lapel,
and it is a historic Christian practice (though one not embraced by numerous

---

55. In Mark 12:32–33 Jesus's interlocutor expresses no surprise at Jesus's combination of the
two primary commandments and immediately affirms it himself; and in Luke 10:25–28 it is the
lawyer, not Jesus, who combines love of God and neighbor as expressing what stands in torah.

Protestants) to make the sign of the cross over oneself. Symbolic Christian marking of doorways has often been present in churches, and sometimes on other buildings also.

In earlier centuries the symbolic marking of entrances was a regular practice, and it can still be viewed today at some of the medieval colleges of Oxford and Cambridge (and elsewhere). Late medieval piety expressed itself more in images than words, but the basic logic is not different from that embodied in Deuteronomy 6:9. For example, the old entrance to New College, Oxford (founded in the late fourteenth century), as approached from New College Lane, is surmounted by a statue of the Virgin Mary, to whom the college is dedicated, flanked by statues of two kneeling figures: on the left, the angel Gabriel, and on the right, in a posture of suppliant prayer, William of Wykeham, patron and benefactor of the college, who had a strong personal devotion to the Virgin Mary. The presence of the angel Gabriel presumably means that the statues represent the annunciation, at which William of Wykeham is devotionally present.[56] The identity and the allegiance of the institution are thereby clearly expressed.[57]

There was, of course, a marked change in the Reformation, when words were preferred to images, and when there was a fresh appropriation of the Bible as a whole. Biblical texts came to be ubiquitous in Protestant domestic decoration, and the instructions of Deuteronomy 6:6–9 were commonly appealed to. In the late sixteenth century, for example, Robert Cleaver wrote: "And this is the meaning of that Law, which Moses gave to the Israelites, Commaunding them to write the word of God upon the Postes of their houses, and upon their Gates. Whereby all under government, were taught, what should be required of them so long as they lived in those houses, namely, to serve God."[58] A few years later Richard Braithwaite wrote:

> And wee are taught what wee must doe, returning from Gods house to our owne: and what wee are to doe sitting in our houses, even to lay up Gods word in our heart and in our soule, and binde it for a sign upon our hand, that it may be as a frontlet betweene our eyes. And not only to be instructed thus our selves, but to teach them [to] our children, speaking of them when thou sittest in thine house, and when thou walkest by the way, and when thou liest downe, and when thou risest up. And not so onely, but thou shalt write them upon the posts of thine house, and upon thy gates. Whence you see, how no place, time, or occasion is to be exempted from meditating of God.[59]

It remains striking that the prime implementation is seen to involve "lay[ing] up Gods word in our heart" and "meditating of God." It seems to be a generalized biblically-focused devotion always and everywhere that constitutes the prime fulfillment of the biblical commandment.

---

56. The presence of a contemporary figure in a Gospel scene, usually the passion, is a common medieval artistic convention, nicely echoed in the modern spiritual folk song "Were You There When They Crucified My Lord?"

57. Despite the real continuity between William of Wykeham's symbolizing the college's identity and Deut. 6:9, it is unlikely that any explicit linkage was intended. Interestingly, the wording of v. 9 in the Vulgate (the form in which a medieval Englishman would have known the OT) is *scribesque ea in limine et ostiis domus tuae*, "and you shall write them on the threshold/lintel and on the doors of your house," which restricts the requirement to domestic space. The Hebrew "gates," which idiomatically signifies "town gates," appears to have been understood (in Deut. 6:9) simply to mean "doors."

58. Robert Cleaver et al., *A godlie forme of householde government* (London: Thomas Man, 1598), 24–25; cited in Tara Hamling, *Decorating the "Godly" Household: Religious Art in Post-Reformation Britain* (New Haven and London: Yale University Press, 2010), 106.

59. Richard Braithwaite, *The English Gentleman* (London: I. Haviland, 1630), 161; cited in Hamling, *Decorating*, 106.

All this poses a nice hermeneutical conundrum. Deuteronomy does not envisage the recital or display of words or a symbol equivalent to the Shema, but of the Shema itself; and indeed, Deuteronomy 6:4–9 is an unusually emphatic passage in its specification of the attention that should be paid to *these* all-important words. Yet the symbolic practices specified in the biblical text are not observed by Christians, but have come to characterize Jews (who put on phylacteries and affix mezuzot) as distinct from Christians (who do neither of these things). This is presumably in large part because the explicitly Christian nature of the Lord's Prayer and the cross, and their role in symbolizing identity as formed by Christ crucified and risen, has contributed to distancing Christians from what is envisaged in Deuteronomy 6. But Christians still hold the Old Testament to be authoritative and regard the words of Deuteronomy 6:4–5 as of high importance.

This "inconsistency" surely captures well something of the dynamics of Christian appropriation of Israel's scriptures as the Old Testament. On the one hand, Christian reading needs to be attentive to the meaning of the text in its pre-Christian frame of reference; on the other hand, it must simultaneously take with full seriousness the recontextualization of the material in a frame of reference not originally its own. This Christian frame of reference both affirms and appropriates some of the content of the Old Testament and relativizes or marginalizes other of its content, according to the pattern of its own knowledge of God in and through Jesus Christ, and its implications for living. The logic of Christian appropriation of the Old Testament is neither "all" nor "nothing," but rather a substantive engagement that has its own distinctive dynamic.

Hermeneutical Considerations (2): How Might Christians Realize the Concerns of the Text?

One possible anxiety that can be raised is whether such a dynamic of selective appropriation makes it, in effect, impossible for the Old Testament to be heard in its own voice or for that voice to make any real difference within a Christian frame of reference: will not Christian faith only hear what it wants to hear, and in the way it wants to hear it? There are interesting hermeneutical issues here, on which I offer three observations.

First, the summons to recognize YHWH as the one and only should rightly inform a Christian understanding of God and life with God, and do so without diminution, if only because there is so much also in the New Testament that has a comparable focus on God. The fact that the knowledge of God is mediated and focused for Christians in the person of Jesus makes no difference to the dynamics of this supreme focus on God. The rootedness of Christian faith in Israel's faith, and the real continuities of many aspects of the life of faith from Old Testament to New Testament and beyond, gives Christian faith, at least in principle, an intrinsic openness to affirm Israel's witness to a love supreme as its own.

Second, the recognition that identity and allegiance may be appropriately displayed on one's person and on buildings surely indicates an important area for fresh thinking, to recognize not just what has been done in the past but also what might now be done in the present. There are many complex issues here as to what is feasible in a secular Western society, especially one whose secularity has been formed through reaction against antecedent forms of Christian identity. In principle, a secular frame of reference is meant to be able to host frames of reference other than its own and enable their peaceful (even if appropriately argumentative) coexistence; Christians can readily acknowledge and flourish in such a context. However, some recent controversies in England and France over people wearing religious symbols in public and/or the context of their work seem indicative of a secularism that feels threatened and hostile, rather than hospitable, toward symbols of religious identity in the public realm.[60]

It has become increasingly clear that secular space is not in fact neutral space, but rather is undergirded by particular moral, political, and economic values and visions, which are contestable. Admittedly, it can be difficult to discern what those undergirding values and visions are, since contemporary secular states are complex, and their values can be both overt (as in the promotion of late capitalism, whose advertising adorns many a building and body) and elusive (as in the nature and basis of notions of the common good and living well). On any reckoning, some fundamental rethinking of "politics and religion" is a pressing Christian need.[61]

Although it may not be feasible (for many reasons, from the hermeneutical to the prudential) to enact the "plain sense" of Deuteronomy 6:8–9, this text

60. Rowan Williams helpfully distinguishes between two kinds of secularism. One he calls "procedural" secularism, which he considers to be arguably a descendant of a Christian recognition of the appropriate limits of state authority; within such secularism Christian presence and perspectives can have a legitimate public role. The other he calls "programmatic" secularism, which is ideologically driven, requires public loyalty, and insists that religious convictions must be wholly privatized. Williams shows this programmatic secularism to be not only inimical to faith but also untrue to the way in which complex societies actually operate (*Faith in the Public Square* [London: Bloomsbury, 2012], 2–3, 23–36, and passim).

61. A trenchant recent account is by William Cavanaugh, *Migrations of the Holy: God, State, and the Political Meaning of the Church* (Grand Rapids: Eerdmans, 2011), although his observations apply more, I think, to the USA than to polities on the other side of the Atlantic.

can nonetheless constrain Christians to rethink the nature of their identity and its expression in the public realm, where so many other identities and allegiances are already vigorously on display. It is hardly necessary to go so far as envisaging a contemporary equivalent of the medieval crusaders, who "took the cross" and displayed a large cross on their clothing (i.e., we need not imagine an extreme scenario so as to bring the whole notion into ridicule or disrepute), in order to ask about possible ways in which Christian identity might meaningfully and legitimately be displayed and practiced in the public realm.

Third, this is an appropriate context in which to note that there are possible legitimate concerns as to whether the practices envisaged in Deuteronomy 6:4–9 might, if taken "seriously," entail a narrowing of interest and outlook upon life that could be unhealthy. Might they encourage a pietism in which overtly religious language is the only acceptable language, and religious texts are required to be the predominant form of artistic expression and decoration? Might they encourage an inward-looking and competitive religiosity, in which each strives to outdo the other in terms of conversation and display? Might they encourage lack of interest in the wider life and activities of the world, other than to see them as more or less threatening to the requisite priorities of piety? Nonetheless, while such moves indeed can be made, and from time to time have been made, they are in no way necessary consequences—although what is considered appropriate as expressing religious faithfulness will undoubtedly vary from culture to culture.

Within a Christian frame of reference, one key to understanding is the classic combination of love of God with love of neighbor, as in the words of Jesus. This makes the fundamental point that love of God and love of neighbor are not competitive, as though the interrelationship of the divine and the human were a zero-sum game in which the more one loves God, the less one can love other people. Rather, the opposite is the case. Love for God enables, and indeed is expressed in, love for others. The classic understanding of love for God is that it is something that will purify all other loves and order them aright, so that they can be what they should be, and be less likely to become unhealthy or idolatrous.

The recontextualization of Deuteronomy's own frame of reference within a contemporary Christian frame of reference both enables Deuteronomy to be heard and taken seriously, and makes for an appropriation that is informed by substantive concerns from beyond Deuteronomy's own horizons. The tension between these differing frames of reference is in principle fruitful and never to be definitively resolved, as it is constitutive of Christian engagement with Scripture generally.

Is Deuteronomy 6:4 Paradigmatic for Monotheism?

Another way of probing further the implications of our text is to ask whether the affirmation that Y H W H is "the one and only" does, or does not, constitute "monotheism."

Discussion of "monotheism" is usually presented in religio-historical terms, to do with when and why Israel's religion became monotheistic—but not to do with the reading of the Old Testament as a literary-canonical collection that in important ways provides its own context of meaning. The once widely held view that monotheism goes back to Moses has generally been discarded, and the consensus view is that monotheism is first articulated in the mid-sixth century by Second Isaiah, largely for religio-political reasons, having to do with the affirmation of Judahite identity and hope over against Babylonian dominance. Here its presence is apparently unquestionable, and indeed can be depicted as "philosophical monotheism,"[62] because of passages such as Isaiah 45:5–7:

> [5]I am the LORD, and there is no other [*'ēn 'ōd*];
>   besides me there is no god [*'ēn 'ĕlōhîm*].
>   I arm you [Cyrus], though you do not know me,
> [6]so that they may know, from the rising of the sun
>   and from the west, that there is no one besides me;
>   I am the LORD, and there is no other.
> [7]I form light and create darkness,
>   I make weal and create woe;
>   I the LORD do all these things.

There is here not only explicit denial that there is any deity other than Y H W H (vv. 5a, 6b) but also implicit denial of other deities through the rhetoric of sovereign power (v. 7). With regard to the Shema, however, the general scholarly consensus is that it, even if not far in time of origin from Second Isaiah, is not monotheistic but rather a staging post on the way to monotheism: the Shema represents monolatry, which requires exclusive worship of one deity without denying the existence of others, rather than monotheism proper.

This apparent conceptual difference between the Shema and Second Isaiah may well be less secure, however, than is generally supposed. The consensus view about the meaning of such passages in Second Isaiah can interestingly be set alongside a comparable consensus view about the meaning of Psalm 14:1, where "the fool thinks, 'There is no God [*'ēn 'ĕlōhîm*]'" (AT). Here commentators

---

62. Thus Baruch Halpern, "'Brisker Pipes than Poetry': The Development of Israelite Monotheism," in his *From Gods to God*, FAT 63 (Tübingen: Mohr Siebeck, 2009), 13–56, esp. 32.

consistently observe that it is "practical" rather than "theoretical" atheism that is envisaged: the point is the denial not of the existence of God as such but rather of the contention that God makes the kind of difference such that He should be heeded. This construal is derived from the tenor of the psalm overall, where "the main emphasis seems to be on the conviction that there is no need to reckon with God in any sphere of one's existence, i.e., for practical purposes God does not matter"; or, "The psalm is not concerned with the question of whether people accept the existence of a supreme being. It is concerned with whether people acknowledge the reality of the LORD, the God of Israel, by calling on the LORD in need and seeking the LORD in the decisions of life."[63] This is in keeping with a clearly attested sense of the Hebrew word *'ayin* (or *'ēn*) ("there is no"), which can mean absence rather than non-existence (as in 1 Sam. 14:17, where Saul's roll call reveals that Jonathan and his armor-bearer "were not there [*'ēn yōnāthān . . .*]").[64] Yet the comparable language in Second Isaiah is not given a comparable meaning, but rather is held to be precisely the kind of denial of existence that should not be ascribed to "the fool." Of course, the concerns in Second Isaiah may be distinct from those of Psalm 14. Nonetheless, in many contexts of regular life, the force of "there is no other" is less likely to have the sense of philosophical denial than of rhetorical persuasion. Thus the political orator who says to the crowd "We have no choice" or "There is only one way" or "There is no alternative" is invariably not denying the theoretical existence of alternatives but rather is urging that these alternatives should be ignored and only the way the speaker is advocating should be embraced as the way ahead. Contextually, the prophet in Isaiah 40–55 is urging the Judahite exiles wholeheartedly to embrace YHWH and to reject other deities as making no difference to them. Thus it may be that the force of a passage such as "I am the LORD, and there is no other; besides me there is no god" is in fact no different from that of the Shema with its focus on YHWH as "the one and only."[65]

If this is on the right lines, it suggests that the familiar distinction between "monotheism" and "monolatry" is not in fact well attuned to the tenor of certain prime Hebrew Bible passages.[66] Is, then, "monotheism" a good cat-

63. Thus Arnold Albert Anderson, *Psalms*, NCB (London: Marshall, Morgan & Scott, 1972), 1:132; and James L. Mays, *Psalms*, IBCTP (Louisville: John Knox, 1994), 82.

64. The Hebrew in itself could mean non-existence; here as elsewhere, questions of context are all-important for determining meaning.

65. For comparable judgments about "monotheism" and Second Isaiah from other scholars, see Nathan MacDonald, "Monotheism and Isaiah" in *Interpreting Isaiah: Issues and Approaches*, ed. David G. Firth and H. G. M. Williamson (Downers Grove, IL: IVP Academic, 2009), 43–61, esp. 50–52.

66. For a valuable and nuanced discussion that helpfully highlights both the differing ways in which "monotheism" and related terms are used and the limits of their usefulness (as well as

egory for interpreting the Hebrew Bible at all? Of course, adherence to one God has been a historic self-defining marker of Jews, Christians, and Muslims down the ages. Nonetheless, "monotheism" as a category, along with "polytheism," "theism," and "deism," was first coined in the early modern period (the seventeenth century). There was then an attempt to find new and better categories for classifying "religion," at a time when religion was starting to be reconceptualized as a distinctive phenomenon—more of a subset within life, rather than an approach to life as a whole.[67] Monotheism as a category can suffer, however, from the Enlightenment tendency to abstract and intellectualize faith, such that faith is defined in terms of a certain conceptual content, in isolation from associated moral, ritual, and symbolic practices. Insofar as the meaning of belief in God/gods is significantly given content by the practices that accompany it, an account that abstracts from these is likely to be misleading.

Admittedly, the danger of intellectualizing and abstracting faith in the one God is perennial. One only has to consider James's scathing critique in the New Testament—"You believe that God is one. You do well. Even the demons believe—and tremble!" (James 2:19 NKJV)—to be reminded that in any age intellectual acknowledgment of God may easily become detached from appropriate responsiveness and life practices. Nonetheless it seems that this danger has been exacerbated in modern times, through the legacy of Enlightenment construals of belief in God. On any reckoning, the term "monotheism" does not intrinsically convey the existential dimensions conveyed by the Shema or Isaiah 40–55—either the call for a loyalty that resists alternative allegiances or a devotion to God as the one and only, as to a lover.

Thus there are important limits to the value of "monotheism" as a category for understanding the Old Testament. It may still have a place, faute de mieux, but it needs at the very least to be a matter of "handle with care."

Conclusion: Deuteronomy, Idolatry, and Christian Faith

Finally, it may be helpful to raise a wider issue that arises from a consideration of the Shema in its Old Testament context.

When the value of belief in the one God has ceased to be self-evident, not least because its associated practices and understandings have largely fallen

---

providing a fresh analysis of both biblical and extra-biblical evidence), see Benjamin D. Sommer, "Appendix: Monotheism and Polytheism in Ancient Israel," in his *The Bodies of God and the World of Ancient Israel* (New York: Cambridge University Press, 2009), 145–74.

67. There is a good introduction to the issues and literature in Nathan MacDonald, "The Origin of 'Monotheism,'" in Stuckenbruck and North, *Monotheism*, 204–15.

away—as is surely the case in contemporary Western society—then numerous time-honored questions come freshly to the fore: Why does it matter to believe in one God rather than many? Why does it matter to believe in one God rather than none? If believing in God makes little essential difference to the way one lives, as often appears to be the case, then why should it continue to be an important issue to consider at all? Why not simply forget about God altogether (and so also dismiss atheism as much as theism, since the one category is predicated on the other) and get on with living as best one can?

One helpful way into some of these issues can be via reflection on "polytheism," a term coined as a correlate for "monotheism."[68] "Polytheism" as a category for classification is arguably meant to be a more dispassionate way of giving an account of religious differences than the older term "idolatry," with its inescapably negative resonances. Yet some scholars recently have sought to reinstate "idolatry," in the context of some fundamental rethinking of what it means to believe in God. Particularly interesting is the work of Nicholas Lash, who says succinctly, "The first question to be asked concerning God, and our relationship with God, is not 'to be or not to be?' but what it is that we worship, that we take as God?"[69] Or, as he puts it more fully in his groundbreaking *The Beginning and End of "Religion"*:

> It is taken for granted, in sophisticated circles, that no one worships God these days except the reactionary and simple-minded. This innocent self-satisfaction tells us little more, however, than that those exhibiting it do not name as "God" the gods they worship.
>
> All human beings have their hearts set somewhere, hold something sacred, worship at some shrine. We are spontaneously idolatrous—where, by "idolatry," I mean the worship of some creature, the setting of the heart on some particular thing (usually oneself). For most of us there is no single creature that is the object of our faith. Our hearts are torn, dispersed, distracted. We are (to use the seventeenth-century term) polytheists. And none of us is so self-transparent as to know quite where, in fact, our hearts are set.
>
> Against this background, the great religious traditions can be seen as contexts in which human beings may learn, however slowly, partially, imperfectly, some freedom from the destructive bondage which the worship of the creature brings.[70]

68. Many contemporary scholars are questioning the value of "polytheism" as a category for the accurate understanding and depiction of religious beliefs and phenomena.

69. Nicholas Lash, "Amongst Strangers and Friends: Thinking of God in our Current Confusion," in his *Theology for Pilgrims* (London: Darton, Longman & Todd, 2008), 36–51, esp. 41.

70. Nicholas Lash, *The Beginning and End of "Religion"* (Cambridge: Cambridge University Press, 1996), 49–50, 21–22.

Lash is reformulating a classic (pre-seventeenth-century) understanding of deity and idolatry. A representative formulation can be found, for example, in the work of Erasmus, in his exposition of Psalm 1 written in 1515: "For each individual, his god is the thing in which he places his greatest expectation of bliss. If he will do and suffer anything for money, his god is not the Lord, but Mammon; if he is a slave to pleasure, his belly is his god; if he wrecks everything for the sake of power, the Lord is not his god: the god he worships is called ambition."[71] Alternatively, Luther writes in his Large Catechism, when expounding the First Commandment: "What does it mean to have a god? or, what is God? Answer: A god means that from which we are to expect all good and to which we are to take refuge in all distress. . . . That now, I say, upon which you set your heart and put your trust is properly your god."[72]

In what way can this insight be used for reading the Old Testament? One difficulty that the Old Testament poses is that it hardly lingers to explain *why* "other gods" are problematic, at least in terms the contemporary reader might hope for: different texts sound different notes, and none offer the kind of theological account that might appeal to someone who did not already accept the importance of following YHWH. In broad-brush outline, the Old Testament presentation of "other gods" has two primary emphases. On the one hand, other gods lead Israel away from allegiance to YHWH and are unacceptable for that reason (a characteristic emphasis in Deuteronomy and Deuteronomically influenced material); this is a stance that implies the reality of other gods, but whose reasoning can appear somewhat circular. On the other hand, images of gods are mocked as mere material objects, lacking life and power (a characteristic emphasis in prophetic literature and the Psalms); this is a stance that appears to imply the unreality of other gods, and its rhetoric is to dissuade Israel rather than persuade those beyond Israel. Nonetheless, I propose that the notion of treating as God that which is not God, which is fundamental to a classic understanding of idolatry, as in Lash's account, may still be heuristically fruitful for reading and appropriating the Old Testament. There are at least two inner-biblical reasons for this.

First, there is an Old Testament reason. John Barton has argued that, although Israel initially distinguished between worshiping gods other than YHWH and the use of images in worship, such a distinction was elided by Isaiah, who thereby set in motion the classic understanding of idolatry:

71. *Collected Works of Erasmus*, vol. 63, *Expositions of the Psalms*, ed. Dominic Baker-Smith, trans. Michael J. Heath (Toronto: Toronto University Press, 1997), 14.
72. Martin Luther, Large Catechism, www.gutenberg.org/ebooks/1722.

The recognition that idolatry really consists in *making gods for ourselves* and putting our trust in them is the great breakthrough in Israel's thinking about the matter, and I have suggested that it may be to Isaiah that we owe it. From Isaiah onwards the conviction grew that there simply were no other powers in the universe to rival Yahweh, the God of Israel, and that . . . however much worshippers might bow down to the idol and acknowledge it as a great power, it was really themselves they were worshipping all the time.[73]

Barton further sees this Isaianic perspective as responsible for a classic interpretation of the initially distinct first commandment ("You shall have no other gods before me" [Exod. 20:3]; i.e., no apostasy) and second commandment ("You shall not make for yourself an idol" [20:4]; i.e., no images) as being in essence a single commandment that prohibits the worship of a human substitute for the true and living God. Two initially distinct commandments are re-read as one commandment. If Barton is right, then already within the Old Testament there appears to be a hermeneutical move toward adopting a particular understanding of idolatry—to treat as God that which is not God—as the definitive understanding.

Georg Braulik, following Norbert Lohfink, makes a move comparable to that of Barton when he argues for the developing traditions of Deuteronomy as the context for Israel's first formulation of monotheism. He discusses passages that refer to YHWH as a "jealous God," which consistently relate to the challenge posed by "other gods," and observes: "As soon as language about God becomes monotheistic, the formula about the jealous God loses its meaning." He then discusses "late texts," such as Deuteronomy 8:1–18 and 9:1–8, which "say nothing about any confrontation with the gods," and he infers from these that "The gods are no longer YHWH's rivals; his rival is the human self-confidence of Israel." He infers from this that a process of re-reading, "theological *relecture*," is "incorporated in the framework of an older text."[74]

Second, there is a New Testament reason, in the form of the famous words of Jesus in the Synoptic tradition: "No one can serve two masters. . . . You cannot serve God and mammon" (Matt. 6:24 NKJV//Luke 16:13). Here Jesus metaphorically depicts money and wealth in a personification as a possible, and tempting, object of allegiance that rivals and can displace allegiance to God.[75] In essence it is a restatement of the logic of the Shema, which is now

73. John Barton, "'The Work of Human Hands' (Ps 115:4): Idolatry in the Old Testament," *Ex Auditu* 15 (1999): 63–72, esp. 71; repr. in *The Ten Commandments*, ed. William P. Brown (Louisville: Westminster John Knox, 2004), 194–203.

74. Georg Braulik, "Deuteronomy and the Birth of Monotheism," in his *The Theology of Deuteronomy*, trans. Ulrika Lindblad (N. Richland Hills, TX: BIBAL, 1994), 99–130, esp. 106, 111. Braulik's thesis is heavily dependent on his confidence in differentiating earlier and later texts within the central corpus of Deuteronomy, a confidence that not all share.

75. Modern translations tend to "clarify" the meaning of "mammon" by rendering it as "wealth" (so NRSV, CEB), but at the cost of diminishing the personification. By contrast, as Martin Hengel observes, "Perhaps the early church left this Semitic loan-word untranslated

formulated in such a way as to specify the danger of treating as God that which is not God. There are comparable moves also elsewhere in the New Testament, as in Colossians 3:5, where "greed" is glossed as "idolatry." The point is that the tempting but misleading reality that can endanger allegiance to God is not some putative invisible entity (i.e., a deity, in a certain "traditional" conception) but rather those things encountered within the life of the world that can draw the human heart away from the one true God.

The classic Christian monastic vows can also be understood in this light. A person who embraces poverty, chastity, and obedience is renouncing three idols/false gods—money, sex, and power—upon which one can be tempted to set one's heart as avenues to fullness of life. The monastic vow dares to affirm that God alone suffices and that Jesus in his poverty, chastity, and obedience displays fullness of life.

My proposal here is that the hermeneutical move in the words of Jesus, in conjunction with the comparable move already in Isaiah, makes available a reading strategy for the construal of "other gods" in the Old Testament. "Other gods" are those realities that, in whichever form they take, threaten allegiance to the true God because they treat as God that which is not God.

In methodological terms my concern is that one should be open to the potential value of later understandings for re-reading earlier texts. This does not depend on supposing that the later understanding was *really* already present in the earlier texts, even though it may already have been incipiently present. (If careful philological and historical study shows that in all likelihood certain biblical texts did not originally mean what they were subsequently taken to mean, that must be respected.) Rather, the point is that this conception of idolatry, "treating as God that which is not God," is something that develops out of Israel's texts and traditions and that represents a deepening engagement with their basic and consistent concern of preserving loyalty to YHWH. The proposed understanding is therefore neither identical with original understanding nor remote from it, but rather represents a development of the original, preserving important aspects of its substance even while reconfiguring that original. Such recontextualization and re-reading of Old Testament content is, of course, well known among biblical scholars. The question is what one is to make of it, and on what basis. As ever, *how* one reads the biblical text surely depends on *why* one reads it, and I am trying to articulate what is appropriate for reading the Old Testament as Scripture for today.

The notion of idolatry as "treating as God that which is not God" is, I suggest, able to do justice to the primary emphases of both of the main construals

---

because they regarded it almost as the name of an idol: the service of mammon is idolatry" (*Property and Riches in the Ancient Church: Aspects of a Social History of Early Christianity*, trans. John Bowden [London: SCM, 1974], 24).

of idolatry within the Old Testament. On the one hand, it incorporates the Deuteronomic emphasis on "other gods" as a reality, as an ever-present and ever-threatening danger, which bears on what people *do*. One cannot take for granted that allegiance to the true God will be sustained in the face of alternatives. The attractions of other allegiances and of structures of life built around them are both real and powerful, and people can only be weaned off them through sustained moral and spiritual discipline, which is what allegiance to God as "the one and only" should entail. As William Cavanaugh puts it with regard to contemporary American civil religion, "Everyone acknowledges verbally that the nation and the flag are not *really* gods, but the crucial test is what people do with their bodies, both in liturgy and in war."[76] On the other hand, this construal incorporates the mocking dismissal of idols as mere human constructs, deceptive appearances unworthy of true allegiance. Here the rhetoric remains primarily to shame those who should know better.

The modern Western tendency is to regard the difference between "monotheism" and "polytheism" and "atheism" as a matter of deciding, in essence, how many invisible beings of theoretical potency should be recognized to exist (or not); this tendency is so deeply ingrained that it is not easy for an alternative construal to gain a hearing. But part of the point of starting the studies in this book with the Shema is to see that issues of allegiance and life priorities together with corresponding moral and symbolic practices are at the heart of what it means to understand, and be able to appropriate, the Old Testament's portrayal of God. A love supreme is an existential issue, with implications that are as wide-ranging and far-reaching as they could be.

---

76. Cavanaugh, "The Liturgies of Church and State," in his *Migrations*, 115–22, esp. 119.

2

○○○

A Chosen People

○○○

The concept of election, understood as the proposition that God chooses some, that is, Israel/Jews, but not others, that is, nations/gentiles, plays a major role within the Hebrew Bible. But it has not generally found much favor—to put it mildly—in modern Western thought. Nonetheless, it is hardly possible to take seriously the biblical portrayal of God (as in the Shema) without also taking seriously the question of what it does and does not mean that God chooses a people—a conception that, with varying modulations, is classically integral to Jewish, Christian, and Muslim faiths. Jon Levenson, for example, speaks of

> the crucial fact, too often overlooked, that Jewish, Christian, and Muslim monotheism focuses not only on the one God but also on the special human community to whom he has graciously revealed himself and his will in sacred scripture—another aspect unparalleled in pagan (or, philosophical) monotheism.

In this chapter I develop two of my earlier essays: "Is Election Bad for You?" in *The Centre and the Periphery: A European Tribute to Walter Brueggemann*, ed. Jill Middlemas, David J. A. Clines, and Else K. Holt, HBM (Sheffield: Sheffield Phoenix, 2010), 95–111; and "Election and the Transformation of Ḥerem," in *The Call of Abraham: Essays on the Election of Israel in Honor of Jon Levenson*, ed. Gary Anderson and Joel Kaminsky (Notre Dame, IN: Notre Dame University Press, 2013), 67–89.

In the context of Judaism, one thus cannot speak very long or very adequately about God without speaking about the people Israel . . . ; conversely, one cannot speak very long or very adequately about the people Israel without speaking about the God of Israel. Something analogous can be said about Christianity and Islam, but not about pagan monotheism.[1]

Something of the difficulty of working with the notion of a chosen people can be illustrated from the work of probably the most widely read and most influential Christian interpreter of Israel's scriptures in recent years, Walter Brueggemann. In his *Theology of the Old Testament*, election remarkably does not feature where one would expect it in part 1 ("Israel's Core Testimony") but only in part 3 ("Israel's Unsolicited Testimony"), where it takes up less than four pages (in a book of 777 pages).[2] Some sense of why Brueggemann thus downplays election may become apparent from his recent dialogues with Carolyn Sharp, where among other things, he says:

You know, deep in the night, I think about the whole scandal of particularity: about the chosenness of Israel and the chosenness of Jesus and the chosenness of the Church. It's kind of chilling to think that that's how we've made our faith claim. I'm haunted by that stuff.[3]

The engagement with the biblical text will be carried out in dialogue with what I judge to be the two prime objections to election as a feasible element within a contemporary appropriation of the Old Testament. Both objections urge that election should have a place only in the history, but not the present reality, of Jewish or Christian faith. The focus of the chapter will be the presentation of election in Deuteronomy since this will not only continue and complement the study of the Shema in the previous chapter but also pose the important issues in a sharp way.

1. Jon D. Levenson, *Inheriting Abraham: The Legacy of the Patriarch in Judaism, Christianity, and Islam* (Princeton and Oxford: Princeton University Press, 2012), 6.

2. Walter Brueggemann, *Theology of the Old Testament: Testimony, Dispute, Advocacy* (Minneapolis: Fortress, 1997), 414–17. One might note, by way of contrast, that the more old-fashioned and much less read (at least outside Germany) work of Horst Dietrich Preuss (*Old Testament Theology*, 2 vols., trans. Leo Perdue [Edinburgh: T&T Clark, 1995]) uses election as the structuring principle for giving an account of Old Testament faith.

3. Walter Brueggemann with Carolyn J. Sharp, *Living Countertestimony: Conversations with Walter Brueggemann* (Louisville: Westminster John Knox Press, 2012), 88. In her response, Sharp struggles comparably with the notion: "Some of us can easily bracket or disclaim the expressions of particularity that are overtly xenophobic or that are overtly exclusivist—'this is the only way; the rest of you are going to hell.' But nevertheless, deep down, even with all the 'grace' words and the generosity and inclusivity that some of us on the left try to muster, it is chilling, isn't it?"

God's Election of Israel: The Basis of Election

Deuteronomy's Portrayal of Divine Election: The Mystery of Love

In Deuteronomy, as in the Old Testament more generally, Israel's adherence to YHWH is closely correlated with an understanding of their own human identity and vocation. Valid affirmations about God are understood to require self-involving language that entails particular human understandings and practices. As the Shema (Deut. 6:4–9) puts it, because YHWH is "the one and only" (*'eḥād*), it follows that Israel should love YHWH fully and unreservedly. This entails for Israel a self-identity and praxis fundamentally oriented to sustaining the recognition expressed in this confession and response, which is the basic thrust of verses 6–9 in relation to verses 4–5; the all-important understanding and requirement is to be constantly pondered, recited, taught, written, and displayed.[4]

It is hardly accidental that the *locus classicus* about YHWH as "one and only" is closely followed in the next chapter, Deuteronomy 7, by the *locus classicus* about Israel as the chosen people of YHWH. Moses, still the speaking voice as in the Shema, says to Israel:

> [6]For you are a people holy to the LORD your God; the LORD your God has chosen [*bāḥar*] you out of all the peoples on earth to be his people, his treasured possession. [7]It was not because you were more numerous than any other people that the LORD set his heart on [*ḥāshaq*] you and chose [*bāḥar*] you—for you were the fewest of all peoples. [8]It was because the LORD loved [*'āhēv*] you and kept the oath that he swore to your ancestors, that the LORD has brought you out with a mighty hand, and redeemed you from the house of slavery, from the hand of Pharaoh king of Egypt.

Here we see one of the conceptually foundational uses of the specific verb "choose" (*bāḥar*), which has led to "election" becoming a mainstream theological concept. Although the books of Genesis, Exodus, Leviticus, and Numbers clearly portray YHWH's singling out of Abraham and his descendants, it is Deuteronomy that introduces a specific term for this, a term that then passes into the theological lexicon.[5] It becomes clear that the love (*'āhēv*) that

---

4. See chap. 1 above.

5. It is likely that the literary location of *bāḥar* in Deuteronomy to depict YHWH's initiating His relationship with Israel, which is the first such usage of *bāḥar* in the canonical sequence of the OT, corresponds with the probable historical development of election terminology in the seventh or sixth century BC, when Deuteronomy introduced *bāḥar* to give a new and specific focus to an understanding that previously had been expressed in other terms. But my argument does not depend upon this correlation.

Israel is to show to YHWH (6:5) is rooted in YHWH's antecedent love (*'āhēv*) for Israel (7:8).

Significant also is the rooting of election in YHWH's antecedent commitment, His oath, to Israel's ancestors (Abraham, Isaac, and Jacob [v. 8]). This is a recurrent motif in Deuteronomy (e.g., 8:18; 9:5, 27) and is subsequently developed in rabbinic tradition. Paul also sees Israel's election as irrevocable because Israel is "beloved for the sake of their ancestors" (Rom. 11:28).[6]

The presence of an appeal to the ancestors in Moses's intercession (Deut. 9:27) was especially formative. As Tigay puts it: "Moses' invocation of the patriarchs became the precedent for invoking the 'merit of ancestors' (*zĕkhūt 'āvōt*) in Jewish prayers. . . . This concept holds that even when Israel lacks merit, . . . its ancestors' merits can sustain it and God may grant mercy for their sake."[7] Although some Christians have been dismissive of this notion, it is analogous to Christian prayer, not least prayer for mercy, "for the sake of your son, our Savior Jesus Christ." Subsequent generations can in some way still seek to enter into the living heritage of a foundational moment of divine blessing—though when one tries to spell this out more fully the issues rapidly become complex and controverted.

Within the Old Testament, it is noteworthy that the one occasion in the patriarchal narratives that God specifically swears an oath is Genesis 22:16–18, the divine blessing pronounced in response to Abraham's exemplary responsiveness to God in offering Isaac. This story appears to be a paradigmatic account of the meaning of sacrificial worship (as practiced in the Jerusalem temple), with Abraham as the archetypal embodiment of Israel, in which sacrifice represents radical self-dispossession.[8] Insofar as it is appropriate to find intertextual resonance with this story in the repeated Deuteronomic reference to YHWH's keeping the oath that he swore to the ancestors, there would be a rooting of YHWH's choosing Israel in His commendation of Abraham's self-dispossession. This to a certain extent would qualify the rooting of election in a gratuitous love that transcends reason by rooting it also in the acceptable self-offering of Abraham, analogous to the acceptable self-offering of Jesus.

YHWH's delight in Israel and commitment to Israel is formulated strongly: the idea of Israel as a "treasured possession" conveys the image of Israel as the object of YHWH's special delight, and the verb "set his heart on" (*ḥāshaq*) is used elsewhere for the passionate emotion of a man's falling in love with a woman and desiring her.[9] The nature of election as rooted in, and expressive of, the act of divine loving is thus clear.

Generally speaking, one of the recurrent notes that is sounded by a responsive individual recipient of love is an astonished "Why me?" This is a question that always looks for more than actual reasons and explanations, however much some reasons and explanations may indeed be given. The question expresses sheer marvel at the gratuitous wonder of being loved (gratuitous, because even the most admirable personal qualities are no guarantee of being loved by another). The reality of love surpasses the realm of reason. In this sense love is a

6. See also the discussion of Rom. 11:29 near the end of chap. 4 below.
7. Jeffrey Tigay, *The JPS Torah Commentary: Deuteronomy* (Philadelphia and Jerusalem: Jewish Publication Society, 1996), 103.
8. I argue this in my work *The Theology of the Book of Genesis*, OTT (New York and Cambridge: Cambridge University Press, 2009), 179–99.
9. As in Deut. 21:11; cf. Gen. 34:8.

mystery, not in the sense of a puzzle to be resolved but in the sense of a reality whose dimensions grow as people engage with it: in convenient shorthand, "the more you know, the more you know you don't know."[10] If this note of astonished wonder at the unpredictable gift of love is lost, then a significant dimension of understanding the nature of divine choosing is thereby also lost.

This note is sounded again a little further on in Moses's discourse, in Deuteronomy 10. As part of summing up the implications of YHWH's dealings with Israel at Sinai/Horeb and in the wilderness, Moses says:

> [14]Although heaven and the heaven of heavens belong to the LORD your God, the earth and all that is in it, [15]yet the LORD set his heart [hāshaq] in love on your ancestors alone and chose [bāhar] you, their descendants after them, out of all the peoples, as it is today. [16]Circumcise, then,[11] the foreskin of your heart, and do not be stubborn any longer.

If everything in heaven and on earth belongs to YHWH as the sovereign God, then all is at His disposal, and He could take His pick of anyone and anything. So it cannot but be an astonishing wonder that it is Abraham and his descendants who have become the special focus of YHWH's delight and concern. It is not through unawareness of other nations that this account of election is articulated, for it is precisely the recognition of other nations that gives Israel's election its cutting edge of wonder.

The wonder, however, is not an end in itself, for it should motivate a more serious response of obedience on Israel's part. They are to internalize the ritual practice of circumcision, with an imaginatively suggestive metaphor for enhancing responsiveness to YHWH; they are also to renounce the stubborn rebelliousness that has characterized Israel hitherto, as Moses has emphasized in his account of Israel's making the golden calf and its aftermath (9:6b–7, 24). Just as a "Why me?" response to being loved by someone will make most sense if the love is entered into, so Israel's wonder at YHWH's electing love will make most sense if it leads to Israel's entering more fully into covenant obedience.

---

10. This is also, of course, the sense in which God is a mystery; cf. chap. 7 below.

11. This is a good rendering of the Hebrew perfect with *vav* consecutive (*vĕqātal*); see the discussion of the comparable form in Deut. 6:5 (chap. 1 above). The *BHS* editor, Johannes Hempel, has a strange note at this point, wondering whether Deut. 10:16–19 should be "deleted" because it has a plural "you" as distinct from the singular "you" elsewhere in 10:12–22. Such speculation, which is not of a text-critical nature and has no text-critical warrant (cf. the absence of any note previously in *BHK* or subsequently in *BHQ*), should have no place in a text-critical apparatus. Even if a case could be made for the verses as secondary in redactional terms (possible but tenuous), the speculation contributes nothing to an appreciation of the thought expressed in the received text (although v. 20 also voices the need for Israel's renewed adherence to YHWH, and so as a sequel to v. 15 it would not change the direction of the text).

YHWH's requirement for Israel to be faithful is regularly spoken of elsewhere in terms of His being jealous (*qannā'*, as in Deut. 4:24; 5:9; 6:15, cf. Exod. 34:14; Josh. 24:19), precisely because jealousy is a corollary of love when it *matters* that the loved one, especially if covenantally committed (as in marriage), should return the love and not faithlessly go elsewhere.

One prime fact about Israel's election, therefore, is that in an important sense it is an end in itself. It is justified in the way that love is justified—and love is its own justification. Beyond that, one can also say that its value is seen in the richer quality of life that it makes possible. Fundamentally, however, love transcends rationalizations.

Is Election Instrumental?

It is important to emphasize that election expresses YHWH's love for Israel, not least because Christians regularly see God's election of Israel in the Old Testament in solely, or at least predominantly, instrumental terms: election is the vocation to serve God so as to bring blessing to others.[12]

The key text for the instrumental understanding of Israel's election is Genesis 12:3b. A reading of this text as making the point that the election of the one is for the sake of all has entered deeply into contemporary Christian literature, scholarly as well as popular.[13] Political theologian William Cavanaugh, for example, says: "God points the way forward to the salvation of the world by the election of a peculiar people of God. Genesis begins with the story of universal creation, but very quickly descends to the local in the election of Abraham and his people. But the local is for the sake of the universal; in Abraham all the nations of the earth will be blessed (Gen. 12:3)."[14] Likewise popular Christian apologist Rob Bell says:

> In Genesis 12, God tells a man named Abram that he's going to bless him, and through him, he is going to bless the whole world. . . . The blessing is instrumental in nature. God wants to use Abraham, to flow through him, to have him be the conduit through whom God can bless everybody else. Abraham is just a vessel.

12. It is also common for Jews to see their election as being on behalf of others, but the nuances of this position differ in a Jewish frame of reference.

13. It is likely that Gerhard von Rad's reading of the passage in these terms has been hugely influential; see his *Genesis*, trans. John Marks (from 9th German ed.), 3rd ed., OTL (London: SCM, 1972), 152–55, 159–61; I discuss his reading in my work *The Theology of the Book of Genesis*, 141–61.

14. William Cavanaugh, *Migrations of the Holy: God, State, and the Political Meaning of the Church* (Grand Rapids: Eerdmans, 2011), 144; cf. 89. Cavanaugh appeals to Gerhard Lohfink, *Does God Need the Church? Toward a Theology of the People of God*, trans. Linda M. Maloney (Collegeville, MN: Liturgical Press, 1999), where Lohfink (appealing to Westermann, who essentially follows von Rad) reads Gen. 12:3b as a "promise of salvation" showing that "God's concern is for the whole breadth of the world of nations" (30).

God doesn't choose people just so they'll feel good about themselves or secure in their standing with God or whatever else. God chooses people to be used to bless *other* people. Elected, predestined, chosen—whatever words people use for this reality, the point is never the person elected or chosen or predestined. The point is that person serving others, making their lives better.[15]

The Christian value of this is on one level incontrovertible. Self-seeking, complacency, and inertia—in essence, self-centeredness and lack of love for others—constantly blight Christian (and other) living. A challenging call to serve others is indeed biblical. However, even if this is a good reading of Genesis 12:3—though, I suggest, it probably is a canonical re-reading rather than the likely meaning of God's words to Abram in their own right—then it does not follow that it should be generalized in such a way that the witness of Deuteronomy, that there are also other dimensions to Israel's election, is silenced.

Daniel Block, in his recent essay on Deuteronomy, "The Privilege of Calling,"[16] is interested in Israel's "missionary calling," in a way that seems to presuppose the common Christian reading of Genesis 12:3 (although he does not here cite it). Although he concedes that "Israel's missionary function does not receive much space in the record of the Sinai revelation,"[17] he nonetheless finds its presence in the divine speech that introduces the Sinai material, Exodus 19:3–6 (part of which is very similar to Deut. 7:6): "Now therefore, if you will indeed obey my voice and keep my covenant, you shall be my treasured possession among all peoples, for all the earth is mine; and you shall be to me a kingdom of priests and a holy nation" (Exod. 19:5–6 ESV). Block comments on Israel's call to be a holy people that "God did not separate Israel from the nations so that he might merely lavish his attention on her as if she were a pet kitten or a china dish on a shelf"; rather, "Israel collectively was to serve as a link between God and the world. The need for mediation was created by the estrangement of the world from its Creator. As YHWH's priests, Israel was to declare the light of his revelation to the nations and to intercede on their behalf before Him."[18] We see the familiar Christian picture of sin and salvation, with salvation mediated by the mission of God's faithful people—although Block points out that the mission is centripetal in the Old Testament, with nations coming to Israel when attracted by Israel's way of living.[19]

The key issue is Block's construal of Israel's special position as directed to the nations. He says, "With the addition of 'for all the earth is mine' (Exod. 19:5), YHWH's implicit universal concern is rendered explicit. And only from this perspective can Israel's law be understood. God gave the law to his people *in order* to declare to the world what his glory and grace could accomplish in the lives of the destitute and enslaved."[20] He correspondingly reads Deuteronomy's references to the nations out of whom YHWH has called Israel as likewise expressing YHWH's "universal concern."

15. Rob Bell, *Velvet Elvis: Repainting the Christian Faith* (Grand Rapids: Zondervan, 2005), 165.

16. Daniel I. Block, "The Privilege of Calling: The Mosaic Paradigm for Missions (Deut 26:16–19)," in his work *How I Love Your Torah, O LORD! Studies in the Book of Deuteronomy* (Eugene, OR: Cascade Books, 2011), 140–61.

17. Ibid., 159.

18. Ibid., 157.

19. Ibid., 160.

20. Ibid., 159.

Block's interesting reading is surely, however, an instructive misreading that subtly but significantly changes the thought of the Deuteronomic text. For he does not consider those texts within the Old Testament indicating that the prime responsibility of a priest is to serve YHWH, to face toward God rather than toward people.[21] Nor does he consider the possibility that reference to the nations of the earth may be not to indicate YHWH's universal *concern* (such that Israel's election is for their benefit) but rather to indicate YHWH's universal *dominion* and *power* so as rhetorically and existentially to highlight the wonder of His choice of Israel: the God who could have chosen anyone or everyone has in fact chosen Israel to be the ones in whom He takes special delight, and He wills to exalt them accordingly, when they are rightly responsive to Him (26:18–19).

Interestingly, both Bell and Block (in the preceding small font section) shy away from YHWH's election of Israel as an end in itself by depicting such a notion pejoratively ("just so they'll feel good about themselves"; "that he might merely lavish his attention on her as if she were a pet kitten or a china dish on a shelf"). It is curious that they are unable here to articulate the nature of love of one to another as a wondrous good, of value in itself, even though I imagine that they would have no difficulty in doing so in other contexts.

This may be connected to a failure also to think through the nature of the blessing that Israel is to mediate to others (on the common Christian reading of Genesis 12:3b). For should not reception of that blessing entail a realization on the part of people in other nations that God loves them for themselves? If not, then in what does the blessing consist? Even if that love brings with it a call to serve, that service is a corollary to being loved, not the core of being loved. So too, the Israelites are loved for themselves, prior to any impact for good that they may have on others.

Is Election Tribal and Unjust?

One classic critique of the notion of election, articulated especially in the eighteenth century, is that it represents something tribal, parochial, and blinkered, and that such narrowness is incompatible with belief in one God, who to be God at all must be God for all. Some Enlightenment thinkers predicated such tribalism of Judaism in order to contrast it unfavorably with the universality of Christianity. Others, however, argued that Christianity also compared unfavorably with the true universality of a "natural" religion in which all particular (or in eighteenth-century terminology, "positive," i.e., humanly posited) religious traditions were judged, and found to be more or less wanting, by the yardstick of rational religious purity. Such purity would best be found in forms of religious belief and practice

---

21. Compare 1 Sam. 2:28. The godward direction of a priest's responsibilities also constitutes the first two of the three priestly functions specified in Deut. 10:8; the third function of blessing, however, envisages orientation toward others.

that abandoned biblical content—which in the eighteenth century meant deism.[22] In this early-modern scenario, election came to be considered as unambiguously negative.

Even if it was Enlightenment thinkers and their intellectual descendants who have repeatedly urged this objection, it is by no means a purely modern phenomenon. The Emperor Julian, known for his rejection of Christianity in the fourth century ("Julian the Apostate"), articulated precisely this problem in his own way. Speaking as a Hellene (that is, identifying himself with historic Greek culture), Julian asked: "For if he is the God of all of us alike and the creator of all, why did he neglect us?"[23]

In recent years, a forceful critique of election has been articulated by Rolf Knierim, in the very context of his seeking to offer an account of the continuing significance of the Old Testament for Christian faith:

> The exclusionary election theology[24] contradicts the Old Testament concept of God's universal, indivisible justice, and that the violation of universally equal justice, especially by violence, is sinful. . . . Also, by subjecting the theology of creation to the theology of exclusionary election, it discredits the claim that Yahweh is truly and justifiably the universal deity. Lastly, it represents the most serious theological perversion of the notion of God and, thus, the most serious among all possible and actual similarly sinful theologized ideologies. . . . For decisive reasons, the theology of creation is not only the widest framework of the Old Testament theology; it is [also] the basis of and criterion for the validity of Israel's or any election.[25]

On the one hand creation (universal) trumps election (particular). On the other hand, because the particularity of election denies the requirements of justice, it can be no more than a self-serving tribal construct inappropriately foisted on others in the much-misused name of God ("sinful theologized

22. For the anti-biblical polemic of Thomas Paine in his advocacy of deism, see chap. 4 below.

23. Julian the Apostate, *Contra Galilaeos* 106d; cited and discussed in John Granger Cook, *The Interpretation of the Old Testament in Greco-Roman Paganism*, STAC 23 (Tübingen: Mohr Siebeck, 2004), 333, 339.

24. By "exclusionary election theology" Knierim means the concept of election that he sees as predominant in the OT, especially in the Pentateuch and Joshua, whereby Israel's election is not for the sake of humanity but rather of benefit to Israel at the expense of others. The status of other nations as blessed, rather than cursed, is not the purpose of Israel's election but the result of their favorable stance ("blessing") toward Israel. So election favors Israel; others are only favored if they too favor Israel: all is for Israel's benefit. Although I have substantial exegetical agreement with Knierim about the construal of the crucial Gen. 12:3 (see n. 13 above), I think that the key interpretive issues can be otherwise, and better, expressed.

25. Rolf P. Knierim, *The Task of Old Testament Theology: Method and Cases* (Grand Rapids: Eerdmans, 1995), 452.

ideologies"). Election is apparently to be removed from a constructive account of the enduring significance of Israel's scriptures.[26]

Alternatively, David Clines regularly challenges Jewish and Christian overfamiliarity with, and apparently unthinking acceptance of, many of the perspectives within Israel's scriptures. He argues that scholars, as scholars, should stand outside the biblical frame of reference, rather than identify with it; they should not share, but rather challenge, the ideology of the biblical text and its authors. Not least, he encourages readers of the Old Testament imaginatively to put themselves in the position of those who were not elected by YHWH. For example, he encourages a reading of Psalm 2 from the perspective of those (whom he calls "Moabites") who in the psalm are subjected to the rule of a king in Jerusalem: "It is not only fictional 'Moabites' who have fetters upon them but real people at the end of the twentieth century also who are constrained by the psalm to believe that God has favorites among the peoples of the earth, has no time for the idea of toleration, and resorts to violence to solve his problems."[27] Elsewhere he says, "How can we modern readers of the Bible cope with the fact that the God represented in the Bible is a national deity? If you adopt the point of view of the Egyptians or the Canaanites, God is not experienced as a saving God, and the only words you will hear addressed to you are words of reproach and threat."[28]

Clearly, there is real force in this kind of objection to divine election. If there are the chosen, then there are also, in some sense, the unchosen. And if one ceases to assume, or at least hopefully expect, that one is among the chosen, but rather adopts, even if only in imagination, the position of the unchosen,[29] then the possible objections to divine election can be numerous.

There are real difficulties here. For example, a classic modern critique of the exodus and conquest narratives is that by Robert Allen Warrior.[30] Its potency lies in his reading the biblical narratives

26. For thoughtful Jewish critiques of Knierim's approach to election, see Joel S. Kaminsky, "Wrestling with Israel's Election: A Jewish Reaction to Rolf Knierim's Biblical Theology," in *Reading the Bible for a New Millennium*, vol. 1, *Theological and Hermeneutical Studies*, ed. Wonil Kim et al., SAC (Harrisburg, PA: Trinity Press International, 2000), 252–62; and Jon D. Levenson's review essay, "Rolf P. Knierim, *The Task of Old Testament Theology: Method and Cases*," *RelSRev* 24/1 (1998), 39–42; and his "The Universal Horizon of Biblical Particularism," in *Ethnicity and the Bible*, ed. Mark Brett (Leiden: Brill, 1996), 143–69.

27. David J. A. Clines, "Psalm 2 and the MLF (Moabite Liberation Front)," in his *Interested Parties: The Ideology of Writers and Readers of the Hebrew Bible*, JSOTSS 205 (Sheffield: Sheffield Academic Press, 1995), 244–75, esp. 273.

28. David Clines, *The Bible and the Modern World*, BS 51 (Sheffield: Sheffield Academic Press, 1997), 100.

29. This can be a potent motif in literature, as in the portrayal of Captain Ahab in Herman Melville's *Moby Dick* (New York: Harper & Brothers, 1851), or of Michael Henchard in Thomas Hardy's *The Mayor of Casterbridge* (London: Smith, Elder, 1886).

30. Robert Allen Warrior, "Canaanites, Cowboys, and Indians: Deliverance, Conquest, and Liberation Theology Today," in *The Postmodern Bible Reader*, ed. David Jobling, Tina Pippin,

"against the grain" from the perspective of the Canaanites. He does this because he is an Osage Indian who is explicitly drawing a parallel with Christian appeal to these texts in modern American history as a warrant for dispossessing Native Americans from their ancestral lands.

The broader phenomenon of postcolonial criticism develops these concerns, often with high levels of unease about biblical content. As R. S. Sugirtharajah puts it, "What postcolonial biblical criticism has done is to treat texts no longer as moral or spiritual reservoirs, but as a system of codes which interpreters must disentangle in order to reveal the hidden power relations and ideologies lurking in supposedly innocent narratives." Unsurprisingly, he sees "the idea of the chosen race," as in Deuteronomy, as "endowing [Israel's] role in history with an imagined importance" and as signifying nothing more than "a form of colonialism."[31]

For the present I would just note, with reference to Warrior's critique, that the American government representatives' appeal to the biblical text was abusive because they were in a position of power and were using the Bible self-servingly. As we will see, the rhetoric of Deuteronomy 7, that Yhwh gives His people the victory, should not be separated from His giving it to Israel when they are small and weak and facing apparently overwhelming odds. Those who use the Bible in a position of strength should not forget that meaning is relative to context, and that what is said to Israel in weakness can differ significantly from what is said to Israel in strength.

A major difficulty in understanding the Deuteronomic conception of election is finding the right frame of reference for it.[32] The problematizing of the particular in the light of the universal, in terms of justice and equity, undoubtedly has a certain logic that can feel compelling. But such a frame of reference, which tends to depend upon a somewhat abstract rationality, is not the only frame of reference. For, as we have seen, Deuteronomy's logic is the logic of love and of the sheer wonder that being the recipient of gratuitous love can entail.

In recent years the nature of election has been discussed especially by Jewish scholars, who have searchingly probed what it does and does not mean.[33] Michael Wyschogrod, for example, has written:

> The love with which God has chosen to love man is a love understandable to man. It is therefore a love very much aware of human response. God has thereby made himself vulnerable: he asks for man's response and is hurt when it is not forthcoming. For the same reason, God's love is not undifferentiated, having the same quality toward all his children. God's love is directed toward who we are.

---

and Ronald Schleifer (Oxford: Blackwell, 2001), 188–94. The essay originally appeared in 1989 and has been reprinted in various contexts.

31. R. S. Sugirtharajah, *Exploring Postcolonial Biblical Criticism: History, Method, Practice* (Chichester: Wiley-Blackwell, 2012), 181, 185.

32. See also the discussion of David's election in chap. 4 below.

33. See esp. Jon D. Levenson, *The Death and Resurrection of the Beloved Son: The Transformation of Child Sacrifice in Judaism and Christianity* (New Haven and London: Yale University Press, 1993); and Joel S. Kaminsky, *Yet I Loved Jacob: Reclaiming the Biblical Concept of Election* (Nashville: Abingdon, 2007); also the account of recent Jewish scholarship on this topic in Joel N. Lohr, *Chosen and Unchosen: Conceptions of Election in the Pentateuch and Jewish-Christian Interpretation*, Siphrut 2 (Winona Lake, IN: Eisenbrauns, 2009), 32–91.

We are confirmed as who we are in our relationship to God. And because God is so deeply directed toward us, because his love is . . . true meeting of the other (and there is an other for God; this is the mystery of creation), there are those whom God loves especially, with whom he has fallen in love, as with Abraham. . . .

What, now, of those not elected? Those not elected cannot be expected not to be hurt by not being of the seed of Abraham, whom God loves above all others. The Bible clearly depicts the suffering of Esau. . . . And yet, in recounting the blessing of Jacob and the exclusion of Esau, no careful reader can fail to notice that the sympathy shown Esau is greater than that for Jacob. God shows Esau compassion even if Jacob does not. The consolation of the gentiles is the knowledge that God also stands in relationship with them in the recognition and affirmation of their uniqueness. . . . The mystery of Israel's election thus turns out to be the guarantee of the fatherhood of God toward all peoples, elect and nonelect, Jew and gentile.[34]

One way of reading Wyschogrod is to see that election makes Israel the embodiment of a vocation greater than itself, to display the priority of divine love in human life (and so there are instrumental dimensions in Israel's election). In an extended way it simultaneously intensifies and transforms the unequal particularities of all life, doing so in such a way as to charge those heightened inequalities with heightened possibilities of responding to God, for those who have eyes to see and ears to hear. Such an account deserves careful reflection.

On any reckoning, however, the wonder of being loved is surely not other than the mystery of grace; it is non-negotiable as a fundamental element in Jewish and Christian faiths. Of course, numerous other factors need to come into any developed account of grace, and the historic disagreements between Jews and Christians (and between distinct Christian traditions) over the difference that Jesus may make to one's account of grace serve as a reminder of the complexity of issues involved. Likewise, the question of how best one should relate the particular concerns of divine love to universal concerns of divine justice is complex and resists easy answers. For the present, my argument is simply that divine election, insofar as it expresses the mysterious grace of God, is something without which neither Jewish nor Christian faiths can survive in recognizable forms.[35] For to lose this would be to lose the particular grace that gives faith its basic meaning and rationale.

34. Michael Wyschogrod, *The Body of Faith: God in the People Israel* (Northvale, NJ: Jason Aronson, 1996), 63–65.
35. I am conscious that in this section I have made claims about what is essential to Jewish faith in a way that does not do justice to the contested place of election in some contemporary Judaism. It is the logic of classic Judaism that I have in mind.

God's Election of Israel: *Ḥērem* as the Consequence of Election

Does Divine Election Entail Violence toward Others?

Although a critique of divine election as tribal and unjust is a long-running critique, it is perhaps not the prime critique of election at the present. Rather, contemporary anxieties seem more to relate to the way in which belief in a chosen people seems to be a corollary of belief in a sole deity (at least, among Jews, Christians, and Muslims), and the way in which such belief makes problematic the relationship between the chosen people and others. A characteristic sign of the times is that essays and books whose titles and content link classic belief in God and election with *violence* are on the increase.[36]

Typical of many is prize-winning novelist Philip Pullman. In an interview, when asked about his apparent antipathy toward God and the church in his novels, Pullman explains his attitude as follows:

> Well, all right, it comes from history. It comes from the record of the Inquisition, persecuting heretics and torturing Jews and all that sort of stuff; and it comes from the other side, too, from the Protestants burning the Catholics. It comes from the insensate pursuit of innocent and crazy old women, and from the Puritans in America burning and hanging the witches—and it comes not only from the Christian Church but also from the Taliban.
>
> *Every single religion that has a monotheistic god ends up by persecuting other people and killing them because they don't accept him. Wherever you look in history, you find that. It's still going on.*[37]

Alternatively, from within a biblically rooted faith, the former British Chief Rabbi, Jonathan Sacks, says: "Since September 11, many reflective people have wondered whether there is something not just about fundamentalism but [also] about religion itself, specifically monotheism, that gives rise to violence in the name of God. This is an old claim but an important one, and we must face it honestly."[38]

---

36. One notable example among many in the biblical sphere is Regina M. Schwartz, *The Curse of Cain: The Violent Legacy of Monotheism* (Chicago: Chicago University Press, 1997), which I have discussed in my essay "Is Monotheism Bad for You? Some Reflections on God, the Bible, and Life in the Light of Regina Schwartz's *The Curse of Cain*," in *The God of Israel*, ed. R. P. Gordon, UCOP 64 (Cambridge: Cambridge University Press, 2007), 94–112. A valuable general treatment (though it does not discuss the OT) is by Miroslav Volf, "Christianity and Violence," in *War in the Bible and Terrorism in the Twenty-First Century*, ed. Richard R. Hess and Elmer A. Martens, BBRS 2 (Winona Lake, IN: Eisenbrauns, 2008), 1–17.

37. Philip Pullman, "Heat and Dust," *Third Way* 25/2 (April 2002): 22–26; repr. in *Church Times* [Anglican, UK], April 5, 2002, 14–15, emphasis added.

38. Jonathan Sacks, "Credo," *The Times* [London], April 20, 2002.

When Sacks refers to this as an "old" claim, I am not sure exactly what pedigree he envisages. To the best of my knowledge, the first modern thinker to argue that monotheism is inherently intolerant and violent was David Hume in the eighteenth century. In Hume's *The Natural History of Religion* (1757) we read, for example: "The intolerance of almost all religions, which have maintained the unity of God, is as remarkable as the contrary principle of polytheists."[39]

In any case, whatever the pedigree, the concern has become widespread that a classic biblically-rooted belief in a single deity who chooses particular people is problematic because it entails attitudes of exclusiveness and/or practices of violence toward those identified as "other." This critique is one that Jews and Christians should take seriously. The critique is not just because of the historical record of Christian societies, but also because of the biblical roots of faith. Deuteronomy in particular, the central Old Testament text on which we are focusing, poses the precise problem.

Deuteronomy's Portrayal of Divine Election: A Rationale for "Holy War" (Ḥērem)

Deuteronomy's prime passage about election, Deuteronomy 7:6–8, begins with the little word "for" (*kī*), which relates it intimately to what precedes. This is what we must now consider.

> [1]When the LORD your God brings you into the land that you are about to enter and occupy, and he clears away many nations before you—the Hittites, the Girgashites, the Amorites, the Canaanites, the Perizzites, the Hivites, and the Jebusites, seven nations mightier and more numerous than you— [2]and when the LORD your God gives them over to you and you defeat them, then you must utterly destroy them [*haḥărēm taḥărīm*, the verb is an emphatic form of the root from which the noun *ḥērem* is derived].[40] Make no covenant with them and show them no mercy. [3]Do not intermarry with them, giving your daughters to their sons or taking their daughters for your sons, [4]for that would turn away your children from following me, to serve other gods. Then

---

39. David Hume, *Dialogues concerning Natural Religion; and, The Natural History of Religion*, ed. J. C. A. Gaskin (Oxford: Oxford University Press, 1993), 162. Whether or not Hume is right is perhaps a moot point. Or to put it differently, one might ask about the sphere in which tolerance or intolerance is exercised. For example, Hinduism, classically an example of what looks to the Western mind like *theological* tolerance—in terms of belief in various deities (though whether Hinduism really is "polytheistic" is disputed)—has for much of its history maintained a rigid caste system and thus has been *socially* intolerant. The relationship between theological beliefs and life practices is almost always more complex than summary categorizing allows.

40. Below I discuss the problems with the rendering "destroy."

the anger of the Lord would be kindled against you, and he would destroy you quickly. ⁵But this is how you must deal with them: break down their altars, smash their pillars, hew down their sacred poles, and burn their idols with fire. ⁶For you are a people holy to the Lord your God; the Lord your God has chosen [*bāḥar*] you out of all the peoples on earth to be his people, his treasured possession.

Israel's elect status provides the basis for the uncompromising practice of "holy war" toward seven other nations who reside in the land that Yhwh is giving to Israel. The fact that verse 6 begins with "for" makes unambiguous that *election is specified here so as to underwrite the just-mentioned practice of "holy war."*

The term "holy war" originated in the study of Islam, was transferred into Old Testament study in the early twentieth century, and was popularized especially by Gerhard von Rad.[41] The appropriateness of the term both within Islam and within the Old Testament is contestable and contested.[42] Nonetheless, since the term is well established in both scholarly and popular usage, there is a case for continuing to use it (akin to that for continuing to use "monotheism")[43] with suitable flexibility and reserve.

I am using the term "holy war" as a provisional rendering of a particular Hebrew noun, *ḥērem*,[44] whose verbal form is used in 7:2. The NRSV, typical among recent translations, translates this verbal form of *ḥērem* (v. 2b), which depicts what Israel is to do to certain other nations, as "destroy." Here, in material that closely follows the Shema in Deuteronomy 6, we surely have *the* prima facie biblical warrant for the contemporary anxiety that "monotheism" and the notion of a chosen people are deeply problematic, because they entail murderous violence toward others. Thus Gerd Lüdemann, for example, is apparently doing no more than highlighting the plain sense of the biblical text when he says, in the course of a more general discussion of Deuteronomy: "The Holy War . . . and the message of Deuteronomy, are loaded with violence, and those responsible for them wanted in their minds to exterminate whole

41. See Ben C. Ollenburger, "Gerhard von Rad's Theory of Holy War," intro. in Gerhard von Rad, *Holy War in Ancient Israel*, trans. and ed. Marva Dawn (Grand Rapids: Eerdmans, 1991), 1–33, esp. 4–6.

42. The issues are well discussed in Stephen B. Chapman, "Martial Memory, Peaceable Vision: Divine War in the Old Testament," in *Holy War in the Bible: Christian Morality and an Old Testament Problem*, ed. Heath A. Thomas, Jeremy Evans, and Paul Copan (Downers Grove, IL: IVP Academic, 2013), 47–67.

43. See chap. 1 above.

44. A useful survey of recent scholarly discussion of *ḥērem*, which serves to show the extent of scholarly disagreement on most issues to do with it (because of the paucity and intrinsic complexity of the evidence), is by K. Lawson Younger, "Some Recent Discussion on the Ḥerem," in *Far from Minimal: Celebrating the Work and Influence of Philip R. Davies*, ed. Duncan Burns and John W. Rogerson, LHBOTS 484 (London: T&T Clark, 2012), 505–22.

peoples in the name of God. . . . Its content is the claim to exclusiveness made by an intolerant deity or, more precisely, the image of an intolerant God who chooses Israel."[45]

Here we face what may be *the* quintessential enigma and challenge of the Old Testament. One moment we are considering the mystery and wonder of divine love as fundamental to the calling and choosing of Israel; the next moment we are considering such choosing as a basis for apparent divinely-sponsored genocide. One moment we see God as loving; the next moment we see a deity who apparently sponsors mass murder. How should this be approached and understood?

Some Approaches to the Problem of Election and Violence

Remarkably, one common approach, at least on the part of Christian Old Testament scholars, is in effect silence. It is commonplace for Old Testament theologians to cite Deuteronomy 7:6–8 as a prime passage for understanding election in the Old Testament, and yet to say nothing about its immediate literary context of *ḥērem* or the role that election plays in relation to *ḥērem*. Nearly every significant work of Old Testament theology in recent years—those of Eichrodt, von Rad, Zimmerli, Clements, Childs, Preuss, Brueggemann, Gerstenberger, Goldingay, Rendtorff, Waltke[46]—mentions the theological importance of Deuteronomy 7:6–8 for understanding election while saying nothing about its immediate context, as though apparently it can and should be understood on its own in an axiomatic way.[47] One can,

---

45. Gerd Lüdemann, *The Unholy in Holy Scripture: The Dark Side of the Bible*, trans. John Bowden from the 1996 German ed. (London: SCM, 1997), 55–75, esp. 73.

46. Walther Eichrodt, *Theology of the Old Testament*, trans. J. A. Baker from German, 2 vols. (London: SCM, 1961–67), 1:256; 2:299, 372; Gerhard von Rad, *Old Testament Theology*, trans. D. M. G. Stalker, 2 vols. (London: SCM, 1965–75), 1:178; Walther Zimmerli, *Old Testament Theology in Outline*, trans. David Green (Edinburgh: T&T Clark, 1978), 45; R. E. Clements, *Old Testament Theology: A Fresh Approach* (London: Marshall, Morgan & Scott, 1978), 87–89; Brevard S. Childs, *Old Testament Theology in a Canonical Context* (London: SCM, 1985), 44; idem, *Biblical Theology of the Old and New Testaments* (London: SCM, 1992), 426; Horst Dietrich Preuss, *Old Testament Theology*, trans. Leo Perdue (Edinburgh: T&T Clark, 1995), 1:31–33, 38, 40; Walter Brueggemann, *Theology of the Old Testament: Testimony, Dispute, Advocacy* (Minneapolis: Fortress, 1997), 415–17, 497; Erhard Gerstenberger, *Theologies in the Old Testament*, trans. John Bowden (Minneapolis: Fortress, 2002), 86; John Goldingay, *Old Testament Theology*, vol. 1, *Israel's Gospel* (Downers Grove, IL: InterVarsity, 2003), 215, and cf. 498; Rolf Rendtorff, *The Canonical Hebrew Bible: A Theology of the Old Testament*, trans. David Orton (Leiden: Deo, 2005), 90, 461; Bruce K. Waltke with Charles Yu, *An Old Testament Theology* (Grand Rapids: Zondervan, 2007), 509.

47. This is a point about recent OT theologies and the implications of their genre. Insofar as Christian scholars write commentaries on Deuteronomy and work sequentially through the text, this problem does not arise in the same way.

of course, make a case for starting with election prior to discussing holy war, as has been done here, so that one can attend to the affirmation of the mystery of divine love without the voice of 7:6–8 being drowned out by clamor about genocide. But for scholars not even to recognize, or mention, the context within Deuteronomy is all too reminiscent of proof-texting; and it does not offer readers of Israel's scriptures the help with understanding its content that they need.

An alternative approach could be to try to ease (evade?) the problem by appeal to traditio-historical and redactional theories about the possible formation of the Deuteronomic text. It has been proposed, for example, that the material about ḥērem in 7:1–5 is a "later accretion" and that the "for" of 7:6 originally justified the observances in 6:20–25.[48] Thus, in an earlier and more pristine version of Moses's discourse, election did not underwrite holy war. But this hypothesis, like many comparable hypotheses that fill discussions of the tradition-history and composition of Deuteronomy, mainly serves to show that it is easy to imagine differing linkages between the differing constituent elements of Moses's discourse. In any case, one still needs to give an account of the thought and flow of the text in its received form, which is the form in which historically it has impacted Jews and Christians, and in which it still impacts readers today.

Another approach is to try to ease the difficulty by arguing that the kind of warfare represented by ḥērem was part of the common cultural coinage of the ancient Near East. That is simply how people thought and what people did then: "We rightly recognize now that in this the Israelites shared very much the same religious outlook as their contemporaries."[49] "The general spirit of the ḥerem coincided with the accepted ethics of the Ancient Near East."[50] Israel's practices made sense in the ancient world and are a reminder that modern Western anxieties about violence were not shared by many previous ages. Unarguably, a good historical awareness of differences across the ages, and an ability to try to see things within their own frame of reference, is always of value; and there are also dimensions of the Old Testament that Christians do not, and should not, wish to appropriate today. But is the assumption of common cultural coinage correct?

There is indeed evidence that ḥērem was a practice of war beyond the context of ancient Israel. Most famously, the language of ḥērem has been found in a rare surviving text from one of Israel's immediate neighbors: the

---

48. So Yair Hoffman, "The Deuteronomistic Concept of the Ḥerem," *ZAW* 111 (1999): 196–210, esp. 202.

49. Rex Mason, *Propaganda and Subversion in the Old Testament* (London: SPCK, 1997), 6.

50. Hoffman, "Ḥerem," 197.

ninth-century Moabite Stone.[51] Here Mesha, king of Moab, tells of how, among other things, "Kemosh said to me, 'Go seize Nebo from Israel.'" Subsequently he was victorious and killed seven thousand Israelite prisoners "for I devoted it [Nebo] to Ashtar-Kemosh."[52] There is also a usage in a Sabaean text (RES 3945) of South Arabia, possibly from the seventh century, that can be interpreted as depicting the military action of a Sabaean king, Karib-ilu, who "devoted the city of Nashan to the ḥērem by burning."[53] However, it would be unwise to generalize on the basis of such evidence. In particular, there is no definite evidence that ḥērem was practiced in the two major centers of civilization of the ancient Near East, Mesopotamia and Egypt, still less that it was linked to their people's own self-understandings as peoples (as is the case for Israel in Deuteronomy).[54] No doubt armies and cities were regularly wiped out in ancient warfare by Assyrians, Babylonians, and Egyptians; but in terms of the available evidence, these were not conceived, or prescribed, in the category of ḥērem.[55] As such, the concern with ḥērem must be seen as characteristically, although not uniquely, Israelite.

A Reading of Deuteronomy 7:1–5

How then might progress be made? Although the issues are complex, prolonged reflection upon Deuteronomy has nonetheless led me to think that there are factors both within the biblical text and within its history of reception that offer a constructive way ahead. In essence, my argument (in classic Christian

51. This is available in all standard collections of ancient Near Eastern material, e.g., ANET 320–21. For detailed analysis of the text and language, see Kent P. Jackson and J. Andrew Dearman, "The Text of the Mesha Inscription"; and Kent P. Jackson, "The Language of the Mesha Inscription"; both in Studies in the Mesha Inscription and Moab, ed. J. Andrew Dearman, ABS 2 (Atlanta: Scholars Press, 1989), 93–130.

52. This is line 17 of the inscription. The verb rendered "devote" represents the root ḥrm, in a verbal form analogous to the hiphil verbal form in Deut. 7:2; 20:17.

53. See Lauren A. S. Monroe, "Israelite, Moabite and Sabaean War-Ḥērem Traditions and the Forging of National Identity: Reconsidering the Sabaean Text RES 3945 in Light of Biblical and Moabite Evidence," VT 57 (2007): 318–41, esp. 333.

54. There are difficulties in knowing what constitutes evidence here, not least if the ḥrm root is not used yet there seem to be similar practices. For a survey of other possible ancient Near Eastern uses of, or analogues to, the ḥrm root, see Philip D. Stern, The Biblical Ḥerem: A Window on Israel's Religious Experience, BJS 211 (Atlanta: Scholars Press, 1991), 5–87.

55. To be sure, in a biblical account the Rabshakeh speaks of Assyria as practicing ḥērem (2 Kings 19:11//Isa. 37:11); but the Rabshakeh's speeches are Israelite compositions, full of rhetoric that in narrative terms is meant to be (1) representative of what an Assyrian might consider persuasive to Israelites/Judahites in a besieged city and (2) deeply ironic from the perspective of an informed reader who understands Deuteronomic theology. Such language should not be taken as evidence for Assyria's own understanding of its military practices.

terminology) is that careful attention to the *letter* of the text indicates that its *spirit* is in fact other than is envisaged by contemporary anxieties about divinely warranted mass murder. I will in effect propose that attention to the *letter* of the text problematizes a *literalist* construal.

> [1]When the LORD your God brings you into the land that you are about to enter and occupy, and he clears away many nations before you—the Hittites, the Girgashites, the Amorites, the Canaanites, the Perizzites, the Hivites, and the Jebusites, seven nations mightier and more numerous than you— [2]and when the LORD your God gives them over to you and you defeat them, then you must utterly destroy them [ḥaḥărēm taḥărīm]. Make no covenant with them and show them no mercy. [3]Do not intermarry with them, giving your daughters to their sons or taking their daughters for your sons, [4]for that would turn away your children from following me, to serve other gods. Then the anger of the LORD would be kindled against you, and he would destroy you quickly. [5]But this is how you must deal with them: break down their altars, smash their pillars, hew down their sacred poles, and burn their idols with fire.

It is important initially to recognize the rhetorical nature of the text and to take this rhetoric seriously without taking it woodenly. On the one hand, the seven nations of 7:1 can hardly be placed on a map of Canaan in terms of historical geography. "Seven" in Hebrew idiom often functions to indicate "many" rather than a precise number (as in "Your enemies . . . shall come out against you one way, and flee before you seven ways" [Deut. 28:7]).[56] Moreover, comparable lists of the peoples of Canaan in other contexts (e.g., Gen. 15:20–21; Exod. 3:8, 17; 13:5), lists that vary both in the number and identity of those mentioned, suggests that the function of the lists is more rhetorical than geographical. In other words, the seven nations are probably symbolic opponents who represent a threat to Israel within its home territory.

On the other hand, the strongly rhetorical character of Deuteronomy 7 as a whole is evident in its depiction of the seven nations as "mightier and more numerous" than Israel, such that they make Israel afraid as to how they can succeed against them (7:1, 17). It stands in obvious tension with the rhetoric elsewhere, that YHWH has made Israel "as numerous as the stars of heaven" (1:10; 10:22), whose purpose is to evoke gratitude to YHWH for fulfilling His promises to their ancestors (cf. Gen. 15:5; 22:17; 26:4). Recognition of this rhetoric, with its formal inconsistencies, suggests that Israel also, like the

---

56. Similarly the idiom "seven times" means "many times" (e.g., Gen. 4:15; Ps. 79:12; Prov. 6:31; 24:16).

seven nations, takes on in this context a symbolic character. Both peoples are perhaps somewhat like "ideal types," who play an imaginative role in enabling one to think about an issue.

Moreover, the rhetoric about the smallness of Israel in relation to the seven nations is explicitly used to put Israel in mind of their exodus from Egypt; as YHWH delivered them once, so He can do again (7:17–19), and this should induce them to have confidence not in themselves but in YHWH. Deuteronomy, like the book of Exodus, portrays Israel vis-à-vis Egypt rather as David vis-à-vis Goliath. The victory that YHWH gives, whether over Egypt or over the nations of Canaan, is a victory against the odds ("These nations are more numerous than I; how can I dispossess them?" [7:17]), which is only possible through divine enabling rather than conventional strength. The implied reader, who identifies with the people of Israel, is one who identifies with a people who are weak in relation to more powerful others and so who look to God for strength. This perspective should be fundamental to any responsible use of the biblical text; for a text that envisages YHWH as enabling David to be victorious over Goliath becomes entirely different if claimed by Goliath as divine warrant for overcoming David.

Besides these issues of rhetoric, the biblical text poses interesting issues of translation and interpretation—especially with regard to the key term *ḥērem*. Despite the frequency with which the verbal form of *ḥērem* (7:2b) is translated with a straightforward English verb that signifies the taking of life ("destroy," KJV, NRSV; "exterminate," REB), I suggest that such a translation may beg the interpretive question. Deuteronomy has two other verbs to express a straightforward sense of "destroy."[57] Moreover, the conceptuality of *ḥērem* is on any reckoning more complex than "destroy," even if in certain contexts destruction might be entailed. It appears that the prime sense is a matter of making something the exclusive possession of YHWH and thereby removing it from the sphere of regular human use. Even though this could entail destruction, it is important to realize that "'destruction' is a secondary implication of *ḥērem* and not its primary meaning."[58] There is thus a case for translating the verbal form with "put under the ban," or simply "ban," not least because such a translation has the merit of being somewhat opaque and thus prevents the contemporary reader from too readily assuming that the meaning of the word is understood.

---

57. Most common is *hishmīd*, which strikingly is used frequently for YHWH's bringing an end to Israel if they are faithless (Deut. 7:4; 9:8, 14; etc.), though it is also used for YHWH's actions on Israel's behalf against other nations (2:21; 9:3) and can be used for the actions of one nation against another (2:12). The other verb, apparently synonymous, is *ha'ăvīd* (7:10, 24; 8:20; 9:3).

58. Chapman, "Martial Memory," 57.

The noun *ḥērem* has a long postbiblical history.[59] In due course it came to be the term for expulsion and exclusion from the synagogue— "excommunication," to use the common Christian term. The historical development and use of the term is complex and controverted. Apparently in part because of this post-biblical history, Norbert Lohfink says that "the usual translation, 'ban,' is and always has been false and misleading."[60] But my purpose in commending "ban" is not to suggest medieval Jewish understandings, but rather to use a word that in a contemporary context combines historic resonance with opacity.

There is also one obvious contextual issue for the translation of the verbal form of *ḥērem*. If the seven nations are to be "destroyed" (v. 2), why should intermarriage need to be prohibited (vv. 3–4)? Since, to put it bluntly, corpses present no temptation to intermarriage, the text surely envisages the continuance of living non-Israelites in close proximity to Israel.[61]

In the light of this, I propose a reading of Deuteronomy 7:1–5 in which the text is construed as a definitional exposition of *ḥērem* as an enduring practice for Israel. The basic idea that something that is designated *ḥērem* is thereby absolutely removed from all use is here given a specific focus. Thus when Israel comes into contact with the seven nations in the promised land and YHWH enables Israel to overcome them, then the requirement is that Israel should practice *ḥērem* with regard to them (7:1–2a). This means refusing normal practices of treaty making or being moved to pity for the vanquished (7:2b). The content of this *ḥērem* is then given in what immediately follows, in terms of two specific practices. Negatively, Israel is to avoid intermarriage (7:3–4), for this would entail religious compromise, since intermarriage as a rule entails acceptance and incorporation of the religious culture of the non-Israelite and thus could lead to dilution of Israel's allegiance to YHWH. Positively, Israel is indeed to carry out destruction—but the specified destruction is not of people but solely of those objects that symbolize and enable

---

59. For an entrée, see William Horbury, "Extirpation and Excommunication," *VT* 35/1 (1985): 13–38.

60. Norbert Lohfink, "*Ḥāram; Ḥērem*," in *TDOT* 5:180–99, esp. 188.

61. This point is commonly recognized by interpreters who argue for the "ideal/utopian" nature of Deuteronomy's legislation; e.g., Andrew David Hastings Mayes, *Deuteronomy*, NCB (Grand Rapids: Eerdmans, 1979), 183. For a concern, however, that this might be overpressing the terminology and its sequence, in a manner insensitive to its rhetoric, see Lohr, *Chosen and Unchosen*, 167–70. Admittedly one could argue that Israel's occupying the land might take time, and the point of the text would be that Israel, in the process of wiping peoples out, is not to intermarry with them; and I do not see how such a reading could be disproved, though I think it goes against the grain of the rhetoric. Any argument in this area must be cumulative to have persuasive force.

allegiances to deities other than Yhwh (7:5). In other words, *ḥērem* is being presented as *a metaphor for unqualified allegiance to Yhwh*.[62] On this reading *ḥērem* is not a "mere" metaphor, for it envisages specific and demanding practices. These practices, however, do not entail the taking of life on the battlefield, but rather the rejection, the absolute non-use, of that which could compromise Israel's covenantal allegiance to Yhwh: intermarriage and the presence of alien religious symbols within Israel's promised land. Deuteronomy uses the language and imagery of warfare for Israel vis-à-vis the "seven nations of Canaan" in a metaphorical mode, so as to depict the real conflicts over identity and allegiance that confront Israel in engagement with its immediate neighbors.

The point that intermarriage "as a rule" requires the embrace of non-Israelite religion and culture requires some consideration of Deuteronomy 21:10–14, which envisages an Israelite soldier taking a non-Israelite wife from among those whom Israel has defeated. This exception has long puzzled interpreters. One obvious approach is to argue that the woman would not be a Canaanite and so would not come under the prohibition of 7:3–4. Yet even if there is some force to this, the basic logic of the prohibition of intermarriage is that *any* non-Israelite spouse would entail religious compromise because of the intrinsic social and familial, and so religio-cultural, dimensions of regular marriage. Some scholars simply argue that this must be an earlier law that was formulated prior to the distinctive Deuteronomic development of *ḥērem*, then preserved unchanged despite the tensions it now creates.[63] Most likely the marriage is permitted because a captive woman would have in effect forfeited her original religio-cultural context and her wider familial context.[64] Thus she would no longer represent religious compromise (whatever her own individual inclinations), as the assumption would be that she would be obliged to conform to her new husband's frame of reference and mode of life, religious and otherwise, or at least not actively dissent from it. Her situation would be analogous to that envisaged by David in 1 Samuel 26:19, where life in alien territory brings strong pressure to conform to local patterns of religious life.

A Reading of Deuteronomy 20:16–18

Alongside Deuteronomy 7:1–5 we must also consider the other passage in Deuteronomy that specifies the practice of *ḥērem*, that is, 20:16–18. In what precedes (20:10–15), the situation of warfare against distant nations is considered, and Israel is given permission to take plunder and captives. But the situation is different for those who inhabit the land of Canaan:

62. See also the similar construal in Christa Schäfer-Lichtenberger, "JHWH, Israel und die Völker aus der Perspektive von Dtn 7," *BZ* 40 (1996): 194–218; and in Nathan MacDonald, *Deuteronomy and the Meaning of "Monotheism,"* FAT 2/1 (Tübingen: Mohr Siebeck, 2003), 108–22.

63. So, e.g., Michael Fishbane, *Biblical Interpretation in Ancient Israel* (Oxford: Clarendon, 1985), 199–200.

64. This original context is what Ruth voluntarily renounces in her famous words that express her determination to stay with Naomi as she returns to Israel (Ruth 1:16–17).

¹⁶But as for the towns of these peoples that the LORD your God is giving you as an inheritance, you must not let anything that breathes remain alive. ¹⁷You shall annihilate them [*haḥărēm taḥărīm*, as in 7:2]—the Hittites and the Amorites, the Canaanites and the Perizzites, the Hivites and the Jebusites—just as the LORD your God has commanded, ¹⁸so that they may not teach you to do all the abhorrent things that they do for their gods, and you thus sin against the LORD your God.

Again, the purpose of the *ḥērem* is unambiguous—it is to preserve undiluted allegiance to YHWH (v. 18). It is unlikely that the text here envisages anything different from 7:1–5. The final words of 20:17, "just as the LORD your God has commanded," indicate that the specification of 20:16–18 is to be read as a restatement of 7:1–5 (on the assumption that the words of Moses represent the will of YHWH, as is specified in 5:22–31; esp. vv. 27, 31). Yet here the language of *ḥērem* is prefaced by an explicit requirement not to "let anything that breathes remain alive," and it could be argued that such specificity overturns the metaphorical sense for which I have argued in 7:1–5 in favor of a reading of *ḥērem* as a practice on the battlefield. Probably the "not let remain alive" (20:16) is envisaged as the same as "make no covenant with them and show them no mercy" (7:2), both being variants of the idiom "take no prisoners."⁶⁵ So although one can argue that if a metaphorical meaning is likely in 7:1–5, then it should be carried over here, the opposite could also be argued: a battlefield sense in 20:16–18 should be carried back to 7:1–5.

However, the real interpretive issue is not whether the text uses the language of warfare, defeat, and killing, for it clearly and consistently does. Rather the issue concerns the genre of the text and the register of the language. For example, whether or not "liturgical poem" is the most precise genre designation of Genesis 1,⁶⁶ the point of such a designation is to try to gain the best vantage point, or frame of reference, for construing the text as a whole. It means that the reader is steered away from some questions (How could the writer really have known what happened? Can the "days" of Gen. 1 be aligned with scientific accounts of the emergence of life upon earth?) toward others (How should humans think about, and live in, the world as God's world? What follows from God's approval and indeed delight

65. The language of Deut. 20:16 is also used in a stereotypical way in the summary account of Joshua's victories (Josh. 10:28, 30, 33, 37, 39, 40; 11:11, 14).

66. Walter Brueggemann, *Genesis*, IBCTP (Atlanta: John Knox, 1982), 26, 30; followed by Ellen Davis, *Scripture, Culture, and Agriculture: An Agrarian Reading of the Bible* (Cambridge: Cambridge University Press, 2009), 43.

in the world?). Comparably, when Jesus speaks in strong, indeed violent, language about the need for undivided allegiance to God and avoidance of sin—"If your right eye causes you to sin, tear it out and throw it away. . . . If your right hand causes you to sin, cut it off and throw it away" (Matt. 5:29–30//Mark 9:43–48)—interpreters have no difficulty in recognizing the metaphorical usage, in a way that does not undermine the text but rather takes it seriously. The basic problem is that we do not *know* what the genre of Deuteronomy 7, or the register of its language, actually is, and so we must heuristically explore possibilities. Thus far the argument is solely that there are at least some indications in the language of Deuteronomy 7 that it may be using *ḥērem* for Israel's actions vis-à-vis the "seven nations of Canaan" in a metaphorical mode.

What Kind of Law Is the Law of *Ḥērem*?

The next step is to ponder a puzzle within modern scholarly work on Deuteronomy and propose a particular resolution. The discussion will be a good example of the difference that judgments about the world behind the text can make to one's judgments about the world within the text (or in other terminology, it illustrates the enduring value of historical-critical insights for good exegesis).

Standard Approaches to the Problem of Ḥerem

The puzzle relates to the scholarly consensus that, despite the specific way in which Deuteronomy 7:1–5 and 20:16–18 promote the practice of *ḥērem*, they in fact promote something that was not actually realized within Israel's history. A representative voice is that of Moshe Weinfeld, who has discussed this issue in various contexts.[67] He consistently contends that "the law of *ḥērem* in Deuteronomy . . . is a utopian law that was written in retrospect."[68] Further, "in reality, the Canaanites were neither expelled nor exterminated, as may be learned from Judges 1:21–33 and 1 Kings 9:20–21, so that the whole question [of *ḥērem*] was a theoretical one, especially raised by the Deuteronomic move-

---

67. Moshe Weinfeld, *Deuteronomy 1–11*, AB 5 (New York: Doubleday, 1991), 357–84; idem, "The Ban on the Canaanites in the Biblical Codes and Its Historical Development," in *History and Traditions of Early Israel: Studies Presented to Eduard Nielsen*, ed. André Lemaire and Benedikt Otzen, VTS 50 (Leiden: Brill, 1993), 142–60; idem, "Expulsion, Dispossession, and Extermination of the Pre-Israelite Population in the Biblical Sources," in his *The Promise of the Land* (Berkeley: California University Press, 1993), 76–98.

68. Weinfeld, "Expulsion," 91.

ment." Deuteronomy's conception of *ḥērem* "is an a priori decree that belongs more to theory than to practice."[69] The consensus nature of Weinfeld's thesis is concisely articulated by Jeffrey Tigay: "Modern scholars hold that this law is purely theoretical and was never in effect."[70]

Why this consensus as to the non-implementation of Deuteronomy's prescription of *ḥērem*? It is inseparable from the question of Deuteronomy's likely context of composition, which a general modern scholarly consensus—to which Weinfeld and Tigay belong—has set in the late seventh century in some kind of relation to Josiah's reform. In a late seventh-century context—and equally in later contexts (if, as some propose, one lowers the date of Deuteronomy or at least of elements within it)—it is most unlikely that extensive military action against non-Israelite peoples within the land of Canaan with a view to wiping them out could have been considered as in any way a meaningful option. The kingdom of Judah did not have the resources, and in any case people from other nations had long since been assimilated within Israel.[71]

The question why Deuteronomy should use the language of *ḥērem* as a way of depicting warfare against the inhabitants of Canaan becomes sharper when one compares Deuteronomy 7:1–5 and 20:16–18 with other, probably older, pentateuchal laws, especially those of Exodus 23:23–33 and 34:11–16, whose content is similar but which do not use the terminology of *ḥērem* and typically speak of YHWH's "driving out" (*gārash*) the Canaanites.[72] If Deuteronomy deliberately introduced the term into older laws—which still seems likely, even though questions of traditio-historical and literary dependence in the legal material of the Pentateuch can increasingly be argued any which way—why should it do so?

Why should Deuteronomy promote and prioritize *ḥērem* if it "was never in effect"? As so often, one is reduced to learned conjecture. Some scholars see the issue as illustrative of the "theoretical" or "idealistic" nature of Deuteronomy more generally. As Susan Niditch puts it, "Much in Deuteronomy is of a theoretical nature, like the second-century Jewish law code, the Mishnah, often planning for a reality that no longer or does not yet exist."[73] Alternatively, Moshe Weinfeld, as already noted, uses terminology such as "utopian," "theoretical," "a priori." Others, however, try to imagine some more concrete scenario or purpose. Jeffrey Tigay, for example, envisages Deuteronomy's *ḥērem* as conceived "when the Canaanites had ceased to exist as a discern-

---

69. Weinfeld, *Deuteronomy 1–11*, 384.

70. Tigay, *Deuteronomy*, 471.

71. One of the most famous of those assimilated is the loyal soldier Uriah the Hittite (2 Sam. 11); Hittites are the first of the proscribed peoples in Deut. 7:1.

72. See, e.g., Weinfeld, *Deuteronomy 1–11*, 382–84; or his "Ban," 142–55, 159.

73. Susan Niditch, *War in the Hebrew Bible: A Study in the Ethics of Violence* (New York and Oxford: Oxford University Press, 1993), 63.

ible element of the population in Israel, to account for their disappearance."[74] By contrast, Rainer Albertz sees the *ḥērem* legislation ("fortunately purely theoretical") as demonstrating "fear of a cultural and religious swamping in the time of the exile."[75] Given the paucity of historical evidence, it is hardly surprising that diametrically opposed conjectures are offered as to the challenges facing Israel/Judah and/or the impact of whichever Canaanites, if any, were contemporary to the Deuteronomic writer(s). Nonetheless, some account needs to be offered.

Noteworthy is Philip Stern's proposal that the Deuteronomic writers restricted the use of the *ḥērem* to certain primordial nations that had ceased to exist, so as "to eliminate the possibility of using the *ḥērem* against others."[76] This is an interesting reading of the language and logic of the biblical text: *ḥērem* is to be practiced by Israel against the inhabitants of Canaan when it enters the land; such a scenario, however, lies in the mists of the past by the time Deuteronomy is written; and so *ḥērem* cannot in fact be practiced. In other words, the law of *ḥērem* is promoted so as to be disabled.

In one form or other, a move with comparable implications is not uncommonly made by interpreters who argue that *ḥērem* is restricted to the past as a one-off command that has no enduring significance.[77] It is comparable to the classic move of the rabbis, about which Moshe Greenberg says: "Now, had there been any inclination to generalize this law, it would have been easy for the talmudic sages to perform an appropriate hermeneutical exercise to that end. But in fact the sages left the ancient *ḥerem* law as they found it: applying to seven extinct nations, while radically meliorating other terms of the obsolete law."[78] The rabbis, of course, took for granted that Deuteronomy was the work of Moses himself. But in terms of the abiding significance of the *ḥērem* legislation, even if one holds to a seventh-century (or later) date

---

74. Tigay, *Deuteronomy*, 471.

75. Rainer Albertz, *A History of Israelite Religion in the Old Testament Period*, trans. John Bowden from the 1992 German ed. (London: SCM, 1994), 2:391.

76. Stern, *Biblical Ḥerem*, 102–3.

77. So, e.g., with reference to either Deuteronomy or Joshua, or to both: Brevard Childs, *Old Testament Theology*, 77–78; and his *Biblical Theology*, 146; Hoffman, "Ḥerem," 205–6; Lohr, *Chosen*, 169–70; John Goldingay, *Old Testament Theology*, vol. 3, *Israel's Life* (Downers Grove, IL: IVP Academic, 2009), 571–72; Stephen Chapman, "Perpetual War: The Case of Amalek," paper presented in Cheltenham (UK) on May 31, 2012, at an International Symposium on the Bible and Spirituality, sponsored by the University of Gloucestershire and the British Bible Society.

78. Moshe Greenberg, "On the Political Use of the Bible in Modern Israel: An Engaged Critique," in *Pomegranates and Golden Bells: Studies in Biblical, Jewish, and Near Eastern Ritual, Law, and Literature in Honor of Jacob Milgrom*, ed. David P. Wright, David Noel Freedman, and Avi Hurvitz (Winona Lake, IN: Eisenbrauns, 1995), 461–71, esp. 469.

for Deuteronomy, one can come to essentially the same construal as those who hold to Deuteronomy as the ipsissima verba of Moses. The move is to maintain a focus on the logic of the world within the text and to see it as a world that in certain ways cannot be carried over into the world in front of the text: ḥērem is confined to the past.[79]

Ḥērem as Metaphor

I find the notion that ḥērem is specified in Deuteronomy only so as to show that it is inoperative to be more ingenious than persuasive. It seems a curious strategy when other more straightforward strategies suggest themselves: either pass over ḥērem in silence so as to indicate that it is no longer a live issue, or even explicitly give it a time restriction ("when you come into the land, . . . but not afterward," vĕlōʾ ʾaḥărē-kēn). I cannot see that it does justice to the rhetoric of Deuteronomy 7, with its picture of Israel's need to focus on YHWH and trust Him for victory against the odds, which is hardly a one-off issue or restricted to the past. Moreover, the location of the primary ḥērem requirement (7:1–5) becomes puzzling. For it is part of a substantial address by Moses, who is expounding the basic principles of the covenant between YHWH and Israel, prior to the detailed laws that begin in chapter 12. It directly follows the keynote issue of the Shema and precedes the account of the enduring lesson to be gleaned from Israel's time in the desert (chap. 8), and to be learned from their faithlessness with the golden calf even at Sinai/Horeb (chaps. 9–10). One would expect such material in context to be about continuing practices of faithful life within the covenant, rather than a coded way of overruling a contemporary assumption that the practice of ḥērem in warfare might still be a good thing to do. Moses's address in chapters 6–11 looks like an articulation of enduring foundations of the covenant, which should enable an appropriate living of the covenant not just for a first generation but also for subsequent generations. In other words, the location of ḥērem in chapter 7 generates an assumption that it should be dealing with Israel's faithful living within the covenant on an ongoing basis.

My positive interpretive thesis is thus straightforward. In response to the puzzle as to why Deuteronomy should promote and prioritize ḥērem if it "was never in effect," I am arguing that to speak of its being "never in effect" misrepresents the issue. It is not that Deuteronomic ḥērem was not envisaged as an actual practice, but rather that the nature of the practice the text envisages is no longer military: ḥērem could be practiced, yet in ways other than on

79. Whether one views the date of Deuteronomy as Mosaic or Josianic will, of course, make a difference as to how the past is envisaged.

the battlefield. My contention is that, although it appears there was once an actual practice of *ḥērem* on the battlefield, both in ancient Israel and among its near neighbors, Deuteronomy uses and indeed privileges the notion of *ḥērem* only because it was seen to lend itself to a particular metaphorical usage for practices appropriate to enabling Israel's everyday allegiance to YHWH within a world of conflicting allegiances.

Although I have argued that there are clues within the language of Deuteronomy 7 that point in this direction, the decision to locate Deuteronomy within a late monarchic (or exilic or post-exilic) context also has considerable hermeneutical implications. If the (apparently) ancient practice of *ḥērem* is promoted when it is not feasible in military terms, then this is a good reason for supposing that it should be feasible in other terms. To put it differently, there is a long history within the Christian tradition of metaphorizing the military language of the Old Testament. Fighting with the whole armor of God in Ephesians 6:10–20 is probably the best-known New Testament example, and a metaphorizing ("spiritualizing") move is basic to Origen and much subsequent Christian reading of the Old Testament. My proposal is that such a metaphorizing move is already present within the text of Deuteronomy itself. Of course, it may be objected that I am anachronistically retrojecting a Christian interpretive tendency into the Old Testament. But my argument is made via a consideration of Deuteronomy's language, both in itself and in relation to its likely context of origin—no doubt informed by an awareness of metaphorizing tendencies in Christian history, but arguing nonetheless that there is reason to find such tendencies already within Deuteronomy itself.[80]

The Reception and Interpretation of Deuteronomy 7 in Ezra 9

If we move beyond Deuteronomy itself, there is support for my thesis in the earliest explicit interpretive engagement with Deuteronomy 7 that has been preserved: the narrative about Ezra's dissolution of mixed marriages in Ezra 9–10. Here the narrative is set in motion through the periphrastic citation of Deuteronomy 7:1, 3 in Ezra 9:1–2:

> After these things had been done, the officials approached me and said, "The people of Israel, the priests, and the Levites have not separated themselves from the peoples of the lands with their abominations, from the Canaanites,

---

80. The argument in my "Election and the Transformation of *Ḥerem*" is that the metaphorizing of *ḥērem* is analogous to the biblical metaphorizing of child sacrifice, for which Jon Levenson has argued persuasively in his *Death and Resurrection*.

the Hittites, the Perizzites, the Jebusites, the Ammonites, the Moabites, the Egyptians, and the Amorites. For they have taken some of their daughters as wives for themselves and for their sons."

The citation of Deuteronomy 7 is not verbatim. The list of nations is changed (in a way comparable to variations in the lists of nations in the Pentateuch). The Ezra citation seems to embody a contemporizing of the text, in conjunction with other portions of Torah. This fits well with what has been argued to be Deuteronomy 7:1's intrinsic significance as a general symbolic depiction of problematic other nations. As the narrative of Ezra 9 develops, the issues are posed entirely in terms of Israel's *separation* from other peoples so as to preserve holiness through the abolition of intermarriage. It is striking that there is no suggestion that other peoples should be put to death, or that the text requires anything other than separation through rejecting intermarriage. Within the continuing narrative, moreover, the one use of a verbal form of *ḥērem* is to depict the "forfeiting" of property by the non-compliant (Ezra 10:8). One might, of course, observe that any action more warlike than dissolving marriages would not have been a feasible option for a provincial people in the Persian context. Nonetheless, within the narrative there is no hint that anything other than full compliance with the Deuteronomic prohibition is what is being enacted, or that separation is in any sense a compliance that is second best because of the constraints of the situation. Such a reading of Deuteronomy 7 may stand closer to the intrinsic sense of Deuteronomy 7 than has generally been recognized.

A Reading Strategy for Ḥērem in the Book of Joshua

A final element in my proposed reading of Deuteronomy 7 must be a proposal for reading the narratives in the book of Joshua, in which Israel is depicted as fighting the Canaanites and under obligation to practice *ḥērem*—though it is not possible here to do more than gesture toward a heuristic reading strategy.

It has long been recognized that the book of Joshua is closely related to Deuteronomy. As such, it is naturally read as spelling out what Deuteronomy envisages (whether or not one formulates this in compositional and editorial categories with some form of DH hypothesis). How then should its narratives of warfare and *ḥērem* be read?

This issue has been set in a new light by recent scholarship. There are well-known debates about the paucity of archaeological evidence that might support the historicity of a conquest under Joshua, and also debates about the nature and purpose of Joshua as a book apparently close in time of composition to Deuteronomy (either seventh or sixth century): both debates serve sharply to pose the question as to what sort of text Joshua is and how it ought to be read. More directly, there have been close readings of the text of Joshua that show how the narrative of Joshua is more surprising than one might have imagined,[81] at least if one was expecting a depiction of YHWH's being on Israel's side and enabling them to defeat and destroy the wicked Canaanites. For YHWH is not "on Israel's side," and the Canaanites are not depicted as wicked.

YHWH's relationship to Israel's war effort is perhaps most explicitly addressed in a brief and intriguing episode that prefaces the capture of Jericho (Josh. 5:13–15): even if it is a latecomer within the development of the text, it nonetheless now serves as an interpretive key:

> [13]Once when Joshua was near Jericho, he looked up and saw a man standing before him with a drawn sword in his hand. Joshua went to him and said to him, "Are you one of us, or one of our adversaries?" [14]He replied, "Neither;[82] but as commander of the army of the LORD I have now come." And Joshua fell on his face to the earth and worshiped, and he said to him, "What do you command your servant, my lord?" [15]The commander of the army of the LORD said to Joshua, "Remove the sandals from your feet, for the place where you stand is holy." And Joshua did so.

Joshua responds to this figure as Moses does to YHWH at the burning bush (Exod. 3). The command to Joshua is to perform an act of reverence that has no apparent connection with warfare, though it anticipates the ritual expressions that replace military actions around Jericho. Most important, the direct question about being "for us" or "for them" is straightforwardly rebutted: despite expectations, YHWH is not "on Israel's side." This articulates what has become a basic principle in classic theology and spirituality. God is not on any human side, though it is possible that humans may come to be on

---

81. A pioneering work is by Robert Polzin, *Moses and the Deuteronomist: A Literary Study of the Deuteronomic History* (New York: Seabury, 1980). A subtle hermeneutic is proposed by Ellen Davis, "The Poetics of Generosity," in *The Word Leaps the Gap: Essays on Scripture and Theology in Honor of Richard Hays*, ed. J. Ross Wagner, C. Kavin Rowe, and A. Katherine Grieb (Grand Rapids: Eerdmans, 2008), 626–45, esp. 630–39. The fullest and most suggestive treatment of which I am aware, and to which I am particularly indebted, is Douglas S. Earl, *Reading Joshua as Christian Scripture*, JTIS 2 (Winona Lake, IN: Eisenbrauns, 2010), whose thesis is accessible in more popular form in his *The Joshua Delusion? Rethinking Genocide in the Bible* (Eugene, OR: Cascade Books, 2010). There is also resonance with the reading offered here in Carolyn J. Sharp, "'Are You for Us, or for Our Adversaries?' A Feminist and Postcolonial Interrogation of Joshua 2–12 for the Contemporary Church," *Interpretation* 66/2 (2012): 141–52.

82. There is a textual variant, *lō* ("to him") rather than *lō'* ("no/neither"), but this is probably an error.

God's side. God cannot be harnessed to human plans, yet human plans may be brought into conformity with God's plans. Even though this principle is not straightforwardly an "Old Testament principle," a passage such as Joshua 5:13–15 is nonetheless an important adumbration.[83]

Something of what this unsettling of expectations involves can be seen in the two most developed depictions of a Canaanite and an Israelite in the wider narrative. The most developed depiction of a Canaanite is what introduces the main narrative action. Rahab is prima facie a maximally unpromising figure: a Canaanite, a woman, and a prostitute. Yet she assists the Israelite spies, she acknowledges YHWH in language that resonates with Israel's primary affirmations—"the LORD your God is indeed God in heaven above and on earth below" (Josh. 2:11)—and she practices the primary divine quality of "steadfast love" (ḥesed, 2:12: "since I have dealt kindly with you").[84] Both her words and her deeds are exemplary from the perspective of Israel's faith. So she is exempted from ḥērem, despite the lack of exemption clauses in Deuteronomy, and enabled (with her family) to become part of Israel (6:23, 25). In subsequent rabbinic tradition, she even marries Joshua and becomes an ancestress of eight prophets and of the prophetess Huldah.[85] Conversely, Achan is a Judahite of impeccable pedigree (7:1). Yet he is disobedient, and he (with his family) dies (7:1–26). The "banned" outsider becomes an insider. A privileged insider forfeits everything. Comparably, the narrative of the altar beyond the Jordan makes problematic any straightforward notion of what territory constitutes the land that YHWH gives to Israel (22:7–34).

When one reads Joshua as a sequel to Deuteronomy, the construal of ḥērem is less than straightforward. Admittedly ḥērem as warfare constitutes the backdrop of the action; but the depiction of battles is perfunctory and formulaic (with a partial exception in Josh. 7–8). The foreground interest is in people and situations that call into question any simplistic in-or-out account of Israel's identity; instead, they searchingly probe what faithfulness to YHWH really entails.

83. The context of 5:13–15 makes it interpretively more significant than 10:42, where in a summary comment on Joshua's later victories the narrator says, "Joshua took all these kings and their land at one time, because the LORD God of Israel fought for Israel."

84. For ḥesed as a divine quality, see esp. Exod. 34:6–7, where it characterizes both YHWH's nature (v. 6) and His actions (v. 7), on which see chap. 6 below.

85. See Louis Ginzberg, *Legends of the Jews*, trans. Henrietta Szold and Paul Radin, 2nd ed. (Philadelphia: Jewish Publication Society, 2003), 2:843–44. Sharp sees Rahab's being "outside the camp" (Josh. 6:23) as indicating that she is "merely tolerated in a marginal position" ("Interrogation," 147). Even if this is a right reading of 6:23, Jewish tradition clearly did not consider it significant, perhaps laying more weight on the potentially positive implications of 6:25.

Conclusion

We have explored two facets of Deuteronomy's presentation of what it means that Israel should be Yʜwʜ's chosen people. On the one hand, we have seen that the particularizing logic of election is an expression of the particularizing logic of love. When there is a dynamic that elicits a wondering sense of "Why us/me?" we can see more clearly the relational nature of call and response that characterizes Israel's election. Although the particularizing focus of love can be puzzling in relation to understanding how God can care for the whole of creation, I have argued that the tension here is constitutive of both Jewish and Christian faiths (*mutatis mutandis*) more generally.

On the other hand, we have seen how Israel's election is closely related to the need to practice *ḥērem*. Although at first sight this seems to justify contemporary anxieties about the likelihood that biblical belief in the one God and a chosen people will generate violence toward others, I have argued that this is most likely a misreading of the text. Rather, the practice of *ḥērem*, apparently originally a battlefield practice involving killing, has been retained, and indeed highlighted, by Deuteronomy only because it was seen to be amenable to metaphorical reconstrual in terms of practices that enhance Israel's covenantal faithfulness to Yʜwʜ in everyday life.

When these two facets are taken together and understood in relation to Israel's confession in the Shema of Yʜwʜ as "the one and only," we see Israel as a people called to a loving covenantal relationship with God that entails strong responsibilities, especially in terms of practices that will prevent that relationship becoming diluted.

If this is on the right lines, many possible questions are still left open. It has not been possible to give a general account either of election or of *ḥērem* in the Old Testament as a whole. Also, even if it has successfully been argued that characteristic objections to the notion of a chosen people need not rule it out from contemporary Christian thought and practice, there is still more that needs to be said about possible contemporary appropriation in terms of what counts as faithfulness. For the conceptuality of Deuteronomy 7:1–5, even when read as metaphor, still jars on the ears of those accustomed to interfaith dialogue, religious tolerance, and more individualistic approaches to marriage options. There are certainly no straightforward conclusions to draw, and there are good reasons, both within the scriptural canon and in historic Christian practice, for resisting any facile replication of Deuteronomy's rhetorical strategy concerning problematic "others." The way in which the story of Rahab rules out any simple account of what counts as the faithfulness represented by *ḥērem* is a prime example within the canon of the need for some imagination and flexibility in thinking about possible ongoing appropriation. I offer some preliminary reflections.

Refusal, or at least discouragement, of intermarriage has a long history within Christian, as within Jewish, tradition (even if it has not been understood as an appropriation of *ḥērem* legislation). It has been a formal requirement in Roman Catholic and Orthodox churches and is a strong, albeit often unwritten, requirement in many evangelical churches. Its logic, and its wisdom, relates to the practicalities of bringing up and forming children—questions about priorities of time and money and community and identity, and also the preservation and transmission of Christian faith and practice. It need not entail a denial that, in a contemporary culture with relatively loose family and community commitments, two mature adults of different outlooks (differing faiths, or faith and non-faith) might well be able to form a good and lasting relationship in which each outlook is respected and preserved. Any child, however, can in principle only be brought up in the faith of one of the parents (although in practice various kinds of compromise and/or syncretism are imaginable). In general, it is likely that the practicalities of formation in such situations will introduce elements of strain even into good adult relational dynamics, strain that can sometimes lead to fracture. Lack of strain would be exceptional, and exceptions that prove the rule are not a good reason to establish a different rule.

Issues about marriage, religion, and identity are, of course, wide ranging and complex. For example, at the time of this writing (early August 2012), the problem of forced marriages for children in certain Asian families who have emigrated to the United Kingdom is in the news. Parental concern that their offspring should not assimilate in ways that abandon traditional religious values and identity can lead to "honor killings." This has been highlighted by the tragic case of Shafilea Ahmed, a teenage Muslim girl who resisted her parents' unilaterally-decided plans for her marriage and was murdered in 2003, a murder for which her parents have just been convicted. Justified outrage at murderous abuse may not, however, be a good guide to the complexity of legitimate concerns that surround upbringing, wisdom in marriage, and the appreciation and preservation of faith within a secular culture.

The destruction of objects that symbolize allegiances other than to YHWH can also be argued to have enduring significance. The concern within Deuteronomy is that Israel is recidivist, so strongly attracted to allegiances other than to YHWH (the constant problem of "other gods") that strong language and action become necessary. Here the already-cited words of Jesus become interpretively important: "If your right eye causes you to sin, tear it out and throw it away. . . . If your right hand causes you to sin, cut if off and throw it away" (Matt. 5:29–30//Mark 9:43–48). Jesus is concerned with the ease with which faithfulness to God can be compromised and metaphorically urges drastic action. In a contemporary idiom, one can think of an alcoholic undergoing therapy in Alcoholics Anonymous, where the only appropriate response to alcoholic drink is to keep away from it and, if necessary, get rid of it ("smash the bottle," "pour its contents down the drain"). For some, there are comparable problems with gambling, pornography, and drugs, which like alcoholism can skew imagination and diminish integrity, and which in medical terms can become addiction and in theological terms can become idolatry. Yet not all people have difficulties here; many can enjoy responsible drinking, films with moderate sexual content, and an occasional modest wager without problems.

Blanket prohibitions of particular (not intrinsically immoral) practices for believers may be meaningful in some situations but are probably of limited value in most contemporary contexts. Different things become destructive for different people. Certainly, when practices do become destructive they require strong measures. But what is necessary for some may not be necessary for all. The Christian church that seeks to enter into Israel's legacy is endlessly diverse. Wisdom in discrimination and discernment is needed if the faithfulness of all is best to be maintained.

3

Daily Bread

The content of the book of Exodus is in many ways foundational for Israel's life with God. The story of the manna in Exodus 16 is the first extended sequence about Israel's life in the wilderness after their deliverance from Egypt and before their coming to Sinai. In such a context one may reasonably suppose that the story deals with Israel's new identity as the people of YHWH and what it means for them to learn to live as such a people; at least, that is my working assumption, to be judged by its fruitfulness in what follows.

When the story is read within a Christian frame of reference, with the assumption that Israel's story is in some sense also the church's story such that Christians should imaginatively identify with Israel, then there are expectations about the story's enduring implications for the life of faith. This means, among other things, that a disciplined use of the imagination should be integral to a good reading of the scriptural text. Of course, what is *disciplined* to one person may seem *fanciful* to some and *constrained* to others. But that simply means that, although some interpretations are better than others, and certain interpretations may enduringly shape the way in which the biblical text is read, the task of reading well remains a continuing challenge.

In this chapter I develop my earlier study "On Learning Spiritual Disciplines: A Reading of Exodus 16," in *Reading the Law: Studies in Honour of Gordon J. Wenham*, ed. J. G. McConville and Karl Möller, LHBOTS 461 (New York and London: T&T Clark, 2007), 213–27.

A Reading of Exodus 16

First, the scene is set:

> [1]The whole congregation of the Israelites set out from Elim; and Israel came
> to the wilderness of Sin, which is between Elim and Sinai, on the fifteenth day
> of the second month after they had departed from the land of Egypt. [2]The
> whole congregation of the Israelites complained against Moses and Aaron in
> the wilderness. [3]The Israelites said to them, "If only we had died by the hand
> of the LORD in the land of Egypt, where we sat by the fleshpots and ate our
> fill of bread; for you have brought us out into this wilderness to kill this whole
> assembly with hunger."

A month and a half after departing from Egypt, Israel is in an unwelcome
place. The specific notation that the wilderness of Sin is "between Elim and
Sinai" may well be interpretively significant.

This passage raises some interesting underlying questions of approach to narrative interpretation.
In antiquity, Origen regularly found substantive significance in place names, rooted in the recognition that many Hebrew place names indeed carry meaning; for example, Massah, a nominal
form from *nissāh* ("test"), means "place of testing" (Exod. 17:7). Thus Origen was famously able
to read the extended list of place names in Israel's itinerary in Numbers 33 as a kind of pilgrim's
progress.[1] Modern commentators have generally resisted finding interpretive significance in places
that appear in itineraries, except where the text itself is explicit (as in Exod. 17:7). Martin Noth's
comment on Exodus 16:1—"This is no more than a reference to [P's] list of stopping places"[2]—
resists Origen's approach yet perhaps shares Origen's underlying assumption about the face-value
significance of the text; for Origen observes on Israel's coming to Elim in Exodus 16:1, "If we
follow only the simple record of facts, it does not edify us much to know to what place they came
first and to what place second."[3] However, the development of attention to the poetics of biblical
narrative surely makes possible various middle ways between maximalizing and minimalizing the
significance of the wilderness itineraries.

The problem with the wilderness of Sin is that it is set between two much
more desirable places. On the one hand Elim, whence they had just departed
(15:27), had twelve springs of water and seventy palm trees (the numbers
being symbolically suggestive),[4] which are surely meant to make it sound like

1. Origen's "Homily XXVII on Numbers" is available in *Origen: An Exhortation to Martyrdom, Prayer, and Selected Writings*, trans. and intro. Rowan A. Greer, CWS (London: SPCK,
1979), 245–69.

2. Martin Noth, *Exodus*, trans. John Bowden, OTL (London: SCM, 1962), 133.

3. *Homilies on Exodus* 7:3; in *Origen: Homilies on Genesis and Exodus*, trans. Ronald Heine,
FOTC 71 (Washington, DC: Catholic University of America Press, 1982), 304.

4. Traditional Jewish interpretation regularly construed the twelve springs as one for each of
the twelve tribes, while the seventy palm trees were for each of the seventy elders. So, e.g., Rashi;
Ibn Ezra, however, was dismissive: "There is no need for this kind of thing. For the 12 springs
and the 70 trees were not created at this moment for Israel" (Michael Carasik, ed. and trans., *The
Commentators' Bible: The JPS Miqra'ot Gedolot*, vol. 2, *Exodus/Shemot* [Philadelphia: Jewish

a wonderful place to stay when in desert regions. On the other hand Sinai, the mountain of God, is where Israel will enter into covenant with YHWH. Other places (and implicitly, times) may be fine, but here and now is awful: "The grass is always greener . . ."

There is also a straightforward implication that, just as soon as the journey becomes difficult, the Israelites complain (a keynote in the portrayal of Israel's wilderness wanderings) and readily view their leaders suspiciously, indeed in the worst possible light. Any moral and spiritual fiber is conspicuous solely for its absence.

Moreover the content of their complaint is remarkable. Entirely gone is any sense of YHWH's deliverance of Israel so as to give them a better place to live and enable them to worship YHWH better, a deliverance to be remembered and celebrated in various ways (Exod. 12–15). Rather, they seem to take it for granted that death is all that awaits them, in which case they would prefer at least to have had stomachs full rather than empty at their end; and so they would rather have died in Egypt before ever setting out. This is not a good advertisement for the quality of Israel's memory! Not only has YHWH's deliverance disappeared from view, but also Egypt is misremembered as a place not of oppression (Exod. 1:13–14; 5:1–23) but of the kind of plenty that, had it indeed been available, would have been available only, one imagines, to the Egyptians and not to their Hebrew slaves. Thus the people are immature, with a distorted perception of their situation, impatient toward their new context of life. As Brevard Childs puts it, "The people's complaint is not a casual 'gripe,' but unbelief which has called into question God's very election of a people."[5] Or as Walter Brueggemann puts it, "The seductive distortion of Israel is that, given anxiety about survival, the immediacy of food overrides any long-term hope for freedom and well-being. The desperate, fearful choice that Israel voices in this contrast is reminiscent of Esau, who was willing to forego his birthright for immediate satisfaction in food (Gen. 25:29–34)."[6] Instead of trust there is craving.

The human problem of selective memory and related fearfulness is recurrent, and in a contemporary context there are many possible analogies. For example, László Tőkés—who as a Protestant pastor helped spark the Romanian revolution in 1989 by denouncing policies of the leader of the country's communist regime, Nicolae Ceaușescu; when harassed by the authorities, he became a fulcrum for popular protest and eventually a member of the European Parliament—recently attributed some of the difficulty in making progress with the admittedly considerable contemporary

---

Publication Society of America, 2005/5765], 121). Nonetheless the evident symbolic resonance of 12 and 70 in relation to Israel can surely be exploited in more than one way.

5. Brevard Childs, *Exodus*, OTL (London: SCM, 1974), 285.

6. Walter Brueggemann, "The Book of Exodus," in *The New Interpreter's Bible*, ed. Leander E. Keck et al. (Nashville: Abingdon, 1994), 1:675–981, esp. 812.

problems within Romania to a tendency to romanticize life under Ceauşescu: "The situation has worsened so much that many people have in their minds, in my view, a mistaken nostalgia for the communist era. Many feel there was at least stability, where they had their portion."[7]

Given Israel's belief that their new life is less desirable than their old life, what will YHWH and Moses do?

> [4]The LORD said to Moses, "I am going to rain bread from heaven for you, and each day the people shall go out and gather enough for that day. In that way I will test [nissāh] them, whether they will follow my instruction [tōrāh] or not. [5]On the sixth day, when they prepare what they bring in, it will be twice as much as they gather on other days."

YHWH communicates to Moses an astonishing undertaking. If food is what the Israelites want, food is what they will get.[8] He will make bread fall like rain from the skies. Although this could depict just one particular downpour, the words that follow make clear that this will become a regular, daily phenomenon with a particular significance. The principle of daily collection, which will be amplified later, is here spelled out in a general formula for a daily task (děvar yōm běyōmō, "the matter of a day in its day," as in the requirement to produce a specified number of bricks each day [Exod. 5:13, 19]); yet it is also made clear that when the end of the week comes, arrangements will be different.

The purpose of this—which is articulated for Moses's understanding and is not necessarily what he is to communicate to the Israelites for their under-standing—is a testing of Israel. What kind of test is it? On first reading one might perhaps think that it is a test simply designed to ascertain whether or not the Israelites will do what they ought to do (analogous perhaps to teach-ers who set tests for schoolchildren to see whether or not they have done their homework). But at most this is only a part of what is involved. The opening depiction of Israel (vv. 2–3) makes it overwhelmingly likely that such a test would be failed, as indeed it is (v. 20); and there would be little constructive point in repeating such a test every day. Analogous use of the key verb (nissāh) suggests, however, that the test has an intrinsic pedagogic dimension. This is clearest in the use of the manna story in Deuteronomy 8:2–3, 5 where initial language of testing (v. 2), similar to Exodus 16:4b, is followed by a statement of purpose (v. 3b), "in order to make you understand that humanity does not live by bread alone, but by every word that comes from the mouth of the

---

7. *The Times* [London], Thursday, December 17, 2009, 45.

8. I take "bread" (*lehem*), as used by both the Israelites (Exod. 16:3) and YHWH (v. 4), to be a generic term for basic food, as in the inference from this story in Deut. 8:3 and elsewhere (e.g., 1 Sam. 14:24 MT).

Lord" (AT); and there is also a generalizing summary of the wilderness period as a time when (v. 5b), "as a parent disciplines a child so the Lord your God disciplines you." Thus, there is good reason to see the test as formative, as contributing to the shaping of Israel into the people that God wants them to be, a people who will live by divine instruction (torah).

> [6]So Moses and Aaron said to all the Israelites, "In the evening you shall know that it was the Lord who brought you out of the land of Egypt, [7]and in the morning you shall see the glory of the Lord, because he has heard your complaining against the Lord. For what are we, that you complain against us?" [8]And Moses said, "When the Lord gives you meat to eat in the evening and your fill of bread in the morning, because the Lord has heard the complaining that you utter against him—what are we? Your complaining is not against us but against the Lord."

Moses says nothing about what is to happen as a test. Rather, he seeks to renew Israel's awareness of Yhwh by depicting what is to happen, the bread from heaven, as enabling Israel's knowledge of Yhwh as deliverer. The provision of the bread would also appear to be tantamount to seeing divine glory. Moses states and reiterates that Israel's complaining against Moses and Aaron (vv. 2; 3b) is really a complaining against Yhwh; but strikingly, Yhwh will meet this complaining graciously.[9]

> [9]Then Moses said to Aaron, "Say to the whole congregation of the Israelites, 'Draw near to the Lord, for he has heard your complaining.'" [10]And as Aaron spoke to the whole congregation of the Israelites, they looked toward the wilderness, and the glory of the Lord appeared in the cloud.
> [11]The Lord spoke to Moses and said, [12]"I have heard the complaining of the Israelites; say to them, 'At twilight you shall eat meat, and in the morning you shall have your fill of bread; then you shall know that I am the Lord your God.'"

Moses and Aaron continue to address Israel in a sequence that is somewhat puzzling for its repetitiveness and unclarity.[10] Nonetheless Yhwh's glory appears (though perhaps not as anticipated in v. 7). Maybe Israel's looking toward

9. This is different from the characteristic tone in Numbers, where in stories comparable to those in Exodus, Israel suffers sharply from the divine anger. The difference appears to be the intervening gift of torah at Sinai, with the accompanying assumption that after Sinai the stakes are higher: much is expected of those to whom much is given (cf. Luke 12:48).

10. The logic of the narrative sequence in this early section is less well ordered than elsewhere in the story. As Childs puts it, "The special problem of understanding the logical sequence of the first twelve verses in the chapter has long been felt" (*Exodus*, 276); yet I think that his own discussion leaves the problem unresolved. Even if there is no entirely satisfactory resolution of

the wilderness is to be imagined as looking toward Sinai and seeing Yhwh's presence there (cf. Exod. 24:15–18). Moses is also to speak to the people so as to remind them that their responsive awareness of Yhwh is to be renewed by the events that follow.

> [13]In the evening quails came up and covered the camp; and in the morning there was a layer of dew around the camp. [14]When the layer of dew lifted, there on the surface of the wilderness was a fine flaky substance, as fine as frost on the ground.

Although the quails come and provide "meat" (bāsār), as distinct from "bread" (leḥem), in accordance with what Yhwh has said (v. 12), they play no further role in the story; indeed, any further provision of quails would diminish the importance and significance attached to the bread.[11] Within the story, therefore, the quails are presumably to be imagined as a one-off gift,[12] unlike the recurrent daily bread. It is this bread, which somehow comes with the dew, that is now the entire focus of interest.

> [15]When the Israelites saw it, they said to one another, "What is it?" [or, "It is manna" (Heb. mān hū')]. For they did not know what it was. Moses said to them, "It is the bread that the Lord has given you to eat."

The striking thing about Yhwh's provision is that Israel has no idea what to make of it. As Deuteronomy 8:3 puts it, drawing out its unprecedented nature, it is something "with which neither you nor your ancestors were acquainted." It fits no existing category within Israel's knowledge and experience. Although Moses explains that it is the promised bread, its intrinsic strangeness is memorialized in its name. For the Israelites' question leads to a wordplay between māh ("what?") and mān (the name that the substance is given [Exod. 16:31])—in English, "manna." The new way of living that Israel is to learn involves accustoming themselves to the strange and unfamiliar.

> [16]"This is what the Lord has commanded: 'Gather as much of it as each of you needs, an omer to a person according to the number of persons, all providing

---

this narrative awkwardness, there is little point in lingering, for this section is still preliminary to the story's main concerns.

11. This is also the implication of Num. 11:4–35, where it is the recurrence of nothing but manna that makes the Israelites long for meat.

12. Thomas W. Mann entertainingly envisages the scenario as "manna with a side dish of quail" (The Book of the Torah: The Narrative Integrity of the Pentateuch [Atlanta: John Knox, 1988], 96).

for those in their own tents.'" [17]The Israelites did so, some gathering more, some less. [18]But when they measured it with an omer, those who had gathered much had nothing over, and those who gathered little had no shortage; they gathered as much as each of them needed.

Moses passes on directions from Yhwh. An initial "as much of it as each of you needs" could, on its own, sound like an invitation to gather according to the extent of their appetite. But there is an immediate qualification: each person is to have a particular specified amount, an omer, and the variation between what people gather is to correspond to the varying numbers of people in the households within the tents (e.g., "collect four omers for a household of four, six omers for a household of six"); for the assumption is that one person collects on behalf of each tent. The wording of verses 17–18 is then a little puzzling, however, as it implies that the people collected first and measured later, when one might have expected from verse 16 that an omer for measuring would have accompanied the act of collecting. Perhaps this indicates that "an omer per person" is to be taken as Moses's indicative guide as to the amount that it is appropriate to collect.

Nonetheless there remains some unclarity as to the precise scenario envisaged: How does the recognized disparity in gathering ("some gathering more, some less") relate to the equality of outcome? Is it the case that, however much or little was collected, Yhwh tacitly superintended the process in such a way as to ensure that parity per individual person was the result?[13] Or perhaps more likely, is it the case that what was gathered was pooled and then redistributed in appropriate amounts, Yhwh's tacit superintending having ensured the right overall amount?[14] Either way, however, the point appears to be that the bread from heaven comes in such a way that the strong and energetic are not privileged over the weak and frail, or the greedy over the abstemious.[15] They exercise their varying abilities, and their needs are equally met. Here is the archetypal original of those words that arguably, more than any others, won many followers for Karl Marx: "From each according to their ability; to each according to their need."

[19]And Moses said to them, "Let no one leave any of it over until morning." [20]But they did not listen to Moses; some left part of it until morning, and it bred worms

13. Thus, e.g., Rashi: see Carasik, *The Commentators' Bible*, 2:127.

14. Thus, e.g., John Calvin in vol. 1 of his *Commentaries on the Four Last Books of Moses: Arranged in the Form of a Harmony*, trans. Charles William Bingham, in *Calvin's Commentaries* (Edinburgh: Calvin Translation Society, 1852–55; repr., Grand Rapids: Baker Books, 2005), 278.

15. "The wondrous reality about the distribution of this bread is that their uncompetitive, non-hoarding practice really does work, and it works for all!" (Brueggemann, "Exodus," 813–14).

and became foul. And Moses was angry with them. [21]Morning by morning they gathered it, as much as each needed; but when the sun grew hot, it melted.

To go out every day to collect could seem like a chore that needs to be eased. Why not collect extra on one day and keep it, so that one does not need to go out the next (but rather, perhaps, sleep in)? Yet Moses rules this out. YHWH's bread is not the sort that can be kept overnight. It can only be collected afresh each new day. Unsurprisingly, some doubt this and try to store the bread overnight anyway. They discover that this cannot be done, for the bread fares badly; or if left on the ground, it melts and so becomes unavailable. Again unsurprisingly, Moses is angered at their reluctance to take him at his word.

In this depiction the heavenly bread is resistant to one of the most basic of human urges: to save up and to hoard. It is part of YHWH's new way, into which Israel is being inducted, in which familiar categories of understanding and yardsticks of behavior are replaced. YHWH's principle is that Israel's bread must each day be provided anew and collected anew. The implicit sense is of a need to appropriate the divine gift always in the present, in the here and now. The Israelites indeed are to know what YHWH has done for them in the past (v. 6), which is the basis for what they do in the present; yet they cannot, as it were, live off the past but must appropriate the implications of the past through a pattern of living that is renewed each new day.

> [22]On the sixth day they gathered twice as much [*mishneh*] food, two omers apiece. When all the leaders of the congregation came and told Moses, [23]he said to them, "This is what the LORD has commanded: 'Tomorrow is a day of solemn rest, a holy sabbath to the LORD; bake what you want to bake and boil what you want to boil, and all that is left over put aside to be kept until morning.'" [24]So they put it aside until morning, as Moses commanded them; and it did not become foul, and there were no worms in it. [25]Moses said, "Eat it today, for today is a sabbath to the LORD; today you will not find it in the field. [26]For six days you shall gather it; but on the seventh day, which is a sabbath, there will be none."
>
> [27]On the seventh day some of the people went out to gather, and they found none. [28]The LORD said to Moses, "How long will you refuse to keep my commandments and instructions? [29]See! The LORD has given you the sabbath, therefore on the sixth day he gives you food for two days; each of you stay where you are; do not leave your place on the seventh day." [30]So the people rested on the seventh day.

The principle and practice of daily provision, daily collection, and no hoarding have been established. So now it is possible to introduce an exception. On the sixth day the principle and practice change. In accordance with YHWH's initial words to Moses (v. 5), the people gather a double amount. When their leaders come to tell Moses that they have done this, Moses explains what they are to do. This can be understood in one of two ways. Either one assumes that Moses has told the Israelites that they will collect more on the sixth day, since he already knows that this will happen (v. 5), and when the leaders report to Moses for directions as to what to do with it all (given the established constraints), Moses then explains the principle of Sabbath. Alternatively, as Childs imagines the scenario, "The people are not informed of the plan. They go blissfully out on the sixth day, gathering a day's portion as usual, and to their amazement, they gather twice the normal amount, two omers apiece. When they come to Moses, he exploits their surprise to instruct them in the nature of the Sabbath."[16] Although this latter is more dramatic, the Hebrew says nothing about amazement or surprise, and so I think the former reading is preferable.[17] Either way, Moses explains that because the following day is holy, a Sabbath, they can do the very thing that they cannot do on all other days: prepare the food, keep it overnight, and eat it fresh the next day. Indeed, as Moses says subsequently, on the seventh day, the holy day, the bread is not given by God to be available for collection.

Certain Israelites, true to form, yet again refuse to take Moses's word for it. They go out to look for the bread, just as previously they tried to avoid having to go out for it. In place of Moses's anger comes YHWH's rebuke. And YHWH reiterates and expands what Moses has said previously about the special status of the Sabbath, which is such that double bread comes on the sixth day to enable rest without lack on the seventh. The rhythm of daily discipline for six days is complemented by a different pattern for the Sabbath.

> [31]The house of Israel called it manna; it was like coriander seed, white, and the taste of it was like wafers made with honey. [32]Moses said, "This is what the LORD has commanded: 'Let an omer of it be kept throughout your generations, in order that they may see the food with which I fed you in the wilderness, when I brought you out of the land of Egypt.'" [33]And Moses said to Aaron, "Take a jar, and put an omer of manna in it, and place it before the LORD, to be kept

16. Childs, *Exodus*, 290.

17. If surprise were intended, the Hebrew would surely introduce *vĕhinnēh* ("and behold/ see"; or in more contemporary idiom, "and what they saw was") just before *mishneh* ("double"), and the text of v. 22 would be something like this: "On the sixth day they collected bread and measured it with an omer, and what they saw was that it was double [*vĕhinnēh mishneh*]: there were two omers apiece." The use of *vĕhinnēh*, which serves to shift the perspective from that of the narrator to that of the character within the story, is a common idiomatic way of indicating that something remarkable or surprising is being seen; cf. Gen. 8:11; 22:13; 24:15; 25:24; 26:8; 28:12, 13; 37:7, 9; etc.

throughout your generations." [34]As the LORD commanded Moses, so Aaron placed it before the covenant, for safekeeping. [35]The Israelites ate manna forty years, until they came to a habitable land; they ate manna, until they came to the border of the land of Canaan. [36]An omer is a tenth of an ephah.

The story of the bread from heaven, and what Israel was to learn thereby, is complete. So the narrative changes mode and concludes with a number of explanatory comments. First (v. 31), there is a note about the bread itself, its name, appearance, and pleasant taste. Second (vv. 32–34), a specimen of manna is to be kept as a holy object,[18] beside the ark,[19] as a memorial for subsequent generations of YHWH's provision in the wilderness.[20] Third (v. 35), there is a note about the duration of the manna for the whole of the wilderness period, and its cessation only when Israel entered the promised land, when YHWH's normal mode of provision became the food that grew in the land (cf. Josh. 5:12). Finally (v. 36), there is a note (perhaps originally a marginal gloss to v. 16 or v. 18, subsequently included in the text at this point, where it does not break the flow?) that explains the quantity of manna that is represented by an omer—on the assumption that one knows how much an ephah is![21]

To summarize: The manna, a divine provision, can be seen to function as a symbolic concretization of divine grace. It testingly challenges Israel to learn to live from an unfamiliar resource; it nourishes the Israelites irrespective of their varying abilities; it resists being accommodated to conventional human desires; it is designed to enable Israel to develop a particular rhythm of life, encompassing both the working week and rest on the Sabbath. In all these ways the manna inducts Israel into the divine pattern for life.

18. How an omer's quantity of manna can be preserved, when usually the manna decays overnight, is not specified; just as there is no explanation as to how it could be baked or boiled on the sixth day, even though it ordinarily melted in the sun's heat. Perhaps one should simply imagine that, given the variable nature of the manna's durability, if a portion of manna is to be kept, then that portion becomes keepable.

19. The Hebrew of 16:34, *liphnē hā'ēdūt*, is rendered "before the covenant" by NRSV. William Propp usefully observes that "*'ēdūt* is often, as here, an elliptical or metonymic reference to *'ārōn hā'ēdūt*, 'the Covenant Ark'" (*Exodus 1–18*, AB 2 [New York: Doubleday, 1999], 599).

20. Stephen Geller sees a concern to connect the manna with the "bread before the Presence" so as to interpret such bread not as food to be consumed by the deity but as a symbol of divine provision for Israel ("Manna and Sabbath: A Literary-Theological Reading of Exodus 16," *Interpretation* 59 [2005]: 5–16, esp. 12).

21. For the general problem of determining weights and measures in antiquity, see standard works of reference, e.g., Marvin A. Powell, "Weights and Measures," *ABD* 6:897–908. Powell reckons that the preservation of a single omer "probably reflects the character of this capacity measure as a daily food ration. The ancient norm for a daily food ration seems to have been widely regarded as ca. 1 liter, usually of barley" (904).

Some Hermeneutical Difficulties

If the story of Exodus 16 has been to some extent understood, we may usefully ponder the question of what kind of material the story is, and how some of the issues it raises may best be handled.

I have offered a reading of the text in its received form, without prejudice to questions as to its possible tradition-history and composition. Conventional pentateuchal criticism tends to ascribe the narrative to the Priestly writer (P), with elements either of the Yahwist (or more recently, non-P tradition) and/or of redactional development;[22] but since, apart from the concern for the Sabbath, neither the terminological nor the conceptual resonances with related Priestly texts are strong, such an analysis offers little illumination here.[23] There is indeed, as noted, some awkwardness in the first part of the narrative, whose explanation is unclear; but this is not such as to disable a meaningful reading of the whole.

On Understanding the Manna

One major interpretive challenge concerns the appropriate conceptual moves to make in construing the nature of the manna. Unsurprisingly, there is a long history of various kinds of rationalization, whereby the manna is understood in terms of a natural phenomenon of the Sinai. Already in antiquity Josephus commented on the manna in the desert: "It is a mainstay to dwellers in these parts against their dearth of other provisions, and to this very day all that region is watered by a rain like to that which then, as a favor to Moses, the Deity sent down for men's sustenance."[24]

Interestingly, rationalizing moves can be made for reasons both sympathetic and unsympathetic toward the biblical text and the faiths rooted in it. This is

22. For details see, e.g., Antony Campbell and Mark O'Brien, *Sources of the Pentateuch: Texts, Introductions, Annotations* (Minneapolis: Fortress, 1993), 41–43, 144; or Thomas Dozeman, *Exodus*, ECC (Grand Rapids: Eerdmans, 2009), 378–79.

23. A possible exception is Ellen Davis's reading, where ascription to P is closely linked to a construal of the manna story as a counternarrative to the economic realities that Israel associated with Egypt—though the heuristic value of such a contrastive reading seems to me largely independent of the ascription to the P writer; see her *Scripture, Culture, and Agriculture: An Agrarian Reading of the Bible* (Cambridge: Cambridge University Press, 2009), 66–79, esp. 72, 74, also 145. An extensive analysis of the text as containing both P and non-P narratives is presented by Dozeman, where the prime interpretive result, as far as I can see, is that one comes to have two narratives rather than one, and the concerns of the received text are divided between them (non-P: oasis, testing; P: wilderness, complaint, and Sabbath) (*Exodus*, 357, 360–64, 374–87); yet each reconstructed narrative is harder to make sense of and less memorable than the received narrative.

24. Josephus, *Jewish Antiquities* 3.31; in *Josephus*, trans. H. St. J. Thackeray, LCL (London: Heinemann; Cambridge, MA: Harvard University Press, 1967), 5:333–35.

presumably because it is such a deep human instinct to want to make sense of the unfamiliar by assimilating it, in one way or other, to the familiar. How this works out in detail then depends upon one's wider frame of reference. The unsympathetic may rationalize to try to show that claims to the supernatural are evidence mainly of popular desires for marvels or else of piety's tendencies toward credulity, when in reality the supernatural is the natural scientifically misunderstood, and therefore awaiting explanation and demystification. Equally, however, believers may find some degree of rationalizing helps rather than hinders faith, though much depends on how this is done. In a culture that is deeply shaped by the technological application of scientific discoveries, it can often feel helpful for faith to assimilate at least some of the biblical content to scientific explanation without thereby denying divine action. The danger is that the short-term gains in plausibility may lay themselves open to long-term overthrow through seeming to make the truth-content of biblical narrative dependent upon the evaluative criteria of the natural sciences.[25]

A striking recent example comes from the distinguished Cambridge physicist Colin Humphreys, whose book *The Miracles of Exodus: A Scientist's Discovery of the Extraordinary Natural Causes of the Biblical Stories*,[26] nicely encapsulates its thesis in its subtitle. Humphreys says:

> A natural explanation of the events of the Exodus doesn't to my mind make them any less miraculous. As we will see, the ancient Israelites believed that their God worked in, with, and through natural events. What made certain natural events miraculous was their timing: for example, the River Jordan stopped flowing precisely when the Israelites were assembled on its banks and desperate to cross. . . . I believe this natural explanation [an earthquake's blocking the flow of the Jordan] makes this miracle more, not less, believable.[27]

Humphreys is consistently upbeat about the positive value for faith of his approach to the biblical text. By way of contrast with "most scholars [who] believe [the biblical text] is riddled with errors and inconsistencies," he argues

25. Michael Buckley, *At the Origins of Modern Atheism* (New Haven and London: Yale University Press, 1987), has become a warning beacon, through a meticulous history of thought, of the danger of theology's self-destruction through well-meaning but conceptually confused self-translation into the concepts and categories of the natural sciences.

26. Colin Humphreys, *The Miracles of Exodus: A Scientist's Discovery of the Extraordinary Natural Causes of the Biblical Stories* (London and New York: Continuum, 2003). For fuller discussion of Humphreys and the appropriate understanding of miracles, see my "Miracle in the Hebrew Bible," in *The Cambridge Companion to Miracles*, ed. Graham Twelftree (Cambridge: Cambridge University Press, 2010), 57–74, esp. 65–68.

27. Humphreys, *Miracles of Exodus*, 5. For the importance of timing in Humphreys's account, cf. 256, 271, 337.

that "modern science suggests that the Exodus text has often been misinterpreted by scholars" and that "the real meaning of the text, suggested in this book, is frequently more dramatic than the traditional interpretation, . . . truly astonishing, amazing, and inspirational."[28]

Humphreys discusses the story of the manna as part of his attempt to identify the geographical location of the desert of Sin (Exod. 16:1). He appeals to the known fact that the stem of the tamarisk tree, when bitten by a particular insect, "exude[s] a sweet, sticky substance that falls to the ground and solidifies"; then he argues that "the biblical description of manna fits so well the present-day manna that I believe we can say, beyond reasonable doubt, that the manna the Israelites ate in the desert was a natural substance produced by suitable trees." According to Humphreys, the manna disappears when the sun grows hot, because insects eat it; a specimen of manna could be kept in a jar because its high sugar content preserved it; and tamarisk trees are plentiful (and thereby able to produce the necessary large quantity of manna) in the Hisma Desert, which is where the biblical desert of Sin is therefore to be located.[29]

Humphreys's contention that "the ancient Israelites believed that their God worked in, with, and through natural events"—and that, by implication, contemporary believers should believe likewise—is, as far as it goes, unexceptionable within a framework of faith. Moreover, there can be little doubt that modern arguments, and confusions, about "natural" and "supernatural" have sometimes led believers to feel that they should stress the supernatural at the expense of the natural in ways that are theologically problematic—either because it encourages a "god of the gaps" mentality, or because it can devalue the reality of God within regular life. This latter concern is expressed by Terence Fretheim in his discussion of the manna:

> If the provisions of God in the wilderness are all subsumed under the extraordinary or miraculous, then the people of God will tend to look for God's providential care only in that which falls outside the ordinary. The all too common effect of this is to absent God from the ordinary and everyday and to go searching for God only in the deep-sea and mountaintop experiences. Consequently, the people of God will not be able to see in the very ordinariness of things that God is the one who bestows blessings again and again.[30]

Yet, valid as these concerns are, it is not clear how far they really help with understanding the manna in Exodus 16. For a prime concern of the narrative

---

28. Ibid., 339.
29. Ibid., 290–92.
30. Terence Fretheim, *Exodus*, IBCTP (Louisville: John Knox, 1991), 182.

is that *God's action, in the form of the manna, reconfigures and reconstitutes the ordinary and everyday for Israel.*

Further, it is telling that when Humphreys cites "the key points as recorded in the book of Exodus," he cites only parts of 16:14–16, 21, 31–35.[31] This means that, quite apart from the biblical narrative's containing no mention in this context of tamarisk trees and its representing the manna as found widespread upon the ground, at least two major concerns disappear from view on Humphreys's reading: first, the story's own framing concern with the manna as a divine test in relation to God's instruction (16:4b); and second, the differing behavior of the manna at the end of each week, when double can be collected on the sixth day, the manna can be kept overnight, and no manna appears on the Sabbath (16:22–30). It is hard not to suspect that precisely because these parts of the story resist Humphreys's rationalizing account of manna as the natural product of the tamarisk tree, they are allowed to drop out of sight. So despite Humphreys's rhetoric about scholarly misinterpretation and the "inspirational" potential of his interpretation, I think it is in fact hard to improve upon the century-old sobriety of S. R. Driver: "It is evident that the Biblical manna, while on the one hand (like the Plagues) it has definite points of contact with a natural phaenomenon or product of the country, differs from the natural manna [meaning the juice exuded from a particular species of tamarisk] in the many praeternatural or miraculous features attributed to it."[32] In trying to make the biblical narrative "more, not less, believable," Humphreys moves well beyond establishing that the story has appropriate local color in relation to particular desert regions. For he is surely in fact replacing it with an alternative narrative that is more believable only because its picture of the divine provision is no longer that of the biblical text. The explanatory "success" of his approach is in inverse proportion to its ability to account for what the text actually says and gives space to, most obviously in relation to the difference on the sixth and seventh days.

On Understanding Exodus 16 within Its Pentateuchal Context

At this point it may be helpful to note two further, though lesser, issues within the biblical narrative, which also, albeit differently than the manna, raise the issue of the appropriateness of some kind of rationalizing explanation.

The first problem is the number of Israelites in the desert. The description of Israel's starting point, Elim (16:1), as having twelve springs of water and

---

31. Humphreys, *Miracles of Exodus*, 288–89.

32. Samuel Rolles Driver, *The Book of Exodus* (Cambridge: Cambridge University Press, 1911), 153–54.

seventy palm trees (15:27) is clearly, as noted above, meant to make it sound like a thoroughly desirable oasis for the Israelites. If, however, twelve springs and seventy trees are to provide for all Israel at once, without long waiting and possible contention as to who gets access and when, then it seems to presuppose a total group of a few thousand at most. Likewise, the ability of Moses and Aaron to address the Israelites as a whole, and to be addressed by them, seems to presuppose a similar-sized group. But what, then, should one make of those passages elsewhere that provide a specific enumeration? If one computes from the statement "The Israelites journeyed . . . about six hundred thousand men on foot, besides children" (Exod. 12:37; cf. Num. 1:2–3, 45–46), and adds women and children proportionally, then one reaches a total of at least two million people. So many Israelites would be too numerous to enjoy twelve springs and seventy trees or to converse with Moses. There is thus a disparity between the implications of the narrative portrayal, not to mention intrinsic feasibility in the envisaged desert context, and the explicit numeration provided.

The issue of large numbers was perhaps most famously aired in the nineteenth century by the Anglican bishop of Natal, John Colenso, in his *The Pentateuch and the Book of Joshua Critically Examined*,[33] which caused considerable controversy.[34] (Eighteenth-century deists, not least Reimarus, had earlier raised the issue but had had limited impact.) The computation of two million people is Colenso's, though he reckons this "a very moderate estimate" (35); he also calculates a further two million sheep and oxen (59). Colenso is acutely aware of the logistical difficulties posed by the face-value implications of certain specifications within the biblical text.[35] However, like many of his nineteenth-century contemporaries, he has a limited conceptual frame of reference within which to discuss the difficulties, and he displays a rather wooden approach to biblical narratives. The bottom line for Colenso is essentially that Christians need to be honest in acknowledging the unhistorical nature of the Pentateuch, and that lack of such honesty was hindering Christian mission.

This is not the place for any full discussion of this issue, yet it is appropriate at least to touch on its possible implications for reading the wilderness narratives as Scripture. A wide range of proposals have been offered. Might the large numbers be a mistranslation? Might they represent straightforward exaggeration? Might they be symbolic (and if so, of what?)? The difficulty with all such suggestions is not only the specificity of the number 603,550, as a total of separate tribal numbers, in Numbers 1:46 (as also in Exod. 38:26). It is also the specificity of the amount of

33. John Colenso, *The Pentateuch and the Book of Joshua Critically Examined* (London: Longman & Green, 1862).

34. Illuminating and complementary accounts of the controversy within Britain are available in Peter Hinchliff, *John William Colenso, Bishop of Natal* (London and Edinburgh: Nelson, 1964), 85–114; and Timothy Larsen, "Bishop Colenso and His Critics: The Strange Emergence of Biblical Criticism in Victorian Britain," in *The Eye of the Storm: Bishop John William Colenso and the Crisis of Biblical Interpretation*, ed. Jonathan A. Draper, JSOTSS 386 (London and New York: T&T Clark, 2003), 42–63.

35. For a recent restatement of the problem, with a computation of the implied population as three and a half million, see Lester L. Grabbe, "*Adde Praeputium Praeputio Magnus Acervus Erit:* If the Exodus and Conquest Had Really Happened," *BibInt* 8, no. 1/2 (2000): 23–32.

silver offered for the sanctuary—100 talents and 1,775 shekels, given at the rate of half a shekel per person (Exod. 38:25–26); for since a talent contained 3,000 shekels, the amount of silver tallies exactly with 603,550 people if each offer a half shekel. This seems to require the numeration to be taken at face value. So an alternative approach, which takes the numeration at face value, is to suggest that the large numbers might represent a conflation of two (or more) different historical periods, whereby the numbers of Israel at a later period of its history are ascribed to the wilderness context, presumably through the assumption of a continuity between Israel past and present. However, a number of two million or more still looks unduly large for the population of Israel at any one time in antiquity. Although I incline toward this last proposal, it must be frankly admitted that there is no unproblematic way of making sense of these large numbers.

Second, there is the problem of the Israelites' food resources. The people speak (16:3), and YHWH subsequently responds, as though they were in the desert without food resources. Moreover, the later complaint about the manna is premised on manna being the only food available (Num. 11:4–9). Yet the account of the Exodus mentions numerous livestock that Israel is said to have had on leaving Egypt (Exod. 12:38; cf. 10:24–26); subsequent narratives apparently refer to these self-same livestock (or their descendants) as still present (Exod. 17:3; Num. 20:4; 32:1); and when the golden calf is made, the Israelites sacrifice and feast in a way that presupposes plentiful livestock (Exod. 32:5–6). Moreover, livestock would also need their own food. How then should one read Israel's expression of hunger, and the divine provision in response, in Exodus 16?

It is, of course, perfectly possible to think of explanations that can give an account of why this apparent tension between the manna narrative and other narratives need not be seen as a problem. One can, for example, think in terms of an unequal distribution of food resources among the Israelites. Thus Umberto Cassuto: "Those of the Israelites who possessed cattle certainly had no reason to complain about the lack of food; but we may easily assume that there were not a few among the people who had no cattle, whilst actual bread, such as they were accustomed to eat in Egypt, none of them had."[36] Alternatively, one can think of the Israelites as desiring a particular kind of food. Thus Alan Cole: "Like all pastoralists, they were very loath to slaughter their own beasts (cf. Num. 11:22), which was the only alternative to a diet of milk and cheese in the desert."[37] Either way, one can thereby read the narrative as though the presence of the livestock was both presupposed and apparently unproblematic.

There are thus major issues as to how best to read the manna story, both in itself and in relation to its wider narrative context, with a proper imaginative

36. Umberto Cassuto, *A Commentary on the Book of Exodus*, trans. Israel Abrahams (Jerusalem: Magnes, 1967), 189.
37. R. Alan Cole, *Exodus*, TOTC (London: Tyndale, 1973), 130.

seriousness that can do justice to its content. How far should one imagine the manna in terms of a sweet extract from tamarisk trees? How far should one imagine the size of Israel in terms of the numbering specified elsewhere? How far should one imagine that Israel, clamoring and then receiving manna, all the while had food resources in terms of their livestock? The persuasiveness of any preferred scenario will depend upon a range of factors.

On Determining the Genre of Exodus 16

One of the most important factors is one's judgment as to the narrative's likely genre. For a judgment about genre entails a sense of which questions a text will, and will not, fruitfully sustain.

There are at least four characteristics of Exodus 16, as of many other pentateuchal narratives, to which one needs to do justice. It is set in a particular historical context of foundational significance; it is a relatively self-contained episode, whose relation to its wider literary context appears loose in certain ways; it reads opaquely and elusively to the contemporary historian of ancient Israel; it functions with high levels of existential and archetypal resonance. There are, however, real difficulties in trying to use any one English word to depict the genre of such a text. Any particular term—myth, legend, saga, folktale, and so forth—tends to be used in so many differing ways by different people that without careful definition it will probably mislead as much as illuminate. Relatedly, people sometimes fix on particular terms and then employ them rhetorically and polemically in ways that lose sight of the specifics of the text that give rise to the use of the term in the first place. Not all manage to be as relaxed and positive about the issue as C. S. Lewis (who was relaxed because of his deep professional immersion in the study of literature), who succinctly observed, "I think He meant us to have sacred myth and sacred fiction as well as sacred history."[38]

One sophisticated modern attempt to handle this issue on a broad canvas has been the German articulation of a difference between *Historie* and *Geschichte*. To the best of my knowledge, this goes back to the late-nineteenth-century work of Martin Kähler, who attempted to distinguish two markedly different understandings of "history" so as to do justice to the biblical portrayal of Jesus in his *Der sogennante historische Jesus und der geschichtliche,*

---

38. From a letter to Janet Wise, October 5, 1955; cited in Kevin J. Vanhoozer, "On Scripture," in *The Cambridge Companion to C. S. Lewis*, ed. Robert MacSwain and Michael Ward (Cambridge: Cambridge University Press, 2010), 75–88, esp. 87. The context of what Lewis says is a general discussion of the nature and genres of literature in the OT and why he was not a "fundamentalist" (the text is available in C. S. Lewis, *Collected Letters*, vol. 3, *Narnia, Cambridge, and Joy, 1950–1963*, ed. Walter Hooper [London: HarperCollins, 2006], 652–53).

biblische Christus.[39] The basic distinction, as it has come to be understood, is conveniently summarized thus by David Jasper: "*Historie* is a description of how events actually happened; *Geschichte* is a description of what events *mean*, both to those who first experienced them and to us now. In other words, *Geschichte* is also concerned with contemporary present-day experience. History is not just about the past; it is also about the present."[40]

The distinction is epigrammatically summed up by Karl Barth: "Not all history is 'historical' [*Nicht alle Geschichte ist "historisch"*]."[41] It was also much used by major figures in twentieth-century German biblical and theological scholarship. Gerhard von Rad, for example, in his introduction to his Genesis commentary speaks of the Genesis narratives as "sagas" whose characteristics are to be understood in terms of the nature of *Geschichte* as distinct from *Historie*. The generalizing way in which he writes suggests the applicability of what he says to a narrative such as Exodus 16:

> [Saga] is the form favoured by a people for depicting its early history. . . . In its sagas a people is concerned with itself and the realities in which it finds itself. . . . For there is another history that a people makes besides the externals of wars, victories, migrations, and political catastrophes. It is an inner history, one that takes place on a different level, a story of inner events, experiences, and singular guidance, of working and becoming mature in life's mysteries; and for Israel that meant a history with God. . . .
>
> There is often an entire world of events—actual, experienced events!—enclosed in a single saga. The saga, therefore, has a much higher degree of density than has history (*Historie*). . . . Anyone who wants to understand such sagas correctly must acquire a broader and more profound conception of "history" (*Geschichte*) than what is often accepted today. At the beginning, the saga in most cases certainly contained a "historical" fact as its actual crystallizing point. But in addition it reflects a historical experience on the relevant community which extends into the present time of the narrator. This second constructional element is, as a rule, the stronger, often dominating to such an extent that it can

39. Martin Kähler, *Der sogennante historische Jesus und der geschichtliche, biblische Christus* (Leipzig: A. Deichert, 1896; repr., Munich: Chr. Kaiser, 1956); ET as *The So-Called Historical Jesus and the Historic Biblical Christ*, trans. Carl E. Braaten (Philadelphia: Fortress, 1964).

40. David Jasper, *A Short Introduction to Hermeneutics* (Louisville: Westminster John Knox, 2004), 93.

41. Karl Barth, *CD* III/I:61–94, esp. 80 // *KD* III/I:87. Barth is writing with reference to the genre of the creation narratives of Genesis. He goes on to express himself robustly on the subject of reductive attitudes toward such biblical material: "We must dismiss and resist to the very last any idea of the inferiority or untrustworthiness or even worthlessness of a 'non-historical' depiction and narration of history. This is in fact only a ridiculous and middle-class habit of the modern Western mind which is supremely phantastic in its chronic lack of imaginative phantasy, and hopes to rid itself of its complexes through suppression" (81).

expand and elevate the material to a historical (*geschichtlich*) type behind which the original historical (*historisch*) fact more and more disappears.[42]

There are, of course, aspects of this account with which one can, in one way or other, argue. But it well captures what is surely an intrinsic aspect of many resonant ancient narratives, non-biblical as well as biblical—narratives that have *mattered over long periods of time* to the people who have preserved them, and that can still matter today.[43] Whatever the origins of the narrative, as the narrative is handed on and retold, it acquires ever greater coloring from the contexts of its retelling. This is because the narrative is seen to be a suitable vehicle for the expression of certain recurrent existential issues and questions of identity that are important to the people who cherish the narrative. Because of such a history of prior use, the narrative in its received form may relate somewhat loosely to its received literary contextualization. One consequence is that it is usually more or less impossible to separate out, or reconstruct, the different elements that have come to constitute the narrative, though sometimes anachronisms can give some clues.[44]

It may be that "legend" is the least problematic word for depicting this phenomenon. However, it is then important to resist pejoratively construing legend as something inferior, a kind of history *manqué* that is frustratingly opaque to the ancient historian who wants to know what really happened. Rather, legend should be recognized as that literary form in which many cultures express foundational narratives and depict particular people and events that are widely taken to be enduringly significant for identity and practice within that culture.

42. Gerhard von Rad, *Genesis*, trans. John Marks, rev. ed. (London: SCM, 1972), 33, 34. Specifically on Exod. 16, von Rad writes: "It is clear that the narrator is not just telling us of a strange occurrence that took place in the earliest days of Israel's history. The event that is recorded belongs to one particular time and place; but at the same time it is typical, that is, it shows forth something that is true at all times and in all places" (Gerhard von Rad, *Moses*, ed. K. C. Hanson, trans. Stephen Neill [Göttingen: Vandenhoeck & Ruprecht, 1940; ET, Cambridge: James Clarke, 2012], 72).

43. The other most resonant and enduring texts from the ancient world—Homer's *Iliad* and *Odyssey*—are a locus for comparable debates as to the nature of the content and its "historicity." In antiquity, Homeric interpretation also provided models and resources for patristic OT interpretation.

44. An unusually clear example, in my judgment, is the way the divine name YHWH has been used in the patriarchal narratives, even though much of the religious logic of the narratives generally remains non-YHWHistic, and the logic of certain individual texts seems to presuppose the name of the deity as "El" rather than as YHWH, as when "Surely YHWH is in this place" is on Jacob's lips, and yet the place is named Bethel rather than Bethyah (Gen. 28:16, 19 AT). For full discussion see my work *The Old Testament of the Old Testament*, OBT (Minneapolis: Fortress, 1992; repr., Eugene, OR: Wipf & Stock, 2001).

If this is on the right lines, then certain things may reasonably follow for an understanding of Exodus 16. First, the large number of Israel as in the millions should not be introduced into one's imaginative engagement with the manna story, for the perhaps least unlikely conjecture is that this is a numeration of Israel originating in a context distinct from that in which the manna story came about. Rather, the numeration may well attest to something of the rich and complex internal tradition-history of the Pentateuch and the way in which later generations of Israel identified with the generation that came out of Egypt.

Second, livestock should not be presumed to be present within the manna story, for this becomes an example of how a story that has had its own history of use may relate somewhat loosely to its received literary contextualization. It is not that there are no connections between Exodus 16 and other pentateuchal narratives, as most obviously Numbers 11:4–9 makes clear, but rather that such connections as there are qualify but do not remove the episodic and relatively freestanding nature of the story. Both the numeration of Israel and the possible presence of livestock raise the same kind of issue for the reader. To be sure, numerous Jews and Christians down through the ages have indeed felt it appropriate, because of their reverence for the text, to the best of their abilities to combine diversity and divergence of biblical content into a harmonious whole. My proposal, however, is that the contemporary theologically-engaged reader should resist the temptation to produce an integration of divergent narrative elements, where the implicit criteria of consistency may in reality be somewhat abstract and not do sufficient justice to the specifics of the biblical text. Imaginative and synthetic reading of the received text must indeed take place, but it needs not to be a forced or heavy-handed reading. If in some places a diamond is polished and in other places it is rough, it still remains a diamond.

Third, an instinct to rationalize the manna as a natural phenomenon, a recurrent instinct for which I have taken Humphreys as representative, should also be resisted as a kind of category mistake. In terms of the preceding discussion, it is an attempt to present *Geschichte* as though it were *Historie*. Or put differently, it wants to render divine grace as symbolized by the manna, and the distinctive rhythm of life associated with it, as though it were a regular feature of the world that is accessible and comprehensible apart from grace. Or in yet other terms, the biblical witness is perspectival, and one's evaluation of it will be significantly affected by whether or not one seeks in some way not only to imagine but also to appropriate its perspective, even if for the contemporary believer it may be fitting to make discriminations as to the nature of the biblical text, discriminations not made by all earlier generations.

To conclude this section, I offer two disparate but nonetheless suggestive articulations of some of the wider issues at stake, one methodological and the other substantive. First, a recent discussion of Sigmund Freud's remarkable work on the Bible concludes with a general observation about the frames of reference within which interpreters may write (and with reference to our discussion, evaluate): "Although we have begun to see that 'different registers of discourse'—personal and public, popular and scholarly, fictional and historical, poetic and scientific—might be interrelated, we have barely begun to consider the possibility that they might be equal and begin to write accordingly. Perhaps we should take our clue from the ancients, for the Bible is engaged in just such cross-disciplinary discourse precisely because it was predisciplinary."[45]

Second, there is a memorable formulation in some oft-quoted words of American poet William Stafford (1914–93), who coins a novel verbal form so as to conclude his poem "Bi-Focal":

> So the world happens twice—
> once what we see it as,
> second it legends itself
> deep, the way it is.[46]

The Manna within a Wider Canonical Context

There is a certain intrinsic tension within the story of the manna. On the one hand it appears to be setting out a fundamental and enduring pattern for Israel's life as the people of YHWH. Yet on the other hand the provision of manna is clearly restricted to Israel's time in the desert, and this could be taken to imply that the story's implications are limited: if the manna ceases, on what basis, if any, should the spiritual disciplines associated with it persist? The prime interpretive move, both within the canon and in postbiblical thought, is to construe the manna metaphorically (figuratively, typologically) in a variety of ways and thereby to articulate its enduring significance.

The Lesson to Be Learned from the Manna in Deuteronomy 8

Deuteronomy 8, one of the earliest construals of the manna story, is structured precisely around the contrast between life in the desert and life in the promised land. Its concern is that Israel's time in the desert, when life was hard, was a time

45. The Bible and Culture Collective, *The Postmodern Bible* (New Haven and London: Yale University Press, 1995), 195.

46. William Stafford, *The Way It Is: New and Selected Poems* (Minneapolis: Graywolf, 1998), 72.

of learning through the manna a fundamental truth, a truth that is in danger of being unlearned and forgotten in the promised land, where life is easier.

> [2]Remember the long way that the LORD your God has led you these forty years in the wilderness, in order to humble [*'innāh*] you, testing [*nissāh*] you to know what was in your heart, whether or not you would keep his commandments. [3]He humbled [*'innāh*] you by letting you hunger, then by feeding you with manna, with which neither you nor your ancestors were acquainted, in order to make you understand that one [*'ādām*][47] does not live by bread alone, but by every word that comes from the mouth of the LORD. . . . [5]Know then in your heart that as a parent disciplines a child so the LORD your God disciplines you.

Moses, the speaking voice throughout Deuteronomy, begins by depicting the forty years in the desert as a time of testing (*nissāh*) in relation to divine commandments, in a way that is, as already noted, similar to Exodus 16:4b. To this is added the concept of humbling (*'innāh*), whose importance is clear from its repetition at the beginning of verse 3. The purpose of testing and humbling is explicitly clarified later in the chapter: "to humble you and to test you, and in the end to do you good" (v. 16). This is fully consonant with the notion of parental discipline in verse 5: what YHWH does with the Israelites is for their good, even if it feels painful and unwelcome at the time, for it is part of the process of forming good character and appropriate lifestyle (a point memorably developed by the writer to the Hebrews, in Heb. 12:5–11).

More specifically, humbling is seen in Deuteronomy 8:3 as making Israel teachable, putting them in a condition to learn something fundamental with reference to themselves and God. It may be helpful here to remember the famous portrayal of Moses in Numbers 12:3 as "very humble [*'ānāw*], more so than anyone else on the face of the earth." The condition of being humble (*'ānāw*) is presumably that which the action of humbling (*'innāh*) is meant to induce (both adjective and verb belong to the same Hebrew root).[48] If one reads Deuteronomy 8:2–3 and Numbers 12:3 in the light of each other, Moses supremely demonstrates the quality that engenders teachability in relation to God—hence his unique and not-to-be-challenged role within Israel as portrayed in the narrative of Numbers 12.[49] It is teachability for Israel generally that Moses in Deuteronomy 8 portrays as the purpose of the manna.

47. This unduly individualizes the generic and collective term *'ādām*. A better gender-inclusive rendering would be "humanity."

48. The *piel* form, *'innāh*, like certain other *piel* forms (e.g., *qiddēsh*, "consecrate/sanctify") here has the sense of bringing about a state or condition.

49. For an illuminating probing of the meaning of Moses's humility in Num. 12:3 as dependence upon God, and some of its wider implications for reading Scripture, see Richard S.

The process of humbling Israel began with making life harder ("letting you hunger" [Deut. 8:3]). This hardship was then resolved by the divine provision of manna, a solution that was unfamiliar and unprecedented. Although nothing further is said here about the manna, this emphasis on its unfamiliarity can reasonably be taken as a summary of the manna's representing a new and distinctive rhythm and practice of life as spelled out more fully in Exodus 16. It is through having their hunger met thus that Israel is opened to learning a fundamental principle about human life: not by bread alone is human life sustained, but by responsiveness to the divine will. Material needs are affirmed, but qualified. Or to put it in other terms, through being fed by manna, Israel is taught a non-reductive account of what it means to be human, for alongside material needs is relationship between humanity and God, which is also constitutive of true human existence. One may not unreasonably see significance in the use of the generic *'ādām*, "humanity," rather than simply "Israel," as making the point that what Israel learns in this particular way is a principle of universal applicability.

Jesus's use of this principle, in the synoptic portrayal, well articulates its nature and purpose in a particular situation (Matt. 4:4//Luke 4:4). The overall nature of the testing of Jesus in the desert appears to be to probe the meaning of his sonship to God as pronounced at his baptism: if Jesus is Son to God as Father, then what follows from this? What does it entail, and does it not entail?[50] The first test is that, if he is hungry through being in the desert (as also was Israel), then he should feed himself; that is, if he is Son of God, he should have divine power, which he could exercise to meet his need. So why not use it? Why not use his power to enact a kind of equivalent to the manna by turning stones into bread? To this possibility Jesus responds with Deuteronomy 8:3, precisely to relativize the importance of material hunger in favor of obedient responsiveness to God. The point in context seems to be that, just as the manna is to direct its recipients to God as constitutive of their lives, so too, only more so, is the meaning of Jesus's sonship; such power as he has is to be used not according to his own preference or for his own benefit but rather as an obedient outworking of his Father's will. And if, in a wider Christian frame of reference, Jesus embodies the nature of humanity at its truest and fullest, then his refusal to prioritize his own welfare out of obedience to his Father should characterize fullness of humanity for others also.

Yet God's gift to Israel of a promised land, where the conditions of life are entirely different from those of the desert, is double-edged:

[7]For the LORD your God is bringing you into a good land, a land with flowing streams, . . . [9]a land where you may eat bread without scarcity, where you will lack nothing. . . . [10]You shall eat your fill. . . . [11]Take care that you do not forget the LORD your God, by failing to keep his commandments. . . . [12]When you have eaten your fill and built fine houses and live in them, [13]and when your herds and

---

Briggs, *The Virtuous Reader: Old Testament Narrative and Interpretive Virtue*, STI (Grand Rapids: Baker Academic, 2010), 45–69.

50. See my work *The Bible, Theology, and Faith: A Study of Abraham and Jesus*, CSCD (Cambridge: Cambridge University Press, 2000), 198–205.

flocks have multiplied, . . . and all that you have is multiplied, [14]then do not exalt
[*rūm*] yourself, forgetting the LORD your God, who brought you out of the land
of Egypt. . . . [17]Do not say to yourself, "My power and the might of my own
hand have gotten me this wealth." [18]But remember the LORD your God, for it is
he who gives you power to get wealth.

In the promised land Israel will be tempted to forget YHWH, that is, to unlearn
what they have learned in the desert. The initial danger is of Israel's "exalting" itself, where the concept of exalting (*rūm*, in v. 14) is the exact opposite
of humbling (*'innāh*, in vv. 2–3). The comfort and ease and prosperity of
their situation may induce in them a sense of self-congratulation and self-
sufficiency, a condition no longer marked by openness and teachability in
relation to YHWH. The consequence is that they would ascribe their well-being
to their own efforts without recognition of YHWH's enabling of those efforts
(vv. 17–18). Or, in other words, they will unlearn the lesson of the manna and
fall back into a reductive account of human life and welfare in which God is
no longer constitutive.

Such is the suggestive potency of this reading of the manna that it can be
a natural move for Jews and Christians to metaphorize the manna into the
spiritual insights that many (though, to be sure, not all) acquire in times of
hardship—insights about relationship with God as constitutive of human
well-being[51]—and contrast this with the spiritual blindness and apathy that
regularly characterizes those who are unduly comfortable in life.

Jewish and Christian Metaphorical Construals of Manna

The Deuteronomic linkage between manna and learning from the mouth
of YHWH received continuing reflection and development in antiquity. One
prime move within a Jewish frame of reference was to draw on the implicit
symbolism of manna as "bread from heaven," and so unlike regular food that
comes from the earth. The result was to understand manna as *wisdom*, and
relatedly as torah, whose content exemplifies and enables wisdom—in other
words, manna as that which comes from God and most nourishes people in
relation to God.

Philo notably exemplifies this pattern of understanding the manna as wisdom. For example, he comments on "bread from heaven" in Exodus 16:4: "Of
what food can he rightly say that it is rained from heaven, save of heavenly

51. There are many testimonies from people who in terrible conditions reach rock bottom
but then emerge with new or renewed faith in God. One of many memorable examples from
the Second World War is Ernest Gordon, *Miracle on the River Kwai* (London and Glasgow:
Collins, 1963; repr., London: Fount, 1995).

wisdom which is sent from above on souls which yearn for virtue by Him who sheds the gift of prudence in rich abundance?"[52] Similarly, elsewhere Philo reflects on the portrayal of the equal distribution of the manna: "The heavenly food of the soul—wisdom—which Moses calls 'manna,' is distributed to all who will use it in equal portions by the divine Word."[53] When the Letter of James portrays wisdom in a similar way—wisdom is "from above" (3:13–18, esp. v. 17) and is readily available, "If any of you is lacking in wisdom, ask God, who gives to all generously and ungrudgingly, and it will be given you" (1:5)—then it is no great stretch for a Christian reader also imaginatively to link the gift of wisdom with the manna.

However, the Jewish linkage of wisdom with torah becomes problematic in the New Testament, especially in John's Gospel, where it is Jesus rather than torah who is the embodiment of wisdom and God's gift to the world. This becomes clear in the prologue to the Gospel and also the most extended New Testament engagement with the manna, in Jesus's discourse about the bread of life in John 6:30–58. Here Jesus speaks in a way that is resonant with other ancient Jewish interpretations, albeit now redirected.[54] The discourse begins:

> [30][The crowd that follows Jesus is speaking] "What sign are you going to give us then, so that we may see it and believe you? What work are you performing? [31]Our ancestors ate the manna in the wilderness; as it is written, 'He gave them bread from heaven to eat.'" [32]Then Jesus said to them, "Very truly, I tell you, it was not Moses who gave you the bread from heaven, but it is my Father who gives you the true bread from heaven. [33]For the bread of God is that which [or, he who] comes down from heaven and gives life to the world." [34]They said to him, "Sir, give us this bread always."
>
> [35]Jesus said to them, "I am the bread of life. Whoever comes to me will never be hungry, and whoever believes in me will never be thirsty."

Here Jesus picks up the people's appeal to the manna—"He gave them bread from heaven to eat" (which expresses the content rather than the exact wording of Exod. 16)—and offers a striking exposition. His initial move is to read this text as depicting something that is not primarily located in the past, as an ancient memory, but in the present, as a living reality (perhaps thereby drawing on contemporary Jewish expectations about an ultimate renewal

---

52. Philo, *On the Change of Names*, 259–260; in *Philo*, trans. F. H. Colson and G. H. Whitaker, LCL (Cambridge, MA: Harvard University Press, 1968), 5:275.

53. Philo, *Who Is the Heir of Divine Things?*, 191; in *Philo*, LCL, 4:379.

54. Peder Borgen, *Bread from Heaven: An Exegetical Study of the Concept of Manna in the Gospel of John and the Writings of Philo*, SNT (Leiden: Brill, 1965), remains a valuable study of this issue.

of the gift of manna). The textual basis for this is twofold: on the one hand, Jesus clarifies that the unspecified subject of the verb "he gave" is not "Moses" (as might be implied by the context, which specifies the performance of an action that could warrant adherence to its agent, such as Jews already had in relation to Moses) but "my Father"; on the other hand, Jesus rereads the verb as a present, "gives," rather than a past, "gave."[55] Jesus then depicts this contemporary reality of bread as "true" and "giving life to the world," thus as embodying what people deeply hope for. So his hearers quite naturally express a desire to receive it—in response to which Jesus identifies himself as this bread, such that he permanently meets the fundamental needs of whoever comes to him in faith.

The following discourse is full of richly suggestive language in terms of what it means to recognize Jesus as the bread of life. Within the general metaphorical sense of hunger and thirst met through coming to Jesus in faith (v. 35), there is language about eating Jesus's flesh and drinking his blood (vv. 51–58), which for a Christian reader is strongly suggestive of eucharistic eating and drinking. An imaginative linkage of Jesus as the bread of life with an actual practice of eating bread and drinking wine can strengthen an imaginative linkage with Israel's eating of the manna, only now re-read and re-envisioned in the light of Christ.

The eucharistic resonance is suggested not only by the specific wording and imagery of Jesus's language of verses 51–58, but also by the way in which Jesus's words almost read as words of institution—and there are no words of institution in the account of the Last Supper and the discourse in the Upper Room (John 13–17). One can compare this with the prayer at the conclusion of Jesus's public ministry in John's portrayal (12:27), which strongly resonates with the synoptic accounts of Jesus's prayer in Gethsemane, a prayer that has no place in John's account of Gethsemane (18:1–11). One of the challenges in understanding John's Gospel is to know how best to interpret John's presentation of material that is strikingly similar in both wording and content to material that is well known in the Synoptic Gospels, yet differs subtly and appears in different narrative contexts.

Even if in a first-century context there was polemic between Jews and Christians as to the respective roles of torah and Jesus as the definitive locus of God's self-revelation—a matter about which Jews and Christians still differ—and even if a reading of Jesus as divine bread was meant in that context to carry a strong implied negative to the Jewish tradition in which torah is divine bread, it does not follow that Christians need simply to replicate that negative today. For although faith in Christ undoubtedly relativizes the role of torah, it is fully possible for Christians, once faith in Christ is established,

55. It is likely that there is an underlying engagement with the Hebrew root *ntn* as implied by the textual quotation, whereby the vocalization provided by Jesus is construed not as past tense, *nātan*, but as present participle, *nōtēn* (see ibid., 62–65, 172).

to read torah more positively than is possible in a polemical context and thus, within an appropriate re-framing, to re-engage torah's enduring value. If Jesus is manna for Christians, part at least of the nourishment that he gives can be the wisdom still to be derived from Israel's scriptures.

The Discipline of Daily Living

One final facet of Exodus 16 to be touched on here is what might be called a "discipline of daily living." The need to start each day with collecting fresh manna readily becomes metaphorical for wider patterns of starting each day through deliberate engagement with God so as to receive grace afresh. One may think, for example, of the testimony of the servant of YHWH, whose work of sustaining others is rooted in his own daily receptiveness to YHWH:

> The Lord GOD has given me
>   the tongue of a teacher,[56]
> that I may know how to sustain
>   the weary with a word.
> Morning by morning he wakens—
>   wakens my ear
>   to listen as those who are taught. (Isa. 50:4)

Alternatively, there is the testimony of the appallingly afflicted man in Lamentations 3 (a testimony that includes saying that God has used him for target practice, and also made his teeth grind on gravel [Lam. 3:12, 13, 16]) who yet affirms the sustaining goodness of God that is renewed at the start of each new day:

> The steadfast love of the LORD never ceases,
>   his mercies never come to an end;
> they are new every morning;
>   great is your faithfulness. (Lam. 3:22–23)

One may reasonably surmise that it is the spiritual discipline of attentiveness and receptivity toward God each morning that enables the testimony to be expressed.

Within the Christian Bible as a whole, a further weighty resonance is with a clause of the Lord's Prayer: "Give us this day our daily bread."[57] The

---

56. The NRSV conjecturally emends the Hebrew "those who are taught" to "teacher," which I consider unnecessary. Either way, however, the point remains clear that the servant's ability to minister to others is rooted in his own daily receptivity to God.

57. This is the familiar liturgical form, taken from Matt. 6:11, whose relationship to Luke 11:3 I will not here discuss.

interpretation of the rare Greek word rendered as "daily" (*epiousios*) has from ancient times been influenced by the story of the manna.[58] Whatever the precise etymology of *epiousios*, the canonical resonance remains strong and is suggestive of reading "daily bread" in a metaphorical way to include whatever is needed for sustaining life in ever-renewed openness to God within the disciplines of grace. Admittedly this is not the only way of reading the text. Ulrich Luz, for example, resists such a reading on the grounds that it "does not agree with the intention of the text [within the ministry of Jesus]" and (implicitly) gives insufficient weight to "the strong rooting of this petition in the situation of the poor."[59] But even if this be granted for the likely primary thrust of the words in the context of Jesus's ministry, it does not necessarily resolve the question of meaning when the words are contextualized within the canon of Christian Scripture; difference of context can appropriately engender difference of meaning and emphasis (as with manna, Jesus, and torah). Even if one should not metaphorize daily bread in such a way as to exclude concern for actual bread—a move that is likely to be made only by those whose provision of actual bread is secure and so able to be taken for granted—it does not mean that one should not metaphorize daily bread at all or fail to recognize that the words of Jesus can function on more than one level simultaneously.

It is worth briefly noting something of the long history of Christian appropriation of the daily provision of manna in terms of the need to trust God for His providential provision. So, for example, Eadmer, the twelfth-century biographer of Anselm of Canterbury, depicts the time in which Anselm was the abbot of the monastery at Bec (1078–93) in a way that has clear biblical resonance:

> The food of the monks was so organized, by God's providence, that they lacked nothing which their necessity required, although very often they were in such straits that they feared the next day might find them utterly destitute. At times they were so nicely poised between having something and having almost nothing, that their "something" was never more than just enough and their "almost nothing" never so little that they suffered want. At such times matters fell out exactly according to the prediction which their abbot used to make when officials of the monastery complained to him about the threat of imminent distress. For he was frequently approached by cellarers, chamberlains, and sacrists, who

58. See, e.g., William David Davies and Dale C. Allison, *The Gospel according to Saint Matthew*, ICC (Edinburgh: T&T Clark, 1988), 1:607–10.
59. Ulrich Luz, *Matthew 1–7: A Continental Commentary*, trans. Wilhelm C. Linss (Minneapolis: Fortress, 1989), 383.

asked for his advice in overcoming the shortages which weighed heavily on their offices; and he would reply, "Trust in God, and I am confident that he will supply whatever is needful for you."[60]

Comparably, a recurrent Christian instinct has linked reception of manna, understood as daily divine provision, with prayer. To be sure, neither Exodus 16 nor Deuteronomy 8 mention prayer, but the intuitive logic is straight-forward, once one reads the manna metaphorically. There is the historic and biblically-rooted practice of praying at the start of the day (i.e., the time when Israel would go out to collect the manna)—as does the servant of YHWH (Isa. 50:4) or those who recite the Shema "when they rise" (Deut. 6:7); and there is the instrinsic nature of prayer as that which constitutes opening oneself to God and thereby becoming receptive to receive from Him. Thus, for example, in the fifteenth century, Sir Thomas Malory's imagina-tion readily associates the manna story with prayer and providence. In *Le morte d'Arthur*, Malory depicts Sir Lancelot as adrift on a boat with the dead body of Sir Percival's sister for over a month: "If ye would ask how he lived, He that fed the people of Israel with manna in the desert, so was he fed; for every day when he had said his prayers he was sustained with the grace of the Holy Ghost."[61]

In the eighteenth century, John Newton, in his famous hymn "Glorious Things of Thee Are Spoken," depicts the faith life of God's people in Old Testament imagery, not least that of the wilderness. He, like Malory, links the reception of sustenance from God, manna from God, with prayer, as in the third verse:

> Round each habitation hov'ring,
> See the cloud and fire appear
> For a glory and a cov'ring,
> Showing that the Lord is near.
> Thus deriving from their banner
> Light by night and shade by day;
> Safe they feed upon the manna
> Which he gives them when they pray.[62]

60. Eadmer, *The Life of Saint Anselm*, ed., intro., notes, and trans. R. W. Southern, Oxford Medieval Texts (Oxford: Clarendon, 1972), 47.

61. Sir Thomas Malory, *Le morte d'Arthur* 17.13; in *Le morte d'Arthur*, ed. John Rhys, Everyman's Library (London: Dent, 1906), 2:254.

62. Ian Bradley, ed., *The Penguin Book of Hymns* (London: Penguin, 1990), 131–33, esp. 133. In most contemporary hymnbooks the fifth line is modified to "Thus they march, the pillar leading," and the seventh to "Daily on the manna feeding."

Around the same time William Williams also memorably depicted the Christian life with the imagery of the exodus narrative, construed in the light of Christ, as in its first verse:

> Guide me, O thou great Jehovah,
> Pilgrim through this barren land;
> I am weak, but thou art mighty;
> Hold me with thy powerful hand;
> Bread of heaven, bread of heaven,
> Feed me till I want no more.[63]

There is of course a danger that such language can be generative of pious fantasy. Yet that is no reason for not taking seriously the imaginative and existential potential of the discipline of daily spiritual living as symbolized by the manna.

Conclusion

I have sought to read the manna story in its pentateuchal context, to reflect on various interpretive issues that arise in relation to that context, and also briefly to consider some of the interpretive moves that Christians have typically made when, following a Jewish lead, they have instinctively read the scriptural text metaphorically. I offer three final comments by way of conclusion.

First, it is difficult to do equal justice to all the story's concerns, especially the differing quantities of the manna on the Sabbath in relation to the rest of the week. The Sabbath dimension does not feature in Deuteronomy's account of what the manna teaches; Sabbath equally recedes from view when manna is metaphorized as wisdom, torah, or Christ, or when daily collection of manna becomes the discipline of daily attentiveness to grace or trust in God's providential provision. The regular six-day pattern tends to displace the distinctive seventh-day pattern. This is presumably in part because the spiritual practices of the six days do not become redundant on the seventh day—the believer should hardly think in terms of non-attentiveness toward, or failure to trust in, God on the Sabbath (whether Jewishly or Christianly construed)! The Sabbath concern with human rest and divine provision needs separate treatment. But this can serve as a useful reminder that there is almost always more to say about such a rich narrative.

Second, a suggestive and memorable development of the manna motif in a broader literary context can be found in J. R. R. Tolkien's *The Lord of*

63. Ibid., 150–52, esp. 152.

the Rings—in the portrayal of the Elven waybread (*lembas*), that is given to the company of the ring in Lothlórien and that particularly sustains Frodo and Sam as they journey at the extremity of their endurance in Mordor. The narrator says:

> The *lembas* had a virtue without which they would long ago have lain down to die. It did not satisfy desire, and at times Sam's mind was filled with the memories of food, and the longing for simple bread and meats. And yet this waybread of the Elves had a potency that increased as travellers relied on it alone and did not mingle it with other foods. It fed the will, and it gave strength to endure, and to master sinew and limb beyond the measure of mortal kind.[64]

In a letter Tolkien acknowledges that his portrayal of the qualities of the way-bread is indebted to his understanding of the Eucharist;[65] and although he does not mention the manna, the linkage is, as we have seen, readily available to a Christian imagination. The waybread's "feeding the will" becomes a suggestive way of thinking of how the living of life "not by bread alone" includes moral and spiritual dimensions that can yet be intrinsic to the very act of eating.

Third, the one New Testament use of the manna story that I have not discussed is Paul's words to encourage the Corinthian Christians to partici-pate in giving money to needy Christians in Jerusalem (2 Cor. 8–9). Among other things, Paul appeals to that remarkable facet of the story, the equality of outcome when all was collected, which he sees as embodying an enduring spiritual principle for God's people:

> I do not mean that there should be relief for others and pressure on you, but it is a question of a fair balance between your present abundance and their need, so that their abundance may be for your need, in order that there may be a fair balance. As it is written,
> "The one who had much did not have too much,
> and the one who had little did not have too little." (2 Cor. 8:13–15)

Paul takes seriously the material implications of the story. We also noted that it was Karl Marx's taking seriously the issue of fair distribution of material goods in relation to labor that made his socio-political program attractive to many. This stands as a reminder that the critical test of a spiritual life's authenticity is its outworking in the mundane world, and not least in the financial realm.

---

64. J. R. R. Tolkien, *The Return of the King* (London: George Allen & Unwin, 1965), 213.

65. "Far greater things [the Eucharist] may colour the mind in dealing with the lesser things of a fairy-story" (J. R. R. Tolkien, *The Letters of J. R. R. Tolkien*, ed. Humphrey Carpenter [London: George Allen & Unwin, 1981], 288).

4

Does God Change?

A 1975 Old Testament monograph by Jörg Jeremias begins: "There is hardly any other Old Testament statement about God which has appeared as offensive to thinkers of all times—philosophers as well as theologians—as the sentence that God felt regret [*Reue*] over something planned earlier or even already performed, and retracted it."[1] A review of the second edition of this book by Lester Grabbe begins: "Many attributions of God in the OT pass without comment to most readers, while others (e.g., anger, wrath, jealousy) cause unease; however, no attribute causes greater problems than the concept of God's 'repentance' because it suggests fickleness."[2]

It is a time-honored ploy for the scholar to try to whet the reader's appetite for what follows by highlighting the scale of the intellectual challenge that is to be addressed and (by implication) resolved in the pages that follow; and I am not averse to following Jeremias's lead myself. In this chapter I

In this chapter I develop two of my earlier discussions: "'God Is Not a Human That He Should Repent' (Numbers 23:19 and 1 Samuel 15:29)," in *God in the Fray: A Tribute to Walter Brueggemann*, ed. Tod Linafelt and Timothy K. Beal (Minneapolis: Fortress, 1998), 112–23; and *Prophecy and Discernment*, CSCD (Cambridge: Cambridge University Press, 2006), 48–55, 95–99.

1. Jörg Jeremias, *Die Reue Gottes: Aspekte alttestamentlicher Gottesvorstellung*, BibS(N) 65 (Neukirchen-Vluyn: Neukirchener Verlag, 1975), 9.

2. Lester Grabbe, "Review of Jörg Jeremias, *Die Reue Gottes: Aspekte alttestamentlicher Gottesvorstellung* (2nd ed., Neukirchen-Vluyn: Neukirchener Verlag, 1997)," in *Society for Old Testament Study Book List 1998*, ed. Lester L. Grabbe (Sheffield: Sheffield Academic Press, 1998), 151.

want to consider a concept, or rather two closely related concepts, where greater-than-usual puzzlement has often been the response of many readers of Israel's scriptures. I will argue, via some extensive discussion of how best to read the primary passages in which the concepts appear, that what is at stake is the intrinsically difficult matter of articulating the nature and logic of love.

Introduction to Divine Repentance and Non-Repentance

A distinctive characteristic of Israel's scriptures is that God, on occasion, "repents" (Heb. *niham*). A range of examples show this (in KJV): "And it repented the LORD that he had made man on the earth" (Gen. 6:6). "Then I said, O Lord GOD, forgive, I beseech thee. . . . The LORD repented for this: It shall not be, saith the LORD" (Amos 7:2–3). "And God saw their works, that they turned from their evil way; and God repented of the evil, that he had said that he would do unto them" (Jon. 3:10).

This has regularly been something of an embarrassment for both Jewish and Christian interpreters. "Repenting" has appeared to be at odds with first principles about the nature of God: is it an appropriate, or even a worthy, predicate of the true God? Might it indicate a defective understanding, a problematic anthropomorphism, in which the divine is all too clearly made in the image of the human? In a long history of theological nervousness about this, the first markers were put down in antiquity, initially by Philo.

In his treatise *On the Unchangeableness of God*,[3] Philo insists that God cannot change, because He is immutable. Philo focuses upon the first appearance, in canonical sequence, of *niham* with God as subject, Genesis 6:6. Although he reads the biblical text in Greek, where *niham* is rendered by *enethymēthē*, which is a softer verb ("he pondered"), he focuses directly on the key issue: "What greater impiety could there be than to suppose that the Unchangeable changes?"[4] If as humans become wiser and more virtuous they also become more steadfast and constant, how much more must this characterize the deity: "Can you doubt that He, the Imperishable Blessed One, who has

---

3. Philo, *Quod Deus sit immutabilis*. I have used the text and translation in the LCL edition: *Philo*, trans. F. H. Colson, G. H. Whitaker, and R. Marcus, LCL (London: Heinemann; Cambridge, MA: Harvard University Press, 1968), 3:1–101.

4. Clearly Gen. 6:6 was a contentious passage in antiquity since it was also fixed on by Celsus, who read it dismissively for its low-grade depiction of the biblical God: "How can he repent when they become ungrateful and wicked, and find fault with his own handiwork, and hate and threaten and destroy his own offspring?" Dismayingly, Origen's prime response is to say that Celsus misrepresents the text of Genesis, which he then cites in its Septuagintal form with "pondered" rather than "repented," with no recognition of possible different wording in the Hebrew *Vorlage*; yet he does then move on to substantive issues about theological language (see Origen, *Contra Celsum* 6.58; in *Origen: Contra Celsum*, trans., intro., and notes, Henry Chadwick [Cambridge: Cambridge University Press, 1965], 374).

taken as His own the sovereignty of the virtues, ... knows no change of will, but ever holds fast to what He purposed from the first without alteration?"[5]

Yet whether or not one sets up the problem by opposing "repentance" to "immutability"—and Philo's way of doing this had a long history of influence—there can be various reasons for unease with the notion of divine "repenting."

It is important to define one's terms, so as to know what one is, and is not, talking about. One prime difficulty here concerns the need to find good, or at least as little misleading as possible, words to depict the issue. For example, in the opening citation I translated Jeremias's *Reue* with "regret" (though "repentance" would also be possible, and how best to render *Reue* as distinct from *Buße* and *Umkehr* is a moot point) while Grabbe uses "repentance," the term widely used in English-language translations of the Old Testament and its scholarly discussions until the latter part of the twentieth century.[6]

Difficulties with the verb "repent," and its related noun "repentance," are obvious, not least because the words are little used in contemporary English, even with regard to humans, never mind with reference to God. There are various reasons for this, which must surely include the fact that this word's register of meaning has become unfamiliar and non-intuitive in a contemporary secular context.

In J. M. Coetzee's recent novel *Disgrace*, South African academic David Lurie, after a sexual liaison with a student, faces disciplinary procedures from his university authorities, who want him "to acknowledge your fault in a public manner and take steps to remedy it"; he declines to do so: "I appeared before an officially constituted tribunal, before a branch of the law. Before that secular tribunal I pleaded guilty, a secular plea. That plea should suffice. Repentance is neither here nor there. Repentance belongs to another world, to another universe of discourse."[7]

Unsurprisingly, therefore, the specific terminology of divine "repentance," which was regularly used in older English translations of the Old Testament

---

5. Philo, *Unchangeableness* 20–32; in *Philo*, LCL, 3:21–27. There is a succinct and illuminating account of Philo's hermeneutical strategy for language about God in Nils Dahl, "Contradictions in Scripture," in his *Studies in Paul: Theology for the Early Christian Mission* (Minneapolis: Augsburg, 1977), 159–77, esp. 166–69.

6. A translation problem is already evident in the LXX, where there is an evident difference of approach among the translators. The translators of the Pentateuch consistently avoid a rendering of *niham* that might imply overt divine "change" (thus in LXX: Gen. 6:6, "pondered"; 6:7, "was angry"; Exod. 32:14, "was appeased/merciful"). The translators of the Prophets, however, mostly use the most obvious Greek equivalent to *niham*, i.e., *metanoeō* (see, e.g., Jer. 18:8, 10 LXX).

7. J. M. Coetzee, *Disgrace* (London: Vintage, 2000), 58. Some of the wider issues at stake are illuminatingly discussed by Rowan Williams in "Remorse," in his *Lost Icons: Reflections on Cultural Bereavement* (Edinburgh: T&T Clark, 2000), 95–138. Williams sees the widespread contemporary disappearance of remorse (which in his discussion is more or less synonymous with repentance) as indicative of a shrunken notion both of self and of others, with a consequent contraction of public life.

(e.g., AV, RV, RSV), disappears in recent translations, which prefer phrases in current parlance such as "change mind," "think again/better," "reconsider," "relent," "regret," "be sorry," "renounce" (e.g., JB, REB, NIV, NRSV, ESV, NJPS, CEB). The CEB, for example, renders the three passages cited above as follows: "The Lord regretted making human beings" (Gen. 6:6). "The Lord relented concerning this" (Amos 7:3). "So God stopped planning to destroy them" (Jon. 3:10).

But even if this eases an immediate difficulty in terms of use of English, it does not address the conceptual problem as to what is implied by God's "regretting" or "relenting," and the fact that such language can still "suggest fickleness" or that God is somehow irresolute or inconstant. More specifically, the diversity of contemporary Old Testament translations can obscure the fact that there is one particular Hebrew verb, niham,[8] which is regularly predicated of God and which poses the problem;[9] though there are also numerous passages where niham is not used but where the same conceptuality is present. Hence for convenience and, I hope, clarity (and in line with not a few scholarly discussions that retain the older terminology), I will here retain "repent" as the working translation of niham when it is predicated of God, although I am aware that this terminology may feel infelicitous to some readers.

As though the apparent irresolution or inconstancy of the biblical deity were not a sufficient difficulty, any consideration of the verb niham as predicated of God quickly runs into another difficulty, which is that certain passages in the Old Testament deny that God does any such thing. Two passages in particular receive pride of place in this regard. In one place Balaam says, "God is not a man, that he should lie, or a son of man, that he should repent [niham]" (Num. 23:19 RSV; cf. CEB: "God isn't a man that he would lie, or a human being that he would change his mind"). In another place Samuel says, "The Glory of Israel will not lie or repent [niham]; for he is not a man that he should repent [niham]" (1 Sam. 15:29 RSV; cf. CEB: "The enduring one of Israel doesn't take back what he says and doesn't change his mind. He is not a human being who would change his mind"). One might suppose that this denial could (at least potentially) solve the theological problem as to what is appropriately predicated of God, on the grounds that it could be

---

8. All the relevant uses of niham as "repent" are in the niphal, in which one nun is assimilated. The piel stem of niham means "comfort." The relationship between the niphal and piel of niham is interesting but need not be discussed here.

9. This is a slight oversimplification since shūv is also sometimes predicated of God, usually in conjunction with niham, as in Joel 2:14a//Jon. 3:9a (on which see chap. 6 below). Nonetheless niham is the dominant and recurrent verb.

taken to anticipate Philo and the classic concern to affirm divine immutability. But such a solution would be at the cost of irresolution or inconstancy within the biblical text, which would apparently have no problem with substantially contradicting itself (though for many this would be a lesser problem).

At any rate, the apparent denial that God "repents" is periodically noted by interpreters as a clear example of "contradiction" within the biblical text. Phyllis Trible, for example, observes: "The theme of divine repentance, present in Jonah through the vocabulary of *nḥm* and *šûb*, cuts across the dominant and the countertestimonies of Israel. First, within even a single text the theme receives contradictory treatment. It is affirmed and denied. God repents; God does not repent (1 Sam 15:11, 29, 35; cf. Num 23:19)."[10] Or Eric Seibert, when outlining "contradictory portrayals" of God in the Old Testament, gives as his first example: "While one passage speaks of God as the kind of being whose mind cannot change, another clearly states that 'God changed his mind' (1 Sam. 15:29; Jonah 3:10)."[11]

Since the question of "contradictions," and the significance to be ascribed to them, recurs frequently in discussions about the Bible, this merits a brief discussion in its own right before we proceed with the main argument.

On Handling "Contradictions"

The claim that there are, or are not, contradictions within the biblical text is a standard trope within discussions of the nature and authority of the Bible, not least with reference to what it should, or should not, mean for the Bible to be authoritative for believers today. Negatively, the presence of contradictions is sometimes appealed to as a reason for greater or lesser dismissiveness toward the Old (and/or New) Testament: why should one bother to take a clatter of contradictory voices too seriously? Correspondingly, denials of contradictions usually are motivated by a desire to uphold the integrity and reliability of the text. There is, in fact, a tricky conceptual question as to what constitutes a genuine contradiction, as distinct from a difference, a disagreement, a tension, or a paradox; but this question rarely receives much attention because the negative rhetorical freight of the word "contradiction" is usually allowed to predominate.

10. Phyllis Trible, "Divine Incongruities in the Book of Jonah," in Linafelt and Beal, *God in the Fray*, 198–208, esp. 204.
11. Eric A. Seibert, *Disturbing Divine Behavior: Troubling Old Testament Images of God* (Minneapolis: Fortress, 2009), 172–73. Unfortunately I cannot here engage with Seibert's constructive thesis.

For example, not long ago Robert Carroll (a respected mainstream Old Testament scholar) fixed on this issue as a prime reason for seeing the Bible as a problem for Christianity.[12] He sets out the issue confidently:

> The problem of the Bible for theology is in the first instance the presence of contradictions in the Bible. Not discrepancies of account or contradictions in narratives about historical events—the Bible has many of these—but contradictions in the representation of God. Theology is about God, so a source for doing theology which contains contradictions is invariably problematic. Discourse about God cannot tolerate formal contradictions.[13]

He then moves on directly to 1 Samuel 15 (which we will discuss below) as apparently the optimal illustration of this problem. He notes that at an early point in the narrative, there is a divine word, "I repent that I have made Saul king; for he has turned back from following me" (v. 11 RSV) but that later, in his exchanges with Saul,

> Samuel finally adds a statement of divine principle to his arguments. "And also the Glory of Israel will not lie or repent; for he is not a human that he should repent" (v. 29). In so far as any theology can be extracted from such a tale it must be the statement in verse 29. . . . Human beings may change their minds or lie but Israel's God is not of that ilk. The statement would be uncontentious were it not for the fact that what is said in verse 11 plainly contradicts verse 29![14]

Carroll is, of course, well aware that there are many depictions of YHWH's repenting and that it is the denial that is remarkable, but this is all grist to his mill, since prospective theological reading of the Old Testament loses either way. On the contradiction in 1 Samuel 15 he says:

> Either Yahweh repents (as humans do) or Yahweh does not repent (unlike humans). Both cannot be true. That, in Western logic, is the law of the excluded middle. It is also a violation of the rules about contradiction. So if theological systems are to be founded on the Bible, they are going to run into serious problems in 1 Samuel 15.[15]

And on YHWH's repenting he says:

12. Robert P. Carroll, *Wolf in the Sheepfold: The Bible as a Problem for Christianity* (London: SPCK, 1991). The title neatly encapsulates the book's thesis.
13. Ibid., 41.
14. Ibid.
15. Ibid., 42.

A deity who regularly changes his mind cannot be equated with the Eternal unmoved mover. As a character in a book of tales, Yahweh is fully entitled to chop and change according to plot and characterization; but between that character and the Spirit behind the universe there is a considerable gap. It is not possible to make any equation between the Yahweh of the biblical narratives and the God of the creeds and confessions of the churches, even though clever theologians may be able to adjust the gap between the two so that it is narrower under certain conditions. The Bible will remain problematic for theology.[16]

Carroll's rhetoric is nicely polemical, in a relatively understated but nonetheless emphatic mode. It is clearly designed to make any attempt to counter his argument look like special pleading on the part of "clever theologians" who can do no more than maneuver ingeniously in exercises of damage limitation.

Carroll's categorical denial that it is "possible to make any equation between the Yahweh of the biblical narratives and the God of the creeds and confessions of the churches" strikes at a fundamental tenet of Christian faith, as also of Jewish faith. For Christian faith makes precisely that equation by affirming that the God of the Bible is the God in whom Christians believe: the God of Israel (of Abraham, Isaac, and Jacob) is the God and Father of our Lord Jesus Christ. The nature of the relationship between the narrative portrayal of YHWH and Christian creedal affirmations about the one God is indeed a genuine issue (though recognized down through the ages, and not a novel recognition), and the "equation" between the two needs to be made in nuanced ways that take seriously the issues of literary genre and of religious language. But without some such equation, historic Jewish and Christian faiths are evacuated of much of their content.

How might one make progress? One may, of course, ask whether Carroll's grasp of the nature of theology and of Christian belief in God is quite as sure as he supposes it to be. On the one hand, in terms of content, he implies that Christian theology is straightforwardly committed to belief in an "Eternal unmoved mover," with no apparent recognition that Aristotle's famous category is a matter about which there has been rather extensive debate among Christian theologians. Karl Barth, for example, says: "If ever there was a miserable anthropomorphism, it is the hallucination of a divine immutability which rules out the possibility that God can let Himself be conditioned in this or that way by His creature. God is certainly immutable. But He is immutable as the living God and in the mercy in which He espouses the cause of the creature."[17]

16. Ibid.
17. Karl Barth, *CD* III/4:108–9.

On the other hand, in terms of method, Carroll says that "discourse about God cannot tolerate formal contradictions," with no apparent recognition of the fact that it often does so, as a brief perusal of, say, the Athanasian Creed would rapidly indicate.[18] Putting it differently, there are at least two distinctions that Carroll ignores but that can usefully be made. One is the difference between contradiction and paradox. Christian theology regularly articulates paradoxes, that is, affirmations of apparent opposites—for example: God is transcendent, and God is immanent; God is sovereign, but humans have free will; God saves by grace alone, yet human actions matter for salvation—where both poles need to be maintained in order to do justice to the complexity of reality and of God. The other difference is between formal and material contradictions. This is an issue that John Goldingay develops with relation to our specific concern:

> Formal contradiction involves a difference at the level of words which is not a difference at the level of substance. . . . The OT both states and denies that God changes his mind, even in the same chapter (1 Sam 15:11, 29, 35; each time *nḥm*). There is a clear formal contradiction, but the presence of both assertions in one text invites us to seek to relate them as well as to contrast them. . . . [A fuller discussion of the nature of each assertion leads to a conclusion:] Both the affirmation and the denial are part of a coherent analogical description of God's involvement in the world, and each would be misleading without the other.[19]

Thus it quickly becomes apparent that both Carroll's thesis about the problematic nature of the Bible for theology (at least on the basis stated above) and his rhetoric are tendentious. He portrays the task of theological interpretation as representing a wooden and naïf approach to the text. In effect, he sets up an easy target for some sure hits. His approach demonstrates well the enduring downside of polemics, which is the temptation to gain a hearing and score points at the cost of misrepresenting the other position.

To be sure, not all biblical scholars consider apparently contrary statements in the Old (or New) Testament to be problematic. Some simply ascribe the phenomenon to the rich diversity of voices contained within the canon, which

18. "The catholic faith is this: That we worship one God in trinity, and trinity in unity, neither confounding the persons, nor dividing the substance . . . The Father uncreate, the Son uncreate, and the Holy Ghost uncreate; the Father incomprehensible, the Son incomprehensible, and the Holy Ghost incomprehensible; the Father eternal, the Son eternal, and the Holy Ghost eternal. And yet they are not three eternals, but one eternal; as also there are not three incomprehensibles, nor three uncreated, but one created, and one incomprehensible" (Church of England, *The Book of Common Prayer* [Cambridge: Cambridge University Press, 1662], 68–69).

19. John Goldingay, *Theological Diversity and the Authority of the Old Testament* (Grand Rapids: Eerdmans, 1987), 16–17; the extract is from a wide-ranging discussion of "degrees of diversity and forms of contradiction" in the OT (15–25).

they see as indicative of the multi-faceted dimensions of ancient Israelite religion—perhaps showing difference according to location (say, between the northern and southern kingdoms), or according to time (say, between differing criteria for acceptable religious practice prior to, and subsequent to, Josiah's reform), or according to socio-religious identity (say, between priestly and popular perspectives). Nonetheless, while such analyses can have value in terms of ancient historical accounts, they can leave unaddressed questions relating to the Old Testament as a religiously authoritative textual collection, and what may be involved in thinking synthetically about its role as Scripture for generations of believers subsequent to ancient Israel, on through until today. History of Israelite religion and theological interpretation of the Old Testament are distinct tasks.

One distinctive voice on this issue is that of Walter Brueggemann in his major *Theology of the Old Testament*. He expresses unease with what he conceives to be "the methods of classical Western theological discourse, which wants to overcome all ambiguity and give closure in the interest of certitude," and with "the ways in which Christian readers of the Old Testament have tended to run roughshod over the relatively playful and open inclination of Old Testament rhetoric in order to serve the less tensive propensities of the Christian tradition." So when, among other things, he says, "There is evidence that Yahweh is a conundrum of contradictions, as though Yahweh's interior life is so convoluted that at some points it lacks consistency," he sees this not as a problem requiring resolution but as an instance of the intrinsically dialectical and dialogical quality of the biblical text and its depiction of God, and of necessary provisionality in whatever claims may be made on its basis.[20] Brueggemann's complex and challenging project—arguably *the* major contribution to theological interpretation of the Old Testament in recent years—cannot be adequately discussed here. I simply note that, whatever the undoubted limitations of much Christian reading of the Old Testament, Brueggemann's dismissive generalizations about the Western Christian tradition, together with his rhetoric that polarizes the generative openness of the Old Testament text over against Christian prepossession with "closure" and "certitude" (always negative terms in his vocabulary), are surely indicative more of a mood of impatience than of considered reflection on the problem of responsible use of theological language or on biblical interpreters from Origen and Augustine to Barth and von Rad.

I conclude this brief discussion with the observation of John Rogerson that "the Old Testament speaks with many voices and is invariably at its most interesting when it appears to contradict itself and to undermine commonly held views."[21] Rogerson's wording leaves open the questions of whether apparent contradictions are actual contradictions or not; it puts the emphasis instead on their value for challenging complacency and being an incentive to harder and more searching engagement with the subject matter at hand.[22] Since

20. Walter Brueggemann, *Theology of the Old Testament: Testimony, Dispute, Advocacy* (Minneapolis: Fortress, 1997), 82, 83, 362.

21. John Rogerson, *A Theology of the Old Testament: Cultural Memory, Communication and Being Human* (London: SPCK, 2009), 184.

22. This is an important issue, to which we will return in the discussion of Pss. 44 and 89 in chap. 7 below.

such a note stands in continuity with classic Jewish and Christian approaches to the issue,[23] it is a good note on which to turn to our specific concern with divine repentance.

The Affirmation of Divine Repentance as a Theological Principle

The Potter and the Clay: Setting the Scene

Although numerous narrative and prophetic texts include a depiction of God as repenting (*niham*), there is one Old Testament passage that formulates this as a theological axiom about the nature of God's dealings with humanity: Jeremiah 18:1–12 (esp. vv. 7–10). I propose that the axiomatic nature of this formulation makes this passage *the* passage whereby all other depictions of divine repentance elsewhere should be understood, when one is reading the Old Testament as canonical scripture.

> [1]The word that came to Jeremiah from the LORD: [2]"Come, go down to the potter's house, and there I will let you hear my words." [3]So I went down to the potter's house, and there he was working at his wheel. [4]The vessel he was making of clay was spoiled in the potter's hand, and he reworked it into another vessel, as seemed good to him.

On one level the picture is straightforward: Jeremiah is to receive a message from YHWH that relates specifically to the work of the potter that he sees. Imaginatively, however, the seemingly simple picture of the potter working and re-working clay is open to be developed in more than one way.

> [5]Then the word of the LORD came to me: [6]Can I not do with you, O house of Israel, just as this potter has done? says the LORD. Just like clay in the potter's hand, so are you in my hand, O house of Israel.

Although Jeremiah is apparently in Jerusalem, the capital of Judah, the divine message is for the "house of Israel"; that is, the address is generalizing, with application to God's chosen people as a whole.

The imagery is also striking. For if a potter's ability to do with clay as he wishes (v. 4) illustrates the power of the maker over that which is made, then such imagery applied to God (v. 6) intrinsically symbolizes divine power. The imagery is *not* that of interpersonal relationships, which is the predominant

---

23. See the illuminating account of Jewish and Christian approaches to apparent biblical contradictions in antiquity in Nils Dahl, "Contradictions."

biblical idiom for depicting God and Israel: king and subjects, master and slave, husband and wife, father and son are perhaps the most common images. However unequal all such relationships were, they were always in principle mutual, engaging the stronger party no less, although differently, than the weaker party. Moreover, sheer pity and compassion might renew the relationship at times when it was in danger of breaking down—as, famously, God cannot restrain compassion toward His errant son Israel (Hosea 11:1–9, esp. vv. 8–9). But with a lump of clay a potter has no relationship or responsibilities—it is an object to be used and shaped at will. When applied to God, therefore, the imagery of potter (*yōtsēr*) does not evoke mutuality, but rather unilateral power. It is an idiom that is readily used in the context of God's work of creation (Gen. 2:7, 19, with the verbal root of *yōtsēr*). Correspondingly, the imagery is used elsewhere in Scripture in two specific contexts: either to emphasize divine strength in contrast to human weakness (Isa. 64:8–9; 2 Cor. 4:7), or to discourage, indeed disallow, dissent from a divine decision that appears problematic and open to objection (Isa. 45:9–13; Rom. 9:19–24).[24] So when Jeremiah hears the word of YHWH at the potter's house initially saying that Israel in God's hand is like clay in the potter's hand, the imagery prima facie encourages the attentive reader/hearer to expect some further message about divine strength or a non-negotiable divine decree.

The Puzzle of Textual Sequence

The sequel is therefore surprising. It explicitly picks up the language of Jeremiah's initial commissioning. At the outset of the book (Jer. 1:9–10), YHWH says to Jeremiah:

> [9]"Now I have put my words in your mouth.
> [10]See, today I appoint you over nations and over kingdoms,
> to pluck up and to pull down,
> to destroy and to overthrow,
> to build and to plant."

Now YHWH says to him (18:7–10):

> [7]At one moment I may declare concerning a nation or a kingdom, that I will pluck up and break down and destroy it, [8]but if that nation, concerning which

---

24. In Isa. 45 the issue appears to be the overruling of Judahite objection to YHWH's use of Cyrus to deliver His people, which includes depiction of Cyrus as YHWH's "anointed" (*māshīaḥ*, 45:1). In Rom. 9 the issue is the overruling of possible objection to the arbitrary-sounding nature of God's both having mercy and hardening whomever He chooses.

I have spoken, turns [shūv] from its evil, I will change my mind [niham] about the disaster that I intended to bring on it. [9]And at another moment I may declare concerning a nation or a kingdom that I will build and plant it, [10]but if it does evil in my sight, not listening to my voice, then I will change my mind [niham] about the good that I had intended to do to it.

Although these words clearly relate to Jeremiah's initial commissioning, they are surprising in the context of the potter's house for at least three reasons. First, the recipient of the divine address shifts from "house of Israel" (18:6) to "a nation or a kingdom" (18:7, 9). Second, the words of verses 7–10 apparently do not depict the expected divine power of verse 6 but rather divine contingency and responsiveness. Third, in this part of the divine address the imagery of the potter simply disappears. In other words, the divine contingency and responsiveness are not expressed in terms of a potter's being responsive to the differing contours of the clay with which he works (not "as he felt the shape of the clay, so he worked it accordingly"), which might perhaps be a complementary image to the initial image of a potter reworking the clay as he wills. Rather, within verses 7–10 the imagery is that of speech and response, which is entirely natural to a prophet's vocation to address people, but it is not what a potter does with his clay.

There is thus a basic interpretive challenge. What is the meaning and purpose of verses 7–10? Commentators are not infrequently baffled, as their choice of language reveals. John Skinner observes: "The following verses (7–10) interpret the analogy in a sense so remote from its plain implications that they must be set down as the well-meant homily of an overzealous commentator." Or William McKane contends that "vv. 7–10 are not fitted for the function of interpreting a parable; they amount to a general, theological statement, with a carefully contrived structure, and they have too abstract an aspect to entitle them to be considered seriously as an interpretation of the parable of the potter and his clay."[25]

Almost paradigmatic is von Rad's combination of paraphrase and puzzlement. He was a generally acute and deservedly acclaimed reader of the biblical text; as a Christian lover of the Old Testament, he was less given to resorting to pejorative terminology than some other commentators. Yet he struggles more or less unavailingly to make sense of this particular Jeremiah passage:

In [Jer. 18:1–12] the content is somewhat obscure, and this detracts from its impressiveness. In the opening verses [1–6] Jeremiah is dealing with his own

25. John Skinner, *Prophecy and Religion: Studies in the Life of Jeremiah* (Cambridge: Cambridge University Press, 1930), 163; William McKane, *Jeremiah*, ICC (Edinburgh: T&T Clark, 1986), 1:426.

people who, by being shown the immense freedom at God's disposal, are to take warning. Then, however, it suddenly passes over into general terms [vv. 7–10]. If Jahweh has purposed evil against a particular nation, and it "turns," then he repents of the trouble he intended to cause; and if he has purposed good for another nation, but it is disobedient, then he will alter his design and punish it. This part, too, is meant to indicate Jahweh's freedom as he directs history, but it does this in an oddly theoretical way by giving imaginary examples which are quite contrary to the sense of the passage, for they almost make Jahweh's power dependent on law rather than on freedom. This middle passage (vv. 7–10), after which Judah is once more addressed [cf. vv. 11–12], should probably be regarded as a theological expansion.[26]

How then should the juxtaposition of verses 7–10 with verses 1–6 be understood? As readily apparent in the above citations, one time-honored reflex of the Hebrew Bible scholar in such a situation is to propose that the text must be composite: its differing content must surely reflect its origins from different hands. In this case, verses 7–10 may be a Deuteronomic or Deuteronomistic, or even post-Deuteronomistic, editing of an earlier, possibly Jeremianic, narrative tradition (though there appears to be little consensus on the matter).[27] The hermeneutical move is that textual complexity is construed diachronically in terms of its conjectured history of formation. But even if it be granted that the text may well be composite in diachronic terms, such a recognition does not resolve the question of how best the text should be read in its received form. It is notable that, in the scholars just cited, the appeal to an editor is in a certain sense a gesture of despair in terms of understanding the text as it stands. Yet, as numerous scholars have urged, any possibly composite text may still have synchronic meaning in its own right: the whole is not simply the sum of, or reducible to, its parts, and the parts may acquire a new meaning when read in the context of a larger whole. Moreover, at least sometimes apparently disparate or incongruous textual voices can be reconceived in the category of paradox.

The Contingent and Responsive Nature of Jeremiah's Prophetic Speech

To make progress it will be best initially to set aside the relationship of 18:7–10 to 18:1–6, and instead to consider its most obvious affinity, which

26. Gerhard von Rad, *Old Testament Theology*, trans. D. M. G. Stalker (London: SCM, 1965) 2:198–99.

27. McKane, e.g., favors the view that 18:7–10 represents "a secondary theorizing" of possibly Deuteronomistic origin, but his survey of the arguments well illustrates the lack of consensus (*Jeremiah*, 420–28, esp. 426).

is 1:9–10. These two passages share common terminology in relation to Jeremiah's prophetic speaking: he is to address "nations and kingdoms" (1:10; 18:7, 9) and to speak in such a way as both "to pluck up, break down, and destroy" (1:10; 18:7) and "to build and to plant" (1:10; 18:9). It thus becomes natural to read 18:7–10 as an interpretive development of 1:9–10, a kind of commentary that articulates certain dimensions of how Jeremiah's prophetic speaking should be understood.

Two interwoven aspects of prophetic speech are highlighted. One is that prophetic words seek response: the cognitive information they convey is designed to generate a particular kind of action in consequence of what is said. The other is that apparently unconditional statements about what will happen in the future are in fact conditional, with their conditional nature being related to the response that is given. Thus whether Jeremiah speaks of breaking down or of building, in neither case is the outcome a foregone conclusion. A crucial factor is how people respond to his words. Human turning from evil ("repentance" in its classic sense) can avert a threatened disaster, while human complacency and wrongdoing can forfeit a promised good. In each case God "repents" (*niḥam*) in response to human responsiveness: God in some way takes into account how people respond such that it makes a difference in what He will do.

Such response-seeking language, while especially characteristic of prophecy, is common in human relationships more generally. Prophetic announcements of coming disaster can be seen to have the logic and dynamics of *warning*. If someone says to a person carelessly stepping onto a busy road, "You're going to be run over," the words are a warning, unconditional in form but conditional in substance, whose purpose is to bring about a response (moving off the road) such that what is spoken of does not happen. Comparably, prophetic announcements of coming good have the logic and dynamics of *invitation*. If one person (with genuine intention) says to another, "I love you," they are inviting a response along the lines of "I love you too," which will lead to enhanced relationship—though of course the person addressed is able to decline the invitation ("Thank you, but no thank you"), and what happens next (how the love of the first speaker will be realized) differs entirely according to whether the invitation is accepted or declined.[28]

A fundamental presupposition within 18:7–10, therefore, is that God's relationship with people is a genuine relationship because it is responsive. The

---

28. Recent work in speech-act theory has been helpful in renewing awareness of the relationships between biblical language and life, relationships especially significant for all those who read the Bible as authoritative scripture and seek to be appropriately responsive to God through their reading.

relationship between God and people is characterized by a dynamic similar to that of relationships between people: they are necessarily mutual, and they can both grow and wither. How people respond to God *matters* to God, and *affects* how God responds to people. To be sure, the writer shows sensitivity to possible problems of theological language here, as evidenced by a variation in terminology: when people turn/repent (*shūv*), God "repents" (*niham*). This variation implicitly recognizes the difference between what may be predicated of humanity and what may be predicated of God: the way in which God changes is not the same as the way in which humans change.

As already noted, contemporary translators struggle to find a good way of rendering *niham* when predicated of God, and the NRSV's "change mind" creates its own problems. The concern of the text is not divine mental states but rather divine responsiveness whereby God may authoritatively reverse a previous pronouncement or decision because of changed circumstances. It may be that "rescind," "revoke," "repeal," or "retract" come closer to the force of the Hebrew. On any reckoning *niham* as a theological term poses translation problems comparable to those posed by some of Paul's terms, such as *sarx* ("flesh") or *nomos* ("law").

Another Comparable Account of the Nature of Prophetic Language

The theological principle of divine responsiveness (*niham*) that is articulated axiomatically in Jeremiah 18:7–10 is presupposed in a wide range of other Old Testament passages.

For example, it recurs importantly within the narrative account of Jeremiah's temple sermon (Jer. 26, esp. 26:3, 16–19). It receives paradigmatic narrative exemplification in the story of Jonah (Jon. 3:1–10), and is even incorporated in Jonah's creedal, albeit complaining, summary of YHWH's character (4:2).[29] The converse, God's retracting promised good in response to human complacency or wrongdoing, is equally illustrated in, for example, the introduction to the flood narrative (Gen. 6:5–8) or in relation to Saul's forfeiting his kingship (1 Sam. 15:1–35; see below); it is also in the account of the house of Eli's forfeiting its priesthood (1 Sam. 2:27–30), although without the explicit terminology of *niham*.

Another comparable axiomatic formulation is Ezekiel 33:12–16, where the principle that in Jeremiah 18 is expressed in terms of divine/prophetic address to nations and kingdoms is expressed in relation to individual people. Interestingly, Ezekiel 33:12–16 comes in a passage that develops the implications of Ezekiel's prophetic vocation to be a watchman ("sentinel" in NRSV: Ezek. 3:16–21; 33:1–9), just as Jeremiah 18:7–10 develops the implications of Jeremiah's initial commissioning. Ezekiel 33:12–16 lays out the principle:

29. See further chap. 6 below.

¹²And you, mortal, say to your people, The righteousness of the righteous [*tsaddīq*] shall not save them when they transgress; and as for the wickedness of the wicked [*rāshāʿ*], it shall not make them stumble when they turn from their wickedness; and the righteous shall not be able to live by their righteousness when they sin. ¹³Though I say to the righteous [*tsaddīq*] that they shall surely live, yet if they trust in their righteousness and commit iniquity, none of their righteous deeds shall be remembered; but in the iniquity that they have committed they shall die. ¹⁴Again, though I say to the wicked [*rāshāʿ*], "You shall surely die," yet if they turn from their sin and do what is lawful and right— ¹⁵if the wicked restore the pledge, give back what they have taken by robbery, and walk in the statutes of life, committing no iniquity—they shall surely live, they shall not die. ¹⁶None of the sins that they have committed shall be remembered against them; they have done what is lawful and right, they shall surely live.

Ezekiel speaks in relation to the two prime Old Testament types of human life: the good/righteous (*tsaddīq*) and the bad/wicked (*rāshāʿ*). His point is that these types are not fixed:[30] it is possible to abandon the one and embrace the other, and it is where people end rather than where they begin that ultimately matters. After an initial general statement of principle (v. 12), Ezekiel envisages two pronouncements, addressed to righteous and wicked respectively, which are unconditional in form and yet clearly conditional in substance. Promised life can be forfeited, and threatened death can be averted—it all depends on the response that is made. Although the terminology differs from that in Jeremiah, with no mention of repentance either human (*shūv*) or divine (*niḥam*), the understanding of prophetic pronouncements as both response-seeking and contingent declarations is the same: as for nations and kingdoms, so too for individuals.

The Paradoxical Nature of Jeremiah 18:1–10

If Jeremiah 18:7–10 is highlighting the response-seeking and conditional nature of prophetic speech in relation to God's own responsiveness to humans, how should it be read in the context of Jeremiah's visit to the potter's house and the initial pronouncement of divine power over Israel by analogy with the potter's power over clay (18:1–6)?

First, the text presents a striking paradox. In a context whose imagery strongly emphasizes divine power (vv. 1–6), we have a strong statement of

---

30. One might compare Paul's use of present participles, "those who are perishing [*hoi apollymenoi*]" and "those who are being saved [*hoi sōzomenoi*]" (1 Cor. 1:18), which also depict categories that are not fixed (as might be implied by past participles) but open to change—as Paul knew from his own experience.

divine responsiveness to human attitude and action (vv. 7–10). Where God is free to act, in effect entirely unconstrained in terms of the potter imagery, God commits Himself to responsive action (*niham*). Verses 7–10 do not deny God's freedom but rather specify that that freedom is moral and relational: it takes into account the responsiveness, or lack of it, that humans display. Divine power is exercised not arbitrarily, but responsibly and responsively, interacting with the moral, or immoral, actions of human beings. The text thus presents a notable formulation of the classic theological antinomy of divine sovereignty alongside human freedom and accountability.

Second, in imaginative terms the contextual setting of the potter at work on his clay makes it natural for the reader to think of the responsiveness of verses 7–10 as qualities both of the potter and of the clay. In general terms, people skilled in a craft are regularly highly sensitive and thus responsive to the nature and texture of the material with which they work.[31] This enables one readily to read, or perhaps rather re-read, verses 7–10 as depicting an interaction between potter and clay; the initial imagery of the potter's power can be complemented by thoughts of his responsiveness. Correspondingly, those identified as clay should think of themselves not as helpless objects dependent solely upon the decisions of the potter, but rather as able to make some difference to him. Since the potter's decision about what to do depends on the quality of the clay, the point becomes clear: "Let the vessel therefore make sure it is worth keeping."[32]

Third, the juxtaposition of "house of Israel" (v. 6) with "a nation or a kingdom" (v. 7) carries the implication that in important respects God's dealings with Israel and with others, the elect and the non-elect, do not differ. The dynamics of responsiveness and contingency apply to all alike.

Two Possible Misreadings of the Text

In the light of this reading of the text in its received form, it is worth briefly commenting on two further potential difficulties in understanding it.

First, the way in which the match between human repentance or complacency and divine responsiveness is formulated sometimes bothers interpreters. For it can be read as implying something inappropriate and indeed patently false: an unvarying and automatic pattern of divine response to human attitude and action. Robert Carroll, for example, comments: "The theoretical nature of vv. 7–10 with their image of a predictable deity contracting with nations and kingdoms a reciprocal agreement of corresponding

---

31. I am grateful to Kathleen Rochester for highlighting this point to me.
32. Douglas Rawlinson Jones, *Jeremiah*, NCB (Grand Rapids: Eerdmans, 1992), 255.

and alternating plans for the future is idyllic and unreal."[33] Even von Rad, as already noted, speaks of the text as "oddly theoretical" and "giving imaginary examples" that "almost make Jahweh's power dependent on law rather than on freedom." When a Lutheran theologian sees a text as tending toward making divine power "dependent on law," this indicates a high level of unease.

Certainly a careful theological formulation could appropriately include a note of contingency about the divine response, so as to respect divine freedom and not presume upon God (just as in good human relationships certain responses may be expected but still not presumed upon). Such a formulation does indeed come elsewhere in the Old Testament—most strikingly upon the unlikely lips of the king of Nineveh when enjoining repentance on his people in response to Jonah's message: "Who knows? God may relent and change his mind [*niham*]; he may turn from his fierce anger, so that we do not perish" (Jon. 3:9).[34]

The potential difficulty posed by Jeremiah 18:7–10 arises, I suggest, for two reasons. On the one hand, the text is making a point about divine responsiveness in a way that, characteristic of Hebrew idiom, is generalizing—and a generalization may permit exceptions and qualifications. It is only if the generalization is read as a universal claim that a problem arises. On the other hand, the Hebrew language is notoriously short of modal forms in its verbs: may, might, should, would, and so forth. One always has to infer the correct nuance from the context (and the context may not always enable one to be precise).[35] It would not be strained to render the verb depicting God's response in 18:8, 10 as "I may relent/retract."

The forms of *niham* in Jeremiah 18:8, 10 and in Joel 2:13–14 and Jonah 3:9 are identical (other than that the former is first person and the latter third person), each being perfect with *vav* consecutive/conversive (*wĕqātal* form). The explicit contingency in Joel's and the king of Nineveh's words is "Who knows?" which makes it contextually unambiguous that "may" is the appropriate modal form of the following verbs. The difficulty with "may" in Jeremiah 18:8, 10 is that the *wĕniḥamtī*,

33. Robert P. Carroll, *Jeremiah*, OTL (London: SCM, 1986), 372.

34. This passage and the related formulation in Joel 2:13–14 are discussed in chap. 6 below.

35. Perhaps the most famous example of this issue is how one renders *timshol* in relation to Cain's struggle with sin (Gen. 4:7), an issue that takes a central role in John Steinbeck's *East of Eden* (New York: Viking, 1952; many editions). In chap. 22 of Steinbeck's novel, the story of Cain and Abel is introduced into the narrative; then in chap. 24 we discover that a central character, Lee, has learned Hebrew precisely in order to try to understand this key word in Gen. 4:7. At one point Lee says: "Don't you see? The American Standard translation ["Do thou rule over him"] *orders* men to triumph over sin, and you can call sin ignorance. The King James translation ["Thou shalt rule over him"] makes a promise in 'Thou shalt,' meaning that men will surely triumph over sin. But the Hebrew word, the word *timshel* [*sic*]—'Thou mayest'—that gives a choice. It might be the most important word in the world."

predicated of God, is parallel to the *věshāv*, predicated of a nation, such that the thought of the sentence is "If X, then Y," in other words, "If they do X, then I will do Y." Nonetheless, a case for "may" rather than "will" in this context could still be made on interpretive grounds, to clarify that the words are generalizing rather than universalizing.

There is also a contextual issue that bears on the interpretation of both Jeremiah 18:7–10 and Ezekiel 33:12–16. Although I am taking each passage at its face value, as an axiomatic statement about the contingent and response-seeking nature of prophetic language, the larger context of each prophetic book makes clear that there can come a time when turning to God will no longer elicit divine repentance, since judgment, in the form of the overthrow of Jerusalem and the exile of its leading inhabitants, has become inevitable (see, e.g., Jer. 15:1–4, or the way in which Ezek. 33:12–16 is directly followed by the report of the fall of Jerusalem, in 33:21). If there is still hope for the future, it lies only on the other side of this judgment. Moreover, each book strongly states that YHWH's restoration of Jerusalem and Judah will be a unilateral divine action, not evoked by their repentance (see, e.g., Jer. 32:1–44 or Ezek. 36:16–32, each of which mentions only Judah's or Israel's sin in the context of YHWH's promised renewal and restoration). However, the fact that there are necessary qualifications and exceptions to the axiomatic statements of Jeremiah 18:7–10 and Ezekiel 33:12–16 underlines the appropriateness of a generalizing "may" rather than a universalizing "will" for a reading of these words about divine repentance in their canonical context.

Thus there are good reasons to read Jeremiah 18:7–10 as a generalizing statement that does not need to be construed as potentially problematic in portraying divine action as fixed or automatic. On any reckoning, however, this is an issue where an interpreter's grasp of the subject matter will inevitably influence how one construes the text.

A second potential difficulty is perhaps an even better exemplification of the principle that one's grasp of the subject matter makes a difference in how one reads the text. Especially if one's sense of the subject matter is driven by a hermeneutic of suspicion, it is easy to offer a very different reading, which essentially sees the text as a rationalizing justification of a religious refusal to admit limitation of insight and indeed error.

In the late eighteenth century, Thomas Paine, famed supporter of the American and French Revolutions, and also advocate of deism, fixed on this passage (among others). His strategy was to remove the Bible from the sphere of rational faith, rubbishing its content so as to promote his deist alternative (establishing by reason that there is a first cause for everything, a first cause that is called God):

> Every thing relating to Jeremiah shows him to have been a man of an equivocal character: in his metaphor of the potter and the clay (ch. xviii), he guards his prognostications in such a crafty manner as always to leave himself a door to escape by, in case the event should be contrary to what he had predicted. [Here follows a full citation of vv. 7–10.] . . . According to this plan of prophesying, a prophet could never be wrong, however mistaken the Almighty might be. This sort of absurd subterfuge, and this manner of speaking of the Almighty,

as one would speak of a man, is consistent with nothing but the stupidity of the Bible.[36]

In other words, the point of Jeremiah 18:7–10 is simply "Heads I win, tails you lose," for it is a way of trying to show that a prophet must have been speaking the truth even when events turned out otherwise than predicted.

More recently, the distinguished ancient historian Robin Lane Fox discusses prophecy in the context of his wide-ranging reflection on the Bible, *The Unauthorized Version*.[37] He sees the prophecies of the canonical prophets as utterances that are "no more impressive or accurate than a moderately able foreign journalist's," and observes that regularly "human predictions from the Lord simply did not come true." Canonical preservation and contextualization, however, conveniently obscure this:

> Prophets . . . were more fortunate in their friends and editors than in the exact course of the future. When we read them nowadays, most of the rivals have been eliminated; contexts have been dropped or altered; hindsight has been brought to bear and failures bypassed by various routes. If a predicted disaster did not happen, was it, perhaps, that people had heeded and repented before God?

In other words, appeal to repentance, either human or divine (which Lane Fox goes on to discuss in comparable terms), is no more than a spurious rationalization that was "invoked to save their [the prophets'] credit, . . . at least until admiring people recast their sayings and turned them into scrolls for a new generation."[38] The thrust of Lane Fox's reading is much the same as Paine's, although he fills out a suitably enlightened imaginative picture of the prophets more than Paine does.

Given the nature of the biblical texts and their interpretive possibilities, it is probably not possible to refute such a reading. But one should at least

---

36. Thomas Paine, "The Old Testament," in *The Age of Reason: Part II* (London: H. D. Symonds, 1795; repr. in *Thomas Paine Collection: Common Sense, Rights of Man, Age of Reason, An Essay on Dream, Biblical Blasphemy, Examination of the Prophecies*, Charleston, SC: Forgotten Books, 2007), 399–400; also at http://www.ushistory.org/paine/reason/index .htm. By contrast, Paine observes elsewhere: "Almost the only parts in the book called the Bible, that convey to us any idea of God, are some chapters in Job, and the 19th Psalm; I recollect no other. Those parts are true deistical compositions; for they treat of the Deity through his works. They take the book of Creation as the word of God; they refer to no other book; and all the inferences they make are drawn from that volume" ("Concerning God, and the Lights Cast on His Existence and Attributes by the Bible," in *The Age of Reason: Part I* (London: printed by Barrois, 1794), in *Collection*, 318.

37. Robin Lane Fox, *The Unauthorized Version: Truth and Fiction in the Bible* (London: Viking, 1991), esp. chap. 18.

38. Ibid., 326–28.

notice not only that there is available a coherent reading that makes moral and spiritual sense and exemplifies well-known relational dynamics, but also that the reading of Paine and Lane Fox is in no way disinterested: there is a strongly dismissive tenor to each of their discussions.

The Immediate Response to Jeremiah's Message

YHWH's address to Jeremiah at the potter's house in chapter 18 continues with further words and a response:

> [11]Now, therefore, say to the people of Judah and the inhabitants of Jerusalem: Thus says the LORD: Look, I am a potter shaping evil against you and devising a plan against you. Turn now, all of you from your evil way, and amend your ways and your doings.
>
> [12]But they say, "It is no use! We will follow our own plans, and each of us will act according to the stubbornness of our evil will."

Interestingly, the content of verses 7–10 has not been something for Jeremiah to say to the Judahites. Rather, it is for the benefit of Jeremiah himself and of readers of the prophetic book. What Jeremiah is actually told to say represents a different development of the potter-and-clay imagery: YHWH is fashioning disaster, which should serve to evoke repentance in the hearers. Yet the reported response is one of heedlessness. The warning is ignored. In context this means that the possible averting of disaster through divine repentance, as just outlined, will not apply.

The Denial of Divine "Repentance" as a Theological Principle

It is against this background of the axiomatic depiction of YHWH as one who repents that one must set the passages denying that YHWH repents, in particular the two passages that deny it as axiomatically as Jeremiah 18:1–12 affirms it.

First, there are the words of Balaam to Balak:

> "God is not a human being, that he should lie [kizzēv],
>   or a mortal, that he should change his mind [niham].[39]
> Has he promised, and will he not do it?
>   Has he spoken, and will he not fulfill it?" (Num. 23:19)

---

39. The Hebrew text here uniquely uses nhm in the hithpael rather than niphal for divine repentance. There is most likely no difference in meaning, the only issue being the not uncommon grammatical interchangeability of niphal and hithpael to express a similar, perhaps reflexive, sense; cf., e.g., the uses of hb' ("hide") in Gen. 3:8, 10.

And then there are the words of Samuel to Saul:

> "Moreover the Glory of Israel will not deceive[40] or change his mind [*niḥam*]; for he is not a mortal that he should change his mind [*niḥam*]." (1 Sam. 15:29)

There is, of course, an immediate interpretive issue related to the possible significance of the fact that these denials that God repents are set on the lips of particular characters at particular moments. They do not have the in-principle reliability that belongs to the voice of the narrator. Not infrequently, characters within narratives say things that are most likely doubtful, things that in all probability the reader is not meant to take at face value; yet as in any good drama, readers/hearers are usually given no explicit direction on this and have to work it out for themselves in terms of making sense of the story as a whole.[41] Nonetheless, the working assumption of most interpreters, that the prophetic voices of Balaam (at least in that part of the narrative where he is pronouncing YHWH's blessings on Israel) and Samuel are reliable, will be our working assumption here until we find reason to modify it.[42]

Certain other passages are also in principle relevant to this discussion. For example, the claim that "God does not repent" (*lō' yinnāḥēm*) appears in conjunction with a specific oath (Ps. 110:4 AT), where the assertion clearly has the sense of underlining the irrevocable nature of a particular divine commitment (whose consonance with 1 Sam. 15:29, which also relates to a commitment to David, will become apparent in due course). Similar expressions are used rhetorically to emphasize the firmness of divine action on particular occasions (Jer. 4:28; 20:16; Zech. 8:14). Nonetheless, we

---

40. Here I follow 1 Sam. 15:29 NRSV mg., "deceive," which renders the MT reading *yshqr*. The NRSV's main text, "recant," surprisingly follows 4QSam[a], reading *yshyb* (apparently *shūb*, *hiphil*), which it considers to be the *Vorlage* of the LXX *apostrepsei*, both meaning "turn." Since, however, both these Hebrew and Greek verbs are transitive yet lack the necessary object, this is an awkward and probably corrupt reading. Thus it is preferable to retain MT, whose text here is straightforward and unproblematic.

41. Ahaz's articulation of an apparently unexceptionable theological axiom, "I will not test YHWH," is shown by Isaiah's response to be a self-serving and evasive use of religious language (Isa. 7:10–13 AT). Aaron's account to Moses about the making of the golden calf (Exod. 32:22–24) appears evasive and self-exculpatory when set alongside the narrator's account of events (32:1–6). An example where the sense of the narrative as a whole depends on how one construes a character's words is Balaam's response to Balak's second embassy (Num. 22:18–19), which I have discussed in my *Prophecy and Discernment*, 140–42, 147–49.

42. Yoram Hazony, in his interesting recent work *The Philosophy of Hebrew Scripture* (Cambridge: Cambridge University Press, 2012), disappointingly assumes, without probing the texts, that Balaam and Samuel are simply denying what numerous other passages affirm; hence Hazony unsurprisingly says that "the view advanced by these figures is not accepted by the biblical narrative" and that "it may be that Samuel is not being fully truthful with Saul" (302n91). On this issue, cf. Yairah Amit, "'The Glory of Israel Does Not Deceive or Change His Mind': On the Reliability of Narrator and Speakers in Biblical Narrative," *Prooftexts* 12 (1992): 201–12, esp. 204.

will focus on Numbers 23:19 and 1 Samuel 15:29, mainly because of their unusually emphatic and indeed axiomatic formulation, but also because it will be easier thereby to interact with existing interpretive debate.

On Approaching the Problem

If to say that God repents implies that God's relationship with humanity in general, and with Israel in particular, is a genuine and responsive relationship, in which what people do and how they relate to God *matters* to God, does the denial that God repents deny such mutuality of relationship? Such a denial would surely be prima facie unlikely, for the simple reason that it would deny something central, rather than peripheral, to Israel's understanding of God and to much historic Jewish and Christian belief and practice.

Of course, such unlikeliness does not rule out the possibility. For one could perhaps imagine particular people at particular times or places disagreeing with the consensus understanding now represented in the Old Testament, and it may be that such disagreement could have been preserved within Israel's scriptures despite its departure from the norm. Redactors and canonizers could have allowed reverence for tradition to override their own theological judgment. And on any reckoning, a collection that includes Ecclesiastes is hardly one whose boundaries were drawn according to narrowly conceived axioms. Nonetheless, as with the working assumption that the voices of Balaam and Samuel are reliable, one surely ought to start with a working assumption that their denial may be not of a central principle but of something else, and only abandon the assumption if one finds that it does not and indeed cannot do justice to the relevant texts.

To put it differently, the concept of "denial," like that of "contradiction," needs some probing as to what it does mean and does not mean in this context. For one not-uncommon approach in the literature is to see the denial of divine repentance not as a repudiation but as a qualification of the notion. That is, the denial may in essence be a necessary element in the dynamics of religious language, a part of the intrinsic problem of the human need to speak of God with analogical language drawn from the human realm, in which affirmations (the kataphatic) need to be balanced by denials (the apophatic): God is like this in some ways but is not like this in other ways.

So, for example, Robert Dentan discusses Numbers 23:19 and 1 Samuel 15:29 in relation to "the limitations and safeguards attached to the vivid anthropomorphic language of the Old Testament" and observes:

What had to be done then—as now—was to keep the two ideas of God's likeness to men and his utter difference from them in a dynamic tension, where each truth is accepted wholly and simply, but kept in balance. This kind of paradox, of ambivalent thought, is inseparable from every human effort to deal with matters of ultimate concern. In the antiphony of two apparently contradictory statements the essential, indefinable truth often manages to shine forth—sometimes brilliantly and excitingly—like the play of lightning between two opposing cloud masses.[43]

Comparably, Walther Eichrodt sees our two passages as dealing with issues of religious language in terms of prophetic resistance to a misreading of the mainstream affirmation of divine repentance:

Wherever the habit of conceiving God in human terms might result in a dangerous obscuring of his true character, they [the prophets] also make their protest. It is not anthropomorphisms as such that are important to them in this connection; indeed it is precisely about these that they seem to be least anxious. The spiritual and physical realms are not for them exclusive antinomies; and, for this reason, they go on presenting the trans-physical in physically conceivable forms as the old sagas had done. . . . [But] when certain anthropopathisms are endangering the purity of the idea of God, their voice is heard in clear condemnation. "God is not a man that he should lie; neither the son of man that he should repent;" the purpose of both Num. 23.19 and I Sam. 15.29 in making this declaration is to combat the erroneous idea that it is easy to talk God round, and that his threats and promises need not be taken seriously.[44]

Such an approach is readily intelligible and makes good sense as a way of tackling the problem of God's both repenting and not repenting. However, the key question is whether our two passages are really playing this role. May it be that they are serving a different purpose?

The Terminology and Conceptuality of Numbers 23:19 and 1 Samuel 15:29

Even a cursory consideration reveals that these two passages share certain features. They both amplify, in similar ways, the statement that God does not repent. It may well be precisely because each passage is aware of the potentially problematic nature of the denial that God repents that, either by design or reflex, some qualifications are specified to help the reader/hearer understand what is, and is not, meant.

43. Robert C. Dentan, *The Knowledge of God in Ancient Israel* (New York: Seabury, 1968), 151–52.
44. Walther Eichrodt, *Theology of the Old Testament*, trans. J. A. Baker from the 5th German ed. (1957; ET, London: SCM, 1961), 1:216.

First, the denial that Israel's God "changes his mind/repents [*niham*]" is each time accompanied by another, presumably elucidatory, verb. In Numbers 23:19a, in parallel with *niham*, the verb *kizzēv* is used, whose meaning is well attested: "lie/deceive."

Proverbs 14:5, for example, says "A faithful [*ĕmūnīm*] witness does not lie [*kizzēv*]," where there is a straight contrast between lying and that prime Old Testament quality of integrity, reliability, and faithfulness (*ĕmūnāh*).[45] Strikingly, the psalmist when speaking "in consternation" declares that "everyone is a liar [*kol-hā ʾādām kōzēv*]" (Ps. 116:11)[46]—people lie, apparently in the sense of not living up to their promises, in contrast to God, who does not disappoint.

In 1 Samuel 15:29, combined with *niham* and immediately preceding it, we read "he will not deceive [*lō ʾ yĕshaqqēr*]" (AT). This is another well-known verb (*shiqqēr*), which has the sense "deal/speak falsely."

The primary form of the root is the noun *sheqer*, which is regularly used with regard to false testimony in legal contexts (Exod. 20:16; Deut. 19:18), and of the speech of prophets not sent by God, the content of whose message is to be disregarded (Jer. 14:14; 23:25, 26). The sense of *sheqer* seems to be not solely that of factual error (for in the case of false witnesses and false prophets such error might be far from obvious), but also, and perhaps predominantly, a self-serving, morally deceitful use of language—a use that can transform even an otherwise accurate saying ("This is the temple of Yʜᴡʜ") into something deceptive and false (Jer. 7:4, 8, within the context of 7:1–15). The noun *sheqer* is used in conjunction with *kizzēv* in Proverbs 14:5 and Micah 2:11, which suggests a related semantic field for the two roots.

Thus both *kizzēv* and *shiqqēr* depict unreliable, untrustworthy use of speech. Insofar as they qualify *niham*, it follows that unreliable speech is being denied in the denial of divine repenting on the lips of Balaam and Samuel.

Second, each passage denies that God is a human being (*lō ʾ ʾīsh/ben-ʾādām*, in Num. 23:19a; *lō ʾ ʾādām*, in 1 Sam. 15:29). In neither passage is this some kind of principle in its own right, but each time it introduces the notion of repenting as something characteristic of humanity, and it is from this that God is distanced: He is "not a human being that he should repent." As such, it appears to be a clear example of "negative/apophatic theology," the denial of positive analogy between God and humanity. This shared feature of Numbers 23:19 and 1 Samuel 15:29, in a context where the question is of the appropriate use of language with reference to God, is striking. The point is that what repent (*niham*) may mean with reference to human beings does not pertain with reference to God. There is a qualitative difference between divine and human repentance.

When these two qualifications are taken together, the general tenor of each of our two texts is clear. The concern is to preserve what is said of God—that

45. The prime nominal form of the root *ʾmn* is *ĕmūnāh*, but the different nominal form in Prov. 14:5 does not differ in meaning.

46. Although the verb is used primarily in the *piel*, this *qal* participial use does not differ in meaning.

"God does not repent"—from possible associations to do with the lack of integrity and lack of faithfulness that regularly characterize human speech; God is true and faithful in a way that people are not. Thus it should be apparent that what is being denied here is not the same as what is affirmed in Jeremiah 18:7–10. It is not mutuality and responsiveness in relationship, but insincerity and faithlessness that are specified for denial. In other words, two different topics are in view in what look like positive and negative statements about one and the same thing.

Why then should such an axiomatic denial be specified in these two passages? We must consider the literary context of each passage.[47]

The Contextualization of Numbers 23:19 within Numbers 22–24

The story of Balaam in Numbers 22–24 revolves around two central concerns.[48] One is discernment, the ability to see God and what God is doing, a theme developed with a certain humor and relish. Balaam initially declines the commission from Balak, king of Moab, to curse Israel since God has instructed Balaam that they are a blessed people whom he cannot curse (22:12). However, when Balak sends a second embassy, which invites him to "name his price" (22:15–17), Balaam lets himself be corrupted by greed (while still, of course, maintaining and even increasing the language of piety and integrity). The consequence is that Balaam, the prophet of renown, the best that royalty and wealth can acquire, loses his powers of vision and needs to learn from his ass, proverbially the dullest of animals, what it means to see what is before his very eyes. Three times he blindly urges his ass onward, when the ass can see death, an angel with a drawn sword, confronting them. Only after Balaam is instructed by his ass are his eyes opened by YHWH, and only after he relinquishes his greedy self-seeking does he become able truly to speak for God. Shortly afterward, when Balaam comes to Balak, roles are then reversed. Three times Balak blindly urges Balaam onward, being unable to see what Balaam can see: YHWH's blessing of Israel. Each time Balaam is urged to try again (with various possible helps; only a partial view, in case the view of the whole is putting Balaam off, or more sacrifices to try to make a difference), yet his vision of Israel becomes more glowing. When Balak eventually dismisses Balaam in anger,

47. It is a curiosity of scholarship—analogous to Christian scholars' almost blanket silence about the location of the *locus classicus* on divine election in a context where election functions as a reason for the practice of *ḥerem* (see chap. 2 above)—that the purpose in their own contexts of Num. 23:19 and 1 Sam. 15:29, when considered in discussions of divine (non-)repentance, is regularly passed over with little or no probing.

48. I offer a fuller account in my *Prophecy and Discernment*, 138–49.

Balaam offers a fourth, unsolicited oracle with a precise sting in its tail: disaster for Moab at the hands of Israel.

The other concern of the story is God's commitment to Israel, expressed in the divine resolve to bless Israel and make Israel prosper against its adversaries. The issue of power to curse and bless sets the dynamics of the story in motion at the outset (22:6) and forms the climax of Balaam's last solicited oracle (24:9). The fact that Israel is blessed is what God communicates axiomatically to Balaam when first he seeks divine guidance (22:12), and it is what he learns to take seriously after his temporary blindness (when he hoped he might be able to get away with cursing, and so earn a fabulous reward). This is therefore the note that Balaam sounds at the beginning of his first two oracles when Balak urges him to pronounce a curse on Israel. In his first oracle Balaam speaks initially of his commission:

> "Balak has brought me from Aram,
> the king of Moab from the eastern mountains:
> 'Come, curse Jacob for me;
> Come, denounce Israel!'" (23:7)

But he immediately speaks, in a rhetorical question, of the impossibility of his doing what Balak wants of him:

> "How can I curse whom God has not cursed?
> How can I denounce those whom the LORD has not denounced?"
> (23:8)

On the contrary, he depicts Israel in glowing terms and aspires, when his own end comes, to be like them (23:9–10).

When Balak tells Balaam to try again, Balaam's second oracle is much like his first, only fuller in the glowing portrayal of Israel. Near the outset, he repeats the initial thrust of his first oracle:

> "See, I received a command to bless;
> he has blessed, and I cannot revoke it." (23:20)

God's resolution to bless Israel is such that he, Balaam, can do nothing to gainsay it. It is this affirmation that is immediately preceded by the words we are interested in:

> "God is not a human being, that he should lie,
> or a mortal, that he should change his mind [niham].

> Has he promised, and will he not do it?
> Has he spoken, and will he not fulfill it?" (23:19)

The sense of the denial that God repents is thus fully clarified. God wills to bless Israel. He will not go back on that, nor will He be false to it. So when Balaam speaks at God's behest, he can only pronounce blessing on Israel. In other words, the Balaam narrative is concerned with the issue we have already considered in Deuteronomy 7, the status of Israel as YHWH's chosen people. The point here is that God's election of Israel is irrevocable.[49] The idea that God could be false or faithless in relation to His commitment to Israel as His chosen and blessed people—as humans are often false and faithless in their dealings with each other (and as Balaam is for a while faithless to his vocation)—is the issue being categorically denied. The location of this within the book of Numbers, in whose other narratives Israel is persistently rebellious and falling under judgment, adds weight to the significance of the denial.

The Contextualization of 1 Samuel 15:29 within 1 Samuel 15

The narrative of 1 Samuel 15 has other, though not unrelated, concerns. If one takes the story as a whole (setting aside, for the moment, the problematic v. 29), it is a good example of a story that illustrates the regular dynamics of divine repentance. Bestowed gift or promised blessing can be forfeited through wrong human attitude and action, as outlined above with reference to Jeremiah 18:9–10 and Ezekiel 33:13. The closest narrative analogy to Saul's forfeiting his particular office of kingship is the account of the house of Eli's losing its priesthood (1 Sam. 2:12–3:21, esp. 2:30). The story is set in motion by Samuel's command to Saul to "put Amalek to the ban [ḥērem]" (1 Sam. 15:1–3). This Saul carries out, but only in part since he spares Agag and the best of the animals (vv. 4–10). But it is part of the all-or-nothing logic peculiar to ḥērem that partial fulfillment is not meant to be a possibility (cf. Josh. 7). Therefore Saul's action in sparing Agag and the animals, although amenable to positive rationalization (saving the best so as to sacrifice it all to YHWH [1 Sam. 15:15, 20–21]), in fact constitutes a sin of disobedience, as Samuel memorably articulates (vv. 22–23), and as Saul himself then comes to admit (v. 24). It is for this reason that YHWH repents (niḥam) of making Saul king, as spelled out after the initial account of Saul's actions:

---

49. Jörg Jeremias appeals to the picture of the victorious Israelite ruler in Balaam's final (unsolicited) oracle (Num. 24:15–19) to support the view that the election in 23:19 is of David (*Reue*, 33–36). Yet although it is no doubt David (or a Davidic king) under whom Israel is to defeat Moab, it is Israel, not David, whose election is the concern of Balaam's three solicited oracles, as well as of the preceding narrative (22:12).

[10]The word of the LORD came to Samuel: [11]"I regret [*niham*] that I made Saul king, for he has turned back from following me, and has not carried out my commands."

The divine repentance is a retraction of the privilege of kingship, on the basis of Saul's failure rightly to respond to YHWH's commands. This point is then reiterated by Samuel to Saul, in the terminology of mutual "rejection," when Saul acknowledges his failing but asks that it not be held against him:

[25]"Now therefore, I pray, pardon my sin, and return with me, so that I may worship the LORD." [26]Samuel said to Saul, "I will not return with you; for you have rejected the word of the LORD, and the LORD has rejected you from being king over Israel."

The extended encounter between Samuel and Saul raises an important question. If Saul's disobedience forfeits his kingship because of divine repentance, is this final or can it be reversed? If Saul turns from/repents of his sin, might YHWH cancel His retraction, that is, repent of His repentance? As just seen, Samuel initially denies this possibility: YHWH has indeed rejected Saul as king. When Saul attempts to renew his request, by taking hold of Samuel's robe, so as to try to prevent him from leaving and so make possible further words about Saul's situation, the robe tears, and Samuel interprets this in a way that gives no ground but rather underlines what he has already said:

[27]As Samuel turned to go away, Saul caught hold of the hem of his robe, and it tore. [28]And Samuel said to him, "The LORD has torn the kingdom of Israel from you this very day, and has given it to a neighbor of yours, who is better than you. [29]Moreover the Glory of Israel will not deceive or change his mind [*niham*]; for he is not a mortal, that he should change his mind [*niham*]." (NRSV mg.)

Yet after this, when Saul again acknowledges his sin, Samuel does appear willing to compromise somewhat, though not with regard to Saul's forfeiture of his kingship:

[30]Then Saul said, "I have sinned; yet honor me now before the elders of my people and before Israel, and return with me, so that I may worship the LORD your God." [31]So Samuel turned back after Saul; and Saul worshiped the LORD.

How should this narrative sequence be read? On any reckoning, it is not straightforward. And it is likely to be difficult for many a contemporary reader, whose sympathies may well lie with Saul more than with Samuel—or by

extension, with YHWH, on whose behalf Samuel speaks. The ban is so repel-
lent that Saul's unwillingness fully to carry it out seems deserving of praise
more than blame; even if his actions deserve blame in their own ancient frame
of reference, then forfeiture of kingship seems a stiff, even disproportionate,
penalty; and Samuel's repeated refusal to respond favorably toward Saul, even
when he acknowledges his sin, seems harsh and forbidding.

One possible approach, which seeks to stay with the grain of the text, is to
argue that Saul is portrayed not only as weak and thus undeserving of being
king, but also as self-seeking rather than genuinely repentant. His weakness
can be seen in the reason that he gives for his sin: "because I feared the people
and obeyed their voice" (v. 24b). Saul's concern that Samuel should "honor"
him publicly (v. 30) can readily be construed as self-seeking in a way that represents less than a genuine turning to God. Saul could be using correct religious
language, but without the corresponding existential reality—as in his initial
greeting of Samuel: "May you be blessed by the LORD; I have carried out the
command of the LORD" (v. 13). If so, then the relational dynamics to enable a
differing divine response remain lacking in Saul. But even if one reads the text
thus, such an interpretation does not fully meet the likely reservations about
the tenor of the text or the sense that a moral rationalizing of Saul's actions
does not fully explain what is going on in the narrative.

It is at this point that we need to consider the meaning of verse 29. What
does it mean in itself, and how does it relate to the wider story? One obvious
interpretation in context is that it underlines what Samuel has just said. The
divine decision to reject Saul as king is nonnegotiable. Thus Robert Gordon
puts it: "Too much can be made of the surface tension between the statements, in verses 11 and 29, concerning the possibility or impossibility of God's
repenting. When God issues a decree that is plainly intended as irrevocable,
as in the rejection of Saul, then, says our text, there is no possibility of that
decree being rescinded (cf. Num. 23:19)."[50] Yet if that is the sole point, it still
leaves the puzzling question of why the text of verse 29 should look so much
like the formulation of a general principle about God, when a more simple
formulation would presumably have sufficed for the purpose of saying that the
decision about Saul was nonnegotiable—such as "and in this matter YHWH
will not repent [*ūbāzōʾt lōʾ yinnāḥēm yhwh*]," as in the denial of YHWH's
reneging on his sworn commitment in Psalm 110:4.

The vital contextual clue to the meaning of verse 29 comes, I suggest, in
the immediately preceding words in verse 28. Here Samuel tells Saul not only
that "the LORD has torn the kingdom of Israel from you this very day," but

---

50. Robert P. Gordon, *1 and 2 Samuel* (Exeter: Paternoster, 1986), 146.

also that "[He] has given it to a neighbor of yours, who is better than you."
Who is this neighbor? His identity is revealed to the reader in the very next
story, when Samuel goes to anoint one of the sons of Jesse to be king, and
chooses David (1 Sam. 16:1–13). Whether or not Samuel is to be imagined
as in some way knowing the identity of the neighbor before his visit to Jesse
(one can envisage the scenario either way), the knowledge that David is the
divinely chosen successor to Saul is presupposed by the narrator of 1 Samuel
15, who tells the story thus. It is this oncoming event—*that God will give the
kingship of Israel to David*—that sets the context for verse 29 and explains
why verse 29 is formulated as a general principle about God, that "God does
not repent." That which is denied is not the responsive dynamics of divine
repentance as presupposed elsewhere in the story. Rather, the text envisages
the positive commitment of God to make David king over Israel. It is this on
which God will not go back, as though it were in any way an equivocal or
deceptive undertaking such as humans commonly make.[51]

What is at stake in 1 Samuel 15:29 is not, as in Numbers 23:19, God's
election of Israel, but the subsequent fundamental election within the Old
Testament, the election of David. It is with reference to this that Samuel says
that God does not repent. As God's election of Israel is irrevocable, so is God's
election of David. Hence the axiomatic statement with regard to each that
"God does not repent."

On Reading 1 Samuel 15 and the Narratives about David

Although the Old Testament is privileged by believers as Scripture, aspects of what is both explicit
and implicit in certain narratives are open to question from more than one perspective. We have
already noticed that a reader's sympathies in 1 Samuel 15 are unlikely to go with the grain of the
text as readily here as in some other passages. One reason for this is the fact that the narrative is
premised upon the logic of *ḥerem*, in a way that clearly does envisage the taking of life. I have argued
in chapter 2 that Deuteronomy retains, indeed prioritizes, the language of *ḥerem* only because it
was seen to be open to metaphorical understanding, where its severe logic is construed in terms of
faithfulness to YHWH through avoiding intermarriage and symbols of rival allegiances (although
the book of Joshua interestingly probes the severity of the logic, especially in the story of Rahab).
That does not resolve the problem in 1 Samuel 15, though it would suggest that from a very early
period there was a certain discomfort with what Saul was expected to do. Perhaps we can do no
more than note that Saul himself accepts the frame of reference of *ḥerem* by which his behavior
is found wanting, and seek imaginatively to read the narrative within that frame of reference.
Beyond that, however, such battlefield *ḥerem* is a time-restricted practice, limited to its ancient
context, which can only be enduringly meaningful for scriptural readers in metaphorical form.

More generally, it has become fashionable for commentators to read the narratives about David
with a high level of suspicion.[52] On any reckoning, one cannot deny a disproportion between the

---

51. See also chap. 7 below for further discussion of the implications of the election of David
in Ps. 89.

52. Typical of a growing bibliography is Baruch Halpern, *David's Secret Demons: Messiah,
Murderer, Traitor, King* (Grand Rapids: Eerdmans, 2001). One suggestive attempt to row against

failings of Saul (impatience,[53] inappropriate mercy), for which he forfeits his kingship, and the subsequent failings of David (adultery and murder, to go no further than the story of Bathsheba and Uriah in 2 Sam. 11), for which he does not forfeit his kingship. This points us to a key element in God's electing purposes: they to a significant extent defy rationalization. However much moral concerns may feature, not least in the principle that much is expected of those to whom much is given, they cannot account for all that the text portrays. This, I suggest, is why attempts to account for God's rejecting Saul from kingship, and Samuel's harshness toward him, in moral terms tend to be unsatisfactory. Even if Saul behaves questionably and so there is some moral reason for his rejection, as the biblical text makes clear, there remains a disproportion between him and David because, at root, David is favored by YHWH, and by Samuel as YHWH's representative, in a way that Saul is not. David is the chosen of YHWH, and the dynamics of YHWH's actions in the narrative are in certain ways analogous to those of someone who has fallen out of love with one person and has transferred that love to someone else.[54]

One way of making some progress with the challenging theological issues here involves recognizing that the Old Testament portrayal of divine election, in which some are favored over others (Israel over the nations, David over Saul)—which is *not* about salvation as Christians understand that term—is not unrelated to recurrent features of life in general.[55] For it is an inescapable fact that some are favored more than others in things that profoundly shape life as a whole. Intelligence, appearance, and health are all unevenly distributed, in ways that bear no relation to the character of a person. One's situation in life and the things that happen to one may likewise be largely or entirely beyond one's control. For many people, especially those less favored, a prime challenge in life is to make the most of a situation beyond their choosing or liking—for there always remains a choice about how to respond to one's situation.[56]

For the purposes of reading 1 Samuel, however, the important thing to recognize is that the imbalance or disproportion in the narrative between Saul and David is an outworking of divine election. I think that the recent tendency to read what is said about David with high levels of suspicion is in certain ways the result of transposing this theological issue into a socio-political dimension and reading it as the pious and rationalizing cover-up of brutal power politics. It is a possible reading strategy. But the basic issue is how best to do justice to a theology of divine election.

---

this tide is J. Randall Short, *The Surprising Election and Confirmation of King David*, HTS 63 (Cambridge, MA: Harvard University Press, 2010).

53. The earlier impatience of Saul in offering sacrifice (1 Sam. 13:8–15) likewise feels undeserving of Samuel's severe censure and the loss of a future dynasty. But here too the key to Saul's rejection is YHWH's preference for David (13:14).

54. Michael Wyschogrod's account of this dimension of election (see pp. 51–52 above) is suggestive, though it does not resolve all the problems.

55. I have discussed this more fully in relation to the story of Cain and Abel in *The Theology of the Book of Genesis*, OTT (New York and Cambridge: Cambridge University Press, 2009), 88–101.

56. Viktor Frankl's best-selling work *Man's Search for Meaning: An Introduction to Logotherapy*, trans. Ilse Lasch (in German, 1946; ET, New York: Pocket Books, 1984) develops his particular understanding and practice of psychotherapy: "logotherapy," which entails learning to weave the threads of a broken life into a pattern of meaning and responsibility. In this he drew on his time in Nazi concentration camps. Frankl was not explicitly religious yet clearly drew deeply on his Jewish roots in ways that resonate with scriptural concerns: "We who lived in concentration camps can remember the men who walked through the huts comforting others, giving away their last piece of bread. They may have been few in number, but they offer sufficient proof that everything can be taken from a man but one thing: the last of the human freedoms—to choose one's attitude in any given set of circumstances, to choose one's own way" (86).

Two New Testament Analogies

Students have sometimes told me that they miss the language of divine repentance in the New Testament, which they find less vivid and engaging than the Old Testament in this respect; for the language of divine repentance and non-repentance does not appear in the New Testament (with one exception). Nonetheless, the concept does, for both the responsiveness and the constancy of God are fundamental features of the New Testament—just as they surely are a fundamental presupposition of the practice of prayer. It may be helpful briefly to note two passages, in different New Testament writers, where what we have seen in the Old Testament is portrayed in fresh ways.

First, in Jesus's teaching in Matthew's Gospel, forgiveness represents a mutuality of relationship between God and humanity. It is a divine gift, yet it may be nullified if it is not extended to others. Thus we read the passage that immediately follows Jesus's giving of the Lord's Prayer and clearly constitutes a commentary upon its "Forgive us our debts, as we also have forgiven our debtors" (Matt. 6:12):

> [14]"For if you forgive others their trespasses, your heavenly Father will also forgive you; [15]but if you do not forgive others, neither will your Father forgive your trespasses."

The human and the divine actions are closely interrelated. But precisely how? Does the text imply that human forgiveness must precede divine forgiveness, as a prior condition? This is clearly a possible reading of the words as they stand, though it could create problems in relation to divine grace.[57] The sequence of the wording, however, with the negatives following the positives, shows that the text is a warning that it is possible not to receive divine forgiveness, even on the part of those who are praying for it. How is this possible?

These issues are clarified later in the Gospel, in another context that focuses on forgiveness: the parable of the unforgiving servant (Matt. 18:23–35). A servant who owes his king ten thousand talents (an astronomical figure, "trillions" in contemporary parlance) cannot pay, but when he begs for mercy, he is forgiven the debt. He then goes to demand from another servant a hundred denarii (substantial, but feasibly payable, if a denarius was a day's wage, as in Matt. 20:1–16). When this second servant asks for mercy, the first servant refuses and has him thrown into prison. When the fellow servants see this,

---

57. The perfect of *aphēkamen* in Matt. 6:12 ("have forgiven") is not determinative one way or the other since the implied user of the Lord's Prayer is someone who has already responded to grace.

they tell the king who summons the first servant: "Should you not have had mercy on your fellow slave, as I had mercy on you?" (18:33). The first servant is then put into prison and left at the mercy of those who will try to wring his initial debt out of him. Jesus then draws the moral: "So my heavenly Father will also do to every one of you, if you do not forgive your brother or sister from your heart" (v. 35). This makes clear that the divine forgiveness precedes human forgiveness, but a failure to respond appropriately—to try to treat grace selfishly and complacently as though it could be kept for oneself, rather than transform one's dealings with others so that grace is in effect passed on—can nullify it. Promised good can be lost. The thought of the parable is similar in substance to that in Jeremiah 18:9–10 and Ezekiel 33:13.

Second, Paul's account of Israel and its ultimate salvation in Romans 9–11 resonates strongly with Old Testament categories. In chapter 11 Paul develops an account of the nature of God's people via the image of an olive tree, which he uses to deliver a warning to certain gentile Christians (v. 13), who were clearly inclined to think dismissively of Jews:

> [17]But if some of the branches were broken off, and you, a wild olive shoot, were grafted in their place[58] to share the rich root of the olive tree, [18]do not vaunt yourselves over the branches. If you do vaunt yourselves, remember that it is not you that support the root, but the root that supports you. (NRSVA)

Paul's initial point is that Israel is the antecedent reality, which was there before the gentiles became part of it. Gentiles need to retain a proper sense of their secondary and dependent position within a larger and older people of God.

> [19]You will say, "Branches were broken off so that I might be grafted in." [20]That is true. They were broken off because of their unbelief [apistia], but you stand only through faith [pistis]. So do not become proud,[59] but stand in awe. [21]For if God did not spare the natural branches, neither[60] will he spare you. (NRSV mg.)

58. The Greek *en autois* is correctly rendered "among them" (so Rom. 11:17 REB, CEB). The Greek for "in their place" would be *anti autōn*. Paul's point is inclusion, not replacement.

59. The Greek idiom here in Rom. 11:20, *hypsēla phronein* ("to think lofty things"), is a similar idiom to that used in Deut. 8:14 LXX (on which see chap. 3 above). It depicts what is classically meant by pride as one of the seven deadly sins: a self-referential attitude that has become resistant to grace.

60. This follows Rom. 11:21 NRSV mg. The extra *mēpōs*, or *mē pōs* ("perhaps he will not"), almost certainly represents copyists' nervous weakening of Paul's categorical statement. The widespread manuscript presence of this qualification attests its acceptability in antiquity. Yet it is inappropriate because Paul gives no reason in context to suppose that ingrafted gentiles might receive from God a "lighter touch" than Jews have received.

Paul develops his image of how God works on His olive tree (i.e., Israel). God both breaks off and grafts in. He does so in accord with human responsiveness, a responsiveness expressed in the prime Christian category of faith/unfaith: when people have faith, they are brought in; when they display unfaith, they are cut off.

> [22]Note then the kindness and the severity of God: severity toward those who have fallen, but God's kindness toward you, provided you continue in his kindness; otherwise you also will be cut off. [23]And even those of Israel, if they do not persist in unbelief, will be grafted in, for God has the power to graft them in again. [24]For if you have been cut from what is by nature a wild olive tree and grafted, contrary to nature, into a cultivated olive tree, how much more will these natural branches be grafted back into their own olive tree.

God's actions of grafting in and breaking off express his kindness and severity. There is, however, something provisional for the present about God's actions, because location within the tree is not yet finalized. It is possible for those grafted in to forfeit their life in the tree if they do not continue to respond in a way that is in keeping with the faith that has enabled them to be grafted in: unfaith/complacency means that those grafted in are subsequently cut off. Likewise, those at present cut off can be restored to the tree if they turn from their unfaith and respond rightly to God.

To someone who has just read Jeremiah 18:7–10 and Ezekiel 33:12–16, the similarity of thought is striking. The initiative lies with God, who adds to and takes away from His tree, but He does so according to the responsiveness of people, and there is a contingency dependent upon how people respond both now and in the future. The dynamics of God as the gardener with the olive tree are in essence those of God as the potter with the clay.

This is the more striking since Paul has earlier used the image of the divine potter with the clay in a different sense, solely to express divine power: "But who indeed are you, a human being, to argue with God? Will what is molded say to the one who molds it, 'Why have you made me like this?' Has the potter no right over the clay, to make out of the same lump one object for special use and another for ordinary use?" (Rom. 9:20–21). Indeed, just prior to introducing the potter image, Paul has spoken strongly of unilateral divine power: "So it depends not on human will or exertion, but on God who shows mercy" (9:16). One of the historic difficulties in interpreting what Paul says about Israel in Romans 9–11 is that his strong statements about divine power and "predestination" in chapter 9 have not always been held in tension with his equally strong statements about the difference that human responsiveness can make in chapter 11. Again, there is a striking parallel of thought with Jeremiah 18, where one has to hold together verses 5–6, the initial statement of divine power, with verses 7–10, the subsequent statement of divine responsiveness, and neither separate the two nor play them off against each other.

A little further on in Romans 11, while Paul is still setting out the relationship between Jews and gentiles within Israel, he says of Jews:

> [28]As regards the gospel they are enemies of God for your sake; but as regards election they are beloved, for the sake of their ancestors; [29]for the gifts and calling of God are irrevocable [ametameletos].

Whatever the grave difficulties posed by the widespread failure of Jews to respond to the gospel of Jesus Christ in his apostolic ministry, Paul does not see these difficulties as ultimately determinative of their status. This is for one basic reason: God's gifts and calling, that is His purposes of election, are "not to be repented of"—where the adjective is a negative of a prime Greek root for "repent" (metamelomai). In verse 28 there are strong resonances with Deuteronomy's understanding of YHWH's election of Israel as rooted in His love and His keeping the oath He swore to the ancestors (Deut. 7:8).[61] The way Paul's thought is worded in verse 29 recalls the Balaam narrative, especially Balaam's words in Numbers 23:19.[62] Moreover, the reader of the Christian Bible can also see a general parallel between the affirmation of Israel's election in Numbers 22–24, in a book in whose other narratives Israel consistently fails to live up to its vocation, and that in Romans 9–11, in the context of widespread Jewish failure to respond positively to the gospel.[63]

Conclusion

I have argued that the passages about God's repenting and non-repenting are easily misread. These passages are often taken in a freestanding way and

61. See chap. 2 above.

62. Yet if Paul was reflecting on Num. 23:19, it was not via the familiar LXX, which does not use "repent" (metanoeō or metamelomai) and indeed changes the sense of the text. For the complex textual issues, see G. Dorival, ed., La Bible d'Alexandrie: Les Nombres (Paris: Cerf, 1994), 438–39.

63. We may also note that Rom. 11 displays inner tensions comparable to those of 1 Sam. 15. In Rom. 11 the necessity of human responsiveness is set alongside an affirmation of non-negotiable divine initiative, as also in 1 Sam. 15. The difference is that in Rom. 11 both emphases relate to the same recipient (though gentiles are included with Jews as needing to respond rightly), whereas in 1 Sam. 15 the principle of responsiveness impacts adversely on Saul, while the divine constancy is directed to David.

related to concerns not their own or played off against each other. Despite all the many things that can be done with texts, the disciplines of careful philologically- and conceptually-alert reading remain foundational, not least for those who seek to read the Old Testament as Scripture. I have argued that both of the basic issues of this chapter—the relational and responsive nature of God ("repentance"), and the unswerving faithfulness of God to those whom He calls ("non-repentance")—are not only not at odds with each other but are also integral to the Old Testament portrayal of God. They are also fundamental to the New Testament and to a Christian understanding of God.

This is an area where synthetic theological thinking in relation to the wider canonical portrayal becomes important. The dynamics of the texts we have considered are commonly expressed in other terms, such as election, grace, and sovereignty (= "non-repentance") and covenant, faithfulness, sin, and forgiveness (= "repentance"), and so other perennial issues also come in view. On the one hand, God acts on His own initiative, calling people with a call that is irrevocable precisely because it depends on God and not on the one called. On the other hand, the relationship thus initiated is a real one in which there is everything to be gained or lost according to how people live within that relationship with God. It depends on God, and it depends on human response. The gift is free and unconditional; yet to respond rightly, so as to enter into the gift and appropriate it, remains crucial. This is surely, in essence, the dynamics and logic of love.

Thus our particular issue directs us to a creative tension at the heart of Scripture. What Carroll saw as a contradiction that disables theology is seen rather to be a facet of the articulation of a tension, intrinsically never to be "resolved" or "relieved." For this tension—unconditional gift and indispensable responsiveness—is the dynamics of love, definitional of what constitutes life as it should be. It enlarges a vision of what it means to live in God's world.

5

Isaiah and Jesus

In one of the most memorable of all the resurrection stories in the Gospels, the risen Jesus, unrecognized, speaks to two of his disciples on the road to Emmaus. The disciples are well informed about Jesus and know what has happened in recent days, including that his tomb was empty and that some women from their group saw angels who said that Jesus is alive. Yet none of this apparently makes any real difference to them. They are disappointed and puzzled by the death of Jesus, not rejoicing in a risen Lord. When Jesus speaks, he reproaches them for their sluggishness of heart and mind; then he proceeds to give what one imagines to be the Bible study to end all Bible studies. "Then beginning with Moses and all the prophets, he interpreted to them the things about himself in all the scriptures" (Luke 24:27).

Presumably the logic of Jesus's expounding the scriptures to his puzzled disciples is that these scriptures provide a context and a content for making sense of Jesus, when all that the disciples already know about him has not "clicked." Israel's scriptures help make sense of Jesus. Yet these disciples are

In this chapter I develop three of my earlier studies: "Christ in All the Scriptures? The Challenge of Reading the Old Testament as Christian Scripture," *JTI* 1/1 (2007): 79–100; "Isaiah and Jesus: How Might the Old Testament Inform Contemporary Christology?," in *Seeking the Identity of Jesus: A Pilgrimage*, ed. Beverly Gaventa and Richard Hays (Grand Rapids: Eerdmans, 2008), 232–48; and "Preaching Christ from the Old Testament," in *"He Began with Moses . . .": Preaching the Old Testament Today*, ed. Grenville J. R. Kent, Paul J. Kissling, and Laurence A. Turner (Nottingham: Inter-Varsity, 2010), 233–50.

Jews who are already thoroughly familiar with these scriptures, much of which they would know by heart. So presumably a further part of the logic of Jesus's exposition is that the disciples need to be able to read these scriptures in a new way, in the light of all that has happened to Jesus, so that they can see in these scriptures what they have not seen before. Jesus helps makes sense of Israel's scriptures. Thus a dialectic between Jesus and Israel's scriptures is envisaged, both being necessary for Christian understanding of the crucified and risen Lord.

On the basis of this, and much other comparable material elsewhere in the New Testament, it has been historic Christian practice to read Israel's scriptures as witnessing to Jesus as the Christ. The book of Isaiah in particular has been seen to play a central role in this witness. What should one make of this today?

The discussion will be in two parts. The first part will consider some of the in-principle issues related to the reading of the Hebrew prophet Isaiah as Christian Scripture. The second part will offer a selective reading of the book of Isaiah in terms of one particular motif within it and the way in which this can be seen to relate to belief in Jesus as the one who "does not abolish but fulfills" the Old Testament.

On Christian Approaches to the Book of Isaiah

Characteristic Emphases in Modern Scholarly Approaches to Prophecy

For much of the history of the church, there have been straightforward appeals to Isaiah as envisaging—that is, predicting—key facets of the incarnation: the life, death, and resurrection of Jesus as the definitive self-revelation of God, and also the role of the church as the place where the gentiles receive God's truth.[1] The distinctive significance of Isaiah in this regard has been encapsulated in the labeling of this prophetic book as a "Fifth Gospel." This originates with Jerome in late antiquity, when he influentially wrote as follows in the prologue to his Latin translation of Isaiah, a prologue that was included in the Vulgate:

> He should be called an evangelist rather than a prophet because he describes all the mysteries of Christ and the Church so clearly that you would not think

1. In this chapter I tend to use a broad brush in somewhat impressionistic mode. I am conscious of giving little space to the specifics of Christian interpretation of Isaiah down the ages. A useful introduction is Brevard S. Childs, *The Struggle to Understand Isaiah as Christian Scripture* (Grand Rapids: Eerdmans, 2004).

he is prophesying [*vaticinari*] about what is to come, but rather composing a history of what has already happened.[2]

On any reckoning the resonances between what is said of the servant of YHWH in Isaiah 52:13–53:12 and the way Jesus is portrayed in the Gospels are striking. It is unsurprising that the Christian vision of Jesus (imaginative, devotional, doctrinal) has often been significantly informed by Isaianic language and imagery.

Modern biblical scholarship has transformed the traditional Christian understanding of the book of Isaiah as envisaging Jesus. Probably the main reason for this has been a clearer grasp of the Old Testament's own primary conception of the role of the prophet and the function of prophecy, together with a concern to read the biblical text in relation to the conventions and concerns of its context of origin. For example, the paradigmatic account of prophetic speech in Jeremiah 18:7–10 shows prophetic speech to be a moral and spiritual challenge that seeks response.[3] The prophet addresses people in such a way that they should seriously engage with God—either break with wrongdoing and turn to God, or not presume upon God and remain in active trust and obedience. Correspondingly, the future is seen to be contingent in relation to the response given: God can take into account people's responsiveness and not carry out the prophet's warning or promise if circumstances have changed. Prophetic speech is predictive, but it is predictive in relation to the near future, to the circumstances that impinge on the lives of the prophet's contemporaries. On such an understanding, the notion that Isaiah should be predicting events to do with Jesus, events that lie centuries in the future, becomes difficult—not that it is inconceivable, but that it is out of place. A future that is contingent in relation to response to the prophetic message is not a future that is sure to be realized regardless of contemporary response.

Although response-seeking prophecy is the predominant mode of prophecy in the Old Testament, prophecy is also found in other modes. On the one hand, in the historical books (mainly Kings) there are some portrayals of prophetic predictions, where fulfillment in the terms specified in the prophecy is of the essence. For example, Ahijah the Shilonite tells Jeroboam that Solomon's kingdom will be divided, and when this happens in the time of Rehoboam, because of Rehoboam's foolishness, this is said to be so that YHWH might fulfill His word spoken through Ahijah (1 Kings 11:29–40;

---

2. *Biblia Sacra iuxta vulgatam versionem*, 2nd ed. (Stuttgart: Deutsche Bibelgesellschaft, 1983), 2:1096.

3. See the discussion in chap. 4 above.

12:15). The fulfillment of the divine word within the course of human history is an important motif.[4]

On the other hand, there is apocalyptic literature, which appears to be continuous with classical prophecy yet to be a particular outgrowth of it. One of the ways in which apocalyptic literature is most often distinguished from prophecy is in the more fixed and less contingent vision of the future that it envisages. Within apocalyptic literature there are sometimes distinctive portrayals of the future, whose purpose appears to be to show how a particular momentous situation, that of which the prediction speaks, fits within a larger providential scheme of God's dealings with His people. The key point is that the life-context of the apocalyptic writer is apparently the time and context of the momentous situation envisaged in the prediction and not the situation some time in the past (from the writer's perspective) in which the making of the prediction is set. In other words, the prediction looks to be a literary trope, an imaginative means of depicting divine sovereignty.

Within the historical books, the most striking prophetic prediction is that of the man of God from Judah who comes to Jeroboam at Bethel and addresses a message to the altar at Bethel: "O altar, altar, thus says the Lord: 'A son shall be born to the house of David, Josiah by name; and he shall sacrifice upon you the priests of the high places who offer incense on you, and human bones shall be burned on you'" (1 Kings 13:2). The man of God's words clearly envisage Josiah's reform in 2 Kings 23, a significant part of the account of which is devoted to Josiah's doings at Bethel, with specific reference to the man of God and his words (23:15–20, esp. 16–18). The time from Jeroboam (probably late tenth century) to Josiah (second half of seventh century) is the best part of three hundred years. However, the prediction should not be interpreted apart from an interpretation of the whole narrative of the two prophets in 1 Kings 13. This is one of the strangest narratives in the whole Old Testament. The most illuminating proposal for understanding it comes from Karl Barth, who suggests that the two prophets are symbols of the northern and southern kingdoms; the account of their interaction is a symbolic summary of the history of the divided kingdoms, at whose outset it stands.[5] Part of the significance of Josiah's reform is that it symbolically reunites the two kingdoms under the divinely chosen leadership of the house of David in Jerusalem. The overall account of the two divided kingdoms is framed by the perspective of Josiah's symbolic reuniting of them; the beginning is told in the light of the end.[6] This does not mean that one should

---

4. Still valuable on this is Gerhard von Rad, "The Deuteronomistic Theology of History in the Book of Kings," in his *Studies in Deuteronomy*, trans. David Stalker from German, SBT 9 (1948; ET, London: SCM, 1953), 74–91, esp. the list of prophecies and fulfillments on 78–81. Von Rad outlines a "theology of the word finding certain fulfillment in history" (83).

5. See Karl Barth, *CD* II/2:393–409; also David Bosworth, "Revisiting Karl Barth's Exegesis of 1 Kings 13," *BibInt* 10/4 (2002): 360–83.

6. Although it is difficult to have much confidence in any specific proposals about the composition of the DH, the particular focus on Josiah's reform seems to me a good reason for entertaining some form of the thesis that a significant edition of the DH should be located then, in the late monarchic period. Still valuable is Frank Moore Cross, "The Themes of the Book of Kings and the Structure of the Deuteronomistic History," in his *Canaanite Myth and Hebrew Epic: Essays in the History of the Religion of Israel* (Cambridge, MA: Harvard University Press, 1973), 274–89.

not take with full imaginative seriousness the scenario in 1 Kings 13 and the man of God's prediction. However, the world within the text should be distinguished from the world behind the text.

Within biblical apocalyptic literature, the most striking prediction is that of the angelic figure who recounts to Daniel in great detail the conflicts of the king of the north and the king of the south (Syrians and Egyptians respectively) that leads up to a devastating assault on the temple and the faithful by a king of unparalleled arrogance and self-aggrandizement (Dan. 11:2–12:4, esp. 11:2–39)—the assault on Jews by Antiochus Epiphanes between 168 and 165 BC. From the context in which the figure of Daniel is set (mid-sixth century) to the time of Antiochus Epiphanes is the best part of four hundred years. The text, however, comes from the time of crisis to which the words of the angelic figure point; it frames the crisis within divine providence and the exemplary witness of Daniel's faithfulness.[7] Again, the world within the text, the message given to Daniel in Babylon about how the faithful are to stand firm, needs to be distinguished from the world behind the text, the conflicts of the second century BC in and around Jerusalem, although the former was meant to be brought to bear upon the latter as resistance literature.

The Challenge of Understanding the Book of Isaiah

The general content of the book of Isaiah displays the characteristics of classical prophecy. However, the case for reading Isaiah as other than long-term prediction comes not just from a better appreciation of the nature and purpose of prophecy as seeking response. It also comes from a consideration of the form and content of the book itself. A paradigmatic instance of the problem can be seen in late antiquity, in the late fourth century, when Ambrose, bishop of Milan, directed the new convert Augustine, who was preparing to be baptized, to read Isaiah.[8] Ambrose apparently did not specify precisely why Augustine should read Isaiah or what he would find there, but Augustine presumed that it was because of the book's heralding of the gospel and the call of the gentiles. Augustine obediently began Isaiah at the beginning—and failed to understand what he was reading. Since he supposed the rest of the book would be comparable, he laid it aside. Although this was with the intention of resuming his reading later, when better fitted for it, in the event he never really did so. It was the Psalms that became the prime place in the Old Testament where Augustine encountered Christ, and it was the Psalms, not Isaiah, that he expounded at length and in depth. Ambrose's expectation that Isaiah could be picked up and read by an intelligent catechumen (indeed, Augustine possessed one of the finest minds in the history of the Christian church) in such a way that Christ would be encountered there came to grief on the simple

---

7. For an understanding of why the content of Dan. 11 and the whole book of Daniel should be situated in the 160s BC, one can still profitably turn to the arguments of Samuel Rolles Driver, either in his commentary, *The Book of Daniel*, CBSC (Cambridge: Cambridge University Press, 1905), esp. xlvii–lxxvi; or in his *An Introduction to the Literature of the Old Testament*, 6th ed., ITL (Edinburgh: T&T Clark, 1897), esp. 497–513.

8. The story is recounted by Augustine of Hippo, in his *Confessions* 9.5.

fact that this is not an obvious or straightforward reading of the text—even for someone predisposed, indeed positively expectant, to find Christ there, for whom prophetic prediction was not a problem, and for whom metaphorical and figural readings, of one kind or other, were taken for granted.

It is unsurprising that Augustine should have found his task so difficult. On any reckoning the early chapters of Isaiah are not an easy read. The organizing principle and purpose of the text is far from self-evident, and its referent is likewise sometimes unclear.

The general concern of the early chapters of Isaiah appears to be the problematic conduct and disposition of the people of Jerusalem, and also its king, and the bearing of this upon the fate of the city in times of enemy aggression. The general historical context envisaged is clearly the time of the Assyrian Empire in the eighth century, which is also the time of the kings mentioned in the heading in 1:1. Assyria is specifically named in 7:17, 18, 20; 8:4, 7; 10:5, 12, 24 and other subsequent passages; though for some reason it is not mentioned in the opening chapter in which Jerusalem's devastation at enemy hands is depicted (1:5–8). This is juxtaposed, however, with language about divine initiative and transformative power, together with images of a glorious Jerusalem in an unspecified future (2:2–4; 4:2–6). In terms of an ancient prophetic concern for YHWH's dealings with Jerusalem and its people, it is possible to make some sense of the text; but it remains unstraightforward.

For example, the vividly sketched context for Isaiah's meeting with Ahaz, and Isaiah's challenge to Ahaz genuinely to have faith in YHWH in time of trouble (in the context of a combined attack by Aram and the northern kingdom of Israel on Jerusalem [7:1–9]) leads into a famous though contextually somewhat puzzling sign of the child Immanuel (7:10–17). This in turn leads into a series of visions of what YHWH will do and how things will be "on that day" (7:18–25) and a series of divine messages to the text's narrating voice, which is presumably (the text does not specify) that of Isaiah himself (8:1, 5, 11).[9] The initial setting fades from view: what follows lacks any clear setting, and the train of thought becomes increasingly difficult to follow.[10]

The advent of a better-developed historical knowledge than was generally available to those living in late antiquity gives readers today a huge potential advantage over Augustine. However difficult the text of Isaiah is, some knowledge of the peoples and events of the eighth century BC helps toward

9. Another difficulty is that the narrating voice in Isa. 8 is in the first person, but in chap. 7 the narrator speaks of Isaiah in the third person.

10. Interestingly, the famous narrative of Nicodemus's visit to Jesus by night poses comparable problems: the context of the conversation recedes into the background, and the flow of thought and identity of the speaking voice become harder to discern (John 3:1–21).

making sense of what is read. Problems of course remain. Indeed, if the predominant scholarly view is correct, that the formation of the text took place over centuries and so incorporates historical perspectives other than those of the eighth century, this may further help explain why making sense of the text is not straightforward.

Within the early chapters of Isaiah come some of the most famous passages with traditional christological resonance—the Immanuel prophecy (7:14) and the glowing accounts of the difference that a faithful Davidic king can make (9:2–7 [1–6 MT]; 11:1–9). These passages are still used in liturgical contexts by Christians during Advent, where the clear implication is that Jesus is the one who fulfills that of which the text speaks. The first passage has a narrative setting: Isaiah's encounter with Ahaz. Isaiah's challenge to Ahaz to take YHWH seriously and not just mouth right-sounding but actually evasive pieties (7:10–13) shows clearly that here we have prophecy in response-seeking mode, such that what is then said about Immanuel will happen in the near future (the birth of Hezekiah?) and is related to the response that Isaiah seeks to induce in Ahaz (7:14–17). Within the world of the text, the Jesus of the Gospels is not envisaged. Jews who have resisted Christian claims about Jesus have not infrequently pointed this out down through the ages, although Christian scholars generally didn't concede the point until the coming of better historical understanding of the ancient Hebrew text and of the world depicted in the text.

Should Christians therefore simply abandon relating the words of Isaiah to the person of Jesus? Does Christian liturgical use of Isaiah deserve to be taken with intellectual seriousness?

The Issue of Long-Term Prophecy

Although mainstream scholars generally give little space any longer to the issue of the depiction of a distant future in certain prophetic texts as genuinely predictive, it perhaps still deserves some attention. In today's world confident academic assumptions about "what all educated people must think or know or consider feasible" may not always fare well out on the streets. The case for not finding long-range prediction to be a significant biblical understanding of prophecy needs to be freshly made in relation to the unpersuaded or those who might see no in-principle objection ("Why not?").

A Conservative Evangelical Approach

For example, there is a persistent presence of evangelical Christian scholars who consider that the denial of long-range prophecy represents a loss of theological nerve and vision because of undue concession to rationalism and positivism. This is not an easy position to respond to, if only because its anxieties may occasionally be justified. The basic concern is well known with relation to the issue of whether or not a single eighth-century prophet, Isaiah, was responsible for the whole book that bears his name, as in the commentaries of John Oswalt and Alec Motyer.[11] As Motyer puts it: "The challenge to unity of authorship began over the issue of predictive prophecy. The rationalistic climate of the last century in which the ground rules of Isaiah-study were laid forbade anything so 'miraculous' as foretelling the future[,] and the prophets became highly sophisticated commentators speaking out of and into their own times."[12] Or as Oswalt puts it: "Surely if there is such a deity, and if he is able to make special knowledge about himself available to his messengers, it is no great feat to make special knowledge about the future available to these messengers."[13] Comparably, Walter Kaiser Jr. says: "As soon as the case for supernaturalism is accepted, the claim that God can announce beforehand what he intends to do in the future is, for all intents and purposes, secured."[14] To some extent this position has developed in reaction to the scornful dismissiveness that not infrequently characterized the deist critique of apologetic arguments from the fulfillment of prophecy in the seventeenth and eighteenth centuries.[15] However, it also has roots within ancient Christian tradition. As we will see in a study of Psalm 44,[16] the Antiochene fathers had no difficulty in understanding the psalm as depicting the Maccabean persecution of the Jews from the perspective of a prediction by David (some eight centuries before the events). As John Chrysostom puts it: "The inspired author . . . recites this psalm . . . not in his own person but in the person of the Maccabees, describing and foretelling what would happen at that time. The inspired authors are like that, you see: they span all times, the past, the present, the future."[17] Chrysostom's confidence in the difference that God can make through inspiration is full and unbounded. Since some such perspective can come readily to some of those who encounter God as a living reality, it needs to be taken seriously.

My present purpose is not to diminish confidence in God, nor to prescribe what gifts God should and should not give to people. Rather my concern is that the form taken by claims about God and inspiration be properly *tested* through facing possibly hard, yet nonetheless responsible, questions—lest words such as those of Chrysostom, however well-intentioned, be deemed glib and fanciful, rather than well founded. Some of the core issues are theological and philosophical, revolving around the perennial issue of understanding the relationship between nature and grace. Kaiser's easy reference to "the case for supernaturalism" hardly does justice to the major conceptual debates in modern times about "supernatural" in relation to "natural," which have sought to clarify the internal logic of Christian faith and its relationship to the world as known by the natural and social sciences.[18] In my judgment, however, disagreements about predictive prophecy often have

11. John N. Oswalt, *The Book of Isaiah, Chapters 1–39*, NICOT (Grand Rapids: Eerdmans, 1986); J. Alec Motyer, *The Prophecy of Isaiah* (Leicester: Inter-Varsity, 1993).

12. J. Alec Motyer, "Three in One or One in Three: A Dipstick into the Isaianic Literature," *Churchman* 108/1 (1994): 22–36, esp. 32.

13. Oswalt, *Isaiah*, 47.

14. Walter C. Kaiser Jr., *The Messiah in the Old Testament*, SOTBT (Grand Rapids: Zondervan, 1995), 235. He says elsewhere, "Care must be exercised . . . lest a brand of theological positivism be allowed to spring up which would dictate what could or did happen in the progress of revelation. God remained sovereign Lord even in this realm" (*Toward an Old Testament Theology* [Grand Rapids: Zondervan, 1991], 9).

15. For a general account of biblical and theological debates in the early modern period, see Henning Graf Reventlow, *The Authority of the Bible and the Rise of the Modern World*, trans. John Bowden from German (London: SCM, 1984).

16. See chap. 7 below.

17. John Chrysostom, *St. John Chrysostom Commentary on the Psalms*, trans. Robert Charles Hill (Brookline, MA: Holy Cross Orthodox Press, 1998), 1:231.

18. The debate has been conducted predominantly among Roman Catholic theologians. Landmark works include Henri de Lubac, *The Mystery of the Supernatural: Milestones in*

to do with the relationship between literature and reality within a biblical frame of reference. In literature generally, the relationship between text and reality varies greatly according to the many genres and conventions of literature. Questions along the lines of "Which literary conventions are apparently being utilized in the biblical text, and how do they relate to literary conventions in other literature of the ancient world and also of other times?" tend to be given little, if any, space in evangelical accounts of predictive prophecy.[19] Yet they are no less important for coming to a good understanding of the biblical text.

Prediction in the Bible Code?

A different kind of affirmation of long-range biblical prophecy arises in the work of journalist Michael Drosnin, whose *Bible Code*, in successive installments, has enjoyed considerable sales and publicity.[20] Occasionally in the past, rabbinic biblical interpreters have made passing observations about certain important words being apparently, as it were, encoded in the biblical text—for example, the foundational term *tōrāh* can be found at the beginning of both Genesis and Exodus if you take the first appearance of *taw* (at the end of *bĕrē'shīt* in Gen. 1:1 and *vĕ'ēlleh shĕmōt* in Exod. 1:1) and then count to every fiftieth letter. This approach has been developed by Eliyahu Rips, a professor of mathematics at the Hebrew University of Jerusalem, who processed the lettering of the whole Hebrew Bible in a computer, then read via a "skip code," or equidistant letter sequence, whereby one skips an unspecified but fixed number of letters and then discovers significant names and phrases formed with these letters (i.e., the method by which the word *tōrāh* is discovered is systematized and computerized). The result, as Drosnin puts it, is this: "A world-famous Israeli mathematician has discovered a code in the Bible that predicts events that happened thousands of years after the Bible was written."[21] Drosnin promotes this discovery in attention-seeking prose in which most individual sentences represent discrete paragraphs.

Drosnin's initial parade example was the assassination of Yitzhak Rabin in 1995. Drosnin wrote an advance warning to Rabin in 1994, to the effect that his name was encoded in the Bible together with the words "assassin that will assassinate" across his name. However, his wider claims are remarkable. Initially he declared, "In addition to the Sadat and Kennedy assassinations, hundreds of other world-shaking events are also encoded in the Bible—everything from World War II to Watergate, from the Holocaust to Hiroshima, from the Moon landing to the collision of a comet with Jupiter."[22] In May 2008, six months before the US presidential election, Drosnin, basing

---

Catholic Theology (New York: Crossroad, 1998); Michael J. Buckley, *At the Origins of Modern Atheism* (New Haven and London: Yale University Press, 1987). An excellent way into the issues is via Nicholas Lash, *The Beginning and the End of "Religion"* (Cambridge: Cambridge University Press, 1996), chap. 9.

19. So, for instance, Alec Motyer handles the man of Judah's prophecy about Josiah in 1 Kings 13 in these terms: "We may, of course, choose at the end to disbelieve what [the OT] attests, but, as with all source documents, we are not at liberty to alter, or diminish the extent of, its claims. Within these claims there is the evidence of 1 Kings 13:2; 2 Kings 23:17, the prediction of the name of Josiah. If prediction is allowed as a feature of the prophet's work, who are we to set limits to its exercise?" ("Dipstick," 34). Apparently it is solely a matter of believing, or not believing, predictive claims. Questions about the possible date, context, and purpose of the texts in Kings, and the literary conventions that they may be utilizing, are nowhere in view. In other words, distinctions between the worlds within, behind, and in front of the text are prematurely collapsed.

20. Three such books of his have appeared to date: Michael Drosnin, *The Bible Code* (London: Weidenfeld & Nicholson; New York: Simon & Schuster, 1997); *The Bible Code 2: The Countdown* (London: Weidenfeld & Nicholson; New York: Simon & Schuster, 2002); *The Bible Code: Saving the World* (London: Weidenfeld & Nicholson; New York: Simon & Schuster, 2010).

21. Drosnin, *Saving*, 1.

22. Drosnin, *Code*, 14.

himself on the code, wrote to Barack Obama, telling him that he would win the Democratic nomination and become president. Moreover, "Every detail of September 11, 2001, was encoded in the ancient text. The rise of Osama Bin Laden, the fall of Saddam Hussein, both Gulf Wars, were all in the code."[23] Alongside such detailed predictions of the affairs of the twentieth and twenty-first centuries, the traditional Christian concern in some way to find Jesus Christ in the Old Testament seems rather trivial by comparison!

Interestingly, Drosnin time and again emphasizes that (unlike Rips) he is not religious but rather secular, so he has no concern with God. However, he thinks that the predictions in the code are contingent, and thus are often warnings of events that can be averted through appropriate action. Although he regards the code as "a miracle proven real by modern science," he also regards it as "a phenomenon we do not yet fully understand"[24]—though in his second book he toys with the idea that some alien "must have" brought the Bible code to earth, most likely the same alien that, according to a notorious speculation by Nobel Laureate Francis Crick, must be responsible for the presence of DNA on earth.[25]

Drosnin is not deranged. His books are published by reputable UK and US publishing houses, and he has access to significant political, military intelligence, and media figures in both the US and Israel. Even if most scholars ignore him, numerous other people apparently do not. My concern here is that it is not self-evident to many in contemporary Western culture that Drosnin's work is utter delusion, still less why it is utter delusion. Of course, it would be unwise to isolate Drosnin from other contemporary phenomena, such as the astonishing popularity and social acceptability of astrology, fascination with Nostradamus, or the interest in conspiracy theories, not least those involving the Bible and the church.[26]

One of the most telling aspects of Drosnin's contentions is that he thinks the Bible code has to be developed and defended entirely in *scientific* terms, because the Bible "is not only a book—it is also a computer program . . . [that] now . . . can be read as it was always intended to be read."[27] His second book offers an appendix in which he responds to critics, in the course of which he solely considers arguments about statistics. The concerns that any education in the *humanities* should bring to bear bother him not at all: the sheer arbitrariness of skip codes (whatever the appeals to the mathematical odds being against certain combinations of letters appearing purely by chance); the criteria by which different rows of letters are aligned in Drosnin's charts, given that word combinations can be found on vertical and diagonal, as well as horizontal, axes; the problems posed by textual variants in antiquity prior to the stabilization of the Masoretic Text; the nature of the language of the code, which appears to combine both biblical and modern Hebrew in an arbitrary way; interpretive difficulties, given the absence of vowels and the varying ways in which certain consonantal combinations can be read; the code's use of a traditional Jewish *anno mundi* chronological system, which was first developed by the rabbis in late antiquity and codified by Maimonides in the Middle Ages; the uncanny predominance of messages of potential interest to modern Americans and Israelis; the importance of testing claims of such enormity by conducting extensive parallel experiments on other substantial textual corpora from antiquity; in short, the basic need to be properly rigorous and self-critical. Drosnin apparently neither knows nor cares about modern scholarly discussions of language, history, and prophecy in the Bible, including the likely formation of the biblical books over time. In essence, it all comes down to the plausibility

23. Drosnin, *Saving*, 1–2.
24. Ibid., xii.
25. Drosnin, *Code* 2, 144–45, 155.
26. Probably the best-known recent example is Dan Brown's ingenious and engaging fictional fantasy, *The Da Vinci Code* (New York: Doubleday, 2003); yet I suspect that a significant part of its success is due to the cultural attractiveness of one of its central concerns, that religious devotion and expectation is most truly directed not to God but to sex.
27. Drosnin, *Code*, 25.

of his basic contention: the Bible "is not only a book—it is also a computer program" that was produced some three thousand years ago by we know not whom, which predicts countless events thousands of years subsequent to its own production, but which "had a time-lock" so that "it could not be opened until the computer was invented."[28]

Rather like astrology, a proposal such as the Bible Code is remarkably difficult to dispose of: what counts as refutation, and how can people recognize it? The underlying assumptions and attitudes appear to be a remarkably resilient pathology of the human mind, which readily looks for patterns of intelligibility and meaning and grounds for hope in self-deceiving ways, a pathology that apparently flourishes in the deracinated social milieus of urban and technological civilization. Until quite recently one would not have expected or needed to defend the proposition that the Hebrew Bible is a book, or rather a collection of books, and not a computer program. The context of biblical interpretation is changing.

Context, Recontextualization, and Canon

One of the first rules that students are customarily taught in biblical study is the importance of interpreting a text "in context." As already noted in relation to the interpretation of the Shema,[29] however, this rule is of limited value unless one also addresses the questions of "Which context?" and/or "Whose context?" The meaning of "interpret in context" was considered to be self-evident as long as the implicit assumption was that "context" meant "context of origin" (whatever the problems in determining what that might be) and/or "immediate literary context." Yet as soon as one takes seriously the phenomenon of the literary preservation of prophetic documents and their continuing use in contexts other than that of origin, the question "In relation to which context should one interpret the text?" becomes unstraightforward. This process of preservation and re-use is epitomized in the scriptural/canonical status that the prophetic documents have received, whereby in some sense they become authoritative and normative for fresh generations, who can never inhabit the context of the documents' origin other than (perhaps) in imagination. This is further complexified when the canon of Israel's scriptures is itself recontextualized in distinct Jewish and Christian frames of reference, where readings and appropriations are made that differ in core assumptions.

The Approaches of Levenson and Childs

A significant contribution to thinking through the implications of this phenomenon can be found in the work of Jon Levenson, who reflects substantively on the significance of differing contexts for interpretation and who within

28. Drosnin, *Saving*, 9.
29. See chap. 1 above.

a Jewish frame of reference articulates concerns that apply also in a Christian frame of reference.[30] Levenson has no doubts as to the value of rigorous historical work; yet context of origin is not the only context. There is also a context constituted by the formation of the literature into a larger whole, a context that is literary and/or canonical: "The problem is that by making *historical* context sovereign and regulative, historical criticism destroys the *literary* context that is the Bible (either Jewish or Christian) as a whole and often even the smaller literary context that is the book, the chapter, or whatever."[31] Levenson recasts a familiar preoccupation of biblical scholars, concerning the difference between what the text meant in its ancient context and how it is to be understood now, into the issue of differing contextualizations of the biblical text. This leads to a restatement of the classic understanding that scripture has more than one sense:

> Just as in medieval Europe there could be interreligious agreement on the *sensus literalis*, so in modern biblical criticism there will continue to be a broad base for agreement on the meaning of textual units in their most limited literary or historical settings. But when we come to "the final literary setting" and even more so to "the context of the canon," we [Jews and Christians] must part company, for *there is no non-particularistic access to these larger contexts*, and no decision on these issues, even when made for secular purposes, can be neutral between Judaism and Christianity. Jews and Christians can, of course, study each other's Bible and even identify analogically or empathetically with the interpretations that the other's traditional context warrants, growing in discernment and self-understanding as a consequence. For the normative theological task, however, a choice must be made: Does the canonical context of the Abraham story, for example, include the Abraham material in Galatians and Romans or not? For Christians it must; for Jews it must not.[32]

Or, in a related formulation:

> In the realm of historical criticism, pleas for a "Jewish biblical scholarship" or a "Christian biblical scholarship" are senseless and reactionary. Practicing Jews and Christians will differ from uncompromising historicists, however, in affirming the meaningfulness and interpretive relevance of larger contexts that

30. Although all the essays in Jon Levenson's groundbreaking *The Hebrew Bible, the Old Testament, and Historical Criticism: Jews and Christians in Biblical Studies* (Louisville: Westminster John Knox, 1993) are important, for present purposes there is particular significance in "The Eighth Principle of Judaism and the Literary Simultaneity of Scripture" (62–81) and "Theological Consensus or Historicist Evasion? Jews and Christians in Biblical Studies" (82–105).

31. Ibid., "Theological Consensus," 100.

32. Ibid., "Eighth Principle," 80–81.

homogenize the literatures of different periods to one degree or another. Just as text has more than one context, and biblical studies more than one method, so scripture has more than one sense, as the medievals knew and Tyndale, Spinoza, Jowett, and most other moderns have forgotten.[33]

In various places Levenson acknowledges the pioneering work of Brevard Childs, whose work on a "canonical approach" to the Christian Bible has made a wide-ranging case for reconceptualizing the task of biblical interpretation. Although "recontextualization" is not Childs's own preferred term, he too is clear that taking seriously the plurality of contexts within which biblical texts are read is a way of retrieving, via significant reconceptualizing, the kind of approach that is needed to do justice to the continuing scriptural function of the ancient texts:

> I would defend the necessity of a multiple level reading of Scripture according to differing contexts. This approach does not suggest a return to the traditional four-fold interpretive scheme of the Middle Ages which proved to be deeply flawed. Not only were the levels of the texts conceived of in a static and arbitrary manner which resulted in the fragmenting of its [sic] unity, but the integral contact of text and subject matter was seriously blurred through clever interpretive techniques. Rather I am suggesting a single method of interpretation which takes seriously both the different dimensions constituting the text as well as distinct contexts in which the text functions.[34]

Moreover, Childs explicitly relates the issue of plural contexts to the issue of reading Isaiah in relation to Jesus:

> How can one claim to read Isaiah as the voice of Israel in the Hebrew Scripture and at the same time speak of its witness to Jesus Christ? It is not only possible, but actually mandatory for any serious Christian theological reflection. Because Scripture performs different functions according to distinct contexts, a multi-level reading is required even to begin to grapple with the full range of Scripture's role as the intentional medium of continuing divine revelation.[35]

In general terms, my proposal is that the phenomenon of recontextualization in a plurality of literary and canonical contexts offers a fruitful alternative to

33. Ibid., "Theological Consensus," 104.

34. Brevard S. Childs, "Does the Old Testament Witness to Jesus Christ?" in *Evangelium, Schriftauslegung, Kirche: Festschrift für Peter Stuhlmacher zum 65. Geburtstag*, ed. J. Ådna et al. (Göttingen: Vandenhoeck & Ruprecht, 1997), 57–64, esp. 61.

35. Childs, "Witness," 63. Whether "multi-level" is the best term for articulating the way in which the meaning of biblical texts can vary according to context need not be discussed here.

using the traditional theological notion of "fuller meaning" (*sensus plenior*) within the biblical text.[36] For the basic issue—that some texts depict significant content with terminology having a semantic potential that can be realized in more than one way, according to interpretive purpose and context—in principle characterizes all texts that come to be recognized as classics and are read and appropriated in a wide variety of contexts. This is not to deny that there may be distinctive features within Christian appropriation of the Old Testament that do not characterize the appropriation of classics generally. The point is that to claim that the meaning of Israel's scriptures may vary according to context is not a matter of special pleading by the Christian theologian, but a recognition of certain facets of the nature of texts as texts. Of course, much depends on how the principle is implemented in practice.

Some Literary Analogies

A general point about the significance of recontextualization is nicely brought out by the literary critic F. R. Leavis in the course of his commenting on the impact of Jane Austen within what Leavis called the "great tradition" in English literature:

> She not only makes tradition for those coming after, but her achievement has for us a retroactive effect: as we look back beyond her we see in what goes before, and see because of her, potentialities and significances brought out in such a way that, for us, she creates the tradition we see leading down to her. Her work, like the work of all great creative writers, gives a meaning to the past.[37]

English literature of the eighteenth century reads differently in the light of that to which it gave rise, which recontextualizes it. A mature distillate and enhancement of a literary tradition constitutes a privileged vantage point for the deeper comprehension of that tradition. If Jane Austen can give meaning to the English literature of the eighteenth century that nourished and helped form her, it may not be unreasonable to propose that Jesus Christ can give meaning to the scriptures of Israel that nourished and helped form him.

36. I do not wish to deny that *sensus plenior* may still be a useful theological notion. However, I prefer to examine the social and epistemological dynamics of privileging certain texts so that they become "canonical": such an approach can help one rethink time-honored issues conventionally discussed under the heading of "biblical authority." Likewise I hope the present discussion offers a fresh way of rethinking issues dealing with the depth and breadth of scriptural meaning.

37. Frank Raymond Leavis, *The Great Tradition* (1948; repr., Harmondsworth: Penguin/Pelican, 1972), 14.

Alternatively, a contemporary frame of reference can make a difference to how Jane Austen's writings are read. As Peter J. Leithart puts it, in relation to the principle that "the original text and its meaning change with time, and our understanding of it must change accordingly":

> Pride and Prejudice has a different cultural meaning in an age of casual dating, living together, hooking up, shacking up, getting down, premarital sex, and feminism than it did when Austen wrote it, or during the Victorian era. For some, the changed circumstances lend Pride and Prejudice a halo of nostalgia that it certainly did not have for Austen: "Oh, for the simple clarities of gentry life" is a twenty-first-century sentiment not shared by the author. For others today, Pride and Prejudice is a stumbling block, a symbol of the oppression and repression from which, in the course of human events, we have happily been liberated. For still others, Pride and Prejudice, authored after all by a sheltered female, is part of that liberation, however much Austen might have played the Straussian and dressed her own feminist agenda in the patriarchal garb of her day. While we can establish more or less the cultural significance of Austen's novel to her and her original readers, that is certainly not what it means for us. The intervening history has given the novel a different meaning.[38]

How best might recontextualization specifically within the Christian Bible be understood? One suggestive approach is that of Reformation historian David Steinmetz, who proposes an analogy with detective stories.[39] Characteristically in detective stories there is a "first narrative": the sequential unfolding of the story, which contains, among other things, clues, intelligent guesses, false leads, and puzzlement. However, there is also a "second narrative, one that is invariably recited by the principal investigator in the last or nearly last chapter":

> This narrative is crisp and clear and explains in considerable detail what was really occurring while the larger narrative was unfolding. The cogency of this narrative is not in the least undermined by the fact that none of the characters except the perpetrator of the crime and, until the very end of the story, the principal investigator himself or herself had any clear notion what the story was really about. . . .
>
> It is important to understand that this second narrative is not a subplot, even though it is short. It is the disclosure of the architectonic structure of the

---

38. Peter J. Leithart, *Deep Exegesis: The Mystery of Reading Scripture* (Waco: Baylor University Press, 2009), 67.

39. David Steinmetz, "Uncovering a Second Narrative: Detective Fiction and the Construction of Historical Method," in *The Art of Reading Scripture*, ed. Ellen F. Davis and Richard B. Hays (Grand Rapids: Eerdmans, 2003), 54–65.

whole story. Therefore, the second narrative quickly overpowers the first in the mind of the reader, who can no longer read the story as though ignorant of its plot and form. The second narrative is identical in substance to the first and therefore replaces it, not as an extraneous addition superimposed on the story or read back into it, but as a compelling and persuasive disclosure of what the story was about all along.[40]

The analogy is straightforward:

> Traditional Christian exegesis reads the Bible very much in this way—not exactly in this way, of course, but close enough to provide useful points of comparison. Early Christians believed that what had occurred in the life, death, and resurrection of Jesus Christ was of such importance that it had transformed the entire story of Israel and, through Israel, of the world. The long, ramshackle narrative of Israel with its promising starts and unexpected twists, with its ecstasies and betrayals, its laws, its learning, its wisdom, its martyred prophets—this long narrative is retold and reevaluated in the light of what early Christians regarded as the concluding chapter [that] God had written in Jesus Christ.[41]

Steinmetz's proposal is that this analogy can help Christians recover a way of reading and understanding the Bible that has been marginalized under the impact of historical criticism's concern to understand texts in their contexts of origin. After relating the notion of a second narrative to the patristic conception of a rule of faith, developing a further analogy between the construction of a second narrative and the work of a historian, and considering various difficulties and objections, Steinmetz concludes:

> I am inclined to think that biblical scholars who are also Christian theologians should worry less about anachronism and more about the quality of the second narratives they have constructed. I can well understand why biblical scholars are wary of a traditional exegesis that ascribes to characters in the Bible, especially characters in the Old Testament, an explicit knowledge of the finer points of Christian theology. Such explicit knowledge would have been impossible for them at the time. But I do not have to believe that Second Isaiah had an explicit knowledge of the crucifixion of Jesus of Nazareth to believe that he was part of a larger narrative that finds its final, though not its sole, meaning in Christ. Like many of the characters in a mystery novel, Isaiah had something else on his mind. But the meaning of his work cannot be limited to the narrow boundaries of his explicit intention. Viewed from the perspective of the way things turned out, his oracles were revealed to have added dimensions of significance that no

40. Ibid., 55.
41. Ibid., 56.

one could have guessed at the time. It is not anachronistic to believe such added dimensions of meaning exist. It is only good exegesis.[42]

The Analogy between Interpreting the Bible and Interpreting the American Constitution

Alternatively, another analogy that can be helpful for understanding the general implications of recontextualization within the context of ecclesial reception is the analogy between interpretation of the Bible and interpretation of the American Constitution.[43] The heart of the analogy is that in each case there is a text whose enduring significance is inseparable from its relation to a continuing community of people (though, of course, the Bible, unlike the Constitution, cannot be amended). Both the Bible and the American Constitution can legitimately and valuably be studied in relation to their meaning in their originating contexts. Yet what makes both important, and generates most of the study that is given to them, is the fact that they continue to matter for how people are to live their lives in settings and circumstances that may differ more or less from those originating contexts. It is the contemporary context of reception that poses the question of how best to understand and appropriate the foundational text.

This generates a never-to-be-finally-resolved dialectic. On the one hand, the intrinsic meaning of the authoritative document matters; the community is bound to, and constrained by, the meaning of its foundational charter, which outlines the community's basic character and its raison d'être; without fidelity to this document, the community ceases to be what it is meant to be. On the other hand, life goes on, things change, and people cannot remain in the founding context. So there must necessarily be some kind of *development* in relation to the authoritative charter. Development is characteristically expressed in terms of *realizing the implications* of the original, or of *determining what is compatible* with it. All of this requires the continuing interpretive activity on the part of the community as a whole, and of its recognized representatives, to explore, via both argument and practice, what does and does not constitute a good implication or an appropriate compatibility. The community must both attend to and be constrained by the original meaning, and also not be restricted by original meaning and be able to move beyond it.

42. Ibid., 65.
43. This analogy is periodically suggested by scholars. The fullest and most helpful discussion of which I am aware is Jaroslav Pelikan, *Interpreting the Bible and the Constitution* (New Haven and London: Yale University Press, 2004), though the book lacks a conclusion to pull the threads together and to draw out their wider implications.

It is because the continuing significance of the Christian Bible is realized supremely in the continuing life of the church, just as the continuing significance of the American Constitution is realized in the continuing life of the American people, that study of original meaning is both necessary but not necessarily determinative. Historical study of the Bible, by the very act of removing the Bible from its primary life setting within the church, can achieve analytical clarity (or at least plausibility) about origins and development at the same time that it risks obscuring the dynamics that actually pertain when the Bible is seen to matter for life now, and decisions need to be taken about what to do.

The challenge for Christian interpretation of the book of Isaiah is to have historical respect for the distinctive Isaianic voices in their own right and then combine that with taking seriously a Christian understanding of God in Christ as the frame of reference within which the Isaianic witness is now to be understood and appropriated. This may be complex. For example, the classic Jewish objection to seeing Jesus as the "fulfillment" of those passages that speak glowingly of a faithful Davidic king who brings justice and peace (Isa. 7:14; 9:1–7 [8:23–9:6 MT]; 11:1–9) is straightforward: "If Jesus is the redeemer, why is the world so unredeemed?" Christian reading of these passages in relation to Jesus is inseparable from the fundamental reconstrual of messiahship and salvation that runs through the Gospels and the rest of the New Testament.

A Christian Reading of the Book of Isaiah

I will attempt a thematic, albeit selective, reading of the book of Isaiah as a whole.[44]

I start in the New Testament, with some of the words of Mary's Song, the Magnificat, which Mary utters when visiting Elizabeth shortly after the annunciation by the angel Gabriel:

> He [God] has shown strength with his arm;
>   he has scattered the proud in the thoughts of their hearts.
> He has brought down the powerful from their thrones,
>   and has [exalted] the lowly;
> he has filled the hungry with good things,
>   and sent the rich away empty. (Luke 1:51–53)

44. I will work with the book of Isaiah in its received form. This is without prejudice to the standard debates about tradition-history, composition, and redaction. I presuppose the substantial recent scholarly writing that has recovered ways of reading of the book as a whole, whatever the possible diversity of its parts. I use "Isaiah" to mean either the book of that name or the speaking voice within the text.

A truth about God has become evident through its impinging upon the everyday world, in this case in God's choice of the (peasant?)[45] girl Mary to be the mother of a child who is to be the sovereign Lord over God's people. The perception of this reality, however, is not straightforward and requires discernment. The unsympathetic and the literalist might insist that unless and until Caesar and his minions are removed from their current positions of power, the language means little. Since the emperor Augustus was still well ensconced in Rome, as also was King Herod in Judea, and Roman imperial power experienced no notable blips around the time of Jesus's birth, then our text could be a pious but vacuous expression of fantasy—at best an opiate for the marginal and miserable. Yet to take Mary's Song seriously means to rethink the nature of human greatness and significance in the light of God, and to recognize that what counts is not necessarily found in the centers of political power, whose significance is thereby re-envisaged.

Mary's Song can be used heuristically to direct our attention to a recurrent yet underappreciated theme in Isaiah:[46] exaltation and abasement.[47] The book of Isaiah in all its parts has a focus on the city of Jerusalem, capital of the kingdom of Judah, and on its inhabitants. In relation to the wider geopolitical world of the Levant in the Iron Age, Jerusalem was a small and relatively insignificant entity, especially when set alongside the historic civilizations of Egypt and Mesopotamia. However, from the perspective of Israel's canonical writers, Jerusalem has a significance quite other than that which would be apparent in political, military, or economic terms. This significance depends upon God. For Jerusalem is a place that YHWH has chosen, where Solomon's temple on Mount Zion mediates YHWH's presence, and where YHWH's chosen house of David rules—all of which is

---

45. Early Christian imagination, in the *Protoevangelium of James*, developed an influential account of Mary as the daughter of Joachim and Anna, who was dedicated to service in the temple from an early age. Matthew and Luke are silent about her background, other than locating her in the village of Nazareth.

46. The motif is absent in various recent accounts of theological issues in Isaiah, such as J. Clinton McCann Jr., "The Book of Isaiah—Theses and Hypotheses," *BTB* 33/3 (2003): 88–94; L. Juliana Claassens, "Isaiah" in *Theological Bible Commentary*, ed. Gail R. O'Day and David L. Petersen (Louisville: Westminster John Knox, 2009), 209–22; and John Goldingay, "The Theology of Isaiah" in *Interpreting Isaiah: Issues and Approaches*, ed. David G. Firth and H. G. M. Williamson (Downers Grove, IL: IVP Academic, 2009), 168–90 (apart from reference to some of the key texts in relation to divine holiness, 172–74).

47. The resonances of the Magnificat with Hannah's song in 1 Sam. 2, and with some of the psalms, is a reminder that this theme within Isaiah is well represented in other parts of the OT also (linkages between Isaiah and Psalms are natural since both are Jerusalem-oriented literary collections). Deuteronomy 8—with its contrast between a divine humbling that teaches the nature of human life (vv. 2–3), and a human self-exaltation that leads to a forgetful narrowing of human sensibility (vv. 14–18)—would also be germane to the discussion (see chap. 3 above).

presupposed by Isaiah. Thus within the world of Isaiah, and the world of the Hebrew Bible, Jerusalem represents importance and greatness. But how is this greatness to be understood?

Two Visions of Exaltation

After an introductory, apparently summarizing, portrayal of the prophet's message in Isaiah 1, the theme of exaltation and abasement is central to chapter 2.

> ²In days to come
>> the mountain of the LORD's house
> shall be established as the highest of the mountains,
>> and shall be raised above the hills;
> all the nations shall stream to it.
>> ³Many peoples shall come and say,
> "Come, let us go up to the mountain of the LORD,
>> to the house of the God of Jacob;
> that he may teach us his ways
>> and that we may walk in his paths."
> For out of Zion shall go forth instruction,
>> and the word of the LORD from Jerusalem.
> ⁴He shall judge between the nations,
>> and shall arbitrate for many peoples;
> they shall beat their swords into plowshares,
>> and their spears into pruning hooks;
> nation shall not lift up sword against nation,
>> neither shall they learn war any more.

A vision of Mount Zion in the future sees it as a mountain of supreme height (2:2), imagery that in the wider ancient world would be symbolic of an appropriate dwelling place for deity (like Mount Zaphon in 14:13, or Mount Olympus in Greek mythology). The fact that geographically, in the time of Isaiah, Mount Zion (the place of Jerusalem's temple) was a modest hill, smaller than many in the hill country of Judah, is of course an integral presupposition of the prophetic vision. The greatness of this future Mount Zion, unlike the present one, will be apparent to all. The corollary of this greatness is that nations near and far will go there: they will not be compelled to come but will want to do so. Why? They will go to learn, to be instructed in desirable ways of living, the content of which will be accessible in Jerusalem. Specifically, YHWH's direction and arbitration will bring justice, and the consequence of justice will be reconciliation and peace (2:3–4). In other words, the future greatness of Zion is focused on divinely given instruction, bringing justice and peace for all.

> [5]O house of Jacob,
> come, let us walk in the light of the LORD!

Eschatology influences ethics.[48] The vision represents something ultimate, a light to look toward, a goal that should make a difference to the orientation of life in the present. Even if the present is far removed from this vision, it should nonetheless encourage Israel to be faithful in the here and now.

For, as becomes clear, the vision stands in stark contrast to present realities.

> [6]For you have forsaken the ways of your people,[49]
> O house of Jacob.
> Indeed they are full of diviners from the east
> and of soothsayers like the Philistines,
> and they clasp hands with foreigners.
> [7]Their land is filled with silver and gold,
> and there is no end to their treasures;
> their land is filled with horses,
> and there is no end to their chariots.
> [8]Their land is filled with idols;
> they bow down to the work of their hands,
> to what their own fingers have made.

The land of Israel is full of things that are widely taken to constitute human greatness: enormous wealth and military resources (2:7). But these are accompanied by problematic religious practices and personnel, of a kind that may characterize the Philistines but should not characterize Israel (2:6).[50] Moreover

48. Brevard Childs comments: "The description of eschatological rule is not part of a human social program" (*Isaiah*, OTL [Louisville: Westminster John Knox, 2001], 31). This is true. Nonetheless it should not be allowed to obscure the fact that eschatological vision is meant to make a difference in how people think and live, in terms of their hopes and priorities. The deficiencies of liberal/cultural Protestantism are probably not a particularly helpful way into fresh thinking about contemporary Christian ecclesial and social responsibilities.

49. The text of the poem, here and in various places, is difficult. The best discussion is by H. G. M. Williamson, *Isaiah 1–5*, ICC (London and New York: T&T Clark, 2006), 189–205. I will for convenience stay with NRSV since the various textual difficulties do not affect the tenor of the whole.

50. This is, of course, Isaiah's judgment as to what should characterize Israel in distinction from other nations, a judgment that has been "received" through the processes of canon formation. It is not incompatible with historical likelihood that Isaiah's perspective was not a majority perspective in his own context: Israelite diviners may well have been commonplace and, in the judgment of many, uncontroversial (which may be an implication of 3:2).

their religious practices are idolatrous (2:8), for they accord divine honor to their own handiwork. True vision of YHWH is lacking.

> ⁹And so people are humbled,
> and everyone is brought low—
> do not forgive them!
> ¹⁰Enter into the rock,
> and hide in the dust
> from the terror of the LORD,
> and from the glory of his majesty.
> ¹¹The haughty eyes of people shall be brought low,
> and the pride of everyone shall be humbled;
> and the LORD alone will be exalted in that day.

In the prophet's vision the consequence is clear—the abasement of humanity, which is reduced to terror before YHWH, and the futility of attempts to find somewhere safe to hide from a God who has become fearful (2:9–10). There is a clear inversion: human attempts at exaltation are brought low, while by contrast YHWH—indeed YHWH alone—is exalted (2:11).[51] Even though YHWH's dealings with Israel, focused upon Jerusalem, still constitute the frame of reference (there is explicit address to "the house of Jacob" in v. 6), the language of the chapter seems deliberately to generalize its referent. The apparent assumption is that the issues to do with Jerusalem paradigmatically represent the situation of humanity more generally.

> ¹²For the LORD of hosts has a day
> against all that is proud and lofty [rām],
> against all that is lifted up [nissā'] and high;
> ¹³against all the cedars of Lebanon,
> lofty [rām] and lifted up [nissā'];
> and against all the oaks of Bashan;
> ¹⁴against all the high [rām] mountains,
> and against all the lofty [nissā'] hills;
> ¹⁵against every high tower,
> and against every fortified wall;
> ¹⁶against all the ships of Tarshish,
> and against all the beautiful craft.
> ¹⁷The haughtiness of people shall be humbled,

51. There is interesting variation in the terminology for abasement and exaltation; e.g., (in 2:11) YHWH's exaltation is depicted with a verb other than that used for attempted human exaltation, perhaps as a tacit differentiation of the genuine from the spurious.

and the pride of everyone shall be brought low;
and the LORD alone will be exalted on that day.

The initial vision of human abasement and divine exaltation opens out into a
more wide-ranging account, which is expressed in terms of YHWH's "day." This
day is emphatically "against" ('al, ten times in 2:12–16) everything that is "high."
Although a variety of Hebrew terms for "high" are used, the predominant adjectives are *rām* and *nissā'*, adjectives from verbal roots that recur resonantly in
both adjectival and verb forms in other important passages in the book. YHWH's
day is spelled out in terms of things that are naturally high in the world around
(great trees, mountains, hills) or that have been humanly constructed in grand
and impressive ways (towers, walls, ships). All of these will encounter the same
inversion as before, as YHWH alone is exalted (2:17b is verbatim identical to 2:11b).
This is not because YHWH has turned against His creation, but because the day
of YHWH here has the sense of judgment, a day of reckoning against human sin
and all that corrupts creation. For it is clear that all the language of height and
exaltation metaphorically depicts human pride and self-aggrandizement.

[18]The idols shall utterly pass away.
[19]Enter the caves of the rocks
   and the holes of the ground,
from the terror of the LORD,
   and from the glory of his majesty,
   when he rises to terrify the earth.
[20]On that day people will throw away
   to the moles and to the bats
their idols of silver and their idols of gold,
   which they made for themselves to worship,
[21]to enter the caverns of the rocks
   and the clefts in the crags,
from the terror of the LORD,
   and from the glory of his majesty,
   when he rises to terrify the earth.
[22]Turn away from mortals,
   who have only breath in their nostrils,
   for of what account are they?

There follows another picture of human terror before YHWH: futile attempts
to find safe places to hide, and recognition at last of the futility of the costly
objects that had become the focus of human priorities (2:18–21). The picture
is unremittingly stark.

The depiction of terrible overthrow may well be, at least in part, a figure for Assyrian and/or Babylonian depredations on Israel and/or Judah, understood as divine judgment, in a proximate historical context; but there is nothing in the imagery to indicate that it should be read primarily with reference to any one historical event. The whole vision of YHWH's day and its consequences appears to be eschatological in the same way as the vision of exalted Mount Zion—an ultimate reality that should bear upon vision and action in the present, to realign priorities and allegiance. So the passage ends with a final appeal to the human audience (2:22),[52] comparable to the appeal in 2:5 following the vision in 2:2–4. The appeal is to "turn away from mortals," to cease to trust in human attempts at exaltation rather than walking in YHWH's way. As Childs puts it, "With this utterly theocentric focus, the reader finds the central pulse beat of Isaianic theology."[53]

There is a sharp contrast between the two visions of what is high. One is divinely approved prominence; the other is humanly attempted prominence. The elevated mountain of the temple brings justice and peace for all under God. The exalted things that humans esteem and create lead to idolatrous priorities that issue in ultimate fear and debasement. The first vision points to the "better way" that those addressed in the second vision should heed.

Who Qualifies for Exaltation?

The exaltation of YHWH is a recurrent theme in the book of Isaiah, perhaps most famously at the beginning of the account of Isaiah's vision of the divine king in the temple: "In the year that King Uzziah died, I saw the Lord sitting on a throne, high and lofty [*rām vĕnissā'*]" (Isa. 6:1). The language of Isaiah 6 recurs toward the end of the book,[54] in a passage that promises divine restoration:

> For thus says the high and lofty one [*rām vĕnissā'*][55]
>   who inhabits eternity, whose name is Holy:
> I dwell in the high and holy place,
>   and also with those who are contrite and humble in spirit
>   [*shĕphal-rūaḥ*],

---

52. The verb at the beginning of Isa. 2:22 is plural and so is addressed to humans. If it were singular it would be an appeal to YHWH for mercy, comparable to that in Ps. 89:46–48 (47–49 MT).

53. Childs, *Isaiah*, 33.

54. For a discussion of the recurrence of language from Isa. 6 elsewhere in the book of Isaiah in compositional terms, see H. G. M. Williamson, *The Book Called Isaiah* (Oxford: Clarendon, 1994), chap. 3, esp. 38–41.

55. The lack of a definite article makes the wording here in 57:15 identical to 6:1; it also suggests that *rām vĕnissā'* functions virtually as a name (as does also *qādōsh*, "the holy one" in 40:25).

> to revive the spirit of the humble,
>> and to revive the heart of the contrite. (Isa. 57:15)

Here the exalted God is seen to be present not just in the temple but also with people who are open to His presence. The notion of "humble [*shāphāl*, "low"] in spirit" makes clear that those who are open to God, and with whom He is present, are the exact opposite of the "high" of 2:6–22. The paradox is that the God who is high is with people who are low.[56] The concern of this passage is expressed more sharply near the end of the book:

> Thus says the LORD:
> Heaven is my throne,
>> and the earth my footstool;
> what is the house that you would build for me,
>> and what is my resting place?
> All these things my hand has made,
>> and so all these things are mine, says the LORD.
> But this is the one to whom I will look,
>> to the humble and contrite in spirit,
>> who trembles at my word. (Isa. 66:1–2)

Here the language of divine sovereignty, rather than exaltation, is used, but the point is similar (and if the earth is a footstool, and heaven a throne, exaltation is implied). Such a sovereign God cannot be humanly constrained, even by the temple in Jerusalem. Yet He is not therefore remote, but rather to be found in those whose disposition is humbly open to Him. The rhetoric of "not in the temple, but in the humble" is a serious critique of complacent assumptions about the divine presence. It is not a proposal to do away with the temple, but a strong statement that certain human dispositions are necessary for the presence of God to be an existential reality.

If YHWH, and YHWH alone, is exalted, does this exclude humans from exaltation? Is the only appropriate thing to say of people that they must be "humble in spirit"? Although this might appear to be entailed by the passages considered thus far, the language of exaltation and abasement is used in other contexts where further dimensions are probed and in which the possibility of human exaltation is recognized. In the next passage in canonical sequence after 2:6–22, in which divine exaltation is spoken of, the relationship between divine exaltation and possible human exaltation is implicitly raised:

---

56. YHWH's presence will also revive (57:15), presumably in the sense of giving both healing from affliction and renewed confidence, matching the content of the divine words as they continue in 57:16–21.

> People are bowed down, everyone is brought low,
>   and the eyes of the haughty are humbled.
> But the LORD of hosts is exalted by justice,
>   and the Holy God shows himself holy by righteousness. (Isa.
>   5:15–16)

At first sight, this may appear to be little more than a repetition of the language of chapter 2. Many see it as a redactional gloss/repetition of little significance, other than to make the point that God's judgment (v. 15) is a demonstration of His justice (v. 16). Contextually, however, it closely follows the "song of the vineyard," in which Israel and Judah are envisaged as a vineyard, planted and cared for by God. But what fruit then grows in the vineyard? The song focuses on this issue with a striking wordplay:

> He expected justice [*mishpāt*],
>   but saw bloodshed [*mispāḥ*];
> righteousness [*tsĕdāqāh*],
>   but heard a cry [*tsĕʿāqāh*]! (5:7)

Justice and righteousness—judicial integrity in disputes and honest/uncorrupt dealings in the public realm—are what YHWH seeks from His people; and this word pair, justice and righteousness, recurs frequently in Isaiah as a whole,[57] appearing already in the opening overture (1:21, 27). If 5:15–16 is read in the context of the song of the vineyard, the language of 5:16 resonates with the language of 5:7, in a way that suggests that its point may not be to depict YHWH's judgment of the greedy and oppressive as just (a thought that is surely axiomatic), but rather to outline a contrast with the abasement of 5:15, which continues the concern of the song of the vineyard. As I have argued in an earlier study:

> The Isaianic text presumes a certain kind of analogy between divine and human which may be summarized: Israel is to embody those moral qualities which characterize YHWH himself—Israel is to practise justice and righteousness because this is how YHWH himself acts. Further, it is a basic prophetic axiom that YHWH acts in and through the actions of his servants, just as YHWH speaks through the words of the prophets. Thus YHWH's actions of justice and righteousness may be seen precisely in the actions of justice and righteousness performed by those accountable to him. . . .

57. A justly acclaimed study is by Rolf Rendtorff, "Isaiah 56:1 as a Key to the Formation of the Book of Isaiah," in his *Canon and Theology: Overtures to an Old Testament Theology*, trans. Margaret Kohl from German, OBT (Minneapolis: Fortress, 1993), 181–89.

The point then of the contrast within 5:15–16 is surely conceptual . . . [or] didactic, an explanation of the true sense of "being high"—of human exaltation as something founded in the kind of moral practice characteristic of God, over against widely held, but mistaken, alternative construals (such as the possession of much property [5:8] or the indulging of pleasure [5:11–12]) which have disastrous consequences. In the attainment of such true [human] exaltation God is exalted and his holiness displayed.[58]

Admittedly, this interpretation of 5:15–16 is contestable,[59] yet it is congruent with other content in the book. In Isaiah 33, which contains oracles of deliverance from a "destroyer" who "will be destroyed" (33:1), familiar language recurs:

> [5]The LORD is exalted, he dwells on high [*shōkēn mārōm*];
>   he filled Zion with justice and righteousness;
> [6]he will be the stability of your times,
>   abundance of salvation, wisdom, and knowledge. . . .
> [And in response to a picture of corruption and desolation in the
>   land—]
> [10]"Now I will arise," says the LORD,
>   "now I will lift myself up;
>   now I will be exalted [verbal forms of *rām věnissā'* are used]." . . . .
> [13]Hear, you who are far away, what I have done;
>   and you who are near, acknowledge my might.
> [14]The sinners in Zion are afraid;
>   trembling has seized the godless:
> "Who among us can live with the devouring fire?
>   Who among us can live with everlasting flames?"
> [15]Those who walk righteously and speak uprightly,
>   who despise the gain of oppression,
> who wave away a bribe instead of accepting it,
>   who stop their ears from hearing of bloodshed
>   and shut their eyes from looking on evil,
> [16]they will live on the heights [*měrōmīm yishkōn*];
>   their refuge will be the fortresses of rocks;
>   their food will be supplied, their water assured.

58. R. W. L. Moberly, "Whose Justice? Which Righteousness? The Interpretation of Isaiah V 16," *VT* 51/1 (2001): 55–68, esp. 63, 67.

59. Hugh Williamson carefully discusses my thesis but still prefers to see 5:16 as depicting the justice of divine judgment. He argues that if the sense of the verb used of God in v. 16b (*niqdāsh*) is "shows himself holy" (a rendering I do not contest), then "it is difficult to see how this could be done by anything other than his own justice and righteousness" (*Isaiah 1–5*, 376). However, God's justice and righteousness remain "his own" and still display Himself when they are seen in human lives that are faithful to Him—for it is in nature transformed by grace that the divine is discerned.

Here again is both the language of divine exaltation and the imagery of divine enactment of justice and righteousness, such that life becomes stable and good (vv. 5–6). Moreover, the repeated imagery of divine exaltation (v. 10) leads into a further picture of divine judgment and the terror that this brings to those in Zion who are corrupt (vv. 13–14). By contrast, however, those who live uprightly and with integrity will "live on the heights" (vv. 15–16a). The same terminology of exaltation is used both for YHWH and for the upright (vv. 5a, 16a). It presumably means that those who display YHWH's own qualities come to share YHWH's own exaltation.

In summary, the passages considered depict an understanding of exaltation as a characteristic of the one God, which may also become a characteristic of humans who are open to God through humility of spirit and who embrace the way of YHWH through living with integrity (practicing "justice and righteousness" [33:5–6]). But the humans who try to exalt themselves on their own terms (money, power, oppression of others) thereby encounter the opposition of YHWH and will, sooner or later, be abased by him.

The Exaltation of the Davidic King and of the Servant of YHWH

Similar language and conceptuality recur with reference to the figures within Isaiah that have most consistently been read (whether predictively, metaphorically, or figurally) in relation to Jesus: the Davidic king, and the servant of YHWH.

Isaiah's encounter with the evasive Ahaz (Isa. 7) is followed by various passages that speak of a Davidic king who will show the appropriate royal qualities that have, by implication, been lacking in Ahaz himself. One of the most famous (9:2–7 [1–6 MT]) speaks of a special royal/Davidic son:

> 6For a child has been born for us,
>   a son given to us;
> authority rests upon his shoulders;
>   and he is named
> Wonderful Counselor, Mighty God,
>   Everlasting Father, Prince of Peace.
> 7His authority shall grow continually,
>   and there shall be endless peace
> for the throne of David and his kingdom.
>   He will establish and uphold it
> with justice and with righteousness
>   from this time onward and forevermore.
> The zeal of the LORD of hosts will do this.

Whether or not this depicts an actual birth at the start of life, or a metaphorical birth at the beginning of a royal reign (as in Ps. 2), the interpretation of the language overall is contested. There is a long history of Christian interpretation that has focused on the divinely resonant epithets used for the royal son: "Wonderful Counselor [*pele' yō'ēts*]" resonates strongly with YHWH's being wonderful in counsel (*hiphlī' 'ētsāh*, 28:29), and "Mighty God [*'ēl gibbōr*]" likewise depicts YHWH (10:21). This has been taken to envisage God incarnate in the person of Jesus the Messiah. Interpreters concerned with Isaiah's originating context, however, have tended to see the language as representative of the ideology of kingship, perhaps influenced especially by Egyptian royal ideology. It can be tempting not to take such language seriously, on the grounds that it may be hardly different in kind from courtiers saying to their monarch, "O king, live forever!" (Dan. 2:4; 3:9; 5:10; etc.).[60] Within Isaiah's frame of reference, however, there is a distinctive vision. I suggest that the key to it is that the titles of the royal son (to which enormous attention has been given) are inseparable from his anticipated actions (to which rather less attention is usually given). The king can be given divine epithets because the king is to display divine qualities: the practice of justice and righteousness, which will bring peace. Although the language of exaltation and abasement is not used, our heuristic key suggests that this royal figure is appropriately imagined as potentially sharing in YHWH's exaltation because of his practice of YHWH's qualities.

A stark contrast with the Davidic king is afforded by the king of Babylon whose overthrow is celebrated in Isaiah 14:4–23. This king of Babylon is depicted in archetypal terms whose resonances extend far beyond his immediate portrayal. Most famous is the middle section of the poem:

> [12]How you are fallen from heaven,
>   O Day Star, son of Dawn!
> How you are cut down to the ground,
>   you who laid the nations low!
> [13]You said in your heart,
>   "I will ascend to heaven;
> I will raise my throne
>   above the stars of God [*'ēl*];
> I will sit on the mount of assembly
>   on the heights of Zaphon;
> [14]I will ascend to the tops of the clouds,
>   I will make myself like the Most High [*'elyōn*]."

---

60. Particularly striking is Bathsheba's use of such words to David, even when the premise of the conversation is that David is dying and needs to decide on his successor (1 Kings 1:31).

¹⁵But you are brought down to Sheol,
   to the depths of the Pit.

The king is depicted as thinking in terms appropriate to a non-Israelite, as he speaks not of Zion but of Zaphon, and not of Yhwh but of El and Elyon—although the informed reader of the Hebrew Bible knows that what Zaphon represents is realized in Zion,[61] and that El and Elyon can be epithets of Israel's God.[62] The king's ambition is boundless and so well depicted in mythological terms. He wants to ascend to heaven and take his place on high, on the lofty mountain where the divine assembly meets, not just as one of the assembly but as its leader. Yet this vaulting ambition is overthrown: he has fallen from the heights of heaven and been brought down (here the passive implies the action of God) to the lowest depths imaginable, and his outcast corpse will be denied even burial, never mind the conventional glory of a royal tomb (vv. 18–19). The resonance with the day of Yhwh, where the high is brought low, is strong. Although the emphasis is predominantly on the imagery of the king's fall, rather than the reasons for it, a reason is nonetheless given: "because you have destroyed your land, you have killed your people" (v. 20a)—that is, in Isaiah's terminology elsewhere, because he did not practice justice and righteousness.

The most Christianly resonant part of the whole book of Isaiah, the account of the servant of Yhwh in 52:13–53:12, is framed at the outset by words on Yhwh's lips:

See, my servant shall prosper;
   he shall be exalted and lifted up [*yārūm vĕnissāʾ*],
   and shall be very high. (52:13)

The terms that have earlier been used of Yhwh and his throne (6:1), and subsequently will be effectively a name for Yhwh (57:15), are now used of a human figure, the servant of Yhwh, as an interpretive preface to the account of his suffering, death, and vindication. On this most famous Isaianic passage, I only make three brief comments. First, no matter how much one tries with historical imagination to think of a figure in the world of captive Judah

61. The Hebrew phrase *yarkĕtē tsāphōn* in Isa. 14:13b (NRSV: "the heights of Zaphon") is also used in apposition to "Mount Zion" in Ps. 48:2 (3 MT; NRSV: "in the far north"). The psalmist appears to be utilizing the mythological resonances of a divine mountain for articulating the significance of Zion.

62. So, e.g., Melchizedek is priest of El Elyon and blesses Abram by El Elyon (Gen. 14:18–20 NRSV mg.). But when Abram picks up Melchizedek's wording, he speaks of Yhwh El Elyon (Gen. 14:22 AT), as though to clarify that it is in fact the God whom Israel knows as Yhwh by whom Melchizedek has blessed him.

as the primary referent for the prophetic vision (where I am inclined to envisage the prophet himself as taking on Israel's role as servant, and suffering on Israel's behalf),[63] the resonance of the language with the New Testament's portrayal of the suffering, death, and resurrection of Jesus is inescapable for the Christian imagination. Whether or not Jesus thought of himself in these terms, Christians think of Jesus thus, because of the congruence between what the servant undergoes and what Jesus undergoes. Second, although the servant does not perform the "justice and righteousness" that is expected of Israel and its rulers, in his own particular way he is fully obedient to YHWH's demanding will. His own qualities are those of patient endurance (53:7), refusal to misuse other people (no "violence"), and honesty (v. 9b): in other words, he is surely "humble in spirit [shĕphal-rūaḥ]" (57:15), and his death is brought about by "a perversion of justice" (53:8). So, third, it is because of the servant's astonishing faithfulness amid suffering and humiliation that he is seen to be raised to that position of exaltation that characterizes God Himself (52:13). The logic is surely as elsewhere: those who embrace and live out God's ways come to share in God's own exaltation.

The servant is a supreme exemplar of motifs associated with exaltation and with what is required for exaltation, motifs in Isaiah as whole. Greatness, as symbolized by exaltation, whether it be for Zion as a whole or for particular figures, is consistently construed by Isaiah in the moral and spiritual terms of faithfulness to God's revealed will and the rejection of self-aggrandizement.

Isaiah and the Portrayal of Jesus in the New Testament

If we turn to the Gospels, there is much that readily resonates with Isaiah's portrayal of exaltation and abasement. The words of Jesus that "all who exalt themselves will be humbled, and all who humble themselves will be exalted" (Matt. 23:12//Luke 14:11; 18:14) could be taken as a one-line summary of my (selective) reading of the book of Isaiah. Elsewhere, Jesus uses Isaiah's depiction of the Day Star, Son of Dawn with reference to the town of Capernaum, where he lived, but where people would not repent: "And you, Capernaum, will you be exalted to heaven? You will descend to Hades" (Matt. 11:23 AT). The imagery used of the king of Babylon is applied to human pride more generally.

Indeed the idea of inverting usual priorities of exaltation and superiority lies at the very heart of Jesus's teaching, not least with regard to his own

---

63. So, e.g., Christopher R. Seitz, "Of Mortal Appearance: Earthly Jesus and Isaiah as a Type of Christian Scripture," in his *Figured Out: Typology and Providence in Christian Scripture* (Louisville: Westminster John Knox, 2001), 103–16, esp. 114; Childs, *Isaiah*, 412.

mission and practice. So, for example, we see this in the passion predictions and their sequels in Mark. When Peter attempts to correct Jesus's depiction of his role as Messiah in terms of suffering and dying, Jesus responds with "Those who want to save their life will lose it, and those who lose their life for my sake, and for the sake of the gospel, will save it" (Mark 8:35). When the disciples argue about their position in some kind of pecking order, Jesus responds with "Whoever wants to be first must be last of all and servant of all" (9:35). When James and John request top places in Jesus's kingdom, and the others become annoyed with them (because they get ahead of the others in their request?), Jesus responds with "Whoever wishes to become great among you must be your servant, and whoever wishes to be first among you must be slave of all." He goes on to point out that this represents his own priorities, which are "not to be served but to serve, and to give his life a ransom for many" (Mark 10:43–45).

At the structural level of the total portrayal of Jesus, there are strong resonances also. Most clear perhaps among the evangelists is John's portrayal of the cross—the place of apparent weakness, shame, and death when Jesus is lifted up on the cross is the place of exaltation and glorification, where humans are drawn to the truth of their being (John 12:32–33; 13:31–32). Alternatively, Paul depicts Jesus's self-emptying as the form of human life whereby Jesus construed his equality with God (Phil. 2:5–8); the consequent exaltation of Jesus to the highest position imaginable (2:9–11) concludes with a citation of Isaiah's vision of general human acknowledgment of the definitive reality of the one God (Isa. 45:23) as realized in and through what Jesus has done (Phil. 2:10–11). Paul's further personal testimony to his own revaluation of what previously he had valued the most, his relinquishment of everything so as to know Christ and the power of his resurrection (3:2–11), can be seen to model a Christian appropriation of Christ's pattern of abasement and exaltation.

Conclusion: The Book of Isaiah and Faith in Jesus

There is, of course, much content in Isaiah that does not feature in the above reading. Nonetheless, the recognition of a significant concern that runs through the book enables some brief concluding reflections.

First, the prophetic portrayal of the paradoxical nature of greatness surely moves the believer to be suspicious of any close alignment between human glory/power and the presence of God. For it is all too likely that what humans admire, esteem, and strive for will be potentially idolatrous, becoming the symbolic embodiment of activity and qualities that are not rooted in concern for God's justice, righteousness, and holiness. However, an alignment between what seems naturally desirable and what is of God is not precluded, at least on a broad Old Testament canvas.

A certain paradox seems to be one of the points of the story of Samuel's anointing of David. After Samuel has had to be reminded that God does not look on the outward appearance but on the heart (1 Sam. 16:6–7), so that the independence of God's choice from conventional human attractiveness is established, it is then possible to recognize that God's choice may indeed be outwardly attractive (16:12). Similarly, those who have been weaned off the self-aggrandizing attractions of political power are those who can then best be entrusted with it.

But despite this caveat, there is much in Isaiah to suggest a certain hermeneutic of suspicion toward common understandings of human grandeur. The servant of YHWH is no David, for he is entirely without the kind of attractiveness that would naturally or instinctively draw human beings to himself (53:2), and recognition of him is inseparable from astonishment (52:14–15; 53:1). So too, Jesus's earthly ministry met more apathy, bafflement, and hostility than it met warmth, understanding, and acceptance, and it ended in abandonment and an agonizing execution. Recognition of Jesus, even resurrected and ascended, is not self-evident.

It surely follows that there should be "nonconformist" dimensions in Christian discipleship, such as the exaltation of the humble and the humbling of the exalted.[64] In this general context, Christians need to give serious and sustained attention to many of the emphases of liberation theology, some of feminist theology, and some of ideological suspicion, with their various critiques of rather too comfortable "establishment" perspectives on theology and life. The suspicion that too much theology and ecclesial life is self-interested and complacent cannot satisfactorily be met by mere denials. Actions speak louder than words.

The content of Christian proclamation, the saving lordship of Christ, should not be separated from a mode of proclamation that enters into the reality of that lordship by itself embodying the pattern of abasement and exaltation, of death and resurrection, as Paul makes so clear in Philippians 2–3 and in 2 Corinthians. If the divine exaltation of Christ is promoted by methods that utilize unregenerate patterns of human power, then its nature is thereby intrinsically distorted and its meaning emptied out, as rather too many people down the years have had good reason to point out.

At the time of this writing (late August 2012) three young women (Nadezhda Tolokonnikova, Maria Alyokhina, and Yekaterina Samutsevich) from the punk band Pussy Riot have just been

---

64. I write as a member of the Church of England, an established church of which the monarch is the supreme governor, whose origins as a distinct church in the murky politics of Henry VIII, and much of whose subsequent history, cannot but make one alert to the ambiguities and compromises of ecclesial establishment, whatever the possibilities it also offers.

sentenced to two years' imprisonment for their "hooliganism" in performing a "punk prayer," which contained abrasive and scatological language, in front of the iconostasis in Christ the Saviour Cathedral in Moscow in February 2012. From the outset Patriarch Kirill, the head of the Russian Orthodox Church, has condemned Pussy Riot's performance in the cathedral as "blasphemous" and "sacrilegious," and this has played a role in their condemnation. The sentencing judge, Marina Syrova, said that the women had been "motivated by religious enmity and hatred" and that their actions had been "blasphemous and insulting to believers."[65]

The symbolic offense of their action is deliberate, real, and undoubtedly hurtful; it has made many Russians unsympathetic to Pussy Riot. Nonetheless, the concern of the women was to protest both at the way Putin was about to resume presidential power (he was re-elected shortly after their protest) and at the unquestioning endorsement of President Putin by Patriarch Kirill. The patriarch's unquestioning support for President Putin is clearly related to Putin's support for the Orthodox Church and his willingness to promote its restoration to a dominant position in Russian culture.

In the course of the trial, all three women appealed to Christian priorities. Yekaterina Samutsevich said that Pussy Riot was trying to "unite the visual imagery of Orthodox culture with that of the protest culture, thus suggesting that Orthodox culture belongs not only to the Russian Orthodox Church, the patriarch, and Putin, but that it could also ally itself with civic rebellion and the spirit of protest in Russia." Nadezhda Tolokonnikova said that Christianity is about a search for truth "and a constant overcoming of . . . what you were earlier." Maria Alyokhina observed that among Orthodox leaders "the Gospels are no longer understood as revelation," but as a collection of quotations that can be manipulated for their own purposes.[66]

It is hard not to see the patriarch's conduct as questionable. One might compare it with the implications of the notorious April 2012 episode of the patriarch's gold Breguet watch, worth roughly 20,000 euros, which was ineffectually airbrushed out of a 2009 photograph on the church's website. It suggests complacency about the return of the Orthodox Church to a position of privilege, power, and wealth in Russia. For the patriarch to focus on the offensive symbolic dimensions of the protest at the expense of taking seriously the content of the protest is surely a clear example of the manipulation of religious symbols and language for self-serving purposes. There is surely a failure both in learning from the Orthodox Church's terrible sufferings in the twentieth century and in heeding the priorities of the prophets and of Christ.

Self-serving use of religious language and symbols is something the prophets consistently target, sometimes in deliberately provocative language. When Isaiah, speaking in Yhwh's name, addresses the leaders of Jerusalem as "rulers of Sodom" and its inhabitants as "people of Gomorrah" and goes on to say, "Your appointed festivals my soul hates. . . . Though you make many prayers, I will not listen" (Isa. 1:10, 14–15), it is not difficult to imagine some of the pious being offended by such language.

Finally, how should Isaiah's vision of "the day of Yhwh" best be understood in a Christian frame of reference? It is an interesting example of the complex relationship between the specific language of the text and an understanding of its subject matter in differing contexts. The vision is of an ultimate reality, by which ill-founded human aspirations to greatness and grandeur are found wanting and overturned, when God appears and confronts human pretension with divine truth. Whatever precisely is envisaged by "the day of

65. Tony Halpin, "Cries of 'Shame' as Pussy Riot Jailed over Anti-Putin Stunt," in *The Times* [London], August 18, 2012, 4.

66. Paul Vallely, "A Protest Founded on the Gospels," *Church Times* [Anglican, UK], August 24, 2012, 11.

YHWH" in its Old Testament frame of reference, the imagery has historically fed into Christian visions of a final day of judgment, when all humanity is held accountable before God's truth, and human priorities in life are finally disclosed for what they really have been—a disclosure with possibly terrifying existential implications. For Christians it is the coming of Jesus, supremely in his death and resurrection, which constitutes that which is final—not in the sense that history does not continue, but in the sense that God has definitively revealed and enacted His judgment on the world. This judgment is such that, at any subsequent point in this world or beyond, that which is revealed in the life, death, and resurrection of Jesus remains the ultimate yardstick by which human aspiration and endeavor is measured by God and either affirmed or found wanting. It is not that human self-aggrandizement cannot continue since Jesus came, but the nature of, and the reason for, its ultimate futility have been definitively disclosed.

It thus becomes appropriate to see the self-revelation of God in Jesus as the supreme realization of Isaiah's vision of "the day of YHWH." This is one way of approaching John's understanding of Jesus as the human face of God, such that Isaiah "saw his glory and spoke about him" (John 12:41). This is not what is envisaged in Isaiah's own frame of reference. But this is how his subject matter can be understood and appropriated when his words are re-contextualized as part of Christian Scripture.

6

Educating Jonah

Reading a text and following what it says is one thing. Understanding what it means is another. All significant literature, of course, poses challenges of understanding to the reader. But the challenges are in certain ways heightened in the Bible. For although words can indeed convey fundamental truths about God and humanity and can touch existential depths, no words can do this automatically (and of course, the affirmation that the Bible conveys such fundamental truths is contested). Words can be read uncomprehendingly, superficially, or suspiciously in ways that can make it difficult or impossible for readers genuinely to grasp what the words convey. Readers can suppose that they understand a text when in reality their grasp is partial, and perhaps seriously impaired. Moreover, familiarity or long acquaintance is no guarantee of comprehension. As John Ames, Congregationalist minister and narrating voice in *Gilead*, puts it: "You can know a thing to death and be for all purposes completely ignorant of it."[1]

A famous example of the problem comes in Matthew's portrayal of Jesus's ministry. In response to the Pharisees' objection to his table fellowship with undesirables (tax collectors and sinners), Jesus says, among other things: "Go

---

In this chapter I develop my earlier study "Jonah, God's Objectionable Mercy, and the Way of Wisdom," in *Reading Texts, Seeking Wisdom*, ed. David F. Ford and Graham Stanton (London: SCM, 2003), 154–68; also issued in *JSR* 3/1 (2003), http://etext.virginia.edu/journals/ssr/issues/volume3/number1.
    1. Marilynne Robinson, *Gilead* (New York: Picador, 2004), 7.

and learn what this means, 'I desire mercy and not sacrifice'" (Matt. 9:13). The prophetic text to which Jesus appeals, Hosea 6:6, was well known to the Pharisees, who knew much of their scriptures by heart. There are no unfamiliar words or difficult syntax such as to make the text puzzling or obscure (apart from the issue of whether "and not sacrifice" could really envisage abolishing rather than, as is rhetorically far more likely, relativizing the practice of sacrifice); and the importance of mercy was already well developed in the Jewish thought and practice of Jesus's day. Yet Jesus sees the Pharisees' grasp of mercy as deficient because of their inability to see his interactions with the socially and religiously marginal as exemplifying it; their understanding of mercy was too narrow and thus defective.

In this chapter I propose to explore a less well-known example of the problem that the understanding of mercy, which God Himself practices and which He expects His people to practice, may be more demanding than is commonly thought. I will do this through a consideration of the story of Jonah. My thesis is that the story of Jonah can well be read as a probing of this basic, perennial problem within Jewish and Christian (and other) faiths: religious language that on one level appears simple and straightforward is in fact harder to understand and appropriate than it initially appears.

Introduction to the Book of Jonah

Some Scholarly and Popular Approaches

The book of Jonah has elicited, and continues to elicit, many diverse interpretations.[2] To approach its interpretation in conventional modern scholarly mode via consideration of its date, context of origin, and authorial purpose has obvious value. Nonetheless it is only moderately illuminating for the simple reason that we do not know when, where, or why Jonah was written. There is a strong scholarly consensus, based on cumulative arguments from language and history, that the book is likely to be exilic or later in origin, and I see no reason to dissent from this. But beyond locating the book in the general time-frame of sixth to fourth century BC, it is hard to be more precise. However, recognition of the likely distance in time between the world within

2. Convenient introductory accounts are by Robin B. Salters, *Jonah and Lamentations*, OTG (Sheffield: JSOT Press, 1994), esp. 51–62; and Uriel Simon, *Jonah*, JPSBC (Philadelphia: Jewish Publication Society, 1999), vii–xiii. An extensive account, lively and with some polemical edge, is by Yvonne Sherwood, *A Biblical Text and Its Afterlives: The Survival of Jonah in Western Culture* (Cambridge: Cambridge University Press, 2000).

the text (eighth century) and the world behind the text (sixth to fourth century) does influence one's judgments about the nature of the book's content.

One recurrent suggestion, based on the book's apparently sympathetic attitude to non-Israelites (sailors in chap. 1, Assyrians in chap. 3), has been that the book relates to the internal debates of post-exilic Judah, as some sort of counter-thrust to the "narrow" ethnic and religious policies of Ezra and Nehemiah. Such a proposal about the book's nature and purpose is possible but is no more than conjecture, an attempt to imagine a context in relation to which the book's emphases might reasonably have been formulated; and numerous other scenarios can also be conjectured. In my judgment, most versions of the proposal that Jonah essentially represents a move within in-house Judahite policy debates offer a remarkably thin construal of a book of notable richness and depth. One does not need to spend long with the biblical text and its history of interpretation to discover that the book's intriguing story line seems endlessly to engage the imagination and to defy all attempts to settle on any one interpretation as *the* interpretation. It is a good example of a narrative that is genuinely open to multiple readings.

Some interpretations, however, are better than others. So by way of preface to my own reading, I identify two approaches that enjoy considerable popularity but belong among the less good interpretations.

First is the assumption, fueled not least by the history of art and by countless children's picture books, that the story is about "Jonah and the Whale." There is indeed imaginative potential in such a scenario; unfortunately, however (at least for the student of the Hebrew scriptures), it tends rapidly to acquire a momentum of its own and to lead one away from the biblical scenario. On the one hand, there is no whale; in Jonah 2:1–2, 11 (1:17; 2:1, 10 ET) the Hebrew simply specifies a "big fish" (*dāg*), and the Septuagint correspondingly specifies a "large fish" (*kētos*). A whale is one possible way among many of imagining this fish. On the other hand, the fish plays a minor, swim-on role in the narrative: it swallows Jonah at sea and spews him out on dry land, each time at YHWH's direction, and thereby preserves Jonah from drowning so that he can have a second chance to fulfill his mission to Nineveh. Unless one counts the space given to Jonah's prayer in the belly of the fish, the fish occupies less narrative space than the bush that shades Jonah and then withers toward the end of the story.

Second, there is a recurrent tendency to focus on the fish in relation to rationalizing concerns about the plausibility of the story, often with specific reference to the issue of God's ability to work miracles. In late antiquity Augustine tackled the issue thus in one of his letters:

The last question is about Jonah . . . [and] is expressed thus: "Please tell me what we are to think about Jonah, who is said to have been three days in the belly of a whale. It is improbable and unbelievable that he should have been swallowed up with his clothing and should have been inside the fish. If it is figuratively said, please explain it." . . . I have noticed that this sort of question is a matter of much jest and much laughter to pagans. The answer to this is that either all the divine miracles are to be disbelieved or there is no reason why *this* should not be believed. We should not believe in Christ himself and that he rose on the third day, if the faith of the Christians feared the laughter of the pagans.[3]

In the nineteenth century the distinguished Anglican scholar and churchman E. B. Pusey took a line similar to that of Augustine in responding to contemporary dismissiveness. He says (assuming that Jonah is author as well as subject of the book that bears his name):

Whether Jonah relates God's ordinary or His extraordinary workings, His workings in the way in which He upholdeth in being the creatures of His Will, or in a way which involves a miracle, i.e., God's acting in some unusual way, Jonah relates it in the same way, with the same simplicity of truth. His mind is fixed on God's providence; . . . he nowhere stops to tell us the "how." How God converted the Ninevites, how He sustained his life in the fish's belly, he tells not. He mentions only the great facts themselves, and leaves them in their mysterious greatness. It is not strange that heathen scoffers fixed upon the physical miracles in the history of Jonah for their scorn. . . . What to men seem the greatest miracles or the least, are alike to Him the mere *Let it be* of His All-holy Will.[4]

Such concerns have recurred and still recur.[5] And it is important not to forget that, as Jonathan Magonet observes, "Until the modern period, the historicity of the book, with a few exceptions, seems to have been taken for granted."[6] What may seem obvious now did not always seem obvious. Nonetheless, Augustine and Pusey are surely clear examples of fighting one's battle on the wrong

---

3. Augustine of Hippo, *Letters* 170.6; cited in Alberto Ferreiro, ed., *The Twelve Prophets*, ACCS (Downers Grove, IL: InterVarsity, 2003), 135.

4. Edward Bouverie Pusey, *The Minor Prophets*, vol. 5, *Jonah and Nahum* (London: James Nisbet, 1907), 44, 52.

5. Gerhard von Rad tells of an eighteenth-century professor from Helmstadt who dared to dispute the historical nature of the Jonah narrative and "was fined one hundred florin and forbidden to hold lectures" ("The Prophet Jonah," in his *God at Work in Israel*, trans. John Marks from German [Nashville: Abingdon, 1980], 58–70, esp. 65). Comparable pressures can still be brought to bear on teachers in some contemporary evangelical seminaries/schools with regard to the historicity of Jonah and other issues that in modernity became, and sometimes remain, evangelical identity markers.

6. Jonathan Magonet, "Jonah, Book of," in *ABD* 3:936–42, esp. 940.

ground. They assume that if unbelievers mock and question God's ability to do the marvelous, then the appropriate response must be to affirm God's ability to do the marvelous and encourage a stance of reverence. Both elements of the response are indeed appropriate to believers—*but this is surely not the place to invoke them.* To put it in other terms, one must first consider the genre of Jonah and the literary conventions that it utilizes, and then consider how best to promote a right appreciation and understanding of the book,[7] rather than meet flatfooted mockery with equally flatfooted piety.

An Indicative Outline of the Book as a Whole

There are at least three aspects of the way in which the story of Jonah is told that are indicative of its genre. First is the repeated use of the adjective "big" (*gādōl*),[8] which comes a total of twelve times:[9] Nineveh is a big city, YHWH sends a big wind such that there is a big storm, the sailors fear YHWH with a big fear, and a big fish swallows Jonah (1:2, 4, 16, 17 [2:1 MT]); this is a story in which *things are big.*

Second, and correspondingly, the story line consistently has a larger-than-life dimension to it. Jonah is given the hardest conceivable assignment (the original *Mission Impossible*): he is to go to the capital city of Assyria,[10] the greatest earthly power in his world, and a power that had no reason to heed Israelite prophets. Jonah is a most unpromising prophet; although it is common for prophets to respond to God's call with an expression of inadequacy and diffidence, Jonah surpasses them all by saying nothing and just running away: when told to go east, he catches a boat to the west. While on the boat, Jonah is more heedless and less prayerful than the non-Israelite sailors, yet these sailors are awed by Jonah's testimony about YHWH, respond readily to God, and even (apparently) convert to Israel's faith.[11] Jonah receives God's

---

7. Compare the discussion of predictive prophecy in chap. 5 above.

8. The impact of the repetition is usually lost in English translations, which tend to use a variety of terms: "big," "great," "mighty," "large" (so NRSV).

9. There are two further uses (3:5, 7) that I do not include, as *gādōl* is used substantively (great and small) rather than to describe something as "big."

10. Nineveh did not formally become capital of the Assyrian Empire until the seventh century (see A. Kirk Grayson, "Nineveh," in *ABD* 4:1118–19), but this makes no difference to the point of the narrative.

11. It is difficult to know how best to read the extended account of Jonah and the sailors. I am inclined to see the sailors' coming to pray specifically to YHWH, after their initial engagement with a generic "god" (*'ĕlōhîm*), and directing sacrifice and vows to YHWH as indicating their embrace of Israel's religious frame of reference, where God is known as YHWH: in contemporary terminology, they "convert." (Some traditional Jewish interpretation also adopts this reading. See Louis Ginzberg, *Legends of the Jews*, trans. Henrietta Szold and Paul Radin, 2nd ed. [Philadelphia: Jewish Publication Society, 2003], 2:1033.) This is distinct from the repentance of the

mercy in a most remarkable way and has to learn to praise God from within the belly of a fish. When Jonah realizes that flight is futile and does go to Nineveh, he finds a city that is astonishingly large. He enters, goes a short way, and preaches what is arguably the shortest sermon on record (in 3:4), five words in the Hebrew.[12] Quite apart from its brevity, this address is surely subversive of his commission. Nothing is said about sin or repentance, and "forty days" is the Hebrew idiom for an indefinite long period of time and thereby would imply "no hurry"; existential urgency would only be conveyed by Jonah's specifying "three days," the Hebrew idiom for an indefinite short period of time.[13] Yet Jonah achieves the greatest success anywhere in the Bible, indeed the greatest success imaginable for any prophet: *everyone* in Nineveh from the king downward turns to God, so much so that even their livestock are to be included in the acts of repentance. Apart from the intriguing inclusion of the livestock, the Ninevites' repentance looks to be a model in every way, as it consists of fasting, prayer, rejection of sinful behavior, and lack of presumption upon God.[14] In response to all this, God rescinds the threatened judgment upon the Ninevites, who become a paradigmatic example of divine mercy. Jonah responds to this not with gratitude but with a self-justifying moan about YHWH's mercy. The story then concludes with a parley and small incident between Jonah and God about the meaning of what has happened.

The final indicative feature is that the story concludes with a rhetorical question, which functions as a punch line. We are told no more about Jonah, because once the punch line is reached the unfolding narrative sequence no longer matters in its own right: the story serves the punch line. Although God's final rhetorical question about His compassion is put to Jonah, it is presumably the reader/hearer who is meant to go away and ponder the appropriate

---

Ninevites, all of whose engagement with God is expressed by the generic "g/God" ('ĕlōhîm). This I take to indicate that their repentance is directed to the one God, but with no suggestion that they adopt Israel's particular knowledge of God; i.e., they truly repent but do not "convert."

12. Of course, this could be read as a summary of a longer message. However, the extended prayer of Jonah in chap. 2 would be a precedent for giving a fuller account, and the narrator's brevity here makes it at least possible to read Jonah's five words as all that was said.

13. Interestingly, "three days" is the wording in the Septuagint (Jon. 3:4 LXX). This may be because the Greek translators, like many interpreters, considered that Jonah had by this time learned his lesson and hence made his wording sound appropriate to a prophet who genuinely wants to engage his audience. The Hebrew text implies that Jonah, while now compliant, remains reluctant. See my "Preaching for a Response? Jonah's Message to the Ninevites Reconsidered," *VT* 53/2 (2003): 156–68.

14. Recognition of the paradigmatic nature of the Ninevites' repentance is surely implicit in Jesus's use of the story in Matthew's narrative: "The people of Nineveh will rise up at the judgment with this generation and condemn it, because they repented at the proclamation of Jonah" (Matt. 12:41).

response. If the reader's imagination is concerned with what happened next to Jonah rather than with the nature of the divine compassion, then the reader has failed to get the point.

From these features of the narrative, it is appropriate to conclude that the story of Jonah is somewhat like the story of Job: an exploration and portrayal of moral and theological issues in memorable narrative rather than abstract form.[15] The Jonah narrative has a drily humorous tenor that the Job narrative lacks, and so the narrative function is by no means identical in these two cases; yet a real analogy remains. There is of course evidence for a historical Jonah, the eighth-century prophet mentioned in Kings, who prophesied territorial expansion for the northern kingdom of Israel and who is the subject of our story (the notation in both contexts that Jonah is "son of Amittai" is presumably meant to identify the two figures; 2 Kings 14:25, Jon. 1:1); but stories about historical figures do not need themselves to be historical. It is a pity that Augustine and Pusey (and others like them), despite their well-meaning piety and high intelligence, entirely miss the humor and the consistently larger-than-life nature of the story, and thus feel obliged to come at the issues heavy-handedly. The quizzical should surely be challenged not with an all-or-nothing acceptance of divine miracles but rather with the need to get the story's point and to ponder the mystery of divine mercy, to reflect upon a story of grace that is amazing.

Jesus's appeal to the "sign of Jonah" in the Synoptic Gospels (Matt. 12:38–42; 16:1–4; [Mark 8:11–12]; Luke 11:16, 29–32; a pericope that is traditio-historically and interpretively complex) is memorable but puzzling. It is an imaginatively serious engagement with the world of the story, which aims to make a point in the context of controversy.[16] Because Jesus regards the request for a sign as faithlessness and so not to be acceded to (presumably because it would diminish the need for responsive discernment and repentance on the part of his audience), the sign of Jonah is enigmatic, and any number of different inferences could be made from his story. The point that "just as Jonah became a sign to the people of Nineveh, so the Son of Man will be to this generation" (Luke 11:30) not only is non-specific but also leaves the sign enigmatically located in the future. Strikingly, in the two ways in which the Matthean and Lucan accounts offer a closer specification for the nature of the sign of Jonah, the enigma remains. The analogy between Jonah in the belly of the fish and the Son of Man in the heart of the earth for three days (Matt. 12:40) is given no specified "point"; and since what will happen to the Son of Man still remains in the future, in the context of Jesus's ministry its sense remains opaque to his hearers (though it should be meaningful after Jesus's resurrection). The appeal to the responsiveness of the Ninevites to Jonah and of the queen of Sheba to Solomon (Matt. 12:41–42//Luke 11:30–32), although less was at stake than

15. See chap. 8 below.
16. There is a still-persisting conservative apologetic argument that Jesus, by his appeal to the story, "clearly" regarded it as historical, and the believer therefore should do likewise. This argument is a good example of category confusion. To enter into the world of the text with full imaginative seriousness reveals nothing about the literary genre of the text. Comparable appeal could be made to the significance of Hamlet, Jane Eyre, or Darth Vader on the part of those who takes their stories with imaginative seriousness.

with Jesus, again gives away nothing to make it easier for his audience to respond to Jesus, but rather emphasizes the seriousness of their failing to do so.

Jonah and the Book of the Twelve

A different issue that has come to the fore in recent scholarship is the potential significance of the Book of the Twelve as a whole as a context for interpreting the particular prophetic books within it. There are undoubtedly fresh insights to be gleaned from this angle. The length and complexity of the Book of the Twelve bears some resemblance to the length and complexity of the book of Isaiah. To read the prophetic books within the Twelve in relation to each other can add depth and nuance to one's reading.[17]

One obvious question for the book of Jonah, where Nineveh is spared, relates to the book of Nahum, where Nineveh is overthrown. How is divine judgment in Nahum to be understood in relation to divine mercy in Jonah? This is an ancient question, and ancient Jewish readings made a range of moves, including the most obvious one, that even if the repentance was genuine it was not lasting (though they also canvassed other possibilities, including that the repentance was only superficial in the first place).[18]

Nonetheless, it is perhaps important not to claim too much for the hermeneutical significance of the context of the Twelve.[19] To be sure, it is sobering when Seitz observes that "we have no evidence that the book of Jonah was ever an independent book or the object of interpretation as a book unto itself—late, early, or otherwise in the history of prophecy in Israel."[20] By the same token, however, there is no evidence, to the best of my knowledge, that any biblical commentator has tried to read Jonah primarily within the context of the Twelve until very recently. It should hardly be controversial to allow hermeneutical weight to the fact that both the form and content of the book of Jonah are markedly distinct from the surrounding prophetic texts within the Twelve. Likewise, stretching back to antiquity is a history of both Jews and Christians seeing fit to interpret Jonah as a text with its own distinctive significance. On the Jewish side, because of its portrayal of repentance, the book of Jonah was anciently prescribed as the haftarah for the afternoon service on the Day of Atonement (b. Megillah 31a). On the Christian side, although Jerome wrote commentaries on all the Minor Prophets, he treated each of them as a distinct book. If the history of reception is to be allowed hermeneutical significance—which should generally,

---

17. A pioneer in recent work on the interpretive significance of the Book of the Twelve has been James D. Nogalski, whose numerous publications on the subject have recently culminated in a commentary (with a good indicative bibliography), *The Book of the Twelve: Hosea–Jonah*, SHBC (Macon, GA: Smyth & Helwys, 2011). Amid the burgeoning literature, Christopher R. Seitz has made suggestive contributions in his works *Prophecy and Hermeneutics: Toward a New Introduction to the Prophets*, STI (Grand Rapids: Baker Academic, 2007), esp. 140–49; and *The Goodly Fellowship of the Prophets: The Achievement of Association in Canon Formation*, Acadia Studies in Bible and Theology (Grand Rapids: Baker Academic, 2009).

18. See Beate Ego, "The Repentance of Nineveh in the Story of Jonah and Nahum's Prophecy of the City's Destruction—A Coherent Reading of the Book of the Twelve as Reflected in the Aggada," in *Thematic Threads in the Book of the Twelve*, ed. Paul L. Redditt and Aaron Schart, BZAW 325 (Berlin and New York: de Gruyter, 2003), 155–64.

19. Useful overviews of the possible interpretive implications of Jonah's position in the Twelve are by Hyun Chul Paul Kim, "Jonah Read Intertextually," *JBL* 126/3 (2007): 497–528, esp. 516–28; and James D. Nogalski, "Recurring Themes in the Book of the Twelve: Creating Points of Contact for a Theological Reading," *Interpretation* 61/2 (2007): 125–36. However, robust and methodologically acute doubts about the whole exercise are expressed by Ehud Ben Zvi, "Is the Twelve Hypothesis Likely from an Ancient Reader's Perspective?" in *Two Sides of a Coin: Juxtaposing Views on Interpreting the Book of the Twelve/the Twelve Prophetic Books*, ed. Ehud Ben Zvi and James D. Nogalski, AG 201 (Piscataway, NJ: Gorgias, 2009), 47–96.

20. Seitz, *Prophecy*, 147.

though not unreservedly, be a characteristic of reading the Hebrew Bible as Scripture—then there is an obvious case for continuing to interpret the book of Jonah as meaningful in its own right.

It may be, however, that once one moves beyond redactional issues to an actual reading of Jonah, relatively little is at stake.[21] In his recent commentary, James Nogalski keeps a clear focus on the story of Jonah in its own right and interprets Jonah's relationship with other parts of the Twelve, especially Joel 2:13–14 and Nahum, much as might a commentator who has no particular view about the Twelve as a book.

By way of contrast, Alan Cooper has proposed that "the denouement of Jonah . . . takes place *outside the book*." This raises complex issues, especially since his reading depends on taking the divine words in Jonah 4:11 not as a rhetorical question affirming God's care for the people of Nineveh but rather as a straightforward denial ("As for me, I do not care about Nineveh") so as to pave the way for Nahum.[22] Grammatically this is possible since there is no explicit indicator of a question in 4:11 (e.g., the interrogative particle *hă*), and the question must be inferred as the best way of making sense of the text. However, the absence of an interrogative particle in what is clearly a question is a common Hebrew idiom. Moreover Cooper's proposal makes it impossible (at least to my mind) to make sense of Jonah 4 as a whole.

Toward a Reading of Jonah's Moaning at Yhwh (Jonah 4:1–3)

The passage on which I want to focus comes at a point in the narrative when Jonah's commission to Nineveh has been carried out and God has been merciful toward the Ninevites. The story's interest shifts to Jonah's response to the divine mercy upon the Ninevites. Remarkably, Jonah moans to God about His mercy and wants to die:

> [1]But this was very displeasing to Jonah, and he became angry. [2]He prayed to the Lord and said, "O Lord! Is not this what I said while I was still in my own country? That is why I fled to Tarshish at the beginning; for I knew that you are a gracious God and merciful, slow to anger, and abounding in steadfast love, and ready to relent from punishing. [3]And now, O Lord, please take my life from me, for it is better for me to die than to live."

This plays a key role in the overall narrative for two reasons.

On the one hand, there is a significant silence, or gap, at the outset of the story. When Yhwh speaks and Jonah flees, we are only told *that* he flees and not *why* he flees. Jonah's possible motives can be guessed in many different

---

21. For example, Aaron Schart, "The Jonah Narrative within the Book of the Twelve," in *Perspectives on the Formation of the Book of the Twelve*, ed. Rainer Albertz, James D. Nogalski, and Jakob Wöhrle, BZAW 433 (Berlin and New York: de Gruyter, 2012), 109–28, focuses entirely on conjectures about the redactional activity that may have led to the familiar text and hardly contributes to a reading of it.

22. Alan Cooper, "In Praise of Divine Caprice: The Significance of the Book of Jonah," in *Among the Prophets: Language, Image and Structure in the Prophetic Writings*, ed. Philip R. Davies and David J. A. Clines, JSOTSS 144 (Sheffield: JSOT Press, 1993), 144–63, esp. 158–59.

ways: Is he fearful for himself? Is he tenderhearted toward Nineveh? Is he vindictive toward Nineveh? Is he simply awkward and uncooperative? Or what? There are different ways of weighting one's reading of the overall narrative sequence according to the nature of one's decision about what has motivated Jonah's flight. It is only when Jonah moans at YHWH that he at last explains why he fled. If we take him at his word—and there is no good reason to suspect that he is dissimulating here[23]—then we have information that impacts our reading of the whole.

On the other hand, in the immediate context, Jonah has just achieved the greatest success imaginable for any prophet, in terms of the universal Ninevite response to his words. One would expect someone in that situation to be pleased, grateful, overjoyed, humbled, . . . yet Jonah sulks and moans. This is as great a surprise as anything else in the book, and it now becomes the issue around which the whole conclusion of the story revolves. So how should it be understood?

For these two reasons, the contention that the interpretation of Jonah's complaint is central to an understanding of the book as a whole is not, I think, controversial.[24] Yet for all that Jonah speaks apparently straightforwardly, there remains one basic problem if we consider his words: although the divine mercy is clearly cited as the reason for Jonah's flight, it still remains unclear precisely what it is about the mercy that he finds objectionable. We now know *that* the divine mercy is a problem, but we do not know *why* it is a problem. Our puzzlement in understanding Jonah's initial flight and present resentment is resolved by an explanation that is itself opaque. It is the attempt to penetrate and clarify that opacity that generates much of the literature on Jonah and accounts for much of the diversity of interpretation. A necessary step, therefore, will be to offer some account of at least some characteristic interpretive moves that are made.

It should be said at the outset that the purpose of what follows is not to try to "disprove" any particular interpretations (even though I indicate which angles of approach I find less and more persuasive). This is because the text is

23. It would not be impossible to take Jonah's words as a secondary rationalization of a flight that took place for some other reason. Yet this is where using one's imagination is in danger of giving a character in a story too much life, as it were, beyond the bounds of the story, in a way that may diminish the story itself. In any case, even if the words were a rationalization of a flight that took place for some other reason, Jonah's words would still be the rationalization that the continuing narrative takes up, to which the interpreter must therefore attend.

24. For example: "The key to understanding the intention of the author of Jonah is surely to be found in ch. 4, in the discussion between God and Jonah" (Salters, *Jonah*, 59); "The answer given [to why Jonah became displeased and so angry that he wanted to die] is crucial for an interpretation of the entire book" (Philip Jenson, *Obadiah, Jonah, Micah: A Theological Commentary*, LHBOTS 496 [New York and London: T&T Clark, 2008], 82).

so intrinsically suggestive and open-ended that it is neither likely nor desirable that any one interpretation could displace all others. Of course, this does not mean that "anything goes" or that some interpretations are not better than others, but simply that the range of interpretations for which a good case can be made through close attention to the text is unusually wide.

Jonah's Citation of Scripture and the Significance of the Passages Cited

A first step, before we consider different readings of Jonah's prayer, is to clarify what stands in the text. A remarkable aspect of Jonah's moan is that its content centers on a citation of two divine pronouncements elsewhere in the Old Testament. One is Exodus 34:6:

Exodus 34:6	Jonah 4:2
"The LORD, the LORD,	"O LORD! . . . You are
a God [ʾēl] merciful [raḥūm]	a gracious [ḥannūn] God [ʾēl]
and gracious [ḥannūn],	and merciful [raḥūm],
slow to anger [ʾerek ʾappayim] and	slow to anger [ʾerek ʾappayim], and
abounding in steadfast love [rav-ḥesed]."	abounding in steadfast love [rav-ḥesed],"

The other is Jeremiah 18:8:

Jeremiah 18:8	Jonah 4:2
I will change my mind about the disaster [vĕniḥamtī ʿal-hārāʿāh].	"and ready to relent from punishing [vĕniḥām ʿal hārāʿāh]."

The wording is not quite identical: the sequence of merciful and gracious is inverted in Jonah 4:2, and the verb in first-person speech in Jeremiah 18:8 becomes adjectival (through use of a participial form) in Jonah 4:2. Yet it is so close (much closer in the Hebrew than in the NRSV translation of Jer. 18:8 and Jon. 4:2) that explicit citation of Exodus and Jeremiah by Jonah becomes the natural way of reading Jonah's words.

My contention about explicit citation is made in terms of a reader-oriented hermeneutic of the Hebrew scriptures as a canonical collection. In compositional terms—what traditions did the author of Jonah know, in what form did he know them, and where were they located?—the same contention could still be made, but it becomes debatable. However likely it may be (in my judgment) that the textual content of Exodus 34 and Jeremiah 18 was stable and well-known by the time of the book of Jonah, the sheer uncertainties concerning the tradition-history and composition of the books of the Old Testament make it possible to envisage alternative scenarios.[25] Here

25. Nathan C. Lane discusses Exod. 34:6–7's role in the OT, utilizing both diachronic and synchronic categories, in *The Compassionate but Punishing God: A Canonical Analysis of Exodus 34:6–7* (Eugene, OR: Pickwick Publications, 2010).

as elsewhere, a theological reading of the documents of the Old Testament in their received form is an exercise distinct from discussions of the history of Israelite literature and thought.

It is perhaps less obvious that Jonah is citing Jeremiah 18:8 than that he is citing Exodus 34:6 because of the brevity of this second citation and the fact that the language of Yhwh's "repenting/relenting [*niham*]" recurs regularly in many parts of the Old Testament. Many commentators reckon Exodus 32:14 to be the source, because of its proximity to Exodus 34:6. Nonetheless, Jeremiah 18:7–10 is the only passage that sets out in an in-principle way that Yhwh "repents/relents [*niham*]," and the wording in Jeremiah 18:8 and Jonah 4:2 is almost identical. Thus the Jeremiah passage becomes the natural source of Jonah's wording.

The first-cited passage, Exodus 34:6, is the opening part of Yhwh's words of self-revelation to Moses at Sinai (Exod. 34:6–7). It is an account of the nature of God, from God's lips,[26] spoken to Moses as privileged recipient. As the fullest statement about the divine nature in the whole Bible, it is located in the context of the aftermath of Israel's breaking the recently made covenant by sinning with the golden calf (Exod. 32), even while they were still at the mountain of God (which could be seen as an equivalent to committing adultery on one's wedding night). This narrative context makes the continuing existence of Israel as the covenant people of Yhwh dependent upon this divine self-revelation of grace, mercy, and steadfast love (and also Moses's faithful intercession). These divine words are thus foundational within Israel's scriptures, and unsurprisingly are often cited, especially in the Psalter, where Israel's prayers are formulated.[27] Equally unsurprisingly, they have played a significant role in Jewish theology and prayer down through the ages, both of which are nicely brought together in the talmudic articulation of the "thirteen attributes" of God.

> R. Johanan said: Were it not written in the text [i.e., Exod. 34:6], it would be impossible for us to say such a thing; this verse teaches that the Holy One, blessed be He, drew his robe round Him like the reader of a congregation [i.e., the one appointed to lead congregational prayers, for whom it is customary to draw his robe over his head] and showed Moses the order of prayer. He said to him: Whenever Israel sin, let them carry out this service before Me [i.e., read from the Torah the passage containing the thirteen attributes], and I will forgive them.[28]

26. Although in terms of the Hebrew of Exod. 34:5–6 either Yhwh or Moses could be speaker of the key words, both the preceding divine words in Exod. 33:19 and Moses's citation of this passage in Num. 14:17–18 specify Yhwh as the speaker, and I see no good reason to read Exod. 34:6 otherwise.

27. E.g., Pss. 86:5, 15; 103:8; 145:8; cf. the words of prayer in Neh. 9:17, 31.

28. From *b. Rosh HaShanah* 17b; cited from Isidore Epstein, ed. and trans., *The Babylonian Talmud: Seder Mo'ed* (London: Soncino, 1938), 4:68. For a famous medieval discussion of the thirteen attributes, see Maimonides, *The Guide for the Perplexed* 1.54; in Moses Maimonides, *The Guide for the Perplexed*, trans. Michael Friedländer (New York: Dover, 1956), 75–77.

Historic Jewish practice is depicted thus by Benno Jacob:

> They ["the thirteen attributes"] have been a leitmotif of the Jewish penitential
> prayers . . . and form the foundation of the countless s'li-hot composed through
> centuries. The repentant people of Israel have used these thoughts to plead to
> HIM with complete contrition, ardor, and zeal. Luther, who reflected upon
> the synagogue of the fifteenth and sixteenth centuries, stated: "I would give
> two hundred golden guilders if I could pray like the Jews. They have learned
> it from the magnificent prayers of their teacher Moses, and he was taught by
> God Himself!"[29]

Jonah's use of Exodus 34:6 in prayer thus stands in the early stages of a long
and rich tradition, though the particular way in which he prays the words is
distinctive!

The second-cited passage, Jeremiah 18:8, is less weighty in Jewish and
Christian history than Exodus 34:6, but it is nonetheless important on its
own terms. For it is part of a passage, Jeremiah 18:7–10, that sets out in an
axiomatic way the nature of prophetic speech in relation to human response
and divine purpose and action.[30] The principle articulated is that prophetic
speech seeks response and is contingent: if an announcement of coming judg-
ment/calamity (*rā'āh*) elicits a response of turning from evil, that is, repentance (*shūv*), then God may be responsive and retract (*niham*) the judgment
(*rā'āh*); and conversely, promised good can be forfeited through complacency
and corruption. The theological and moral point is that YHWH, through His
prophets, seeks a rightly engaged human response, and such response *matters*,
not least in relation to a future that is contingent upon such responsiveness.

It should readily be seen that Exodus 34:6 and Jeremiah 18:8 are complementary. The one passage articulates the gracious and merciful character of
God, and the other articulates how that grace and mercy works out, through a
responsiveness that can act mercifully rather than enact a predicted judgment.
It is thus a natural move to bring the two passages together.

Jonah and Joel

Interestingly, this combination of Exodus 34:6 and Jeremiah 18:8 is found
not only in Jonah's words but also, with virtually identical wording, in Joel's

---

29. Benno Jacob, *The Second Book of the Bible: Exodus*, trans. Walter Jacob (Hoboken,
NJ: Ktav, 1992), 985. Unfortunately Jacob gives no source for the Luther quotation, and I have
been unable to locate it. The wording has a genuinely Luther-like ring to it. Given Luther's
notorious anti-Jewish pronouncements elsewhere, it would be interesting to know its context.

30. See the fuller discussion of Jer. 18:7–10 in chap. 3 above.

account of the God to whom Judah should turn in time of disaster, where Joel's words express a theologically-nuanced quasi-creedal or quasi-liturgical summons to the people of Judah:

Joel 2:13	Jonah 4:2
Return to the LORD, your God,	"O LORD! . . . You are
for he is gracious [*ḥannūn*]	a gracious [*ḥannūn*] God
and merciful [*raḥūm*],	and merciful [*raḥūm*],
slow to anger ['*erek* '*appayim*], and	slow to anger ['*erek* '*appayim*], and
abounding in steadfast love [*rav-ḥesed*],	abounding in steadfast love [*rav-ḥesed*]
and relents from punishing	and ready to relent from punishing
[*věniḥām* '*al-hārā*'*āh*].	[*věniḥām* '*al-hārā*'*āh*]."

There is also a clear further verbal link (not fully apparent in NRSV) in the continuation of the Joel passage, though with an interesting difference: what Joel goes on to say is found not on the lips of Jonah but on the lips of the king of Nineveh in the previous chapter as he enjoins repentance on his people (Jon. 3:9).

Joel 2:14	Jonah 3:9
Who knows [*mī yōdē*'*a*]	"Who knows? [*mī-yōdē*'*a*]
whether he will not turn [*yāshūv*]	God may relent [*yāshūv*]
and relent [*věniḥām*],	and change his mind [*věniḥam*];
and leave a blessing behind him?	he may turn from his fierce anger."

The compositional relationship between these two passages is impossible to determine.[31] If, however, one reads Joel and Jonah in literary and canonical sequence as part of the Book of the Twelve, then Jonah is read in the light of Joel. The near identity of wording between Joel 2:13 and Jonah 4:2 also means that the immediate source of Jonah's scriptural citation should probably be read as Joel.[32] But insofar as Joel 2:13 should itself be recognized as citing and combining Exodus 34 and Jeremiah 18 (for the reasons given above in relation to Jonah 4:2), then the substantive point about the textual source of Jonah's words remains unaffected.

But how might this parallel between Joel and Jonah affect one's reading of

31. Thomas B. Dozeman, "Inner-Biblical Interpretation of Yahweh's Gracious and Compassionate Character," *JBL* 108 (1989): 207–23, remains a valuable study of the relationship between the two passages.

32. This is a common observation in the literature, as in Michael Fishbane, *Biblical Interpretation in Ancient Israel* (Oxford: Clarendon, 1985), 345–46.

Jonah?[33] Most importantly, I suggest, the sense of contingency expressed by Joel's "Who knows?" is theologically sure-footed and is best read as classic prophetic theological insight. It represents what Jewish and Christian traditions have learned from this (and comparable passages) to be a right reading of the strong affirmation of divine mercy and responsiveness. God is indeed merciful and responsive, but although this can be relied upon, it should not be presumed upon. God's mercy remains His to give, and He interacts sovereignly and relationally but not mechanically. The repentant may hope for God to retract disaster and bring blessing, but they hope in trust rather than presumption, and so they cannot know in advance what form the divine mercy will take.

When one takes seriously the imaginative world of Jonah 3–4 in the light of Joel 2:13–14, it means that the king of Nineveh is portrayed as having excellent theological insight, trusting and not presuming upon God. It becomes an element in the exemplary nature of the Ninevite repentance. It also means that the king of Nineveh is portrayed as having better theological understanding than Jonah. The Ninevite construes divine mercy rightly in both word and action, while Jonah knows enough only to become upset.

Does Jonah Have a Problem with Unfulfilled Prophecy?

The citation of weighty scriptural passages serves to underline the remarkable nature of Jonah's moaning prayer. That which God's people should normally be grateful for, and find to be a source of life and hope, is something that makes Jonah miserable and wanting to die. Jonah clearly is familiar with scriptural material of fundamental importance. He knows what stands at the heart of Israel's faith; as Leslie Allen puts it, "Jonah is a specialist in creedal confessions."[34] Yet for some reason he does not "get it": "You can know a thing to death and be for all purposes completely ignorant of it." Why?

As a glance at the history of interpretation quickly shows, Jonah's words can be read in more than one way. Broadly speaking, there are probably two main streams of interpretation, each with numerous variations. One sees the

---

33. It is often suggested that the concern in Jonah is to extend the divine mercy beyond its application to Jerusalem in Joel. Hans Walter Wolff, e.g., says that "what is proclaimed to Jerusalem in the book of Joel now applies to Nineveh" (*Obadiah and Jonah: A Commentary*, trans. Margaret Kohl from German [1977; ET, Minneapolis: Augsburg, 1986], 167). The point can also be expressed in sharper terms, such as "Jonah [is] a response to the exclusivity of Joel" (Lane, *Compassionate*, 107; cf. 109). Such a reading is directed more, I think, to the world behind the text than the world within the text; it is analogous to proposals to read Jonah as a response to Ezra and Nehemiah.

34. Leslie C. Allen, *The Books of Joel, Obadiah, Jonah, and Micah*, NICOT (Grand Rapids: Eerdmans, 1976), 228. Allen draws attention also to Jonah's wording in 1:9.

issue as an aspect of unfulfilled prophecy; this, in general, has been advocated by Jewish interpreters. The other has to do with the divine mercy as problematic, especially in its extension beyond Israel to the Ninevites; this, in general, has been advocated by Christian interpreters.

Jonah as a False Prophet

The issue of unfulfilled prophecy is depicted by Childs as "either . . . Jonah's effort not to be a false prophet, or as analysing the relation of conditional to unconditional prophecy, or as dealing with the lack of fulfillment of the prophecy against the nations."[35] The basic logic of a concern with unfulfilled prophecy is that it follows the flow of the story line. Jonah announces coming divine judgment on Nineveh; the Ninevites repent; God retracts the coming judgment; Jonah objects. It puts particular emphasis upon Jonah's final two words, *věniḥām 'al-hārā'āh* ("and ready to relent from punishing"), following directly after "God changed his mind about the calamity" (*vayyinnāḥem 'al-hārā'āh*, 3:10b) as the real focus of Jonah's objection.

The idea that Jonah might have been worried about appearing to be a false prophet is well represented in classic midrash. A convenient synthetic account of such midrashic readings, which draws especially on the eighth/ninth-century work *Pirqe de Rabbi Eliezer*, yet many other texts also, is provided by Louis Ginzberg. Jonah, understood to be a disciple of Elisha,

> was to proclaim their destruction to the inhabitants of Jerusalem. The doom did not come to pass, because they repented of their wrong-doing, and God had mercy on them. Among the Israelites Jonah was, therefore, known as "the false prophet." When he was sent to Nineveh to prophesy the downfall of the city, he reflected: "I know to a certainty that the heathen will do penance, the threatened punishment will not be executed, and among the heathen, too, I shall gain the reputation of being a false prophet." To escape this disgrace, he determined to take up his abode on the sea, where there were none to whom prophecies never to be fulfilled would have to be delivered.[36]

This is charming; but I find its logic unpersuasive.[37] For it seems to depend upon an elementary failure on the part of both Jonah and the Jerusalemites to

---

35. Brevard Childs, *Introduction to the Old Testament as Scripture* (London: SCM, 1979), 419–20. Childs is discussing the purpose of the book as a whole, but what he says readily applies to 4:2–3, given its central role in the book.

36. Ginzberg, *Legends*, 2:1031.

37. Calvin adopts essentially the same reading as the rabbis, though he angles it in terms of Jonah's concern as being less for himself as false but for the honor of God's name, lest it be impugned and ridiculed (*Commentaries on the Twelve Minor Prophets*, vol. 3, *Jonah, Micah,*

comprehend the response-seeking and contingent nature of prophetic language. The reason for warning people that something terrible is going to happen if they carry on as they are doing is to get them to change what they do. So if they change and the envisaged disaster does not take place, and they then turn to confront the one who warned them with "It didn't happen, so you're wrong," the one who warned should hardly be fazed by this. A response along the lines of "The averting of the disaster was the point of why I said what I said. That's how warnings work. Don't you get it? Can't you see?" would be in order. And if people refused to take the point, then they would command no respect, and their scorn of Jonah would not be worth worrying about.

Although my own thesis is that Jonah does not understand the religious language that on one level he knows well, the supposition that Jonah fled because he did not want to look stupid or be called a false prophet for pronouncing something that did not then take place seems to me to make him *so* dim and/or immature that it somewhat diminishes the story as a whole. The mistakes of a child or an ignoramus are less interesting than the mistakes of an accountable adult. A more substantive misunderstanding makes for a more worthwhile story.

Is Jonah Concerned about Prophecy That Is Unfulfilled Because It Is Conditional?

Unsurprisingly, most modern scholars who have wanted to maintain some form of this approach to the story have offered a more subtle rendering, usually in terms of Childs's second option: an engagement with the relationship between conditional and unconditional prophecy.

The most sophisticated attempt of which I am aware is an influential essay by Elias Bickerman,[38] which I will take as representative of such an approach. According to Bickerman, Jonah knows of Jeremiah's axiom about divine responsiveness but objects to the "almost mechanical reciprocity between man's repentance and God's changing His mind" (41). Jonah protests against the popular post-exilic view that "penitence reinstates the sinner in divine favour" (43). Jonah is seen instead to uphold a distinction between two different types of prophecy—"conditional fate" (*fata conditionala*), which "gives man an alternative"; and "declaratory destiny" (*fata denunciativa*), which "works like a spell" (31)—and to be an advocate of the latter. Bickerman commends Augustine's terse "Jonah announced not mercy but the coming anger," and presents Jonah thus: "Jonah was not a missionary preacher threatening divine punishment as *fata conditionala*. Herald of God's wrath, Jonah declared the immutable and inevitable *fata denunciativa*: 'Yet forty days, and Nineveh shall be overthrown'" (32). Thus Jonah's protest is against a theological view represented by major

---

Nahum, trans. John Owen [Edinburgh: Calvin Translation Society, 1847; repr., Grand Rapids: Baker Books, 2005], 118–26). I find this even less persuasive.

38. Elias Bickerman, "Jonah *or* The Unfulfilled Prophecy," in his *Four Strange Books of the Bible* (New York: Schocken Books, 1967), 1–49. Parenthetical page references in the next four paragraphs are all from this essay.

canonical prophets: "The author of Jonah's story makes a confrontation between the thesis of Jeremiah, Ezekiel, Joel, and Malachi that if you repent God will also change His mind, and the antithesis, of Jonah, that God's word once spoken must be steadfast" (43). What then is the purpose of the book? "The thesis of Jeremiah and the antithesis of the prophet Jonah are reconciled and surmounted in a so-to-say Hegelian synthesis by the author of the book, who, as the ancient Jewish commentators noted, wrote a parable for Jerusalem. . . . To the restored [post-exilic] and still sinful city [Jerusalem], the author tells his parable. If God once did spare Nineveh, would He not save Jerusalem by His sovereign decision?" (44–45). The mystery of divine omnipotence—that YHWH spares for His own reasons—is the message of the book (47–48).

Fascinating though Bickerman's interpretation is, I do not find it persuasive. First, Bickerman does not properly establish that the category of "declaratory destiny" is a genuine category in Israel's scriptures. A couple of quick allusions, to Amos 1:4 ("I will send fire into the house of Hazael") and to Nahum 1:14 ("I will make your grave"—which is addressed to Nineveh) (31–32) hardly suffice to establish the category, let alone to give it the kind of status necessary for Jonah to be able to appeal to it.[39] Since Jeremiah and Ezekiel establish that a prophetic warning that is unconditional in form may in fact be conditional in purpose,[40] it cannot suffice simply to point to an unconditional form; it is necessary also to show that the unconditional form cannot plausibly be conditional in purpose. It is of course possible that Jeremiah innovated with the notion of conditional prophecy and a contingent future; but it needs to be shown that this is a genuine innovation, and not rather a making explicit of something already implicitly present.

Second, although Bickerman extensively discusses prophecy as immutable over against prophecy as contingent, he hardly touches on the major part of Jonah's moan, which has to do with the divine mercy as expressed in Exodus 34. Nor does he discuss the way in which an understanding of prophecies of judgment as conditional merges seamlessly with an affirmation of divine mercy.

Finally, there is some irony in the way Bickerman objects to characteristic modern Christian tendencies to find opposition between Israel and the gentiles, on the grounds that this introduces into the book "more than is really there" since in fact "the morality play of Jonah has a cast of three characters: God, the prophet, and the Ninevites" and "there is nothing about Israel" (28). Fair enough. Yet he himself introduces post-exilic Jerusalem as necessary for understanding the book's concern.

The enduring appeal of an approach in terms of unfulfilled prophecy can be seen in the way Ehud Ben Zvi presents it as *the* reading in the *Jewish Study Bible*: "Jonah is upset, but why? Because his proclamation did not come true from his perspective (see Deut. 18.21–22). . . . One has to infer that Jonah thought that God should behave according to the paradigm advanced in another set of biblical texts (see Num. 23.19, 1 Sam. 15.29), but he was sure that God's behaviour would not follow this paradigm. So God was in the wrong, from his perspective."[41] Admittedly I have not here discussed the difficult Deuteronomy 18:21–22, though I have tried to show that Numbers 23:19 and 1 Samuel 15:29

39. Bickerman appeals to the idiom of "cry against" (*qārā' 'al*) as demonstrating declaratory destiny (32). But even on the understanding that prophecy is intrinsically conditional, a message of judgment is a genuine message of judgment unless and until it evokes repentance.

40. See the discussion of Jer. 18:7–10 and Ezek. 33:12–16 in chap. 4 above.

41. Ehud Ben Zvi, "Jonah," in *The Jewish Study Bible*, ed. Adele Berlin and Marc Zvi Brettler (Oxford and New York: Oxford University Press, 2004), 1198–1204, esp. 1203. Ben Zvi mentions other interpretations but suggests that they are insufficiently grounded in what the text of Jonah actually says.

should not be read as opposing the paradigm of divine responsiveness;[42] no doubt, however, it would be possible to imagine Jonah misreading these also!

I must confess that I find this whole line of approach, holding that the issue at stake is unfulfilled prophecy, to be unpersuasive—though of course it may be that this mainly shows that I am a Christian and happy to align myself with characteristic Christian interpretation! In terms of the narrative, I am unpersuaded because the primary emphasis in Jonah's words in 4:2 is on divine mercy; and the final two words, *věniḥām 'al-hār'āh* ("and ready to relent from punishing"), specify how divine mercy operates in the context of prophetic announcements, rather than introducing a distinct issue. Moreover, divine mercy, not prophetic contingency, is the issue that is further developed in the remainder of the narrative: it is the divine caring for Nineveh, rather than the unfulfilled nature of Jonah's prophecy, that is the note on which the book ends.

Some Different Ways in Which Jonah Could Have a Problem with Divine Mercy

If, then, Jonah's problem is with divine mercy, we are still left with the question of whether it is possible to specify exactly what it is about divine mercy to which he takes exception. There is more than one way in which the issue can be imagined, and I will try to articulate the moral and existential logic of a number of different readings. Each reading raises some facet of divine mercy that can in practice be found objectionable, and so merits reflection.

Possible Danger to Those Who Show Mercy

One recurrent construal of Jonah's complaint is to see it as expressing his worry that his being a channel of Yhwh's showing mercy to the Ninevites might mean risk to Israel. This depends upon reading the text with two particular assumptions to the forefront. On the one hand, there is the role of Assyria elsewhere in the Old Testament as the great enemy of Israel, an enemy that overwhelms the northern kingdom in 721 BC. On the other hand, there is the strong likelihood that the book is written at a time subsequent to the Assyrian destruction of Israel, when knowledge of that could be presupposed on the part of author and audience alike. Thus Jonah can be read as lamenting the fact that to be an agent in the sparing of Nineveh could mean preserving Nineveh for its subsequent destruction of Israel. According to Renaissance Jewish scholar Abravanel, Jonah "knew the evils and exiles that [Nineveh]

---

42. See chap. 4 above.

would bring on the tribes of Israel in the future; hence he yearned that the nation of Assyria be destroyed and Nineveh its capital be utterly smitten. This is why he fled instead of going there."[43] Or as John Sawyer succinctly puts it, Jonah "was being asked in effect to sign his own people's death warrant."[44]

Although neither of the two assumptions on which this reading depends are specified in the text of Jonah, that hardly invalidates the reading, for almost all readers will be aware of aspects of the wider canonical context. Indeed, the point at issue is important: the recognition that the bestowal of mercy may be costly, even potentially or actually fatal, for the one who bestows it (or is the agent of divine bestowal). For even a repentant recipient of mercy may only be repentant in the short term. What is to prevent that recipient from turning against the benefactor in the longer term?

A memorable outworking of this theme constitutes one of the major subplots in Steven Spielberg's film *Saving Private Ryan*. In the aftermath of the Normandy landings on D-Day, Captain Miller (Tom Hanks) leads a group of soldiers into occupied France to recover Private Ryan (Matt Damon), who has parachuted into an advanced location, because Ryan's three brothers have already been killed in the landings. Miller takes as an interpreter Corporal Upham (Jeremy Davies), who is a good linguist but otherwise naïf and thoroughly unmilitary; whenever there is fighting, he shrinks and cowers and does not use a weapon, and he is not good even at his role of providing ammunition to the others in battle. While en route, Miller and his men have a skirmish, which leaves them with the problem of a German soldier (Joerg Stadler) as prisoner of war, whom they can hardly take with them. When Miller's other soldiers want simply to shoot him, Upham (who has also been prepared to chat with the German over a cigarette) protests and insists that that would not be right. Miller eventually releases the German soldier, blindfolded, and on his honor to hand himself in to an allied patrol.

When Private Ryan is found at the town of Ramelle, he does not want to be saved. Rather he insists on staying with his fellow soldiers with whom he had parachuted into action. So Miller and his soldiers decide that the only way to rescue Ryan is to stay with him and help to defend Ramelle, whose bridge makes it a strategic location for a German assault. When in due course the Germans do attack Ramelle, the released German soldier is among them. At the climax of the battle, the German soldier carefully targets and shoots

43. Don Isaac Abravanel, *Commentary on the Later Prophets* (Pesaro, 1520); cited in Simon, *Jonah*, ix. A similar interpretation runs through Marvin Sweeney's "Jonah," in his *The Twelve Prophets*, BO (Collegeville, MN: Liturgical Press, 2000), 1:301–34; e.g., 306–7, 318, 328.

44. John F. A. Sawyer, *Prophecy and the Prophets of the Old Testament*, OBS (Oxford: Oxford University Press, 1987), 114; see also Jenson, *Jonah*, 38, 83.

Captain Miller, who is fatally wounded—all of which Upham sees. At this point allied reinforcements arrive, and the Germans quickly surrender. For the first time Upham takes a gun and uses it to help round up the surrendered Germans, among whom is the particular German soldier. Although the German soldier speaks confidently and reassuringly to his fellow Germans ("I know this man"), Upham brusquely tells him to be quiet and after a brief moment's hesitation shoots him dead. Although the German soldier had received mercy from Captain Miller, he did not reciprocate. So Corporal Upham does not want to extend it to him again.

Steven Spielberg offers a brilliant exploration of the potential danger in showing mercy to someone. To imagine that Jonah dislikes divine mercy because of potential future danger from Assyria for Israel opens up an engagement with an enduring issue that can arise in many different ways.

Is Mercy Subversive of Moral Effort?

Another way of envisaging Jonah's objection is to see his concern in terms of divine mercy's being morally and spiritually debilitating: it can undercut the need to live before God with faithfulness and integrity. Hans Walter Wolff, for example, adopts this approach (alongside others) in his commentary on Jonah: "This exposes the essential reason for Jonah's despair. . . . Jonah chimes in with the voices of the people with whom Malachi quarrels: 'It is pointless to serve God' (3:14[–18]). What difference is there 'between the person who serves God and the person who does not serve him' (3:18)?"[45] In other words, why bother to serve God by fulfilling the responsibilities of election and covenant through the often-demanding requirements of torah if those who do not do so receive divine mercy in the same way as those who do? On this approach, divine mercy can be generative of cynicism—that whatever the rhetoric attached to the importance of faithfulness and obedience, the reality of mercy undercuts it and exposes it as empty.[46]

Interestingly, Wolff articulates this understanding of Jonah's moan through intertextual appeal to Malachi—where, because of a possible similarity of

45. Hans Walter Wolff, *Obadiah and Jonah: A Commentary*, trans. Margaret Kohl (1977; ET, Minneapolis: Augsburg, 1986), 168; cf. 176. Similarly Terence E. Fretheim, *The Message of Jonah: A Theological Commentary* (Minneapolis: Augsburg, 1977), imagines the author's contemporaries, in a time of severe hardship, as saying: "'Our faith in God must have been in vain. All of our lives wasted on this commitment'" (121; cf. 34–37).

46. Compare a further expression of this outlook: "How can God expect the faithful to persevere with religious rectitude and justice when evil escapes punishment merely because of a moment's convenient 'repentance'?" (David M. Gunn and Danna Nolan Fewell, *Narrative in the Hebrew Bible*, OBS [Oxford: Oxford University Press, 1993], 139).

date between the two books, he may be envisaging the same specific historical problem of existential spiritual hopelessness being voiced in each text. This is possible. Within the book of Jonah itself, however, there is nothing else that would appear to point in this direction—which may make this a less likely reading. Nonetheless, an intertextual resonance with Malachi remains a possible reading strategy, with or without the conjecture of a shared historical context.

The value of this reading is that the problem it identifies is a real and recurring one. For example, it regularly appears in Christian faith in the context of the relationship between universalism, in the sense of a belief in ultimate salvation for all, and the motivation for mission. Undoubtedly much historic Christian mission has been driven by a sense that people can be ultimately lost; and if people can be brought to salvation, the sacrifices entailed by mission are worthwhile. Conversely, if one holds to universalism and so ultimate destiny is not at risk, is mission and its possibly sacrificial cost really essential? May they rather be only optional? But the basic issue can easily arise in everyday situations in relationship to the cost of daily discipleship, with a "Why bother?" attitude.

The problem is not peculiar to the life of faith. For example, one contemporary realization is surely the increasingly problematic and complex issue of welfare dependence. Social welfare is in essence a political policy of social compassion. Welfare benefits are provided to try to ensure that those who are hard up are not deprived of a position within society; and in principle they are a temporary expedient, until these needy are better placed to fend for themselves. However, the intended purpose of welfare provision can be subverted. It has become clear that it can readily engender a frame of mind in which the unemployed can reckon that it is not worth getting a job or trying to better oneself if the financial and social benefits of work are not greatly different from those of social security (though the problem is often exacerbated by dysfunctional familial and social settings). The attempt to preserve welfare from such subversion is a major contemporary socio-political challenge. The basic problem is simple: though the intention of compassion may be one thing, its result may be another. Compassion can undercut existential struggle and moral effort. In the terms of Jonah's imagined perspective, why should the hard-working and law-abiding put in all that effort so as to support welfare scroungers?

To read Jonah's complaint in the way Wolff does opens up a wide-ranging subject matter with significant moral and existential dimensions.

Is Mercy Morally Objectionable?

A third reading of Jonah's complaint, which has some overlap with the previous point but merits distinct discussion, is that Jonah is protesting against unfairness and/or injustice. As Yehezkel Kaufmann put it, "Jonah is outraged, not because he is a narrow-minded zealot, but because he is a champion of divine justice. He is the voice of the ancient idea that sin must be punished."[47]

A commonly cited parallel is the elder brother of the prodigal/wasteful son, who is angrily resentful at his father's generosity to his undeserving younger brother. The point of Jonah's objection would be that the Ninevites are so undeserving that to be merciful toward them and to spare them is morally offensive. Within the book of Jonah, the basis for this could be that the Ninevites are notorious sinners ("Their wickedness has come up before me" [1:2]), though elsewhere the narrative makes no special point of their sin. Alternatively it could be that they are gentiles; although the Jonah story itself never makes a point of this, such a perspective could readily be introduced from elsewhere in the canonical collection. Or these could be combined.

The overlap with the previous point can be seen in the words of the elder brother: "Listen! For all these years I have been working like a slave for you, and I have never disobeyed your command; yet you have never given me even a young goat so that I might celebrate with my friends. But when this son of yours came back, who has devoured your property with prostitutes, you killed the fatted calf for him!" (Luke 15:29–30). Again there is a clear sense in which mercy appears subversive of moral effort. The difference, however, is in perspective and tone. In the previous section the perspective was looking to the future and disenchanted in tone: "Why bother?" Here the perspective is looking to the past, and the tone is indignant: "It's outrageous!"

The text of Jonah is surely open to such a reading, inasmuch as I cannot see that any part of the story ceases to make sense or jars in the light of it. Again, its appeal lies in the way it raises an enduring existential issue. One form in which it can be developed relates to the difficulty some have with mercy or forgiveness in relation to those from whom they, or those dear to them, have suffered much: mercy toward such people can be not a moral marvel but a moral offense. The problems posed by the Holocaust/Shoah are paradigmatic of the difficulties here.[48] However, the lack of specificity in Jonah about actual wrongdoings perpetrated by the Ninevites suggests that

47. Yehezkel Kaufmann, *The Religion of Israel*, trans. and abridged by Moshe Greenberg (New York: Schocken Books, 1972), 285.

48. The issues here are too complex for brief discussion. One famous posing of some of the key issues is by Simon Wiesenthal, *The Sunflower: On the Possibilities and Limits of Forgiveness*, 2nd ed. (New York: Schocken Books, 1997). It explores the issue not just of forgiveness for atrocity but also more specifically of whether someone other than the victim(s) has the right to forgive. A fine general discussion of the challenges in understanding and practicing forgiveness is by Anthony Bash, *Forgiveness and Christian Ethics*, NSCE (Cambridge: Cambridge University Press, 2007).

particularly heinous offenses and the moral problems they pose are not in view in the book.

Is Jonah Selfish?

Finally, Jonah's complaint can be read as an attempt to limit divine mercy for no reason other than simple selfishness. In the narrative one can contrast the fact that Jonah himself receives divine mercy—which he celebrates with the psalm inside the big fish (with its resounding conclusion "Deliverance belongs to the LORD!" in 2:9b [10b MT])—with his moaning response to the Ninevites' being spared by YHWH. This can be read as a straightforward unwillingness to see what he himself has enjoyed being extended to others. Such an unwillingness does not necessarily need moral rationalizing ("They are gentiles / particularly undeserving"), for it can be existentially meaningful on its own terms. This is a reading that initially appeals to the internal logic of the story, without introducing assumptions from elsewhere in the canon.

A possible biblical parallel might be the teaching of Jesus in Matthew's Gospel where the receipt of forgiveness from God must be accompanied by the extension of forgiveness to others. This issue, which features in the Lord's Prayer (Matt. 6:12) and is underlined in the comments immediately following the Lord's Prayer (6:14–15), is illustrated in the parable of the unforgiving servant (18:23–35), which concludes the discourse on church discipline (18:1–35): to refuse to extend to another the mercy that oneself has received is by that very token to nullify the mercy.[49]

However, it is doubtful that Jonah's complaint about divine mercy is a precise analogy to the Gospel narrative, such that Jonah is in effect nullifying the mercy that he has received. Certainly, on this reading strategy, Jonah is indeed selfish like the unforgiving servant. But as the narrative continues, the point is not that Jonah is in danger of nullifying divine compassion but rather that he needs to learn that its scope is greater than he has hitherto appreciated, such that its extension to the Ninevites should not be a problem. This selfishness is instructed rather than penalized, if one reads the story in this way.

YHWH's Response to Jonah

The thesis at the heart of our reading is that Jonah does not understand divine mercy and responsiveness, even though he knows its prime canonical formulations. The diversity of ways in which Jonah's complaint about

49. See the discussion in chap. 4 above.

divine mercy can be read, for each of which a case can be made, does not enable us to pinpoint the precise reason for Jonah's taking exception to Yʜwʜ's merciful sparing of Nineveh. Although I have some inclination to the view that Jonah is straightforwardly selfish (narcissistic even?), a reading that imports a minimum of assumptions from beyond the world of the narrative, I do not think it possible, or even desirable, to try to establish this reading as *the* reading. Indeed, I would suggest that this inability to pinpoint Jonah's problem should be seen as a strength rather than a weakness.[50] The openness of the narrative to be read in a variety of ways corresponds to the variety of reasons for which people can find mercy problematic. Those who would appropriate the story in a contemporary context have considerable freedom in choosing which particular objections to mercy should be developed as a focus.

Nevertheless, it remains for us to see how God responds to Jonah's complaint, and what this also might imply for contemporary appropriation.

> [4]And the Lᴏʀᴅ said, "Is it right for you to be angry?" [5]Then Jonah went out of the city and sat down east of the city, and made a booth for himself there. He sat under it in the shade, waiting to see what would become of the city.
>
> [6]The Lᴏʀᴅ God appointed a bush, and made it come up over Jonah, to give shade over his head, to save him from his discomfort; so Jonah was very happy about the bush. [7]But when dawn came up the next day, God appointed a worm that attacked the bush, so that it withered. [8]When the sun rose, God prepared a sultry east wind, and the sun beat down on the head of Jonah so that he was faint and asked that he might die. He said, "It is better for me to die than to live."
>
> [9]But God said to Jonah, "Is it right for you to be angry about the bush?" And he said, "Yes, angry enough to die."

Perhaps the first thing to note about this narrative is what it does not say. If Jonah's problem relates to his (mis)understanding of central theological affirmations within Israel's scriptures, one possibility would be for Yʜwʜ to respond with scriptural argument of some kind or other—say, to discuss the meaning of the passages cited, perhaps with an injunction "Go and learn what this means," or to appeal to a different passage. Yet of this there is nothing. Further, it is worth noting that although the book repeatedly portrays God's

---

50. For a valuable account of different readings of Jonah and the hermeneutical issues of what, if anything, constrains their diversity, and why, see Ehud Ben Zvi, "Infinite but Limited Diversity: A Heuristic, Theoretical Framework for Analyzing Different Interpretations of the Book of Jonah," in his *Signs of Jonah: Reading and Rereading in Ancient Yehud*, JSOTSS 367 (London: Sheffield Academic Press, 2003), 129–54.

sovereignty (over sea, fish, plant, worm, wind),[51] a sovereignty that can apparently readily engender responsiveness among sailors and Ninevites, there is no exercise of this sovereignty upon Jonah in any such way as to "compel" his response. Jonah outside Nineveh is left to decide how he will respond to what has happened and what God makes to happen around him.[52]

God opts for an enacted parable (perhaps analogous to the symbolic actions sometimes performed by prophets?). He makes a bush grow and die. He correspondingly gives Jonah some initial comfort that is then replaced by greater discomfort, so as to initiate a further dialogue. Here we may recollect a commonplace of the study of Israel's Wisdom literature. Wisdom literature characteristically eschews themes peculiar to Israel's identity and vocation (election, covenant, prophecy, priesthood, holiness—or indeed, the citation of Scripture) and appeals rather to characteristics of the created order. In schematic terms, instead of the authoritative voice "from above," as in "thus says Yнwн," we have an approach "from below," as in "Go to the ant, you sluggard; consider its ways, and be wise!" (Prov. 6:6 NIV). As Phyllis Trible puts it, "Yнwн develops the argument through natural rather than revealed theology."[53]

God's question to Jonah about the bush is perhaps initially a little surprising since Jonah's concern is surely not really the withering of the bush but rather the loss of his shelter and his consequent discomfort: his concern is not for the bush but for himself. But the question appears to be a persuasive redescription of Jonah's situation, which thereby allows Jonah to see himself as not merely selfish, but rather also concerned about something else's well-being. At any rate Jonah does not resist the suggestion that his misery may in some sense be altruistic. One can read his words in 4:9 as implying, "Why yes, my misery is

51. The sovereignty is expressed in the repeated use of the verb *minnāh* (in the vav-consecutive/ *vĕqātal* form *vayĕman*), "he appointed" (4:6, 7, 8; cf. 2:1 [1:17 ET]), a verb used elsewhere of royal executive action (Dan. 1:5).

52. The puzzle represented by Jonah's "waiting to see what would become of the city" (4:5)—does he not know of the divine decision in 3:10? is the verse perhaps misplaced?—may simply indicate (as numerous readers down the years have surmised) that Jonah is waiting to see whether the Ninevites remain repentant, probably in the hope that if they soon cease to be so, then the divine judgment might be reinstated. (For a survey of the interpretive options here, see Jack M. Sasson, *Jonah*, AB 24B [New York: Doubleday, 1990], 287–90).

There is also some unclarity as to the relationship between Jonah's booth (4:5) and the plant (4:6) since the purpose of each is to give shade. However, these two sources of shade can easily be rationalized if one is so inclined: "Anyone who has sat in a tent for a day in the Near East understands that additional shade is always welcome!" (Fretheim, *Message*, 123).

53. Phyllis Trible, "Divine Incongruities in the Book of Jonah," in *God in the Fray: A Tribute to Walter Brueggemann*, ed. Tod Linafelt and Timothy K. Beal (Minneapolis: Fortress, 1998), 198–208, esp. 207.

because of my concern for that poor plant." Jonah can claim the moral high ground.[54] However, Jonah's acceding to the way in which God has posed the issue opens the way for a final riposte:

> [10]Then the LORD said, "You are concerned [*ḥūs*] about the bush, for which you did not labor and which you did not grow; it came into being in a night and perished in a night. [11]And should I not be concerned [*ḥūs*] about Nineveh, that great city, in which there are more than a hundred and twenty thousand persons who do not know their right hand from their left, and also many animals?"

First and foremost, Jonah's compassion is too limited and narrowly focused. He cares for what does not matter (or hardly matters) and does not care for what does matter. What is a bush in relation to a great city of people and animals? Like Jonah's moan about mercy, this riposte makes a general point that is open to be read in more than one way. He only wants to be merciful where to do so is safe and carries no risk; he selfishly cares only for himself and not for others; he wants to restrict divine mercy to the elect and does not want to see Israel's enemies (or gentiles, or sinners . . .) receive what Israel receives. Rather than try to say that any one of these different angles is the correct one, it would be better to say, "If the hat fits, wear it." The restricted and parochial nature of human care is a perennial phenomenon, which takes countless forms among believers and others alike. It is part of what gives the story of Jonah its enduring resonance.

The Ninevites, for whom YHWH cares, are solely characterized as utterly ignorant, ignorant in the way that small children are ignorant (for it is small children who cannot tell the right hand from the left). It would have been possible, in the light of depictions elsewhere in Israel's Scriptures, to ascribe morally reprehensible qualities to the Ninevites (e.g., arrogance, as in Isa. 10:5–15; cruelty, as in Nah. 3:19) and to present the challenge of compassion in relation to such offensive qualities. However, our text simply stresses ignorance *tout court*. YHWH's redescription of Jonah's selfish misery as care for the plant is surely dwarfed by this depiction of the most powerful nation of Jonah's world as marked by the ignorance characteristic of small children. In this divine perspective, Assyrian power and wealth apparently do not count, because as people they do not know what really matters—which presumably is located in the moral and spiritual realm.

---

54. There are also resonances with prophetic death wishes elsewhere in the Hebrew Bible, such as those of Moses (Num. 11:11–15), Elijah (1 Kings 19:4) or Jeremiah (Jer. 20:14–18). Such resonances heighten the sense of Jonah's posturing.

Although YHWH's dialogue with Jonah takes the form of natural theology, there is nonetheless a presupposition of a scale of values that is far from self-evident, of a sort generally associated in the Hebrew scriptures with torah and prophecy; if it can be said of Israel that they are "a wise and discerning people," this is because they live by YHWH's gift of torah (Deut. 4:5–8). However, YHWH's point is that the insight of wisdom, to which Israel has access in torah, should engender toward those who lack it not arrogance or disdain but rather compassion. The way in which the Gospels overturn conventional assumptions about power and importance, and present knowledge of God's priorities as a reason for active compassion toward others, stands in strong continuity with this.[55]

The keyword in what YHWH says is *ḥūs* ("pity," "care about," "be concerned for"). One might have expected a repetition of one of the keywords characterizing YHWH in Jonah's moaning citation of Exodus 34:6, either *ḥānan* ("be gracious to," the verbal form of the adjective *ḥannūn*) or *riḥam* ("show mercy on," the verbal form of *raḥūm*). But maybe the point is that *ḥūs* is a term lacking the resonances of association with the character of God that mark the terms in the well-known quasi-creedal formulation; and so it may help Jonah think freshly about what the familiar affirmation of divine mercy really means.[56] The most common usage of *ḥūs* is with the eye as subject,[57] so that its primary resonances are with the human phenomenon of a tear coming to the eye—the spontaneous and unpredictable bodily response to other creatures in need. One needs no special intelligence, never mind the special revelation of torah, to recognize and understand the tear that shows the care of the heart. How much more then should something so basic to human experience be recognized as characterizing humanity's Creator, especially when it is a matter not just of something trivial but rather of the condition of living beings, both humans and animals. But what is true of God should also, by implication, be true of the creature who claims in some way to know this Creator. This is what Jonah and the readers/hearers are left to ponder.

55. The point, that moral and spiritual ignorance on the part of the powerful is pitiable, is a particular emphasis in Luke-Acts, especially in the famous words of Jesus on the cross, "Father, forgive them; for they do not know what they are doing" (Luke 23:34; cf. Acts 3:17; 13:27; 17:23, 30).

56. It should be noted, however, that *ḥūs* appears in Joel 2:17 ("Spare your people, O LORD"), and its use in Jon. 4:10–11 could be read as part of an intertextual resonance between Joel and Jonah additional to that which has already been discussed.

57. Wolff succinctly says about *ḥūs*, "The word occurs 24 times in the Old Testament. On 15 of these occasions the eye is the subject" (*Obadiah and Jonah*, 173). For general discussion, see S. Wagner, "*Chûs*," *TDOT* 4:271–77.

Conclusion

I have suggested that a fruitful way to read the story of Jonah, with Jonah's moaning prayer to God as a key element, is in terms of Jonah's not knowing what he ought to know.[58] On one level he indeed knows that YHWH is gracious, merciful, and sparing—for he can, as it were, cite chapter and verse, and he knows it from his own experience en route to Nineveh. Yet he does not really understand it, for when YHWH acts thus toward the Ninevites, he is not grateful but upset, and so YHWH must try to enable Jonah to rethink what mercy means. In this way Jonah depicts a recurrent problem within the life of faith: deficient understanding of familiar words that play a foundational role in Scripture and the creeds. There is probably nothing in either Scripture or the creeds that is not misunderstood by someone, somewhere, sometime, as much within as outside communities of faith. The ease with which truths that should inspire gratitude, worship, and self-giving service can become slogans to be bandied around in point-scoring or self-justification is dismaying. All of this means that theological learning, like the moral and spiritual growth from which it should be inseparable, must be an unending process.

One of the distinctive contributions of the story of Jonah is the way in which the problem of incomprehension is tackled. When Jonah's problem is that he knows the scriptural words but cannot grasp their true meaning, the narrative moves the issue onto a different level. The appeal is not to Scripture but to reason, not to revelation but to natural theology, not to an injunction but to a parable, not to a divine imperative but to a divine question. Although such an approach is well known in the parables of Jesus, it is less well known in the context of the Hebrew Bible. To be sure, the book of Jonah (in itself and still more when read in canonical context) does not question the foundational role of Israel's particular knowledge of God through torah, nor does it suggest that appeal to natural theology could somehow dispense with the word of YHWH to Moses or Jeremiah.[59] Rather, natural theology plays a subordinate and critical role,

58. This is not, of course, a novel reading, even if I have particularly developed its implications here. Jonathan Magonet, e.g., observes: "The extent and quality of Jonah's knowledge is also questioned. . . . He *knows* his tradition. . . . Yet . . . the irony lies here in the fact that what he quotes has a paradoxical relationship to what he does, his very disobedience illustrating the distance between his *formal* knowledge of tradition and his *experienced* knowledge" (*Form and Meaning: Studies in Literary Techniques in the Book of Jonah*, BLS 8 [Sheffield: Almond, 1983], 91–92).

59. For example, the contention that "the book of Jonah appears to be a cautionary challenge to standard theological formulations (4:2)" and that "the great authority of the prophetic voices . . . was under attack from Jonah" (Bruce Birch, Walter Brueggemann, Terence Fretheim, and David Petersen, *A Theological Introduction to the Old Testament* [Nashville: Abingdon, 1999], 439) unhelpfully allows a conjecture about religious conflict at the time of the book's

to enable fresh re-engagement with the given content of revelation when that content has for some reason become stale or problematic. It is a reminder that the contemporary quest for understanding needs to use all possible resources.

Finally, the book of Jonah shows how theological understanding is exemplified in a person's attitudes and actions: what Jonah does flows from his understanding of YHWH. The more deficient the understanding, the more questionable the actions. So when the task of educating Jonah is extended to educating believers today, it is important not to intellectualize the problems of understanding in an abstract way. As Colin Gunton puts it: "Theology is a practical, not a merely theoretical discipline: it aims at wisdom, in the broad sense of light for the human path. Our theological enterprises must therefore be judged at least in part by their fruit."[60] Good pedagogy sees learning and life as belonging together.

---

composition (analogous to conjectures about responses to Ezra and Nehemiah) to have undue influence on, and surely skew, the reading of the text.

60. Colin Gunton, *The One, the Three and the Many: God, Creation and the Culture of Modernity* (Cambridge: Cambridge University Press, 1993), 7.

7

Faith and Perplexity

Down through the ages, the most read and most used part of Israel's scriptures, on the part of Jews and Christians alike, has been the Psalter. In the book of Psalms countless people have discovered and learned the language of prayer. They have made the words their own, and they have used these words when other words have failed. No attempt to hear some of the representative voices of the Old Testament would be complete without at least some attention to the Psalms.

The Hebrew name for the Psalter is *Tehillim* (Praises). Many psalms articulate praise and thanksgiving, and this is the note on which the Psalter ends, with a run of psalms that all end with *halĕlū-yāh*, "Praise the LORD." To praise, to express wonder and joy and gratitude for life and its blessings, and to direct this to the one who gives it all, is fundamental within the life of faith.

Nevertheless, the single most common type of psalm is not the praise but the lament. In recent years much attention has been directed to psalms of lament, not least from a renewed appreciation of the spiritual and psychological importance of honesty in facing the many difficulties and perplexities that can be part of the life of faith, and of giving expression to this in prayer and worship. In line with this, I will consider here Psalms 44 and 89, which are broadly two psalms of lament, though a distinctive kind of lament.

In this chapter I develop two of my earlier discussions: "*Qyn*/Lament," in *New International Dictionary of Old Testament Theology and Exegesis*, ed. William A. VanGemeren (Carlisle: Paternoster: 1997), 4:880–82; and *The Theology of the Book of Genesis*, OTT (New York and Cambridge: Cambridge University Press, 2009), 66–68.

A Reading of Psalm 44

This psalm is conventionally recognized as a psalm of communal lament; indeed it is the first such in the sequence of the Psalter.[1] Its date is uncertain, and any decision about date and origin depends on which context one might infer from the words of the psalm itself. I will suggest, however, that the nature of the psalm is such that, whenever it was written, its interpretation resists being closely attached to any one historical context, for its purpose is to address a recurrent issue within the life of God's people.

The psalm is in four parts (vv. 1–8, 9–16, 17–22, 23–26),[2] or perhaps five if one divides verses 1–8 into two sections (but nothing of substance hangs on this possible subdivision). Despite the differences in content and tone between the parts, it is important to read them in relation to the whole if the psalm is to be understood.

Although much contemporary scholarship is open to unitive readings of biblical texts, it is worthwhile not to forget that a former generation of scholars tended to read differently. For example, in T. K. Cheyne's 1904 commentary, Psalm 44 is divided into two separate texts. One (vv. 1–8 of the canonical text) was "probably the preface to a lost historical psalm" and so ends with an editorial "conclusion lost." The other (vv. 9–26 of the canonical text) was "a prayer of the innocent martyr-nation," which is prefaced by an editorial "some stanzas lost."[3] As ever, interpretive judgments are integral to the process of reading, and the question of which judgments "come naturally," and why, deserves more attention than it often receives.

To the leader. Of the Korahites. A Maskil.[4]

[1]We have heard with our ears, O God,[5]
    our ancestors have told us,

1. If any significance is to be attached to this, it would need to be in relation to recent discussions about the shaping of the Psalter as a whole. One might, e.g., take Ps. 44 in close connection with the individual laments of Pss. 42–43 and see this as a deliberate opening of the second book of the Psalter in terms of lament both individual and communal—perhaps leading up to the Davidic prayer for Solomon as model king (Ps. 72), with which the second book concludes.

2. I am following the English verse numeration. In the Hebrew, because the psalm title is v. 1, every verse number is greater by one.

3. T. K. Cheyne, *The Book of Psalms* (London: Kegan Paul, Trench, Trübner, 1904), 1:191–94.

4. I find no particular interpretive significance in these titular notations, other than *maskil*, which appears also in the title of Ps. 89. *Maskil* is a puzzling term: it is used in the headings of thirteen psalms, where it is far from obvious what, if anything, they all have in common. However, in philological terms the form and meaning is clear: "something that gives understanding" (*maskil* is a *hiphil* [causative] participle used as a noun, of the verbal root *sākal*, "to be prudent/ intelligent"). Thus a *maskil* is "an instructive song" or "contemplative poem" (cf. *DCH* 5:505; *BDB* 968). I suggest that, irrespective of the difficult historical question of how *maskil* was understood by the compilers of the Psalter, it is appropriate for a reader to adopt the philological sense of *maskil* as part of a reading strategy for Pss. 44 and 89. These two psalms represent material to be pondered prayerfully and at length by believers, so that they may thereby deepen their grasp of God's ways in the world and be better able to endure the inexplicable.

5. Psalm 44 is part of the "Elohistic Psalter" (Pss. 42–83) in which, for some reason, there is a consistent preference for referring to the deity as "God" (*'ĕlōhīm*) rather than "the Lord/Yhwh"

what deeds you performed in their days,
>   in the days of old:
²you with your own hand drove out the nations,
>   but them you planted;
you afflicted the peoples,
>   but them you set free;
³for not by their own sword did they win the land,
>   nor did their own arm give them victory;
but your right hand, and your arm,
>   and the light of your countenance,
>   for you delighted in them.

The psalm begins with what is in essence a creed—an official recitation of what is believed to be true about God and His dealings with Israel.⁶ Here the creedal recitation is directed to the past—what "we," those within Israel reciting the psalm, affirm about what God did for Israel in its foundational and formative period long ago, the story of which has been passed down over the generations (v. 1). The content of this is that God gave Israel their land, Canaan, by dispossessing its former inhabitants and settling Israel in their place. The broad canonical story, from God's promise to Abraham to Israel's occupation of Canaan under Joshua, is assumed rather than specified; the focus is on God's action in giving Israel victory over others (v. 2). Moreover this victory was marked by no sense of self-achievement on Israel's part, but rather by a dependence on God, who in effect did the real fighting—not that Israel did not fight, but that they fought in recognition of their God as the one enabling and overruling their efforts. In brief, they fought in faith, and God approved of this (v. 3). This is content appropriate to Israel's present identity as still the people of this God.

⁴You are my King and my God;⁷
>   you command⁸ victories for Jacob.

(*yhwh*). In this psalm the Tetragrammaton does not appear (44:23 [24 MT] has *'adōnāy* rather than *yhwh*). It is doubtful that this has significance for a contemporary reader, other than as a historical peculiarity.

6. Although the OT does not contain the kind of creed with which Christians are familiar (Apostles' Creed, Nicene Creed), and although von Rad's once-influential thesis about the formative nature of the creedal formulation in Deut. 26:5–10 has not undeservedly fallen on hard times, one still should recognize the presence of material that fulfills a role best depicted by the concept of a creed.

7. There are occasional first-person-singular expressions (44:4, 6, 15) among the predominant first-person plurals of the psalm. They may represent a particular individual speaking on behalf of the community, or they could be a personification of the community. In any event, the focus throughout remains on Israel as a community.

8. The NRSV (in 44:4 [5 MT]) is surely right to read a participial form, *mĕtsavveh* ("one who commands"), following LXX and Syriac, rather than MT's imperatival form, *tsavvēh*

[5]Through you we push down our foes;
    through your name we tread down our assailants.
[6]For not in my bow do I trust,
    nor can my sword save me.
[7]But you have saved us from our foes,
    and have put to confusion those who hate us.
[8]In God we have boasted continually,
    and we will give thanks to your name forever. *Selah*[9]

The creedal form continues, but with a difference. The difference is temporal: the creedal content no longer looks to the past but rather to the present, and the affirmation no longer comprises what has been passed down from the ancestors but is a contemporary recognition of what God does. Other than this difference of tense, the content of the affirmation is similar, relating to God's giving Israel victory over their enemies. God gives Israel victory in the here and now, as their faithful sovereign lord (vv. 4–5). Moreover, present Israel, like their ancestors, do not trust in their own martial abilities but rather in the enabling and overruling God: it is He who gives the victory (vv. 6–7). Thus the Israelites find their identity in joyful praise to their God, who is the focus of their confidence and thanksgiving (v. 8). When these creedal affirmations are taken together, they express two things: continuity of faith in God over the generations—as they then, so we now; and confidence in God, who gives deliverance and victory to His people—in God we trust and triumph. This sets the context, and also serves as a foil, for the next part of the psalm.

[9]Yet you have rejected us and abased us,
    and have not gone out with our armies.
[10]You made us turn back from the foe,
    and our enemies have taken spoil for themselves.[10]
[11]You have made us like sheep for slaughter,
    and have scattered us among the nations.
[12]You have sold your people for a trifle,
    demanding no high price for them.

("command"). The MT makes poor sense, and an initial *mem* of *mĕtsavveh* has most likely been lost. This could be through its becoming attached to the end of the previous word, which now reads *'lhym* ("God") but could initially have been *'lhy* ("my God," though this would also require a connective *vav*, i.e., *v'lhy*, "and my God"); or it could be through haplography if the scribe wrote *mem* only once (*'ĕlōhīm tsavvēh*) instead of twice (*'ĕlōhīm mĕtsavveh*).

9. I have nothing to offer about the possible significance of *selāh*, other than to observe that both here and in Ps. 89 it comes at the end of a distinct section within the psalm.

10. Verse 10 is from the NRSVA translation.

¹³You have made us the taunt of our neighbors,
    the derision and scorn of those around us.
¹⁴You have made us a byword among the nations,
    a laughingstock among the peoples.
¹⁵All day long my disgrace is before me,
    and shame has covered my face
¹⁶at the words of the taunters and revilers,
    at the sight of the enemy and the avenger.

The problem is that what has happened is the direct opposite of what Israel creedally confesses. The God who commands victories for Jacob has given victory to Jacob's enemies (vv. 9–10). Instead of "through you we push down our foes" (v. 5), what has happened has been that "you made us turn back from the foe" (v. 10). Instead of Israel's being a formidable presence, they have been as easy to deal with as sheep: easy to kill, easy to scatter (v. 11). Indeed their enemies have gained victory almost effortlessly, for Israel has been like something worthless, whose owner cannot wait to get rid of it and so sells it at reduced price to the first buyer who comes along (v. 12). The result is constant mockery and abuse from the peoples surrounding Israel (e.g., Philistines, Moabites, Aramaeans), who now have a simple way of referring to Israel: "Who's a loser? Israel" (vv. 13–14). Thus the present reality is humiliation, with nothing to say in response to those who scorn and scoff (vv. 15–16). Instead of the creedal affirmation "In God we have boasted continually" (v. 8), what is happening is that "all day long my disgrace is before me" (v. 15). In place of victory, there is defeat; in place of glory, there is shame; in place of confidence, there is confusion.

Why? How could this be? Is there some ready way of understanding why God has treated His chosen people thus?

¹⁷All this has come upon us,
    yet we have not forgotten you,
    or been false to your covenant.
¹⁸Our heart has not turned back,
    nor have our steps departed from your way,
¹⁹yet you have broken us in the haunt of jackals,
    and covered us with deep darkness.
²⁰If we had forgotten the name of our God,
    or spread out our hands to a strange god,
²¹would not God discover this?
    For he knows the secrets of the heart.
²²Because of you we are being killed all day long,
    and accounted as sheep for the slaughter.

Israel knows that sin can incur judgment. The problem is that they have not
been faithless: they have kept God's covenant and have walked in His way (vv.
17–18). Yet although such obedience could anticipate divine blessing (Deut.
28:1–14), they are in a bad place—devastation and ruins (i.e., the kind of
place where jackals live), a place with no glimmer of light, even in the distance (v. 19). They know that faithlessness to their God would be found out,
even if their faithlessness had been kept secret, away from the public eye, for
God can see what humans can hide (vv. 20–21). So, if they had been faithless,
their present distress would make sense, for it could be understood as divine
judgment upon sin. But that is not the case. Rather, it is precisely *because*
they have been faithful to their God that they are being killed as easily as
defenseless sheep (v. 22).

It is important that this protestation of faithfulness be taken at face value,
not undercut by some explicit or implicit theological axiom about the ubiquity
of human sin and self-deception—as though they only *thought* they had been
faithful, whereas *in reality they must have been faithless*.[11] The point of the
text is not a claim to sinlessness (in some abstract sense), but rather a claim
to faithfulness (in actual practice); and if faithfulness is to be a meaningful
and not an empty category, then it needs to be recognized here. Otherwise
the logic of the psalm is destroyed. The psalm would then become in essence
a testimony to human lack of self-awareness. The solution to the disparity
between creedal faith and contemporary distress would then most likely be
that canvassed in verses 17–22: it would be an act of divine judgment on sin,
even if the shallowness of the psalmist's awareness of the realities of sin puts
this recognition beyond his grasp. Such a hermeneutic, however, is uncomfort-
ably reminiscent of Job's comforters.

Conversely, one should not ascribe too much weight to this protestation of faithfulness, in which
verses 4–8 would need to be included alongside verses 17–22, as though it depicts a rare and
golden moment in Israel's history (vv. 1–3 also presents a comparable issue for Israel's early history). Franz Delitzsch, for example, makes much of the psalm's "lofty self-consciousness" (which
he ascribes to the time of David), such that "in this respect Ps. 44 stands perfectly alone: it is like

11. Gerald H. Wilson, e.g., introduces a discussion of Ps. 44's contemporary significance
with a recognition of this tendency: "Too often our first reaction to Psalm 44 is to dismiss the
protestation of innocence as a rather deceitful manipulation of God by a people in a state of
deep denial. After all, we say, 'all have sinned and fall short of the glory of God' (Rom. 3:23)"
(*Psalms*, NIVAC [Grand Rapids: Zondervan, 2002], 1:694). Wilson himself resists the move.
Others, however, cannot resist making the move in one way or other. So, e.g., Samuel Terrien
says: "But what does the psalmist mean by not forgetting the name of God, or not worshiping
a foreign deity? Does he ignore the ethical demands of the Sinai covenant? Innocent of idolatry,
Israel may not be blameless in social equity. . . . The psalmist insists on the purity of the cult.
He is silent on the oppression of the poor" (*The Psalms: Strophic Structure and Theological*
Commentary, ECC [Grand Rapids: Eerdmans, 2003], 360–61).

the national mirroring of the Book of Job, and by reason of this takes a unique position in the range of Old Testament literature side by side with Lam. ch. 3 and the deutero-Isaiah. . . . In this Psalm, Israel stands in exactly the same relation to God as Job and the 'Servant of Jahve.'"[12] This idealizing and historicizing move risks downplaying the specific function of verses 17–22, which is not to memorialize a golden moment but to remove the possibility of "resolving" Israel's affliction by appeal to sin and its consequences.

The one obvious theological explanation does not apply. So what is to be thought or done?

> [23]Rouse yourself! Why do you sleep, O Lord?
> Awake, do not cast us off forever!
> [24]Why do you hide your face?
> Why do you forget our affliction and oppression?
> [25]For we sink down to the dust;
> our bodies cling to the ground.
> [26]Rise up, come to our help.
> Redeem us for the sake of your steadfast love (ḥesed).

The only thing to do is to appeal to God. Although God is the problem—He is apparently unaware or unconcerned about Israel's plight (vv. 23–24)—He must also be the solution. There is nowhere else to go. Although Israel's situation is deathlike, it is still possible to appeal to God's fundamental quality of "steadfast love" (ḥesed) (vv. 25–26), and so this is the note on which the psalm ends.

The fact that ḥesed is fundamental to the character of Israel's God is spelled out in the Exodus narrative of Sinai, where YHWH reveals Himself to Moses in response to Moses's intercession in the aftermath of Israel's breaking the covenant with the golden calf (Exod. 34:6–7). Here ḥesed characterizes both the divine nature (v. 6) and the divine actions (v. 7): "The LORD . . . abounding in steadfast love (ḥesed) and faithfulness, keeping steadfast love (ḥesed) for the thousandth generation." It is natural that the language of this passage regularly appears in Israel's prayers.[13]

Yet if appeal is made to God, it is made in stark terms. The language of the previous two sections has already generated uncomfortable resonances, if one sets the repeated image of "like sheep for slaughter" (Ps. 44:11, 22) alongside depictions elsewhere in the Psalter of YHWH as the caring shepherd of Israel (Pss. 23; 95:7; 100:3). But in verse 23 the psalmist's language is as jarring as it could be. The reproach that God is sleeping and needs to wake up is at odds, of course, with the trusting affirmation of faith in Psalm 121:4, "He who keeps Israel will neither slumber nor sleep." But the most jarring

12. Carl F. Keil and Franz Delitzsch, *Commentary on the Old Testament*, trans. Francis Bolton, vol. 5, *Psalms* (1866–91; repr., Peabody, MA: Hendrickson, 2006), 319–20.

13. See the fuller discussion of Exod. 34:6 in chap. 6 above.

canonical resonance is with the story of Elijah and the prophets of Baal on Mount Carmel, which is presented as a contest between the true God and a false god: "The god who answers by fire is indeed God" (1 Kings 18:24). Elijah, fully confident, is happy to let the prophets of Baal go first; and unsurprisingly, when they call on Baal "there was no voice, and no answer" (18:26). As more time passes, Elijah mocks the futility of their efforts: "Cry aloud! Surely he is a god; either he is meditating, or he has wandered away, or he is on a journey, or perhaps he is asleep and must be awakened" (18:27). The climax of the four possible problems with Baal's responding to his prophets is that he might have fallen asleep and might need to be awakened. There is a flourish in the telling—falling asleep on the job is only what you should expect when dealing with a deity other than YHWH. Soon afterward YHWH answers Elijah's prayer by fire, and He is acknowledged by previously wavering Israel as the true God (18:38–39). It is a stirring story and is unforgettable. But perhaps precisely because it is unforgettable, Psalm 44:23 becomes uncomfortable reading.[14] It is all very well to mock the prophets of Baal, because their god is no true god. But what if that is how YHWH now appears? If He sleeps and needs to awake, how is He better than Baal? Of course, the psalm does not present YHWH as no different from Baal, for it ends with the appeal to His *ḥesed* and in this way reaffirms something of the creedal stance with which it began. Nonetheless, if the jarring quality of the language is not taken seriously—in essence, that the true God may in time of trouble be felt to be no god—one will most likely not do justice to the existential anguish that the psalm expresses.

Calvin instructively struggles with knowing how to handle such language. In commenting on verse 23, he initially observes that "God allows the saints to plead with him in this babbling manner." He goes on to note that "the insensibility of our nature is so great, that we do not at once comprehend the care which God has of us" and so "the faithful familiarly give utterance before God . . . which they conceive from the state of things as it is presented to their view; and in doing so, they discharge from their breasts those morbid affections which belong to the corruption of our nature, in consequence of which faith then shines forth in its pure and native character." Earlier on, in commenting on verse 17, he has recognized the problem that, if God is accused inappropriately, then "what is here spoken would no longer be a holy prayer, but rather an impious blasphemy." This problem resurfaces in verse 23: "If it is objected, that prayer, than which nothing is more holy, is defiled, when some froward imagination of the flesh is mingled with it, I confess that this is true." Yet he still wants to make some space for forceful language: "But in using this freedom,

14. My argument about the resonance between Ps. 44:23 and 1 Kings 18:27 does not express an authorial hermeneutic (unlike my argument about the nature and purpose of the psalm as a whole, which is author-focused), since the psalmist may or may not have had the Carmel narrative in mind (who knows?); rather it exemplifies a reader-oriented hermeneutic, a judgment about what is an appropriate intertextual linkage for a reader to make, given the combination of the biblical documents in a canonical collection. In other words, it is not a question of what it *meant* to the author but of what it *means* for the reader.

which the Lord vouchsafes to us, let us consider that, in his goodness and mercy, by which he sustains us, he wipes away this fault, that our prayers may not be defiled by it."[15]

On one level this is an admirable strategy of serious piety—to recognize that God graciously gives a certain freedom of utterance, but that we should nonetheless recognize it for what it is, an expression of a defective, not fully faithful, understanding of God and His ways. Yet on another level, Calvin may be failing to give the text its due. He mentions neither of the jarring Old Testament resonances (Ps. 121:4; 1 Kings 18:27), even though he could hardly have been unaware of them; and I wonder whether this might have been because attending to these parallels would make it hard to escape the labeling of Psalm 44:23 as "impious blasphemy." Moreover, his concern to maintain the holiness of true prayer makes him apparently unable to recognize that utterances that may formally (i.e., in the abstract) be blasphemous may nonetheless in practice be more like passing discords within a larger harmony, and so acceptable as the expression of honest and bewildered anguish. Words matter, but faith is surely unwise to police its linguistic boundaries too tightly.

How should this psalm be understood? My thesis is that the parts make sense in relation to the whole: so unless the whole is kept in view, the parts will be misunderstood. The psalm differs from regular laments in that it is explicitly designed not only to pose a problem that is both theological and existential but also to leave it without resolution. The opening creedal sections are juxtaposed with the middle section of disaster and disgrace in such a way as deliberately to present the apparent contradiction between creedal faith and actual circumstances, and to do so in such a way that it cannot be resolved by the obvious theological move (judgment on sin) but rather must be held unresolved in anguished appeal to God. The point is not lament or complaint as such, but rather the conflict between creed and circumstance, a conflict that may regularly occur, may be agonizing, and may not admit of any straightforward or immediate resolution.

There has been a recurrent tendency to locate the psalm in the Maccabean period, in relation to faithful Jews suffering persecution then.

One can trace this dating from antiquity to the present. More than one of the Antiochene church fathers advocated it, though strikingly in terms of David's predicting the Maccabean persecution. In the fifth century, Theodoret of Cyrus says: "The psalm predicts the Macedonian savagery, the godless and fierce attitude of Antiochus Epiphanes, and the bravery and piety of the Maccabees."[16] John Chrysostom similarly says: "The inspired author ... recites this psalm ... not in his own person but in the person of the Maccabees, describing and foretelling what would happen at that time. The inspired authors are like that, you see: they span all times, the past, the present, the future."[17] Calvin notes: "The complaints and lamentations ... may be appropriately referred to that miserable and calamitous period in which the outrageous tyranny of Antiochus destroyed

15. John Calvin, *Commentary on the Book of Psalms*, vol. 2, in *Calvin's Commentaries*, trans. James Anderson (Edinburgh: Calvin Translation Society, 1845; repr., Grand Rapids: Baker Books, 2005), 171–72, 163.

16. Theodoret of Cyrus, *Commentary on the Psalms: Psalms 1–72*, trans. Robert Charles Hill, FOTC 101 (Washington, DC: Catholic University of America Press, 2000), 254.

17. John Chrysostom, *St. John Chrysostom: Commentary on the Psalms*, trans. Robert Charles Hill (Brookline, MA: Holy Cross Orthodox Press, 1998), 1:231.

and wasted every thing."[18] Wellhausen succinctly observes (on v. 22, "because of you"): "It is in defense of their religion that the Jews are now slaughtered by the heathen and are waging war against them. The only period when this happened was the Maccabean, in the second century BC."[19]

Such a date may be correct—though it is contested by many interpreters, and we will never know. At least it is imaginatively appropriate. My argument, however, is that the world of the text constructs its own scenario of conflict without resolution, a scenario that, whenever first formulated, has its own integrity and depicts something recurrent in the life of the people of God. As Robert Davidson puts it: "Whatever its original historical context, the psalm had continuing historical relevance in any situation where the religious community found itself facing events which it was powerless to prevent and for which it could find no rational or satisfactory theological explanation."[20]

Although there are further things to say about Psalm 44, it will be best to defer such discussion until we have considered Psalm 89. For Psalm 89 presents matters in a way comparable to Psalm 44, only more so.[21]

A Reading of Psalm 89

This psalm has four parts (vv. 1–18, 19–37, 38–45, 46–51),[22] though with a couple of structural complications within the first two parts. As with Psalm 44, the parts need to be understood in relation to the whole.

Although once it was commonplace to interpret Psalm 89 as a composite, compiled more or less successfully from several originally independent elements, some scholars have argued for its original unity.[23] Such arguments tend to be inconclusive and are surely of secondary importance. It is certainly not difficult to imagine verses 1–18 (in whole or in part) as a freestanding hymn of praise, which is how it is often used in Christian liturgy. The important issue is whether or not the parts, even if once independent, have been formed into a coherent whole.

18. Calvin, *Commentary on the Book of Psalms*, 148.
19. Julius Wellhausen, *The Book of Psalms*, trans. Horace Howard Furness and John Taylor, SBONTNET (New York: Dodd, Mead, 1898), 183.
20. Robert Davidson, *The Vitality of Worship: A Commentary on the Book of Psalms* (Grand Rapids and Cambridge, UK: Eerdmans, 1998), 145.
21. Compare John Goldingay's observation that Ps. 89 might appropriately be seen "as a heightened version of Ps. 44" (*Psalms*, vol. 2, *Psalms 42–89*, BCOT [Grand Rapids: Baker Academic, 2007], 663). Substantive affinity between Pss. 44 and 89 receives some, though not extensive, recognition in the secondary literature.
22. As with Ps. 44, I am following the English verse numeration. In the Hebrew, because the psalm title is v. 1, every verse number is greater by one.
23. See, e.g., James M. Ward, "The Literary Form and Liturgical Background of Psalm LXXXIX," *VT* 11 (1961): 321–39; Richard J. Clifford, "Psalm 89: A Lament over the Davidic Ruler's Continued Failure," *HTR* 73 (1980): 35–47.

A Maskil of Ethan the Ezrahite.[24]

[1]I will sing of your steadfast love [*ḥesed*], O LORD, forever;
   with my mouth I will proclaim your faithfulness [*'ĕmūnāh*] to all
   generations.
[2]I declare that your steadfast love [*ḥesed*] is established forever;
   your faithfulness [*'ĕmūnāh*] is as firm as the heavens.[25]

The first section of the psalm, verses 1–18, is a hymn of praise to YHWH.[26]

The hymn of praise has two keynotes, one of which is sounded at the very beginning: YHWH is characterized by two prime qualities: steadfast love (*ḥesed*) and faithfulness (*'ĕmūnāh*). He is committed to His people, as in the covenant at Sinai (*ḥesed*, supremely in Exod. 34:6–7), and He is dependable (*'ĕmūnāh*—closely akin to *'ĕmeth* in Exod. 34:6, which NRSV also renders as "faithfulness").[27] Moreover because these qualities are enduring and unshakeable (v. 2), the psalmist will be able unendingly to praise YHWH for being so: he will never cease to be the beneficiary of God's love and faithfulness.

The identity of the speaker, the "I," is not specified, but the "I" does not appear further in this hymn of praise, and its identity does not bear on grasping the content of the hymn. One can readily think of the "I" of personal appropriation by the user of the psalm, rather than wonder about who an original "I" might have been.

[3]You said, "I have made a covenant with my chosen one,
   I have sworn to my servant David:
[4]'I will establish your descendants forever,
   and build your throne for all generations.'" *Selah*

Here we encounter the first structural complication. These two verses interrupt the flow of the hymn: they do not focus on praising God, but rather they articulate God's promise to David. This promise will be further developed

24. Ethan the Ezrahite is mentioned elsewhere as a famous wise man (surpassed, however, by Solomon; 1 Kings 4:31 [5:11 MT]). Whatever precisely one makes of this linkage, it suggests an understanding of the psalm as associated with wisdom—the kind of transformative understanding and ability to live well that may come from taking seriously the psalm's content.

25. There are some textual complexities in the opening verses, also in various other verses of the psalm; but unless they affect the overall sense or the substantive interpretive issues, I shall not discuss them.

26. It is also possible to read 89:1–2 as a distinct introductory declaration, followed by the distinctive vv. 3–4, with the hymn proper in vv. 5–18.

27. Whether or not the psalmist intended reference to Exod. 34:6–7 is a moot point. For intertextual issues I am proposing a reader-oriented rather than an authorial hermeneutic (cf. n. 14 above).

in the second section of the psalm. Their meter is also distinctive, being 3:3, unlike the fairly consistent 4:4 of the rest of verses 1–18. So it is not difficult to understand why the New English Bible took the liberty of transposing these two verses to the beginning of the second section. Nonetheless, as will be seen, the parts of Psalm 89 need to be understood in relation to the whole. Even if verses 1–2, 5–18 were once an independent hymn of praise, they have now been tied into a larger whole, not least by this inclusion of the divine promise to David. An opening reference to God's promise to David not only anticipates the second section but also introduces a concern that frames the psalm as a whole.

The content of these two verses relates to YHWH's commitment to David and his descendants,[28] the primary canonical formulation of which is in Nathan's oracle in 2 Samuel 7. When David wants to build a house for YHWH, a house in the sense of a temple, he is refused permission. However, Nathan then conveys YHWH's promise to David, a promise to build him a house, in the metaphorical sense of a dynasty—a dynasty, moreover, that is to be established in perpetuity ('ad-'ōlām, 2 Sam. 7:13, 16; Ps. 89:4 [5 MT]).[29] Because verse 4 expresses the promise to David in the second person, it is best read as a quotation of the known content of the divine promise mentioned in verse 3 (hence the single quotation marks enclosing v. 4 NRSV)—and it corresponds closely, though not verbatim, to 2 Samuel 7:13, 16 ("I will establish the throne of his kingdom forever . . . Your house and your kingdom shall be made sure forever before me; your throne shall be established forever").

This is one of the amazing moments in the Old Testament, a gratuitous undertaking of great magnitude by YHWH. Partly because of its familiarity in Jewish and Christian tradition, and partly because of a hermeneutic of suspicion that has been directed toward it by some interpreters (among the more memorable formulations is Robert Pfeiffer's "monkish drivel"),[30] it can be difficult to hear the divine promise as an overwhelming and humbling gift, which is the note that David sounds in his prayer that follows (2 Sam. 7:18–29).

28. The parallelism of v. 3 is instructive: "I have made a covenant" parallels "I have sworn," thereby illustrating a prime sense of covenant as promise, and "my chosen one" parallels "my servant David," thereby illustrating that election entails service of God.

29. Although 'ad-'ōlām can simply be rendered "forever," I think that "in perpetuity" better conveys that what is at stake is a bequest whose termination is not envisaged.

30. Robert H. Pfeiffer, *Introduction to the Old Testament* (London: A&C Black, 1948), 370. Pfeiffer is here approving the characterization of 2 Sam. 7 by his own teacher, William R. Arnold (cf. ibid., xii), which he has clearly made his own. He apparently reckons the Davidic covenant to be of a genre similar to that of the Donation of Constantine, whose exposé by Lorenzo Valla in the fifteenth century remains a famous paradigm of the value of historically alert philological study.

Nonetheless, such a note is entirely in accord with the joyful praise of the psalm, which now surrounds verses 3–4.

> ⁵Let the heavens praise your wonders, O Lord,
>   your faithfulness [*ĕmūnāh*] in the assembly of the holy ones.
> ⁶For who in the skies can be compared to the Lord?
>   Who among the heavenly beings is like the Lord,
> ⁷a God feared in the council of the holy ones,
>   great and awesome above all that are around him?
> ⁸O Lord God of hosts, who is mighty as you, O Lord?
>   Your faithfulness [*ĕmūnāh*] surrounds you.

The hymn resumes by again praising Yhwh's faithfulness (v. 5). But it moves also onto its other keynote theme, which is His sovereign power. Yhwh is incomparable, sovereign over other deities (vv. 6–7). The divine power and the divine faithfulness are explicitly celebrated together (v. 8).

> ⁹You rule the raging of the sea;
>   when its waves rise, you still them.
> ¹⁰You crushed Rahab like a carcass;
>   you scattered your enemies with your mighty arm.
> ¹¹The heavens are yours, the earth also is yours;
>   the world and all that is in it—you have founded them.
> ¹²The north and the south—you created them;
>   Tabor and Hermon joyously praise your name.

Yhwh's power is sovereign over all—the restless and unruly sea (v. 9), the mythological monster, any opposition (v. 10). Above and below, all is His work (v. 11), and the world from end to end, even great mountains (which might be locations where deities other than Yhwh were worshiped), all things joyfully acknowledge their sovereign Creator (v. 12).

> ¹³You have a mighty arm;
>   strong is your hand, high your right hand.
> ¹⁴Righteousness and justice are the foundation of your throne;
>   steadfast love [*ḥesed*] and faithfulness [*ĕmeth*] go before you.
> ¹⁵Happy are the people who know the festal shout,
>   who walk, O Lord, in the light of your countenance;
> ¹⁶they exult in your name all day long,
>   and extol your righteousness.
> ¹⁷For you are the glory of their strength;
>   by your favor our horn is exalted.

> [18]For our shield belongs to the LORD,
>   our king to the Holy One of Israel.

The psalmist continues to extol YHWH's power and His mighty arm poised for action (v. 13). But he reprises also YHWH's moral qualities, including his utter dependability (v. 14), such that His power is not arbitrary, but for the good. He then moves to the wonderful situation of those who know such a God and can joyfully acknowledge Him for who He is (vv. 15–16). But the hymn ends on the note of divine power, which God graciously gives to His people, whose strength (the idiomatic sense of "horn") is enabled by Him (v. 17). In particular, God strengthens Israel's/Judah's king, who protects his people because God enables him (v. 18).

Thus we have a hymn that celebrates YHWH's faithfulness and power in strong terms: absolute faithfulness and sovereign power. Although it is a hymn of praise and not a creedal recitation, there is nonetheless no great distance between the two since the faithfulness and power that are praised are clearly core affirmations in Israel's knowledge of God. These qualities are linked, moreover, with God's promises to David, God's chosen king. And so the scene is set for the second section of the psalm.

> [19]Then you spoke in a vision to your faithful one,[31] and said:
>   "I have set the crown on one who is mighty,
>   I have exalted one chosen from the people.
> [20]I have found my servant David;
>   with my holy oil I have anointed him;
> [21]my hand shall always remain with him;
>   my arm also shall strengthen him.

Although the second section of the psalm, as also verses 3–4, has common ground with Nathan's oracle in 2 Samuel 7:4–17 (//1 Chron. 17:3–15), this psalm says both less (nothing about the temple) and more (the content of the divine promises is much fuller here and is also called a covenant that has been sealed by an oath), and it also speaks about David rather than to David. So the relationship between the psalm and the narrative is unclear (and has been argued every which way).[32] Nevertheless, it is clearly God's covenant with David, announced in verse 3, that is here developed, and the present

31. The Hebrew of 89:19 (20 MT) has a plural, "your faithful ones," which may be preferable since it could indicate God's people as a whole being the recipients of the prophetic message.

32. A valuable study of the relationship is Nahum Sarna, "Psalm 89: A Study in Inner Biblical Exegesis," in his *Studies in Biblical Interpretation* (Philadelphia: Jewish Publication Society, 2000), 377–94. Sarna surveys the debate and argues that Ps. 89:19–37 displays "a pattern of

account has strong resonances with certain other royal psalms, especially Psalm 2. Here "David" is the known figure from the book of Samuel and also the eponymous representative of the royal dynasty that descends from him (esp. in vv. 29–37).

These first verses of the second section lay emphasis upon God's initiative in choosing David, making him king, and undertaking to accompany and support him. The Davidic covenant is an expression of divine grace.

> 22"The enemy shall not outwit him,
>   the wicked shall not humble him.
> 23I will crush his foes before him
>   and strike down those who hate him.
> 24My faithfulness ['ĕmūnāh] and steadfast love [ḥesed] shall be with him;
>   and in my name his horn shall be exalted.
> 25I will set his hand on the sea
>   and his right hand on the rivers.

Part of God's commitment to David is to give him victory over his enemies (vv. 22–23)—language that is reminiscent of the creedal affirmation of God's commitment to Israel in Psalm 44:4–8. God's commitment and dependability with regard to Israel, celebrated already in the opening hymnic section, are here affirmed with regard to David, whose strength God will enable (v. 24). Consequently David's dominion will be great (v. 25); whether "the sea" and "the rivers" indicate geographical boundaries of a large kingdom (bounded by Mediterranean, Euphrates, and Nile) or are symbolic of the restless watery powers that YHWH Himself subdues (v. 9), David's kingly rule will in some way be a microcosm of YHWH's kingly rule (as in Ps. 2).[33]

> 26"He shall cry to me, 'You are my Father,
>   my God, and the Rock of my salvation!'
> 27I will make him the firstborn,
>   the highest of the kings of the earth.
> 28Forever I will keep my steadfast love [ḥesed] for him,
>   and my covenant with him will stand firm.[34]

---

deliberate and original exegesis on the part of the psalmist, who has adapted an ancient oracle to a new situation" (383).

33. There are numerous resonances between the qualities attributed to David in 89:20–28 and those attributed to YHWH in vv. 6–19, which suggest that David's earthly rule is a counterpart to YHWH's heavenly rule (see Marvin Tate, *Psalms 51–100*, WBC 20 [Dallas: Word, 1990], 422–23, where he draws on the work of J.-B. Dumortier).

34. The verb "stand firm" (in v. 28 [29 MT]) is the Hebrew root from which the noun 'ĕmūnāh is derived.

> ²⁹I will establish his line forever,
>   and his throne as long as the heavens endure.

YHWH's commitment to David is now developed in terms of David's favored relationship with God and favored status over all other human kings (vv. 26–27). This cumulative picture of YHWH's choosing, strengthening, and exalting David now leads into the keynote, sounded already at the outset (vv. 3–4), of His granting David a dynasty in perpetuity, as the enduring sign of YHWH's gracious commitment to him (vv. 28–29).

Two further things remain to be said in this second section of the psalm.

> ³⁰"If his children forsake my law
>   and do not walk according to my ordinances,
> ³¹if they violate my statutes
>   and do not keep my commandments,
> ³²then I will punish their transgressions with the rod
>   and their iniquity with scourges;
> ³³but I will not remove from him my steadfast love [hesed]
>   or be false to my faithfulness ['ĕmūnāh].

What if David's descendants are faithless? Will this annul the covenant? The answer is no. Certainly they will suffer for their sins, which will not be excused or overlooked (vv. 30–32). Nevertheless a severe divine discipline will be the outworking of, not an alternative to, the divine covenantal commitment; God's discipline will in no way signal or lead to the ending of that commitment, for that commitment expresses YHWH's character as a God of hesed and 'ĕmūnāh (v. 33).

This is the second structural complication within the psalm, though not in the same way that the location of verses 3–4 can appear structurally awkward. Rather, in terms of the parallel between Psalm 89 and 44, this could have been an independent section in the mode of 44:17–22, for its function is to rule out one possible theological explanation for disparity between expectations and experience. However, it is not structurally problematic in its own terms since it is quite naturally included within the account of the promises to David as part of what they do and do not mean.

The point that YHWH will not be false to His faithfulness leads now into a striking peroration:

> ³⁴"I will not violate the covenant,
>   or alter the word that went forth from my lips.
> ³⁵Once and for all ['aḥat] I have sworn by my holiness;
>   I will not lie to David.

> [36]His line shall continue forever,
>   and his throne endure before me like the sun.
> [37]It shall be established forever like the moon,
>   an enduring witness in the skies." *Selah*

Initially there is a straight statement of a firm commitment: the covenant is inviolable, and what Y<small>HWH</small> has promised He has promised (v. 34). Yet, as though this were not enough—as though one might conceivably doubt that the divine yes is yes, or no is no—the divine undertaking is further strengthened in three ways (as though in capital letters, bold, and underlined). First, it is depicted as an oath, which is the expression of a promise in its most solemn and binding form.[35] Second, Y<small>HWH</small> has sworn *'ahat*, "one thing," which is a clear idiom of emphasis: "this one thing" or "once and for all." Third, Y<small>HWH</small> has sworn "by my holiness," an idiom of supreme emphasis.[36]

There is an obvious logical problem in a depiction of God's taking an oath, as nicely brought out by the writer to the Hebrews (6:13–18). In an oath one appeals to a solemn and binding authority so as to end all uncertainty about what is said.[37] "Human beings, of course, swear by someone greater than themselves, and an oath given as confirmation puts an end to all dispute" (v. 16). But to whom can God appeal when He is already the supreme authority, the ultimate point of appeal? "When God made a promise to Abraham, because he had no one greater by whom to swear, he swore by himself" (v. 13). The point of this is assurance of the most solemn and binding nature: "When God desired to show even more clearly to the heirs of the promise the unchangeable character of his purpose, he guaranteed it by an oath" (v. 17).

Thus Y<small>HWH</small>'s oath is the strongest affirmation conceivable (v. 35). In the light of this, the enduring nature of David's dynasty is imagined in terms of those enduring elements, the sun and the moon, without which the world would not be what it is—so one can look to God's commitment to David in the same way as one looks up at the moon in the sky.[38]

35. There is no reference to an oath in 2 Sam. 7 or Ps. 2. There is a divine oath in Ps. 110:4, that David is a priest in perpetuity after the order of Melchizedek, which implicitly bears on the status of the Davidic covenant.

36. This idiom of God's swearing "by his holiness" appears also in Amos 4:1–3 to underline what in God's eyes is the utterly heinous nature of careless and selfish oppression of the poor and needy.

37. This point depends, of course, on people having a fundamentally religious frame of reference. Some whose mind-set is secular regard traditional oaths as mumbo jumbo, no more or less binding than any other undertaking since in reality nothing ultimate is at stake.

38. The sense of 89:37b [38b MT] is unclear because there are difficulties in vocalization that are to some extent reflective of uncertainty whether or not MT should be retained. There is a significant secondary literature, whose results are, in my judgment, inconclusive (see, e.g., Timo Veijola, "The Witness in the Clouds: Ps 89:38," *JBL* 107 [1988]: 413–17; Veijola has written extensively on possible religiohistorical dimensions of the psalm's language and imagery). The NRSV reads the problematic *'d* as "witness" and construes the moon (v. 37a) as that witness. If my gloss on this reading is on the right lines, the symbolism in this context could be that as the moon waxes and wanes and yet remains ever present, so too the Davidic covenant will endure

Thus the rehearsal of God's covenant promises to David conclude with what is, to the best of my knowledge, the single strongest commitment on God's lips anywhere in the whole Bible.[39] Moreover, the context of this has already been set by the initial hymnic praise of YHWH's faithfulness and power. The God who is faithful and powerful is the one who can deliver on His promises, for He has both the will and the ability to do so. And if this God has promised and indeed sworn in the strongest way possible, then there should be no doubt whatever that this is a promise He can and will keep.

> [38]But now[40] you have spurned and rejected him;
>   you are full of wrath against your anointed.
> [39]You have renounced the covenant with your servant;
>   you have defiled his crown in the dust.
> [40]You have broken through all his walls;
>   you have laid his strongholds in ruins.
> [41]All who pass by plunder him;
>   he has become the scorn of his neighbors.
> [42]You have exalted the right hand of his foes;
>   you have made all his enemies rejoice.
> [43]Moreover, you have turned back the edge of his sword,
>   and you have not supported him in battle.
> [44]You have removed the scepter from his hand,
>   and hurled his throne to the ground.
> [45]You have cut short the days of his youth;
>   you have covered him with shame. *Selah*

It could not happen. But it has. The impossible has taken place. The evidence of events is that YHWH has turned against his anointed king, and that this is not the chastisement spoken of in verse 32 but something more fundamental: renunciation of the covenant (vv. 38–39). The imagery is primarily of military defeat, with terminology strongly reminiscent of Psalm 44: enemies triumphing and plundering at God's behest (the opposite of the promises in 89:22–23), with nothing but defeat and scorn and shame for God's chosen one.[41] This

---

through ups and downs; but this may be fanciful. The important point is that, whatever one's decision on v. 37b, the overall tenor of vv. 34–37 is unaffected.

39. There are solemn divine commitments elsewhere, such as Jer. 31:35–37. I am unaware of any other biblical passage that equals Ps. 89:34–37 for sheer rhetorical emphasis.

40. The NRSV rendering (v. 38) is not inappropriate in terms of general sense. However, the Hebrew (v. 39 MT) begins not "but now" (*vě'attāh*) but "but you" (*vě'attāh*), rhetorically pointing the finger at God.

41. So, e.g., each lament begins with "you have rejected" (*zānaḥtā*, 44:9a [10a]; 89:38a [39a]), then enemies "plunder" (*shāsū*, 44:10b [11b]; 89:41a [42a]), and Israel/the king has become the "taunt of neighbors" (*ḥerpāh lishkēnīm*, 44:13a [14a]; 89:41b [42b]).

is the only one of the psalm's four parts in which there is no mention of
Yhwh's steadfast love (*ḥesed*) and faithfulness (*'ĕmūnāh*), for such qualities
are nowhere in evidence.

How should this be read? Given the strength of wording in the first two parts
of the psalm, and the fact that affliction could be construed as punishment of a
faithless king, one might be inclined to think that when the psalmist says "You
have renounced the covenant" (v. 39) he cannot really mean it. Commentators
not infrequently make such a move. Thus Charles Briggs comments on verse 39:

> This seems inconsistent with the perpetuity of the covenant vv. 4–5, its firmness
> v. 29, and the promise that Yahweh would not profane it v. 35. But the Psalmist
> certainly had in mind that the chastisement would be temporary, and that the
> covenant kindness and faithfulness could not be removed v. 34. That has been
> so strongly expressed in the previous context that it is implied here.[42]

Or A. A. Anderson says about verse 39: "This verse is not a contradiction of
the previous promises of Yahweh; rather it is an illustration of the punishment
threatened in verses 30ff."[43] Yet this way of posing the interpretive issue is surely
wrong. It does justice neither to the structure and development of the psalm
as a whole, nor to the tone of the final portion that follows, nor to the parallel
with Psalm 44. What has preceded in verses 1–37 is designed not to mitigate the
harsh circumstances of verses 38–45 but to be a foil to them. In other words,
neither commentator allows that the inconsistency with what has preceded may
be precisely the point. The hermeneutical move of downplaying verse 39 is akin
to the move of downplaying the protestation of faithfulness in Psalm 44:17–22:
it has the same effect of deflecting the real concern of the psalms—that the expectations of faith go one way, but experiences in life may go the opposite way.

Recognition that there is no ready way of theologically rationalizing the
situation leads into the final portion of the psalm:

> [46]How long, O Lord? Will you hide yourself forever?
> How long will your wrath burn like fire?
> [47]Remember how short my time is—
> for what vanity you have created all mortals!
> [48]Who can live and never see death?
> Who can escape the power of Sheol? *Selah*
> [49]Lord, where is your steadfast love [*ḥesed*] of old,
> which by your faithfulness [*'ĕmūnāh*] you swore to David?

42. Charles Augustus Briggs, *Psalms*, ICC (Edinburgh: T&T Clark, 1907), 2:262. Briggs is
using the Hebrew numeration of verses.
43. Arnold Albert Anderson, *Psalms*, NCB (London: Marshall, Morgan & Scott, 1972), 2:645.

> [50]Remember, O Lord, how your servant is taunted;
>   how I bear in my bosom the insults of the peoples,
> [51]with which your enemies taunt, O LORD,
>   with which they taunted the footsteps of your anointed.

There is no resolution of the conflict, but rather an anguished appeal to YHWH. The psalmist appeals to his human frailty, which may imply that if YHWH does not soon show mercy to him and restore him, then he will no longer be there to receive it. He appeals to YHWH's steadfast love (*ḥesed*) and faithfulness (*'ĕmûnāh*) in the belief that somehow they are still there even if he cannot see them. And finally he appeals to the reproaches and taunts he suffers, because they undercut any reason for people to recognize the rule of Israel's God through the rule of Israel's earthly king.

The picture of Israel's enemies' *taunting* (Heb. *ḥāraph*, in vv. 50–51 [51–52 MT]) takes on virtually iconic status in two famous Old Testament narratives. First, in the story of David and Goliath, the prime repeated term for Goliath's stance toward Israel is *ḥāraph*, which the NRSV here renders "defy." It sums up Goliath's opening challenge (1 Sam. 17:10), characterizes Israel's account of Goliath (17:25), and represents David's sense of why Goliath must be opposed and defeated (17:26, 36, 45); as much as Goliath is gigantic, he is also defiant. Similarly in the Assyrian siege of Hezekiah's Jerusalem, the prime term for the Assyrian attitude is *ḥāraph*, which the NRSV here renders "mock," and which consistently has YHWH as the object (2 Kings 19:4, 16, 22, 23). These two archetypal enemies, Goliath and Assyria, are consistently *scornful*, dismissive of Israel and Israel's God. It may be appropriate to find intertextual resonance with the *taunting* from the unnamed enemies in Psalm 89, insofar as such taunting scorn represents an archetypal human attitude that is heedless of YHWH and YHWH's chosen people.

As in Psalm 44 there is appeal to YHWH and His faithfulness. But there is no indication of how to resolve the conflict between the absolute promise of the faithful and mighty God on the one hand, and the deathlike situation in which the recipient of the promises finds himself on the other hand.

In this final section (vv. 47, 50) a first-person human voice is heard for the first time since verses 1–2. If one reads the psalm as a whole, then it is a natural move for the reader to link the one who sings unending praise with the one who bears unceasing mockery, and to wonder how it is conceivable to hold together the differing things said.

There is yet one last verse:

> [52]Blessed be the LORD forever.
>   Amen and Amen.

Although this verse is now enumerated as part of Psalm 89, it is clearly not original to the psalm. It is one of those liturgical biddings ("Blessed . . .") with response ("Amen . . .") that conclude each of the books of the Psalter, and thus it is part of the structure of the Psalter rather than of the psalm as such.[44] Nonetheless, its present position is the sharpest reminder that Israel preserved Psalm 89, with its astonishing content, for its life of prayer and the worship of God.

A subject that has received considerable recent attention is the possible significance of Psalm 89 within the shaping of the Psalter as a whole.[45] It has been suggested that the second book ends on a confident Davidic note in Psalm 72, but the conclusion of the third book with Psalm 89 represents a sense that the Davidic kingship has failed. Hence book 4 starts with the one psalm ascribed to Moses (Ps. 90), going back behind David, as it were, and continues with not a few psalms about the kingship of God (and not David). This is a possible reading, although what can seem clear at the beginning or end of a book in the Psalter can seem much less clear in the middle of that book. However, insofar as this approach involves a construal of Psalm 89 as depicting "the downfall of the monarchy,"[46] I am not concerned with it here, because I consider this a simplifying reduction of the psalm. To be sure, a compiler of the Psalter might have read Psalm 89 thus. But this is a reminder that the sequential ordering of the psalms in the canonical collection, although potentially of interpretive value, need not always be followed, especially if it mutes the distinctive voice of a psalm.

Toward Interpreting Psalms 44 and 89 Together

I have put Psalms 44 and 89 together because they display a common structure and concern. Each is structured so as to pose a theological dilemma. The dilemma is the disparity that may arise between what faith trustingly affirms about God (Ps. 44), or what believers expect of a faithful and powerful God who has made promises (Ps. 89), and circumstances in life that are entirely otherwise. Moreover, neither psalm offers a resolution other than to appeal afresh to Yʜwʜ's known character as a faithful God. Each psalm poses a tension that the worshiper who uses the psalm must in some way understand, embrace, and live with. (In form-critical terms I am proposing that the distinctive configuring within the two psalms is such as to make each psalm as much a psalm of wisdom as of lament.)

The Interpretive Implications of the Psalms' Language

A common interpretive strategy has been to try to "pin down" each psalm in terms of date of formation and original context of referent (which defeat?

44. Compare Pss. 41:13; 72:18–19; 106:48.
45. A good starting point for the possible significance of the shape of the Psalter as a whole is Patrick D. Miller, "The Psalter as a Book of Theology," in *Psalms in Community: Jewish and Christian Textual, Liturgical, and Artistic Traditions*, ed. Harold W. Attridge and Margot E. Fassler, SBLSS 25 (Atlanta: Society of Biblical Literature, 2003), 87–98. The seminal work is by Gerald H. Wilson, *The Editing of the Hebrew Psalter*, SBLDS 76 (Chico, CA: Scholars Press, 1985).
46. Miller, "Psalter," 89.

which king?). Yet each psalm remains elusive and is in effect undatable, other than to the general period of ancient Israel and Judah. The language in which the adverse circumstances are depicted in each psalm is conventional language of defeat and disaster, which is not indicative of any one historical setting. Indeed, the language of Psalm 89 (esp. vv. 38–51) has been interpreted in terms of a periodic ritual humiliation ceremony for an Israelite/Judahite king in the temple.[47] Whatever its merits as a historical hypothesis, this suggestively illustrates how seemingly military language cannot necessarily be pinned down to a military context. It may be that the psalms' elusiveness is to some extent precisely because they are designed to evoke not a specific situation but recurrent situations of unresolved and inexplicable tension.

The metaphorizing of the language of defeat in terms of a possible royal ritual humiliation in Psalm 89 is indicative of the potential of conventional language of warfare to be metaphorized and envisaged in more than one way. Previously, in chapter 2, I have suggested that Deuteronomy 7 is metaphorizing the language of ḥērem so as to use it to depict the need to be faithful to YHWH in non-military ways. There is certainly a long post-biblical history of using biblical military terminology to depict moral and spiritual conflict. If there is reason to think that Psalms 44 and 89 were devised to articulate a recurrent problem, then the interpreter may not unreasonably construe their language of victory and defeat, glory and disgrace, metaphorically—that is, in moral and spiritual terms as ways of articulating inexplicable tensions in the life of faith, experienced in various situations of success and failure, expectation and disappointment.

On Living with Unresolved Tensions

How should the unresolved tension that each psalm presents best be handled? I noted in chapter 4 that there is recurrent discussion of "contradictions" within Scripture, often of a distinctly trivial and point-scoring nature. Curiously, to the best of my knowledge, such discussions do not include Psalms 44 and 89 as standard texts, or even mention them at all. Yet surely here we have the real problem of contradiction within the Bible: these two psalms explicitly set up a contradiction between the expectations of faith and the disappointing and perplexing realities that are the opposite of expectations, and they refuse to resolve the contradiction. Here are *the* prime contradictions in the Bible. They are here because the life of faith contains such contradictions, and so learning to live with them is important.

47. For a convenient introduction to this once widely held position, see John H. Eaton, *Kingship and the Psalms*, SBT, 2nd series, 32 (London: SCM, 1976), 109–11, 121–22.

I have already observed how easily one can lessen the tension within the world of the text by denying or at least qualifying one of the premises of each psalm: Israel in 44:17–22 could not really have been faithful, and the psalmist in 89:39 could not really have supposed that YHWH had renounced the covenant with David. On a broader canvas also, that is the world in front of the text, it is possible to try to ease the existential anguish that the psalms depict by denying, or at least qualifying, one horn of the dilemma of contradiction.

One approach is that believers should so tightly embrace and affirm their creedal trust in God and their hymnic affirmations about God that they in effect close their eyes to, or deny, the reality or the awfulness of conflicting circumstances: "Really, everything is all right, for that is how it is when you know God." The danger then, if faith no longer opens eyes but closes them, is that a greater or lesser degree of unreality creeps in. The consequences are unsurprising. If pain and puzzlement cannot be acknowledged and indeed embraced, then for some this becomes a sufficient reason to abandon their community of faith—"They were nice enough people, but somehow they weren't real and couldn't actually face life"—while those who remain acquire an ever-narrower vision of what really counts and matters in the world.

The other approach, probably more widely appealing in contemporary Western culture, is so to fix on the painful circumstances of life that one gives up on faith. The harsh realities of life show that Christian (or other) faith in God is no longer tenable. It might have been once, when one was a child, perhaps in Sunday school. But when one grows up and acquires scientific understanding of how the world works, together with an awareness of increasingly uncertain general prospects—global warming, continuing wars, terrorism, famines, growing disparities between rich and poor, transience of romantic relationships, familial instabilities, social anomie, disillusionment with grand claims about the world, or just existential moments of "Why?" when confronted by needless and innocent suffering—then it becomes clear that "Our God reigns" is empty language that trivializes the realities of the world. Better to discard it and embrace disillusioned honesty rather than pious self-deception. But one consequence can be an increasing difficulty in finding good grounds for sustaining hope and confidence in life and resisting the acids of despair.

Psalms 44 and 89 refuse both these approaches. Rather they insist that one should recognize a painful contradiction, refuse any easy rationalization, and live with unresolved conflict. One should neither abandon faith nor deny painful and disappointing circumstances. Moreover, the presence of these psalms as part of the prescribed texts of prayer for Jews and Christians means that the content of worship, at least in part, needs to include recognition and indeed appropriation of pain and perplexity.

Some New Testament and Christian Perspectives

Jesus as the One Who Fulfills God's Promises

Some of the most famous passages in the New Testament portray Jesus as the descendant of David in whom the divine promises are fulfilled. In Luke's account of the annunciation, the angel Gabriel says to Mary:

> "Do not be afraid, Mary, for you have found favor with God. And now, you will conceive in your womb and bear a son, and you will name him Jesus. He will be great, and will be called the Son of the Most High, and the Lord God will give to him the throne of his ancestor David. He will reign over the house of Jacob forever, and of his kingdom there will be no end." (Luke 1:30–33)

Resonances with the language of the Davidic covenant are readily apparent. Moreover, Jesus in his ministry is recognized to be the Messiah who fulfills God's promises to David and to Israel. In Matthew's famous account:

> Jesus said to them [his disciples], "But who do you say that I am?" Simon Peter answered, "You are the Messiah [*or*, the Christ], the Son of the living God." And Jesus answered, "Blessed are you, Simon son of Jonah! For flesh and blood has not revealed this to you, but my Father in heaven." (Matt. 16:15–17)

There is an important sense in which Jesus's relation to Israel's expectations in their scriptures is constitutive for his identity—so that the title, the Messiah/Christ, soon becomes part of his name: no longer Jesus the Christ, but simply Jesus Christ.

In general terms Christians see Jesus as the demonstration of God's commitment to the house of David, as in Psalm 89, which means that God fulfills His promises through Christ. As John Eaton puts it: "With the church's use of the psalm [89] on Christmas Day, the whole context of worship proclaims that the faithfulness of God is vindicated in the mystery of the incarnation (cf. Luke 1.32ff.)."[48] This vindication comes in God's way and God's time; and the fulfillment is no less a fulfillment even if it might have been unrecognizable to the psalmist.

However, the best way of understanding Jesus in relation to Israel's scriptures is not straightforward. Although, for example, "anointed" (Heb. *māshîaḥ*, Gk. *christos*) is a recognized designation for a royal figure, who may be but

---

48. John Eaton, *The Psalms: A Historical and Spiritual Commentary with an Introduction and New Translation* (London and New York: T&T Clark, 2003), 321. Eaton continues: "Nevertheless, the psalm can also be heard to warn of the suffering that will be known in the new era."

is not necessarily Davidic (he is in Ps. 89:51 but not in Isa. 45:1, where the Persian Cyrus is addressed), "*the* Messiah" is not a category in the Hebrew text. Rather it developed in early Jewish reflection on the continuing implications of their scriptures. Moreover, Peter's acknowledgment of Jesus as "the Messiah/Christ," as Matthew portrays it, is hardly straightforward. Jesus certainly approves his words. Yet as soon as Jesus begins to explain what his vocation as "the Messiah/Christ" will mean, using terms of suffering, death, and resurrection, Peter protests and is firmly put in his place as someone who does not understand, "for you are setting your mind not on divine things but on human things" (Matt. 16:23). Peter is both right and wrong.[49] This is because of the way in which Jesus transforms the meaning of "the Messiah/Christ" even as he appropriates it: hence an understanding of what it means to confess Jesus as the Messiah/Christ depends on the content that is given to the key category of "the Messiah/Christ."

Within the New Testament the content of Jesus's messiahship is given definitively in his death and resurrection, which occupies prime position in the Gospels and in the Letters of Paul. This directs the reader/hearer to issues of suffering and perplexity, and to a resolution that is glorious but mysterious, for Jesus does not linger to explain all that his death and resurrection entail, nor does he, when risen, confront those who crucified him with the error of their ways. So if the Christian says that Jesus fulfills Israel's hopes and realizes God's promises to David, what kind of claim is this?

Suffering and the Life of Faith

The knowledge of God in Christ is perhaps less a resolution of the tensions of Psalms 44 and 89 than a transposition into a different frame of reference. The affirmation that "Jesus is Lord" is open to the same basic objection as "our God reigns": too much in the world does not look as though that is the case, or rather looks as though it is definitely not the case. But the New Testament gives a sufficiently full account of what it means to say that "Jesus is Lord" so that certain kinds of objection can be given a good answer, although hardly a refutation.

One feature of the New Testament portrayal is the greater role given to suffering in the life of faith, in terms of both expecting it and enduring it, by way of following the Master who went to the cross. As Derek Kidner puts it

---

49. I have tried to probe the dynamics of Peter's recognition and blindness in my "'Who Is Jesus Christ for Us Today?' Peter's Confession (Matthew 16:13–28) Reconsidered," in *Christology and Scripture: Interdisciplinary Perspectives*, ed. Andrew T. Lincoln and Angus Paddison, LNTS 348 (London and New York: T&T Clark, 2007), 7–21.

(in the course of commenting on Psalm 44): "Suffering may be a battle-scar rather than a punishment; the price of loyalty in a world which is at war with God."[50] The recognition that faithfulness may entail suffering of various kinds is already present in the Old Testament (Moses, Jeremiah, Psalms, Job, the Isaianic servant), but it is nevertheless given greater weight in the New Testament, such that a Christian frame of reference for Psalms 44 and 89 in certain ways reshapes one's expectations. Thus Paul cites Psalm 44:22 in the context of his passionate and joyful peroration about the Christian's confidence in God:

> Who will separate us from the love of Christ? Will hardship, or distress, or persecution, or famine, or nakedness, or peril, or sword? As it is written,
>
> > "For your sake we are being killed all day long;
> > we are accounted as sheep to be slaughtered."
>
> No, in all these things we are more than conquerors through him who loved us. For I am convinced that neither death, nor life, . . . nor anything else in all creation, will be able to separate us from the love of God in Christ Jesus our Lord. (Rom. 8:35–39)

Paul's point is that Christian faith will indeed bring opposition and suffering, in accord with Scripture. But because of Jesus's death and resurrection, this should not be puzzling in the way it is within Psalm 44 itself, nor should it be debilitating as though it were simply an evil to be endured. For whatever the possible defeats on one level, on another level God's love in Christ makes Christians "more than conquerors." Opposition and persecution may still defy certain kinds of rationalization, but the Christian vision can contextualize such things within the life of discipleship.

The First Letter of Peter reinforces the Pauline vision:

> Beloved, do not be surprised at the fiery ordeal that is taking place among you to test you, as though something strange were happening to you. But rejoice insofar as you are sharing Christ's sufferings, so that you may also be glad and shout for joy when his glory is revealed. If you are reviled for the name of Christ [ei oneidizesthe en onomati Christou], you are blessed [makarioi], because the spirit of glory, which is the Spirit of God, is resting on you. (1 Pet. 4:12–14)

Within the New Testament the primary intertextual resonance of verse 14 is the words of Jesus in Matthew's presentation: "Blessed [makarioi] are you when people revile [oneidisōsin] you and persecute you . . . on my account" (Matt. 5:11). Jesus warns that his way will engender opposition. However, the verb "revile/insult" (oneidizō) appears regularly in the Septuagintal rendering of the Psalms to depict the attitude of those who oppose YHWH and Israel (and also in the accounts of Goliath and the Assyrians in 1 Sam. 17 and 2 Kings 19). Not least is it used in Psalm 89:50–51 (88:51–52 LXX), where the noun "reproach" (oneidismos) is followed by two uses of the verb

---

50. Derek Kidner, *Psalms 1–72*, TOTC (London: Inter-Varsity, 1973), 170.

"reproach" (*oneidizō*) before the noun "anointed" (*christos*).[51] Again, the effect of the linkage is to recontextualize the perplexed anguish of the psalm in a frame of reference where allegiance to God's anointed, Jesus Christ, makes insulting opposition something not only to be expected but also even to be a mark of blessedness, in the confidence that God in Christ has overcome evil and death and Christians can enter into this victory.

Some Jewish Perspectives

Within Psalm 44 one verse in particular has a long and weighty history of Jewish use: verse 22, "Because of you we are being killed all day long, and accounted as sheep for slaughter." As Herbert Levine puts it:

> Few other verses in Psalms have been as important as this one in the history of Jewish response to catastrophe. It adumbrates a theory of martyrdom that has been drawn on since biblical times to explain the inexplicable, and justify the unjustifiable. If Israel cannot understand why it is being persecuted, despite its loyalty to God through adherence to the covenant, then it can always fall back on the idea that "it is for Your sake that we are slain."[52]

Hence the notion of *kiddush ha-Shem* (*qiddūsh ha-Shēm*), the sanctification of God's name, which, although originally depicting various kinds of faithfulness to God, has come especially to mean martyrdom for being Jewish, for the sake of Judaism. This means that Jewish thought has developed in a way analogous to Christian thought, through ceasing to find suffering because of faithfulness to God to be a problem, as in the psalm, but rather recognizing it as something to be expected on account of the various kinds of enmity that faithfulness to God and to Jewish tradition can arouse.

The events of the Holocaust/Shoah, however, have made the language of Psalm 44:22 more two-edged, often with less emphasis on "for your sake" than on "sheep for slaughter." Levine reports, "Throughout the literature of the Holocaust—in memoirs, in poems, in rabbinic response, in public arguments over Jewish resistance or passivity—the phrase 'as sheep to the slaughter' echoes its singular death knell." Although "memorial prayers recited in the contemporary synagogue have . . . cast Holocaust victims in the role of martyrs for the sanctification of God's name," many Jews have protested and rejected traditional imagery and theological understandings.[53] The issues are intractable precisely because so many different dimensions are involved.

---

51. Whether or not the author of 1 Pet. 4:14 intended allusion to Ps. 89 is impossible to say. Again, I am utilizing a reader-oriented rather than an authorial hermeneutic (cf. n. 14 above).

52. Herbert J. Levine, *Sing unto God a New Song: A Contemporary Reading of the Psalms*, ISBL (Bloomington and Indianapolis: Indiana University Press, 1995), 183.

53. Ibid., 204–12, esp. 205, 212.

There is perhaps an analogy with the way in which individual people may believe in God and also know that there is inexplicable and innocent suffering, and yet when confronted by a particular example of such suffering may suddenly question or reject their faith: in one sense "nothing has changed," but in terms of existential awareness and engagement, everything has changed. Might it be that in one sense the Shoah/Holocaust brought nothing that Jews had not already encountered—gratuitous and irrational hatred, persecution, and murder of the innocent, response to which was traditionally encompassed under *kiddush ha-Shem*? Nevertheless the sheer scale and systematization of the murderousness, in a secularizing culture with less confidence in the value of theological understandings and religious practices, brought a major change in existential awareness for many Jews.

One of the best-known Jewish writers who has probed what it means to live in the aftermath of Auschwitz is Elie Wiesel. Wiesel seeks to retrieve faith and also resists rationalizations. In his *One Generation After* he tells, among many others, the following story:

> A disciple came to see Rebbe Pinhas of Koretz.
>
> "Help me, Master," he said. "My distress is great; make it disappear. The world is filled with anguish and sadness. Men are not men. I have no faith in them, or in myself. I have faith in nothing. What shall I do, Rebbe, what shall I do?"
>
> "Go and study. It's the only remedy I know."
>
> "Woe unto me, I cannot even study," said the disciple. "So strong are my doubts, so all-pervasive, that they prevent me from studying. I open the Talmud and contemplate it. For weeks, months on end, I remain riveted to the same page. I cannot go further, not even by a step, not even by a line. What can I do, Rebbe, what can I do?"
>
> When a Jew can provide no answer, he at least has a story to tell. And so Rebbe Pinhas of Koretz replied: "Know that what is happening to you also happened to me. When I was your age I stumbled over the same difficulties. I too was filled with questions and doubts. About the Creator and His creation. I too could not advance. I tried study, prayer, meditation. In vain. Fasting, penitence, silence. In vain. My doubts remained doubts, my questions remained open. Impossible to proceed. Then, one day, I learned that Rebbe Israel Baal Shem-Tov would be coming to our town. Curiosity led me to the house where he was praying. When I entered he was finishing the *Amida[h]*. He turned around and the intensity in his eyes overwhelmed me. I knew he was not looking at me alone, yet I knew that I was less alone. Suddenly, without a word, I was able to go home, open the Talmud and plunge into my studies once more.
>
> "You see," said Rebbe Pinhas of Koretz to his disciple, "the questions remained questions, my doubts were still as heavy with anguish, but I was able to continue."[54]

54. Elie Wiesel, *One Generation After*, trans. Lily Edelman and the author (New York: Random House, 1970), 66–67.

Conclusion

Among the substantive issues that Psalms 44 and 89 raise is the nature of theological rationality. In seeking to understand the dynamic of each psalm, I have emphasized the importance of recognizing when to resist rationalizing a situation (an emphasis that in various ways recurs in other chapters of this book).[55] By way of conclusion I offer some brief reflections on ways of developing this approach to theological thinking.

The recognition that contradiction plays a central role in these psalms might lead one fundamentally to question the role of conventional rationality in the life of faith. One time-honored form this can take is to focus on the famous phrase *Credo quia absurdum*, "I believe because it is absurd." So, for example, Robert Pfeiffer confidently assigns the notion of the Davidic covenant in its prime formulations in 2 Samuel 7 and Psalm 89 to a post-exilic period, when there no longer was a Davidic dynasty, and in the course of his memorably negative account ("monkish drivel") poses the question of why people should articulate belief in an eternal dynasty when no such dynasty any longer exists. He comes out with a striking generalization:

> Belief in the eternity of something that has ceased to exist is characteristic of Judaism in its early stages, and furnishes one of the secrets of its extraordinary vitality. In general, the vigor of a religion seems to be proportionate to its disregard of reason and logic. When a faith ceases to cry out defiantly *Credo quia absurdum* and becomes rational, its days as a vital, inspiring force in the lives of men are numbered.[56]

On one level, Pfeiffer certainly has a point. A faith whose content at no point is other than the "sweetly reasonable" is probably unlikely to move many people to live by it, still less to die for it. But it hardly follows that a vital faith must "disregard reason and logic" in order to retain vitality, or that good use of the axiom can disregard the particular content of biblical faith in God.

Credo quia absurdum has become a freestanding axiom, though its origin is generally traced to Tertullian in the early third century AD in a passage where he seeks to adopt something of Paul's account of the foolishness of the cross in 1 Corinthians 1:18–25: "Crucifixus est Dei filius; non pudet quia pudendum est. Et mortuus est Dei filius; prorsus credibile est quia ineptum est. Et sepultus resurrexit; certum est quia impossibile" (*De carne Christi* [*The Flesh of Christ*] 5.4).[57] This can be rendered: "The Son of God was crucified; there is no shame because it is shameful. And

---

55. Compare, e.g., the discussions of election (chap. 2 above), manna (chap. 3 above), and wisdom (chap. 8 below).

56. Pfeiffer, *Introduction*, 371.

57. See, e.g., Jean-Pierre Mahé, ed., *La chair du Christ*, 2 vols., SC 216–17 (Paris: Cerf, 1975): 1:228–29 (Latin text and French trans.); 2:339 (commentary).

the Son of God died; it is entirely believable because it is unfitting. And the buried one rose again; it is sure because it is impossible."

The notion of *Credo quia absurdum* was adopted by Kierkegaard in the nineteenth century as part of a strategy of *opposing the domestication of Christian faith*, its restriction within familiar categories of philosophy and ethics—which is surely where the axiom rightly belongs. Or to put the point in other terms, it is a matter of taking seriously and maintaining the mystery of God. In Christian theology, mystery is not a puzzle awaiting resolution, if only a little more were known (as in a detective story), although it is often assumed to be such.[58] Rather it is a reality recognized to be ever greater the more one engages with it: in the classic shorthand, "The more you know, the more you know you don't know." So it is a reality that requires openness and willingness to think and rethink, if one is to begin to do justice to it.

In terms of the specific content of Psalms 44 and 89, it is probably best if the contradiction they contain is redescribed as a paradox. Although there is explicit contradiction between promises and circumstances, this contradiction plays a specific rhetorical and conceptual role within each psalm, where faith in YHWH and His steadfast love remains the premise. The problem is not the conflict of opposites in itself, but rather a probing of surprising and difficult dimensions of what is entailed by trust in God. The paradox is also apparent when the psalms are recontextualized within Jewish and Christian faiths, where there is a deeper understanding of the role of persecution, perplexity, and suffering within the mysterious purposes of God—purposes that are focused for the Christian in the person of Jesus at Gethsemane, Calvary, and the Easter tomb.

An alternative way of approaching the issue of appropriate theological rationality is to reflect on the necessary relationship between language and life. On the classic understanding of theology as "faith seeking understanding,"[59]

58. Robert Oden, in his *The Bible without Theology: The Theological Tradition and Alternatives to It* (San Francisco: Harper & Row, 1987), sees the tendency by theologians and biblical scholars to appeal to mystery, which he takes to be a tendency to "explain" by reference to the inexplicable, as evidence of intellectual obfuscation and/or laziness. Oden argues that the value of interpreting the Bible without utilizing theological categories is that the adoption of other categories, say from anthropology, can shed light on and explain that which hitherto appeared inexplicable. For the serious scholar, "the apparently inexplicable presents a challenge and not a solution" (160). I concede entirely that theologically oriented scholars may have appealed prematurely, and improperly, to the notion of mystery—as though the detective gave up before searching out all the clues. But misuse of the notion of mystery does not remove its right use.

59. This conception of theology has perhaps been most famously articulated by Augustine, Anselm, and Barth. For its biblical roots see my "How Can We Know the Truth? A Study of John 7:14–18," in *The Art of Reading Scripture*, ed. Ellen F. Davis and Richard B. Hays, (Grand Rapids: Eerdmans, 2003), 239–57; for its historical and contemporary significance see Nicholas

theological articulations should not lose touch with the life of faith that gives rise to them (which is not to deny that demanding levels of technicality and/or abstraction may sometimes be appropriate to certain kinds of argument). Part of the problem relates to the recognition that it is possible for Christians to say things that are on one level theologically correct, and yet on another level potentially inadequate to do justice to the existential issues at stake. Artur Weiser, for example, concludes his exposition of Psalm 44 with a christological affirmation that makes use of Paul's imagery of a veil in 2 Corinthians 3:

> It is true that in the psalm the love of God appeared to the eyes of the people at that time to be obscured by a veil because of the mystery of suffering for which the Old Covenant was not able to find an entirely satisfactory resolution; it is only through the suffering of Christ that the last veil drops from the face of God and his hidden love is made manifest; it is only in the New Testament that the discords of the psalm are dissolved in the harmonious melody of the hymn of those who have overcome their temptations so that nothing in the world can separate them from the love of God which is in Jesus Christ (Rom. 8.37ff.).[60]

I would not simply disagree, and yet the wording makes me nervous (and the notion of the last veil dropping needs some probing as to what it does and does not mean). It seems to me to be open to be read as a rather glib affirmation of a classic Christian understanding, where the smoothness of the wording risks losing touch with the realities of life. On the one hand, it shows no recognition of the depths of Jewish engagement with God, often in extreme suffering (and often at Christian hands). On the other hand, it says nothing about the existential struggles that Christians may face as they seek to understand and enter into the love of God in Christ, and how they often fail. It is not only what is said but also how it is said that matters if rationality and the life of faith are to be held together rightly.

Finally, if Psalms 44 and 89 articulate a theological paradox, a paradox that is affirmed and deepened within classic Christian faith, what difference should this make in practice to those who read (hear, sing, recite, pray) these psalms and seek to appropriate them? If the paradox is to be pondered, as part of growing in understanding the nature of the life of faith, then there are surely implications for the kind of qualities, communal and individual, that believers should over time acquire: such qualities as to dig deeper in trust, be

Lash, "Anselm Seeking" in *The Beginning and End of "Religion"* (Cambridge: Cambridge University Press, 1996), 150–63.

60. Artur Weiser, *The Psalms*, trans. Herbert Hartwell from the 5th German ed., OTL (1959; ET, London: SCM, 1962), 360.

less glib in speech and prayer, to look beyond the immediate to the long term, and to offer more support to those currently in pain and perplexity. For when the psalms are contextualized in prayer and worship, their language is not only expressive but also transformative, able to make a difference to those who use these ancient and enduring words.

8

<hr>

Where Is Wisdom?

<hr>

One of the prime categories of the Hebrew Bible, and of the faiths rooted in it, is wisdom. Scholarly work often approaches wisdom as a phenomenon characteristic of certain books in the Old Testament: "Wisdom literature." My concern here, however, is with the nature of wisdom as an existential reality: what might it mean and look like to be wise?

Solomon is the Old Testament figure with most historic resonances in relation to wisdom. However, I want to argue here that the figure of Job valuably illustrates one primary dimension of wisdom. My argument will focus on two excerpts from the book of Job, chapters 1–2 and 28: taken together, they offer a striking account of wisdom and of the human qualities that make for wisdom. In particular, the focus will be on the nature of the wisdom that is appropriate in response to the inexplicable afflictions and tragedies that can be a part of life.

On Reading the Book of Job

I start with two brief preliminaries about my approach to the book of Job.

First, I recognize that there are a further thirty-nine chapters within the

<hr>

In this chapter I develop two of my earlier studies: "Solomon and Job: Divine Wisdom in Human Life," in *Where Shall Wisdom Be Found?*, ed. Stephen C. Barton (Edinburgh: T&T Clark, 1999), 3–17; and *The Bible, Theology, and Faith*, CSCD (Cambridge: Cambridge University Press, 2000), 84–88.

book, where there are voices quite distinct from those in focus here, and which need to be taken into account for an understanding of the book as a whole. The question of how the differing voices in the book relate to each other is complex: Do they complement, bypass, contradict, or undermine each other? How best should one decide which voices, if any, to privilege? Regrettably, these questions will not be discussed here. The scope of this chapter is to offer an account that is meaningful in its own right and a contribution to the larger study of the book of Job as a whole, but whose relationship to the whole book of Job is left open.

Second, since, as Stuart Weeks puts it, "We can say little or nothing . . . about the context within which it [the book of Job] was composed, and even the date is largely a matter for speculation,"[1] the compositional context of the book of Job and its possible bearing on a reading of the text will not be discussed. Even if the general consensus that Job is an exilic or post-exilic text is correct (and I have no good reason to dissent), the important point is that the world within the text, both in the narrative of Job 1–2 and in the poem of Job 28, makes full sense on its own terms. Of course, the text must be read as an ancient Hebrew text that works with literary conventions and conceptual assumptions from its world of origin; but it need not be located in any precisely defined period of Israelite or Judahite history in order to be understood.

Other approaches are also possible and indeed more common. Ellen Davis, for example, argues that "Job is Israel in exile" and that "Job's suffering and persistent faith were to be offered as a model for exilic Israel."[2] Undoubtedly the text of Job is open to be read this way. My reasons for declining such an approach are threefold. First, the date remains uncertain, and so a compositional relation to "Israel in exile" is conjectural, though this remains a possible reader-oriented strategy, if one is so inclined. Second, Job is from Uz, not Israel. In my judgment this should caution against an interpretive focus specifically on Israel. Third, the concerns within the narrative of Job 1–2 and the poem of Job 28 are, as we will see, perennial concerns that have no particular relationship to the exilic or post-exilic period more than any other period.

A Reading of Job 1:1–2:10

The scene is immediately set, and the main character is introduced:

¹There was once a man in the land of Uz whose name was Job. That man was blameless and upright, one who feared God and turned away from evil.

1. Stuart Weeks, *An Introduction to the Study of Wisdom Literature* (London and New York: T&T Clark, 2010), 50.
2. Ellen Davis, "Job and Jacob: The Integrity of Faith," in *The Whirlwind: Essays on Job, Hermeneutics and Theology in Memory of Jane Morse*, ed. Stephen Cook, Corrine L. Patton, and James W. Watts, JSOTSS 336 (London: Sheffield Academic Press, 2001), 100–120, esp. 108, 113.

This initial depiction of Job, in which he has four strongly positive characteristics—blameless, upright, fearing God, turning from evil—is the most glowing and positive character depiction in the whole Hebrew Bible. The most closely comparable figure in this regard is Noah, though arguably his depiction is slightly less glowing: "Noah was a righteous man, blameless in his generation; Noah walked with God" (Gen. 6:9). Particularly important among Job's qualities is the fact that he is "one who fears God" (*yĕrē' 'ĕlōhîm*),[3] which is the prime term in Israel's scriptures for appropriate human response to God.

In the Old Testament the primary significance of "fearing God" can be seen in various ways. First, in two famous summary statements about appropriate response to God, "fear" is the first thing specified: "So now, O Israel, what does the LORD your God require of you? Only to fear the LORD your God . . ." (Deut. 10:12). "The end of the matter; all has been heard. Fear God, and keep his commandments; for that is the whole duty of everyone" (Eccles. 12:13). Second, the term is a clear shorthand depiction of those who respond rightly to God, especially in poetic texts. Psalms 111 and 112, for example, are a well-known pair of acrostic psalms: the former depicts the qualities of God, and the latter depicts the substantially similar qualities of the godlike person, the one who "fears YHWH" (112:1 AT). Comparable is the repeated commendation of those who fear God in Psalm 103 (vv. 11, 13, 17), or on the lips of Mary in the Magnificat when she uses the familiar Hebrew idiom: "His mercy is for those who fear him from generation to generation" (Luke 1:50). Third, the "fear of God" plays a central role in two paradigmatic narratives about right response to God, this present Job narrative and the testing of Abraham in Genesis 22, where the purpose of the test relates to the confirmation of the central character as "one who fears God."

The Old Testament use of "fear of God" is thus more or less equivalent *in function* to the New Testament's use of various forms of "believe/trust" and "have faith" (*pisteuō* and *pistis*) to depict appropriate human response to God; so in terms of function a Christian way of conveying the tenor of "one who fears God" might be "a believer," "a person of faith." The *meaning* of the term will emerge from the present narrative.[4]

Given that Job is an outstanding example of right response to God, it is the more striking that he is from Uz. Wherever Uz might be located on a map,[5] Uz

---

3. The Hebrew verb "fear" (*yārē'*) is not in the form of a past-tense indicative ("he feared"), but rather is a participle used as a noun in a construct with "God"; that is, it depicts a particular kind of person, "a fearer of God," "God-fearing person," as also is Abraham in Gen. 22:12.

4. David J. A. Clines has interestingly argued, against scholarly consensus, that "fear of God" does *not* mean moral or religious behavior but rather always denotes "the emotion of fear," such that if people act because of the "fear of God," they are acting "because they are afraid of God and of the consequences he may exact of them"; see "'The Fear of the Lord Is Wisdom' (Job 28:28): A Semantic and Contextual Study," in *Job 28: Cognition in Context*, ed. Ellen van Wolde (Leiden: Brill, 2003), 57–92, esp. 64. Nowhere, however, does he consider the possible role of a narrative such as Job 1–2, or alternatively Gen. 22, for displaying the sense in which "fear of God" should be understood.

5. Although the location of Uz is unknown, the region of Edom is readily imagined, partly because Lam. 4:21 closely connects Uz with Edom, and partly because "the east" (where Job lives, v. 3) is a traditional location for wise people (1 Kings 4:30 [5:10 MT]). However, "the east" has strong mythical resonance (it is where Eden is located, Gen. 2:8), and it may well be that Uz is a symbolic name, "Land of Counsel" (the sense of the Hebrew root *'ūts*), appropriate to a place where Job and his friends talk at length. This would be analogous to the "Land of Nod/

is not Israel. This means that Job is not an Israelite, but someone who stands outside the chosen people. What difference does this make? In general terms, it is a reminder that true relationship with God is not restricted to the household of faith. In terms of the specifics of this narrative, the point is most likely that the dynamics of Job's story are not dependent upon the particularities of Yhwh's dealings with Israel (election, covenant, torah, etc.) but represent what is true or possible for the human condition in itself.

Thus Job, though not an Israelite, is an exceptional human being, whose exceptional qualities are rooted in his relationship with God.

> ²There were born to him seven sons and three daughters. ³He had seven thousand sheep, three thousand camels, five hundred yoke of oxen, five hundred donkeys, and very many servants; so that this man was the greatest of all the people of the east.

Job is fabulously well-off, in terms both of his family and his possessions. Since the groupings of numbers for both family and possessions all add up to ten (seven and three; five and five), they are presumably symbolic large numbers. Although large quantities of livestock in an apparently pastoral context may not say much to the imagination of many a modern urban/suburban reader, the point in context—that Job is exceptionally wealthy—could easily be rendered in comparable contemporary categories (mansions, yachts, airplanes, offshore bank accounts, stock holdings . . .). The kind of prosperity about which most people can only dream is what Job enjoys.

Thus far we have been told two things about Job: that he is exceptional in piety and integrity, and that he is exceptional in prosperity. What we have not been told is the possible relationship, if any, between these. A reader may suppose that divine promises elsewhere in the Old Testament, which say that obedience to God brings blessing,[6] should be brought to bear upon the text, such that Job's prosperity is a consequence of his piety. This is indeed possible. However, it can often be an important principle of narrative interpretation to attend to what is not said as well as to what is said. So we should recognize that the narrator in fact says nothing about the relationship, if any, between Job's piety and his prosperity, but rather has simply juxtaposed these two facts and has left them uninterpreted, in silence. Such a silence, which constitutes a "gap" in narrational terms, is open to be filled—and this will be crucial to

---

Wandering" to which the ever-roaming Cain is exiled (Gen. 4:14, 16 mg.). Presumably neither land would be locatable in terms of the regular conventions of a modern geographical map.

6. So, e.g., Prov. 3:33, "The Lord's curse is on the house of the wicked, but he blesses the abode of the righteous"; or Deut. 28:1–14.

the story as it develops—but it is important to be aware of what one is doing in filling it.[7]

> [4]His sons used to go and hold feasts in one another's houses in turn; and they would send and invite their three sisters to eat and drink with them. [5]And when the feast days had run their course, Job would send and sanctify them, and he would rise early in the morning and offer burnt offerings according to the number of them all; for Job said, "It may be that my children have sinned, and cursed God in their hearts." This is what Job always did.

This fuller account of Job's family appears to serve two purposes. One is to underline the delightful and enviable nature of Job's family, with its regular celebrations where all are included (v. 4). The other is to underline Job's piety, inasmuch as, in this pastoral/patriarchal context, where there is apparently neither temple nor priesthood (as also in Gen. 12–50), Job appropriately acts as a priest, in a way that brings together his concern for God with his concern for his family (v. 5). Although some modern interpreters have difficulty with such a portrayal of Job—on the grounds that it looks like neurosis and obsession rather than healthy piety[8]—this is almost certainly to read against the grain of the text because of inhabiting a different frame of reference (and arguably to ignore how difficult sustained feasting is without drunkenness, lusts, rows, and other behavior later regretted). The narrative's own concern is to portray the exemplary quality of all that Job has and does.

> [6]One day the heavenly beings came to present themselves before the LORD, and Satan [or, the Accuser; Heb. ha-sātān] also came among them. [7]The LORD said to Satan, "Where have you come from?" Satan answered the LORD, "From going to and fro on the earth, and from walking up and down on it." [8]The LORD said to Satan, "Have you considered my servant Job? There is no one like him on the earth, a blameless and upright man who fears God and turns away from evil."

The scene shifts abruptly and dramatically, from earth to "heaven." Here a dialogue takes place that is determinative for the whole story.

7. It is dismaying that some commentators fill the gap without apparently realizing what they are doing; so, e.g., Samuel Rolles Driver and George Buchanan Gray: "Job's piety, according to the narrative (1–3), had led to his being prosperous beyond all the children of the East" (*The Book of Job*, ICC [Edinburgh: T&T Clark, 1921], 13); or Ellen van Wolde, "As readers we get the feeling that it all goes together. There is a direct relationship between the man's piety and his prosperity, between his extreme wealth and his extreme piety" (*Mr and Mrs Job* [London: SCM, 1997], 8).

8. Athalya Brenner, e.g., thinks that "the religiosity of Job the pious is almost a parody of faith" ("Job the Pious? The Characterization of Job in the Narrative Framework of the Book," *JSOT* 43 [1989]: 37–52, esp. 44).

First, we must clarify the identity of Y<small>HWH</small>'s interlocutor. Here the NRSV rendering "Satan" is seriously misleading because it implies that this is a proper name, and consequently encourages readers to suppose that here we have Satan who is the devil.[9] This is wrong because of a simple rule of Hebrew grammar: proper/personal names never take the definite article.[10] Yet here, as the NRSV marginal note reveals, we have the definite article (*ha-*) before the Hebrew word *sātān*. So the Hebrew *ha-sātān* designates not a name but a function or role, and that role, in terms of the meaning of the Hebrew root, is perhaps less "the Accuser" than "the Opponent."[11] In other words, the heavenly being here is not Satan, the figure in much subsequent Jewish and Christian theology, but an otherwise unknown member of the heavenly court—"the satan/opposer"—about whom we know only what we are told here: he gets around on earth so as to be familiar with its inhabitants (vv. 7, 8a), and (as we will see) asks awkward questions.[12]

Y<small>HWH</small>, having initially established that the satan has been carrying out his regular function of familiarizing himself with what is happening on earth, then rhetorically commends Job as an exemplary person, of whom the satan should be well aware. Y<small>HWH</small> uses the same terminology as that with which the narrator has initially introduced Job, thus underlining the truly exceptional nature of Job's piety ("none like him on the earth"). Moreover, Y<small>HWH</small>'s wording "Have you considered . . . ?" appears to imply the kind of awareness that should lead to action.

Y<small>HWH</small> might have said, "Have you seen / do you know my servant Job . . . ?," using the common Hebrew verbs for sight and knowledge (*rāʾāh, yādaʿ*), simply to introduce Job and allow the conversation to continue. However, the actual Hebrew phrase used, "place your heart/mind on [*sīm lēv ʿal*]" is used in contexts where awareness implies corresponding action, analogous to the common idiomatic use of "remember" (*zākar*, e.g., Gen. 8:1; Exod. 20:8). Thus, when certain Egyptians "did not regard [*sīm lēv ʾel*] the word of the LORD," despite the warning of coming hail,

9. This occurs also in some other modern translations, e.g., NIV, ESV, perhaps out of undue deference to the KJV and certain traditional readings of the text.

10. This is distinct from place names, which generally do not take a definite article but can do so occasionally. For the rule, see *GKC* §125, d–f; *JM* §137, a–d.

11. I wonder whether the common rendering "the accuser" may perhaps be influenced by the NT depiction of Satan as "the accuser" (*ho katēgōr*) in Rev. 12:9–10; and also by the LXX rendering of *hasātān* by *ho diabolos*, which can mean someone who speaks in a hostile or slanderous way. This LXX and NT usage perhaps also plays back on common renderings of Zech. 3:1, where, in the vision shown to the prophet, a figure called *hasātān* stands beside Joshua the high priest so as to *sātān* him. Despite the common rendering of the verb *sātān* here as "accuse," no words at all are ascribed to *hasātān*, and accusations require words, or if not words, strong and clear gestures—yet no gestures are mentioned; so it is probably better to render the Hebrew verb with its consistent sense elsewhere: "oppose." For a helpful survey of the usage of *sātān*, see K. Nielsen, "*sātān*," *TDOT* 14:73–78.

12. Henceforth I will replace "Satan" with "the satan" in citations of the NRSV.

they took no action to move slaves or livestock to shelter (Exod. 9:21). When Abigail begs David not to "take seriously [*sîm lēv 'el*] this ill-natured fellow Nabal," she is begging him not to take violent action against Nabal (1 Sam. 25:25). When David's men say of Absalom's men that "if we flee, they will not care about [*sîm lēv 'el*] us," they mean that Absalom's men would not bother with pursuing them (2 Sam. 18:3).[13]

Thus YHWH holds up Job as a model not just for consideration but also implicitly for emulation. Although, within the constraints of the scenario depicted, the implication about emulation is addressed to the satan, in terms of narrative conventions it is intended for those overhearing the conversation—that is, the reader/hearer of the story. Job is being commended *to us* as an exemplary human being, worthy of imitation.

> [9]Then the satan answered the LORD, "Does Job fear God for nothing [*ḥinnām*]? [10]Have you not put a fence around him and his house and all that he has, on every side? You have blessed the work of his hands, and his possessions have increased in the land."

Despite YHWH's commendation, the satan is not impressed; or more precisely, he is suspicious. His suspicion is directed toward what we were told in the opening three verses. From Job's four commended qualities the satan focuses on the most resonant of them, his "fear of God," and puts his question with regard to it. Specifically, the satan fixes on the silence about the relationship between Job's outstanding piety and his outstanding prosperity, and he fills the gap. He does not deny that, in a real sense, Job fears God. But he wonders about what is going on under the surface: What is Job's motivation? It is possible that there is no relationship between Job's piety and his prosperity (it just happens that both are in evidence), and it is also possible to read the narrator's silence as implying that Job's prosperity is a *consequence* of his piety (YHWH blesses Job *because* he is faithful). However, the satan asks whether the real relationship is not in fact that of *purpose* (Job is faithful *so that* YHWH will bless him). Job's piety, though formally directed toward God, is at heart directed to what Job receives from God. Indeed, he does so well out of his piety that his piety is hardly surprising—rather, he would presumably be foolish not to fear God, given the extensive protection and prosperity he receives from God. In short, Job is in it for what he gets out of it.

One could reframe the satan's suspicion by regarding him as suggesting that Job is the religious equivalent of someone who marries for money. Whatever

13. Although the preposition accompanying *sîm lēv* is *'al* in Job 1:8 and *'el* in all the other examples cited, it is unlikely that there is any difference of meaning. Indeed *BHS* notes manuscript variation between *'al* and *'el* in all the passages except 2 Sam. 18:3.

the declarations of love, and whatever the apparently loving gestures and actions, the insidious purpose of it all is not to love but to *exploit* someone—to proclaim love for the person, yet in reality to be in love with their possessions. Although to love is to be self-giving toward another, this is a matter of being self-seeking, of using someone else as a means to one's own ends. Such self-seeking is the more reprehensible when it is disguised by language and actions that purport to be its opposite.

There is a real question, however, as to how this suspicious question should be heard. What is its tone and tenor? Robert Alter, for example, remarks that "the dialogue suggests . . . an element of jealousy (when God lavishes praise on Job) and cynical mean-spiritedness."[14] Certainly the question can be taken this way. But need it be? After all, is it not legitimate to want to know whether a person really is what he appears to be? Especially when someone is held up as exemplary, is it not appropriate to seek assurance that this person is genuine? To raise such a question may not leave the questioner sounding "nice," but that is beside the point.

In this context, it is worth recollecting the former practice of the Roman Catholic Church with regard to the procedures for the canonization of saints. The Vatican used to employ someone who, with nice irony, was entitled "the devil's advocate," whose role was to ask hard questions of someone proposed for sainthood. To recognize someone as a saint means, among other things, that their life is held up as exemplary, a trustworthy model for the faithful to emulate, whose name they can take for their children, and so on. The role of the devil's advocate was "quality control." For if the church proceeds hastily and proclaims someone to be a saint without first checking carefully, it is possible that an investigative reporter could then do some work and discover, say, Mafia links, money laundering, and a mistress; then the resultant publication of the findings would bring shame, confusion, and turmoil to the church that had precipitately declared a plausible crook to be a saint. The devil's advocate had to do the investigating and establish whether or not there were hitherto-unknown difficulties in the life of the proposed saint; if there was dirt to dig, it was his responsibility to dig it. Interestingly, the role of devil's advocate was abolished by Pope John Paul II, precisely to try to speed up the process of canonization, which traditionally was notoriously slow, not least because of the devil's advocate (though the politics could be complex and still are). He wanted to have more saints whose lives were still known in living memory, saints who could serve as, among other things, contemporary role models to commend the faith. It may be that these revised procedures will work well

14. Robert Alter, *The Wisdom Books* (New York and London: W. W. Norton, 2010), 12.

and that the old ones were unduly cumbersome. Nonetheless, the concern represented by the devil's advocate remains a valid one: the greater the claim made on behalf of someone, the greater the importance of rigorous validation of the grounds for the claim.

If, as I have suggested, Yʜwʜ's commendation of Job to the satan as exemplary is implicitly a commendation to the audience of the book, then the audience in every generation can recognize their own legitimate concern being voiced by the satan: Is this apparently exemplary person really what they appear to be? If Job is being commended as (apparently) a "saint" even while he is still alive, then can this commendation withstand rigorous validation?[15]

If the concern of the text is with how to validate the apparently exemplary, two interpretive consequences may briefly be noted. First, if the concern for validation is in principle legitimate, need one take the satan's question to display "cynical mean-spiritedness"? That is, if the satan's role is, by definition, *to oppose*, might this not be *appropriate* opposition? A possible analogy might be the way in which modern Western democracies have developed the notion of the "loyal opposition," people who do not form the executive government but whose job is to be part of the wider government and to constitute a critical check with regard to what the executive does; their role is to ask hard questions and to propose possible alternatives (a task that increasingly takes place outside government and within the media, yet where there may be less obligation to be "loyal"). To be sure, it may be imaginatively difficult to envisage the satan in this narrative as "loyal opposition," given the long history of construing his role negatively. But whatever one's imaginative construal, the important thing is to appreciate the legitimacy of the suspicious question he raises, as to whether Job really is what he appears to be.

Second, it becomes beside the point to generalize the satan's question into an overall skepticism, as is often done: "The Satan doubts that any man loves God for God's sake," or "The Satan expresses a total cynicism about human nature: he implies that true piety among humans does not exist."[16] The point is how to test the reality of the apparently exemplary, rather than to doubt its existence as such.

Once the suspicion—that Job's apparently exemplary fear of God may in reality be a self-seeking using of God—is voiced, how best can it be dealt with? It is clear that mere re-affirmation of the initial commendation would get nowhere, since it would not take seriously the nature of the objection raised; it could lead to a fruitless "Yes, he does," "No, he doesn't." A different way

15. If one can see the critical test as integral to the portrayal of Job's piety, it can, I think, change the frame of reference within which the reader thinks about the "saintly" Job, whose integrity may otherwise make him appear "remote." Michael V. Fox expresses a common reader response when he says, "We first see Job as a puzzlingly perfect character too distant from human normality to be anything other than a spectacle, certainly not a representative of humanity" ("Reading the Tale of Job," in *A Critical Engagement: Essays on the Hebrew Bible in Honour of J. Cheryl Exum*, ed. David J. A. Clines and Ellen van Wolde, HBM 38 [Sheffield: Sheffield Phoenix, 2011], 145–62, esp. 147–48).

16. David Robertson, *The Old Testament and the Literary Critic*, Guides to Biblical Scholarship: Old Testament (Philadelphia: Fortress, 1977), 35; Norman Whybray, *Job*, Readings: A New Biblical Commentary (Sheffield: Sheffield Academic Press: 1998), 33.

of handling the issue is needed, if progress is to be made. Job must be *tested* in such a way as to display the kind of person he really is.

> [11]"But stretch out your hand now, and touch all that he has, and he will curse you to your face." [12]The LORD said to the satan, "Very well, all that he has is in your power; only do not stretch out your hand against him!" So the satan went out from the presence of the LORD.

If the suspicion is that "he's in it for what he gets out of it," then the only sure test is to remove "what he gets out of it" and then see whether or not he remains "in it." If Job is deprived of everything he has, will he retain his fear of God, or not? The satan expresses his expectation in the negative: Job's piety will turn into profanity. And since there is no way of YHWH's genuinely showing that His commendation of Job is right other than by acceding to the proposed stripping from Job of all that he has, the testing sequence of events to follow is set in train without more ado—other than that, since the suspicion has been expressed with regard to all Job has, as enumerated in verses 2–3, it is to these alone, and not Job's person, that what happens next must be directed.

It is almost certainly a distraction (in terms of following the narrative) to focus on the agency of what is going to happen to Job, or reflect on the possible implications of YHWH's saying to the satan that Job is "in your power" (literally, "in your hand"), as though it were significant that the satan, not YHWH, is the one who afflicts Job; as Norman Habel puts it, "The Satan must do the dirty work, the *opus alienum* of God. It is the Satan's 'hand,' not Yahweh's, that will actually 'strike' Job's possessions."[17] On one level, that is what the text of verse 12 implies. Yet in the sequence that follows, there is no reference to the agency of the satan, while fire "of God" ('*ĕlōhīm*, v. 16) falls from heaven, and a "great wind" (*rūaḥ*, v. 19; elsewhere in the Old Testament wind is a prime symbol of divine presence/agency) destroys the house of Job's children and those within it. Thus there is no reason to think that the narrative is somehow distancing YHWH from what happens and implicating the satan instead. (There is a comparable issue in 2:3, where YHWH says, "You incited me against him," in relation to 2:6, where YHWH again says to the satan that Job is "in your power.") The concern in the narrative is that what has been resolved "in heaven" is now worked out "on earth"—though to be sure, as Job himself will articulate, whatever happens on earth must necessarily be in some way related to divine sovereignty.

> [13]One day when his sons and daughters were eating and drinking wine in the eldest brother's house, [14]a messenger came to Job and said, "The oxen were plowing and the donkeys were feeding beside them, [15]and the Sabaeans fell on them and carried them off, and killed the servants with the edge of the sword; I alone have escaped to tell you." [16]While he was still speaking, another came and said, "The fire of God fell from heaven and burned up the sheep and the servants, and consumed them; I alone have escaped to tell you." [17]While he was still speaking, another came and said, "The Chaldeans formed three columns,

17. Norman Habel, *The Book of Job*, OTL (London: SCM, 1985), 91.

made a raid on the camels and carried them off, and killed the servants with the edge of the sword; I alone have escaped to tell you." [18]While he was still speaking, another came and said, "Your sons and daughters were eating and drinking wine in their eldest brother's house, [19]and suddenly a great wind came across the desert, struck the four corners of the house, and it fell on the young people, and they are dead; I alone have escaped to tell you."

[20]Then Job arose, tore his robe, shaved his head, and fell on the ground. . . .

In a stylized and somewhat breathless sequence, Job loses almost everything. To be precise, everything and everyone specified in verses 2–3 is either killed or carried off by others (apart from the four who escaped to tell Job!). That which Job had received "out of" God is gone—so will he remain "into" God? The moment of truth has come. Job initially responds with the common actions of grief in response to death and disaster. He embarks on presumably time-honored rituals of mourning in such a way that the next thing we expect is to hear him speak, presumably to utter a lament of some kind or other in which he will bewail his situation—a lament that could easily degenerate into cursing.

. . . and [he] worshiped. [21]He said, "Naked I came from my mother's womb, and naked shall I return there; the LORD gave, and the LORD has taken away; blessed be the name of the LORD."

[22]In all this Job did not sin or charge God with wrongdoing.

Job speaks memorable words of creaturely acceptance of finitude and loss. He ignores the human agents of his disaster and focuses instead on God, whose sovereign will he affirms and whose name he blesses. Indeed, although he is not an Israelite, at this key moment he uses language characteristic of Israel's praise of God (the wording of Ps. 113:2a, "Blessed be the name of the LORD," is identical to Job's wording in v. 21b). He even, uniquely in the book, names God as Israel knows God, YHWH, a name that otherwise is reserved to the narrator.[18] Job's usage underlines the congruence of his knowledge of God as here displayed with Israel's knowledge of God.

The narrator's note in verse 22 in one sense states the obvious and would not be needed in the context of this narrative alone. It has presumably been included because of what Job says later in the book, and Job's possible reputation as someone who does, more or less, charge God with

---

18. There is one exception to this non-use of the Tetragrammaton on Job's part in his reference to "the hand of the LORD" in 12:9. Unsurprisingly, some manuscripts read "Eloah" (see BHS ad loc., and E. Dhorme, A Commentary on the Book of Job, trans. Harold Knight [London: Nelson, 1967], 174). However, it may be that Job should be read as citing Isa. 41:20 or the general theological stance of his friends (so David Clines, Job 1–20, WBC 17 [Dallas: Word, 1989], 294–95).

wrongdoing—as notably in his speeches in Job 21 and 24. Thus the narrator is clarifying that, even if some of what Job says later may be open to question in certain ways, no such reservation applies at this point in the book.

In other words, because Job blesses and does not curse, he defies the satan's suspicion and proves it to be unfounded. His fear of God is shown to be a genuine fear *of* God and not disguised self-seeking. He has passed the test with flying colors.

Or has he?

> ²:¹One day the heavenly beings came to present themselves before the LORD, and the satan also came among them to present himself before the LORD. ²The LORD said to the satan, "Where have you come from?" The satan answered the LORD, "From going to and fro on the earth, and from walking up and down on it." ³The LORD said to the satan, "Have you considered my servant Job? There is no one like him on the earth, a blameless and upright man who fears God and turns away from evil. . . .

Thus far the scenario and the wording (with two minor and insignificant variations in the Hebrew) is identical to the previous occasion.

> ". . . He still persists in his integrity [*tŭmmāh*], although you incited me against him, to destroy him for no reason [*hinnām*]."

YHWH continues to commend Job to the satan as exemplary and now includes reference to what has taken place since first they spoke, in effect commenting on Job's demeanor and words in 1:20–21. He changes the leading category for depicting Job from his "fear" to his "integrity," where the Hebrew noun for "integrity [*tŭmmāh*]" is formed from the same root as the adjective "blameless [*tām*]" that has been repeatedly used to describe Job (1:1, 8; 2:3); so one might render it "blamelessness" to keep the verbal continuity, though "integrity" better captures the sense in English. But the point is unchanged: Job continues to display those qualities for which he has been commended as exemplary, despite their not "benefiting" him.

Moreover, YHWH depicts what has happened to Job with the same term with which the satan has articulated his suspicion of Job in 1:9: "for no reason / for nothing [*hinnām*]." The point is not that there was no reason at all for what happened to Job, for the concern to test was explicit. Rather, there was nothing deficient in Job himself or in his relationship with YHWH that gave rise to what has happened. The fact that Job really does fear God "for nothing," as has become apparent, underlines that what has happened to him in some sense corresponds to this: the rightness of his disinterested relationship with

God ("for nothing") is reflected in the fact that what has happened to him has no cause in his way of living ("for no reason").

> [4]Then the satan answered the LORD, "Skin for skin! All that people have they will give to save their lives. [5]But stretch out your hand now and touch his bone and his flesh, and he will curse you to your face."

The satan, however, is unpersuaded, and that for a simple reason. The terms of the previous test related only to all that Job had (1:2–3) and explicitly excluded his own person (1:12). But this exclusion allows the suspicion to be expressed again in severer form. Job is not only self-seeking but also nasty about it and indeed ruthless: he will sacrifice anyone and anything in the cause of self-preservation. What does he ultimately care if his family, servants, and livestock perish, as long as he himself is preserved unscathed? The initial test was not sufficiently searching, the satan insinuates, and therefore must be renewed so as to include Job himself. He must experience devastation and desolation in his own person. When this happens, and Job's piety no longer results in his personal well-being, then at last the true nature of Job as indeed unscrupulously self-seeking in relation to God will be revealed. This time, his piety really will turn to profanity.

Whether or not the satan's suspicion is a "fair" response to Job's words and deeds so far is beside the point. The fact that it remains a *possible* interpretation of what is going on is all-important. So something further must happen to Job that will lead him to reveal and express his inner reality.

> [6]The LORD said to the satan, "Very well, he is in your power; only spare his life."
> [7]So the satan went out from the presence of the LORD, and inflicted loathsome sores on Job from the sole of his foot to the crown of his head. [8]Job took a potsherd with which to scrape himself, and sat among the ashes.

The terms of the further test dictate themselves. Job's life must be deprived of all that makes it worthwhile and become deathlike, but he must remain alive. This necessary reservation is not, as in the first test, restricting the scope of the test, but is simply so that Job remains able to respond to his situation. So he is afflicted in a way that is agonizing and also makes him an object of disgust to himself as much as to others. The point of these loathsome sores covering him from bottom to top is that *all of him* is afflicted, with no part left as some kind of comfort zone, where he might still feel all right. His consequent sitting among ashes—ashes being the useless and unlovely remnants of that which once was living and/or had shape and purpose but is now located at the rubbish dump—is an eloquent symbol of his new situation.

⁹Then his wife said to him, "Do you still persist in your integrity [*tŭmmāh*]? Curse God, and die." ¹⁰But he said to her, "You speak as any foolish woman would speak. Shall we receive the good at the hand of God, and not receive the bad?" In all this Job did not sin with his lips.

Job's wife now articulates in her own way the issue at the heart of the satan's suspicion. What is the point of integrity if this is what integrity leads to? Once you see that nothing good comes of it, why bother with it? So be done with it, give up on God, and say what you must surely now think about God, perhaps thereby hastening the end that is now welcome and must surely be coming soon anyway.

Job's response (again differentiated in an aside from his later poetic speeches) is simple and clear. After reproving his wife for speaking "foolishly," presumably because of her assumption about the "point" of integrity, he articulates his own understanding of his integrity / fear of God.[19] In essence, it is no good being a fair-weather friend; true relationship is sustained through the hard times as well as the good times. Indeed, if one reflects on all that Job has been through, then it is appropriate to depict his relationship with God in time-honored and hallowed language: "for better, for worse; for richer, for poorer; in sickness and in health." These marriage vows both describe and constitute true relationship. Job's integrity / fear of God has the dynamics of true love. It thereby becomes fully clear that the content of "fear of God" is far from being "afraid of God and of the consequences he may exact"—for the worst that could happen to Job has happened, and he sustains his fear of God regardless. In terms of the narrative, it is as final a refutation as there could be of the suspicion that Job is self-seeking, that his piety is merely instrumental, or that he does not relate to God for God's own sake.

The Genre of Job 1:1–2:10 and Criteria for Good Reading

What kind of narrative have we just read? The issue is nicely raised in the Talmud:

19. Although in 2:3, 9 "integrity" has replaced "fear of God" as the quality of Job that is under scrutiny, the way in which Job in 2:10 relates "integrity" to an attitude toward God shows that in this narrative "integrity" is closely related to "fear of God" in a way in which it may not be for many a modern Western reader. Today "integrity" can readily be a human characteristic independent of God, not least because of eighteenth- and nineteenth-century debates that entirely reasonably (within their frame of reference) established that one did not need to believe in God to be a moral person. An alternative frame of reference in which positive human qualities are enabled and enhanced by participation in God, even if that participation may not be conscious or articulate, has become opaque to many.

A certain Rabbi was sitting before R. Samuel b. Nahmani and in the course of his expositions remarked, Job never was and never existed, but is only a typical figure. He replied: To confute such as you the text says, *There was a man in the land of Uz, Job was his name.* But, he retorted, if that is so, what of the verse, *The poor man had nothing save one poor ewe lamb, which he had bought and nourished up* etc. [2 Sam. 12:3, Nathan's parable to David]. Is that anything but a parable? So this too is a parable. If so, said the other, why are his name and the name of his town mentioned?[20]

On the one hand, the anonymous rabbi sees the story as a parable, while Samuel ben Nahmani insists that the particularities of the text indicate that Job was a real historical figure. Both views can still be found today, though most scholars would favor the anonymous rabbi. The issue is not one of rationalism but of literary judgment, and it is worth briefly reviewing the reasons for construing the text as parabolic, or alternatively expressed, as an example of narrative theology, in which the imaginative world of a story is used to explore and commend a particular understanding.

The story is constructed around an important moral and theological issue: can a human relationship with God be other than self-serving, and if so, how could one tell? The story depicts an extreme scenario, from the man who has everything to the man who has nothing (indeed, in a sense less than nothing). The presentation of the issues takes no account of the ambiguities and mixed motives that so regularly characterize life, but presents everything in stark terms. The account of Job's loss of possessions and family is highly stylized. Perhaps most significantly, the narrator reports two dialogues "in heaven" between YHWH and the satan, scenarios in which, by definition, there could be no human auditor/spectator. This is surely somewhat analogous to stories with the time-honored scenario, familiar to both Jews and Christians,[21] in which people arrive at the gates of heaven and have a conversation there that relates to their possible entrance through the gates and/or what they find once through those gates. Such stories, although set "in heaven," are invariably to make a point (often dryly humorous) that illuminates some facet of life "on earth," and they wholly and solely serve that purpose. So too, surely, does our Job story. Specificity of name and place indicates nothing more than narrative coloring.

Recognition of a narrative's genre can be important for how one reads its story line, not least in avoiding some misreadings. As already indicated in

---

20. From *b. Baba Batra* 15a; cited from Isidore Epstein, ed., *The Babylonian Talmud: Seder Nezikin*, trans. Maurice Simon (London: Soncino, 1935), 2:74.

21. Christian versions differ, of course, in that the imaginatively appropriate figure with whom people have their conversation is usually St. Peter with his keys.

the above reading, what YHWH and the satan say to each other is implicitly directed to us, the readers/hearers of the story who, as it were, overhear their conversation. If Job is commended as a model to be emulated, that is for our benefit. If YHWH accepts the necessity of testing Job, that too is for our benefit. We need to see what is involved in establishing that someone's fear/faith is genuine, and hence the rigor of the test. One will surely misread the story if one supposes that the story is about the character and/or state of mind of God (e.g., "Does the satan outmaneuver God?"[22] "Is God cruel?" "Is God ignorant?") rather than about the logic of what may in principle be necessary to establish, when challenged, the authenticity of human character. This is a prime instance where recognition of the genre of the story becomes important for the interpretive moves one should, and should not, make with it.

Unfortunately, moves to find fault with YHWH for at least ignorance but usually also for improper harshness, or cruelty, seem to fill the literature. Old Testament specialist Norman Whybray, for example, was only able to see a range of possible negative ("immoral") portrayals of God: "God's decision to test Job could be for any number of reasons; to gain the information about Job's character that he lacked; to salvage his dignity and reputation for omniscience; or for idle entertainment. In any case, the picture presented of God in these chapters is hardly a flattering one."[23] The distinguished classicist Gilbert Murray memorably suggested that God's afflicting Job was like "torturing your faithful dog to see if you can make him bite you."[24] The story of Job becomes a context in which "abuse" of a human person, a highly charged concept in contemporary culture, can be directly ascribed to God and divine action.[25]

The pioneering psychiatrist C. G. Jung offers a particularly striking example of developed critique of God's character:

> His faithful servant Job is now to be exposed to a rigorous moral test, quite gratuitously and to no purpose, although Yahweh is convinced of Job's faithfulness and constancy, and could moreover have assured himself beyond all doubt on this point had he taken counsel with his own omniscience. Why, then, is the

22. For example, Michael V. Fox says: "The Satan goes right for Yahweh's weak spot, namely his hopes for human loyalty. . . . The Satan goads Yahweh into an experiment. . . . Why does Yahweh give in? . . . The reason is that the Satan is probing God's vulnerable spot. The Satan knows how to play to vulnerabilities" ("Reading," 149).

23. R. Norman Whybray, "'Shall Not the Judge of All the Earth Do What Is Just?' God's Oppression of the Innocent in the Old Testament," in *Shall Not the Judge of All the Earth Do What Is Just? Studies on the Nature of God in Tribute to James L. Crenshaw*, ed. David Penchansky and Paul L. Redditt (Winona Lake, IN: Eisenbrauns, 2000), 1–19, esp. 15.

24. Gilbert Murray, *Aeschylus: The Creator of Tragedy* (Oxford: Clarendon, 1940), 93.

25. See, e.g., Nehama Verbin, *Divinely Abused: A Philosophical Perspective on Job and His Kin* (London and New York: Continuum, 2011), in which God is a perpetrator of abuse on Job.

experiment made at all, and a bet with an unscrupulous slanderer settled, without a stake, on the back of a powerless creature? It is indeed no edifying spectacle to see how quickly Yahweh abandons his faithful servant to the evil spirit and lets him fall without compunction or pity into the abyss of physical and moral suffering. From the human point of view Yahweh's behaviour is . . . revolting. . . .

One must bear in mind here the dark deeds that follow one another in quick succession: robbery, murder [1:13–19], bodily injury with premeditation [2:6–7]. . . . This is further exacerbated by the fact that Yahweh displays no compunction, remorse, or compassion, but only ruthlessness and brutality. . . . He flagrantly violates at least three of the commandments he himself gave out on Mount Sinai.[26]

Two comments on this. First, whatever one makes of in-principle issues about divine "omniscience," various Old Testament writers are in no doubt that God knows what goes on in the human heart. Best known is probably Psalm 139, but it is notable that Job himself in the subsequent poetic dialogues says, "Will it be well with you when he [God] searches you out? Or can you deceive him, as one person deceives another?" (Job 13:9). But even if God knows what goes on, *we do not*. So if YHWH had responded to the satan's suspicious question by saying, in effect, "I can see the inner reality of Job's heart and mind, and I know that his fear of me is genuine," that would be no help whatever *to us* in knowing how to determine whether or not someone who is held up as exemplary really lives up to the appearance. The logic of the human realm is that humans can only know the "invisible" realities of heart and mind insofar as these are expressed in word and deed—which, generally speaking, is what routinely happens in daily life, at least at a superficial level. But when the question is put as to whether word and deed may in fact be dishonestly concealing and misrepresenting a very different inner reality— which is also a common enough issue—then one can hardly make progress in answering the question without special circumstances that in some way do lead to an exposure of a person's wellsprings, which sometimes happens and sometimes does not.[27] Sometimes we are simply unable to answer the question of authenticity, at least at the time when a decision must be taken about trusting the person in question; the revealing circumstances may only come later (sometimes too late). In Job 1:1–2:10 the whole point of the "heavenly" scenario between YHWH and the satan is that it is posing, paradigmatically in an extreme case, what is necessary for us human beings to know whether

---

26. Carl G. Jung, *Answer to Job*, trans. R. F. C. Hull (Cleveland and New York: Meridian, 1970), 38, 40.

27. Solomon's ability to get the two prostitutes to reveal what was otherwise hidden is paradigmatic for the problem in a formal judicial context (1 Kings 3:16–28).

a purported exemplar is truly an exemplar (whether someone proposed as a saint should be recognized to be a saint). The narrative displays the logic of critical testing for human, not divine (or satanic),[28] comprehension, via an imaginative scenario. Jung misreads.[29]

Second, the fate of Job's animals, servants, and family is, in the story's own frame of reference, a diminution of Job. They are considered not in their own right but only for their bearing upon Job as paterfamilias. Thus there is a genuine difference of assumption between the ancient world of the narrative and that of today, where most people rightly would not make that particular "patriarchal" assumption. Historical distance and difference can be real and problematic. However, the way Jung formulates his objection is surely tone-deaf to the dramatic tenor of the text, in which the narrative is speedy and stylized, not to be lingered on.[30] An analogy might be a hypothetical complaint by a viewer of an action war movie such as *Where Eagles Dare*. Here the action revolves around a small team of Allied soldiers, led by the British Major Smith (Richard Burton) and the American Lieutenant Schaffer (Clint Eastwood), who have to gain access to an "impregnable" German-occupied Alpine fortress, which they duly succeed in doing. Amid the various twists in the plot, there is a sequence in which armed German soldiers keep coming at the escaping Allied soldiers and just as fast are shot down in large numbers by Lieutenant Schaffer, who himself remains unscathed. The viewer could perhaps object to this sequence along the lines of saying, "These are human beings, with their own lives and families, their own hopes and fears; how can they be brushed aside thus?" But these German soldiers are not dramatically significant: they play a minor role, to create dramatic tension and action in the struggle around

28. The frequently raised puzzle as to what happens to the satan, and why he does not reappear later in the book, seems to me to be comparably based on a misreading of his role. If his role is to ask the hard question, and so set in motion the testing sequence, there is no need for him to reappear once that testing is resolved. As long as we, the readers, understand what is going on in Job's affliction and response, then that is all that is needed.

29. A reading of Jung's *Answer to Job* is, like a reading of Sigmund Freud's *Moses and Monotheism* (trans. Katherine Jones [London: Hogarth, 1939]), a sobering experience. Both Jung and Freud were brilliant and are rightly acclaimed as pioneers of psychiatry. Yet they each read the Bible with a strong agenda, related to their psychiatric concerns, and each is a standing reminder of how easy it is even for great minds to read the Bible in ways that illuminate far more the nature of the reader than the content of what is read.

30. It is likewise surely beside the point to feel sorry for Job's wife. Stuart Weeks, e.g., in relation to the longer speech on the wife's lips in 2:9 LXX, observes that "she is herself, it is easy to forget, also a victim of what has happened," and characterizes Job's response to his wife in 2:10 as "perhaps rather brutal" (*Introduction*, 54). In ordinary life these would be appropriate sentiments. But in a narrative where Job's wife has no existence other than the narrative function of expressing an inappropriate thought (i.e., she is not really a character at all), one's imaginative energies are better directed elsewhere.

escape from the fortress. To concentrate on the carelessness with which they are gunned down, or to lament the abuse of their human dignity, is to fail to appreciate or follow the nature of the drama.[31] One is not obliged to like a certain kind of action movie, but that is a different issue from not understanding how its conventions work. Comparably, Jung comes across as a superficial reader of the ancient text, so eager to make it serve his own agenda that he does not bother to attend properly to its (hardly obscure) conventions.

Thus the narrative of Job 1:1–2:10 should not be read as a portrayal of the limitations and brutality of the God it depicts; rather, it should be read as a portrayal of the meaning of the prime Old Testament category for right human response to God. The way in which Job retains his relationship with God, and when severely afflicted articulates its trusting and non-instrumental dynamics, narratively displays the meaning of "fear of God."

A Reading of Job 28:1–28

Now we turn to a famous and beautiful poem, located toward the end of the speeches of Job and his comforters. The question that the poem both raises and answers is "Where shall wisdom be found?"

Two preliminary issues need to be raised. First, whose voice is speaking in this poem? My proposal is that the voice in the poem is that of the narrator whom we have already heard in 1:1–2:10. Second, why is the poem located at this point in the book? We do not know.

As it stands, the poem has no separate heading, and it both follows and precedes discourses by Job, which might imply that Job should be understood as the speaking voice. Nonetheless, in both content and tone the material is so uncharacteristic of all that Job says elsewhere in the poetic dialogues that most readers reckon Job to be an inappropriate speaker. Yet the content does not at all match the characteristic emphases of Eliphaz, Bildad, or Zophar (or Elihu) either.[32] So how should it be heard?

Many interpreters unsurprisingly conclude that the poem is an independent piece that has fortuitously been preserved within the context of the book of Job, and insofar as its content is independent of the book, so should its interpretation be also. Why is it here? Perhaps it was inserted

---

31. It is hardly different in kind from a child at play who knocks down and "kills" a whole group of models/figurines with a sweep of the hand.

32. The thought of Job 28 is perhaps less distant from that of Elihu than of the others. Thus David J. A. Clines suggests that Elihu was the original speaker (and that his speeches originally came after chap. 27) (*Job 21–37*, WBC 18A [Nashville: Nelson, 2006], 889–926). However, both the tone and the thought of chap. 28 are distinct from the speeches of Elihu. In such matters it is easier to conjecture than to persuade. Moreover, such conjectures, because they "improve" the flow of the text, can readily distract us from attending to the logic of the book in its received form, even if one allows that the received form of the text may well be, at least in part, the result of a complex history of formation.

to sound a pious note that might somehow mitigate the challenging tenor of Job's surrounding speeches. Yet even if the poem has a prehistory prior to incorporation within its received location (which is possible, though we will never know), it does not follow that it should not be interpreted substantively, rather than just adventitiously, in relation to its present context.

The narrator, who has told the story of Job in chapters 1 and 2, is a promising candidate for the speaker of the poem. There are three main reasons for understanding the narrator, whose voice we have heard previously, to be the voice here too. First, the measured and reflective tone of the poem is comparable to the tone of the opening narrative. Second, the climactic terminology and content of the poem relate to that of the opening narrative. Third, there is a comparable didactic concern intrinsic to both narrative and poem, distinct from the more opaque nature of the surrounding poetic speeches.

If, as sometimes suggested, one should imagine the book of Job as a dramatic onstage presentation, with differing live characters speaking their parts, the presence of the speaking narrator for chapter 28 would remove most of the difficulties. The only snag is that we lack the appropriate rubrics.

Admittedly the ascription of the poem to the narrator, which I believe enables the best sense to be made of it, still does not resolve the puzzle as to its location. Perhaps one should see it as introducing a second part to the book, with subsequent speeches by Job, Elihu, and God replacing those by Job and his three "comforters." Nonetheless, it must be frankly admitted that the present unascribed location of the poem amid speeches of Job defies neat explanation and will always remain more or less puzzling to interpreters. Moshe Greenberg nicely observes that "the literary complexity of the book is consistent with and appropriate to the nature of the issues with which it deals."[33]

> [1]Surely there is a mine for silver,[34]
>   and a place for gold to be refined.[35]
> [2]Iron is taken out of the earth,
>   and copper is smelted from ore.
> [3]Miners put an end to darkness,
>   and search out to the farthest bound
>   the ore in gloom and deep darkness.
> [4]They open shafts in a valley away from human habitation;
>   they are forgotten by travelers,
>   they sway suspended, remote from people.
> [5]As for the earth, out of it comes bread;
>   but underneath it is turned up as by fire.
> [6]Its stones are the places of sapphires,
>   and its dust contains gold.

33. Moshe Greenberg, "Job," in *The Literary Guide to the Bible*, ed. Robert Alter and Frank Kermode (London: Fontana, 1989), 283–304, esp. 284.

34. The NRSV prefaces this line, as it prefaces the start of each paragraph of the poem, with a beginning quotation mark, indicating that the poem is being construed as on the lips of Job. Since I am taking the poem to be a contribution by the narrator, not a speech by one of the characters, I omit the quotation marks for the paragraphs throughout.

35. The poem poses numerous philological and interpretive difficulties, especially in the earlier verses (of which there is interesting discussion, and suggestion that the imagery is of journeying instead of mining, in Scott Jones, *Rumors of Wisdom: Job 28 as Poetry*, BZAW 398 [Berlin and New York: de Gruyter, 2009]), but since these features do not substantively affect the question and answer about wisdom, they will not be discussed here.

⁷That path no bird of prey knows,
    and the falcon's eye has not seen it.
⁸The proud wild animals have not trodden it;
    the lion has not passed over it.

⁹They put their hand to the flinty rock,
    and overturn mountains by the roots.
¹⁰They cut channels in the rocks,
    and their eyes see every precious thing.
¹¹The sources of the rivers they probe;
    hidden things they bring to light.

The poem begins with an elaborate account of human ability to discover that which is widely held to be supremely precious: silver and gold. Human ingenuity is represented by mining underground in remote and difficult locations where precious stones of many different kinds (iron and sapphires as well as silver and gold) can be found (vv. 1–6). To penetrate underground means that humans can reach places inaccessible to birds and beasts, creatures who are restricted to what is above ground (vv. 7–8). Humans who delve for precious metals are not only bold in undertaking (v. 9b) but also successful in execution: they see, they bring to light (vv. 10–11). Human ingenuity and ability is wonderful.

Yet it is precisely this wondrous resourcefulness that poses the issue of the poem:

¹²But where shall wisdom be found?
    And where is the place of understanding?
¹³Mortals do not know the way to it,[36]
    and it is not found in the land of the living.
¹⁴The deep says, "It is not in me,"
    and the sea says, "It is not with me."

The ability to discover precious stones does not suffice to discover that quality which, by clear implication, is even more precious than such stones: wisdom (v. 12). This cannot be found in the way that humans find other things (v. 13). Even if they delved undersea rather than underground, it would make no difference—wisdom is no more in the one place than the other (v. 14). In the places and by the means whereby they discover and get hold of other things, humans cannot get hold of wisdom.

36. The NRSV margin (for 28:13) notes that it is following the Greek ("its way") rather than the Hebrew ("its price"). This is indeed preferable since the contextual issue is wisdom's location; its value will only be addressed in v. 15. A Hebrew *Vorlage* for "its way" would be *drkh*, which differs in only one letter from MT's *'rkh*.

> ¹⁵It cannot be bought for gold,
>   and silver cannot be weighed out as its price.
> ¹⁶It cannot be valued in the gold of Ophir,
>   in precious onyx or sapphire.
> ¹⁷Gold and glass cannot equal it,
>   nor can it be exchanged for jewels of fine gold.
> ¹⁸No mention shall be made of coral or of crystal;
>   the price of wisdom is above pearls.
> ¹⁹The chrysolite of Ethiopia cannot compare with it,
>   nor can it be valued in pure gold.

The thought changes from the possibility of discovering wisdom to that of buying it. If ingenuity fails, might wealth, especially exceptional wealth, succeed? Might the precious stones dug out from the earth be used to acquire wisdom? To which the answer—in a series of elegant variations on precious materials whose own precise identity is not always clear, but unfailingly represent high value—is simply no. Wisdom is indeed supremely valuable, but its value is incommensurate with financial value. Wisdom cannot be bought: it is not that kind of thing.

> ²⁰Where then does wisdom come from?
>   And where is the place of understanding?
> ²¹It is hidden from the eyes of all living,
>   and concealed from the birds of the air.
> ²²Abaddon and Death say,
>   "We have heard a rumor of it with our ears."

And so the poet repeats, with variation, the refrain of verses 12–14. If one cannot obtain wisdom by the prime means that humans use to acquire things—ingenuity, discovery, wealth—then where on earth is it to be found? To which the answer is "Nowhere on earth." Those on the earth, above the earth, or below the earth alike agree that it is not there.

But where then is wisdom?

> ²³God understands the way to it,
>   and he knows its place.
> ²⁴For he looks to the ends of the earth,
>   and sees everything under the heavens.
> ²⁵When he gave to the wind its weight,
>   and apportioned out the waters by measure;
> ²⁶when he made a decree for the rain,
>   and a way for the thunderbolt;

²⁷then he saw it and declared it;
  he established it, and searched it out.
²⁸And he said to humankind [*'ādām*],
  "Truly, the fear of the Lord [*yir'at 'ǎdōnāy*], that is wisdom;
  and to depart from evil [*sūr mērā'*] is understanding."

That which is beyond humans is not beyond God. Where wisdom is, and how to get there, is known to God (v. 23); and God is able to see what no one else can (v. 24; contrast vv. 13, 21). When at creation He regulated wind and rain (vv. 25–26), then He established what wisdom is and where it is to be found (v. 27).³⁷ God, however, did not keep this knowledge of wisdom to Himself, but rather declared it to His human creation [*'ādām*], to those who would have the capacity to understand it and for whom it would be of fundamental importance. The content of this primordial revelation is that wisdom and understanding is in fact constituted by the fear of the Lord and departing from evil (v. 28).

These key terms that define wisdom are, however, precisely the qualities that have been seen to characterize Job in the opening narrative. Not only did the narrative introduce Job as "one who feared God [*yěrē' 'ělōhīm*] and departed from evil [*sār mērā'*],"³⁸ but the narrative also probed the meaning of this "fear" and showed that it means true relationship with God, a relationship to be sustained even when the worst that could happen does happen. If the opening narrative establishes a meaning for "fear of God," and the poem of chapter 28 identifies such "fear of God" with "wisdom," then these two passages should be interpreted in conjunction with each other. Job's unswerving adherence to God in the midst of disaster and desolation represents true wisdom and understanding. Thus if we the readers/hearers want to know what wisdom looks like, we should look at Job—and, in principle, emulate him.

37. The language of vv. 25–26 does not sound particularly like creation language (at least, to the contemporary reader), and on its own it could be read as divine preparation of a thunderstorm. However, v. 27, with its "then" and its verbs of definitive action in the past, indicates that the context of creation is most likely the concern of vv. 25–26.

38. The wording of "depart from evil" is identical in 1:1, 8; 2:3; and 28:28, except that in the former context (Job 1–2) *sār* is a participle, appropriate to the narrative description, while in the latter *sūr* is an infinitive, appropriate to a definitional use. More surprising is that 28:28 uses "Lord" (*'ǎdōnāy*) rather than "God" (*'ělōhīm*), when the use of "God" would be expected because of "God" in both immediate (28:23) and more distant (1:1, 8; 2:3) contexts. Although some manuscripts have *yhwh* instead of *'ǎdōnāy*, none have the expected *'ělōhīm*. I see no persuasive explanation for this. (The suggestion that 28:28 may be an addition resolves nothing, for one could expect someone to make the wording of the addition appropriate to its new context.) However, the present wording appropriately emphasizes the intrinsic lordship of God over His creation. The LXX neatly smooths things out by using *theosebeia* in 28:28, which lines up perfectly with the adjective *theosebēs* in 1:1, 8; 2:3.

Why then does the poem so stress the inaccessibility of wisdom? This is surely in part because, in an important sense, wisdom is like God Himself. On the one hand, God is impossible to find within the world. One might say, in a post-biblical idiom, that God is not an item in an inventory of the universe, for anything thus discovered would by definition be a creature rather than the Creator. Nor is God accessible by those means with which humans regularly attain their goals (ingenuity, hard work, wealth). On the other hand, it is the common testimony of countless people down through the ages that God is accessible both here and now. The way God is "accessed" is different in kind from the way things that humans commonly value are accessed; so too wisdom.

This general point receives specific focus in the context of Job: How should one live when life itself falls apart? When things go wrong, it is common either to rationalize or to resent affliction (or to do both). Job does neither. Although we the readers/hearers know the rationale for what Job goes through, he does not when he makes his responses in 1:21 and 2:10, nor does he ever. Job also does not resent catastrophe but rather maintains his stance of trust in God (which then becomes the premise for his passionate questioning). So where is wisdom in a world in which there are incomprehensible tragedies and disasters? It is found in "fearing God and turning away from evil," in maintaining integrity and trust toward God even *in extremis*. This is both hopelessly hard and elusive (as evidenced by the many down through the ages who have responded otherwise) yet entirely possible (as evidenced by the many down through the ages who have displayed Job-like qualities).[39]

One corollary of this interpretation is surely that the poem is using "wisdom" in a specific sense, appropriate to the concern of the book: knowing how to live well in extreme situations. "Wisdom" as defined here is not the ability to utilize knowledge in such a way as to live well in general, which is the consistent concern in Proverbs. This probably relates also to a difference of wording. In Proverbs, the principle that "the fear of YHWH is the beginning of wisdom" (9:10 ET; cf. 1:7; 15:33)—which most likely means that "fear of YHWH" constitutes access to the high road by which wisdom is attained[40]—has a didactic import appropriate to the young person whose life is being shaped: first learn to live in the fear of God, and thereby you will be enabled to live wisely.

---

39. At the time of this writing, a notable recent example is Tariq Jahan, a Muslim in Birmingham (UK), whose son, twenty-one-year-old Haroon Jahan, was killed, along with two others, when someone drove a car directly into them in the course of the riots that swept some of England's major cities for several days in August 2011. His Muslim faith enabled him to speak without bitterness of his loss, understanding it in terms of divine fate and destiny, and his appeal for calm was widely reckoned to have played a significant role in calming the riots.

40. See, e.g., Michael V. Fox, *Proverbs 1–9*, AB 18A (New York: Doubleday, 2000), 67–68.

In Job 28 wisdom is equated with "fear of the Lord," rather than being the result of it, because it is a reading of Job's fear of God, maintained in extreme adversity, as being the wise way to respond to apparently random affliction.

One Wisdom or Two?

Since my reading of Job 28 differs from that in most modern studies, it may be helpful briefly to set out the generally favored alternative readings. I hope that a restatement of my reading, in relation to differing readings, will help clarify its significance.

The key issue in all readings is whether the term "wisdom" is used univocally or equivocally in the poem: does it have one meaning or two different meanings? In my reading, "wisdom" has the same sense throughout. When first used, it is not defined but assumed to be something familiar and desirable. This familiar and desirable quality then receives definition at the end. Certainly there may be a narrowing of a reader's assumptions if initially "wisdom" is assumed to be about living well in general without specific reference to the context of the book of Job; but there is no narrowing if the issues of Job are assumed from the outset.

Predominantly, however, modern scholars have argued otherwise. A. B. Davidson finely formulated a common view in the late nineteenth century:

> The Wisdom spoken of throughout the chapter is a possession of God alone, it is His who is Creator; man has a wisdom also, which is that of the creature, to fear the Lord. . . . [Wisdom] is a thing possible to God alone; and man does not attain to it through the fear of the Lord,—the fear of the Lord is the substitute ordained for man instead of it; for as the absolute Wisdom belongs to the Creator, so the fear of the Lord is the wisdom that befits the creature.[41]

What then is the wisdom that is peculiar to God?

> Wisdom is the idea or principle lying under the order of the Universe, the world plan. . . . Intellectual apprehension of the scope of the phenomena of the world and the events of man's life is beyond the reach of man; such knowledge belongs only to God, who made the world.[42]

Some such interpretation has regularly been rehearsed, often with the added suggestion that the final verse of the poem, largely because it uses "wisdom"

---

41. Andrew Bruce Davidson, *The Book of Job*, CBSC (Cambridge: Cambridge University Press, 1895), 200–201.
42. Ibid., 201.

in a sense different from that earlier in the poem, may well be a later addition to a poem that originally concluded without it. So, for example, Gerhard von Rad says of wisdom in the body of the poem:

> Wisdom, the order given to the world by God, is the most precious thing of all. But while man has eventually found a way to all precious things, he does not find the way to the mystery of creation. Only God knows its place, he has already been concerned with it at creation. . . . [Man] never gets it into his power as he does the other precious things. The world never reveals the mystery of its order.

Then with regard to verse 28 he comments:

> It is highly probable that the last line of the poem is to be regarded as an addition. It stems from someone who did not wish to leave the reader only with the magnificent, negative result. Its interest in wisdom remains undiminished. The way to wisdom is *via* the fear of Yahweh. In this way, the person who made this addition not only departed from the theme of the poem, but he is suddenly using the word "wisdom" in a quite different sense, namely the sense of human wisdom.[43]

Some, however, whether or not they see the final verse as an addition, read it more negatively than Davidson or von Rad, opining that it is disappointing, a loss of nerve that prefers platitude to the acknowledgment of mystery (rather as Job's restoration at the end of the book is often considered to be a bathetic disappointment).[44]

The prime justification for this interpretation in terms of two different meanings for wisdom is, as far as I can see, the textual emphasis on wisdom as inaccessible to humans and known to God. If this means what it says, then such a wisdom must be different from what is accessible to humans in the final verse; it must therefore represent some ultimate divine principle or divine understanding that underlies everything. On such a reading, the thrust of Job 28 becomes comparable to the thrust of the divine speeches in Job 38–41, with their portrayal of the created order as beyond Job's comprehension. Certainly, if a major concern of the book of Job is that God's ordering of the world is

---

43. Gerhard von Rad, *Wisdom in Israel*, trans. James D. Martin (1970; ET, London: SCM, 1972), 148–49.

44. Carol Newsom comments: "There is something shocking and outrageous about coming to the end of such a profound poem and being met by a cliché. These are the shopworn phrases of conventional instruction found in Prov 1:7; 3:7; 9:10; and in Ps 111:10"; and she speaks further of "unbearable smugness" and "dross instead of gold" ("The Book of Job," in *The New Interpreter's Bible*, ed. Leander E. Keck et al. [Nashville: Abingdon, 1996], 4:533).

beyond human comprehension, then its being made in two contexts is hardly impossible.[45] However, it is also possible that the divine speeches in Job 38–41 are being allowed imaginatively to override this earlier poem, which in fact has its own voice. I suggest that there are good reasons for making a clear distinction between the concern of the poem of Job 28 and the concern(s) of the divine speeches in Job 38–41.

First, the poem's refrain, which asks where wisdom is to be found, speaks of wisdom as a familiar concept. No unusual definition of "wisdom" is offered: the poem's sole definition of wisdom is in v. 28. Rather, "wisdom [hokmāh]" is paired with "understanding [bīnāh]," and the pairing of various forms of these Hebrew terms is common within the Old Testament.[46] This surely means that a reader's working assumption should be that "wisdom" and "understanding" here have a familiar meaning—that quality of character and mind in relation to God that enables people to handle life well (albeit in the extreme situation represented by Job)—and not an unfamiliar sense ("the idea or principle lying under the order of the Universe," "the order given to the world by God"). When the same pairing of "wisdom" with "understanding" is found in the conclusion (v. 28) as in the refrain (vv. 12, 20), one's working assumption (corrigible indeed, but not without good reason) is that it is the same wisdom and understanding in each context.

Second, the strong rhetorical picturing of wisdom as inaccessible and unknown to all living creatures is restricted to the refrains of the poem (vv. 12–14, 20–22) and does not feature in the two sections that spell out what are surely the leading ideas—that whatever one's ingenuity and energy or one's wealth, none of these enable a person to attain wisdom. I suggest that it is best to read this as indicating that wisdom is unobtainable by the best and generally most successful resources within human control, rather than that it is unobtainable altogether. The rhetoric of the refrain is designed to sharpen the question of how wisdom can be found, by emphasizing that it

45. "In the poem's denouement, Yahweh will appear and denounce human pretensions to understanding the wisdom of his management of the universe. The Meditation on Wisdom [Job 28] anticipates this very point, but in a serene tone rather than in the dramatic one of Yahweh speaking from the storm. When we encounter the Meditation here, we may not grasp its importance in the scheme of the book. But after reading chapters 38–41, we realize retroactively that its purpose is to prepare us for the book's conclusion" (Raymond Scheindlin, *The Book of Job: Translation, Introduction, and Notes* [New York and London: W. W. Norton, 1998], 203). Some commentators, however, feel that the poem's anticipation of the divine speeches makes those speeches anticlimactic.

46. The adjectival forms "wise" (hākām) and "understanding" (nābôn) are regularly combined (e.g., Gen. 41:39; Deut. 1:13; 4:6; 1 Kings 3:12; Prov. 16:21), as is the nominal form "wisdom" (hokmāh) with "understanding" (bīnāh, e.g., Deut. 4:6; Job 38:36; Prov. 23:23; Isa. 29:14).

does not have a "place" in the world like other things. This underlines that it is, in essence, a category mistake to suppose that one might attain it by the means whereby one attains other precious things. Wisdom's inaccessibility *tout court*, as in the refrains, is thus a trope for reinforcing wisdom's inaccessibility via human ingenuity and resources, as in verses 1–11 and verses 15–19.

A third issue concerns how best one should read the poem's ascribing knowledge of the "place" of wisdom to God (the generic *'ĕlōhîm*, v. 23). As already seen, it is commonly assumed that such an ascription should, in context, be read as restricting such wisdom to God, who alone has access to it. Over against this, however, there are other passages in the Old Testament that ascribe certain qualities to God (the generic *'ĕlōhîm*) in ways that clearly do not envisage that this means inaccessibility to humanity.

A prime example is Deuteronomy 1:17 where justice/judgment (*mishpāt*) is epigrammatically ascribed to God: "For the judgment [*or*, justice] is God's [*kî hammishpāt lē'lōhîm hû'*]." The context is Moses's recounting how he selected and commissioned leaders within Israel to assist him in the administration of justice (Deut. 1:9–18). His commissioning reads thus:

> "Judge rightly between one person and another, whether citizen or resident alien. You must not be partial in judging: hear out the small and great alike; you shall not be intimidated by anyone, for the judgment [*or*, justice] is God's. Any case that is too hard for you, bring it to me, and I will hear it." (Deut. 1:16–17)

Initially Moses charges Israel's judges to resist the common ways in which the judicial process is corrupted: they should not favor their own (Israelites) over others (non-Israelites), nor should they be swayed by or defer to money or power. This account of the qualities that true judges should display, which clearly envisages something hard but attainable, is followed by the epigram in question, whose immediate sequel shows that it is absolutely not about leaving to God something that is too hard for humans (for the really hard cases are to be referred to Moses himself), but about enabling justice genuinely to be done. What is the thought in the epigram? Is it simply that judges should fear God more than they fear fellow humans (which is, of course, an appropriate thought and is well-represented in Jewish and Christian traditions: "Fear Him, ye saints, and you will then / have nothing else to fear")? Is not rather the logic that when judges act with integrity (by avoiding the corruptions just mentioned), then they will be displaying something of the qualities or characteristics of God Himself? As God is, so are the judges to be, for they are acting on God's behalf. In other words, the purpose of ascribing justice/judgment to

God is the very opposite of removing it from the sphere of human attainment. Rather it is firmly to locate it in humans who are open and accountable to God, so that their human action embodies a divine quality.[47] Thereby God's will may be done on earth as it is in heaven.

My proposal is to use the ascription of justice/judgment to God in Deuteronomy 1:17 as a suggestive analogy for understanding the ascription of wisdom to God in Job 28:23. When read thus, the point of the strong contrast between that which is inaccessible to humans but accessible to God is not to make wisdom inaccessible but rather to prepare for specifying its location among humans of a particular kind, those who display the appropriate qualities.

A fourth issue concerns the logic of the depiction that God "established" wisdom at creation (v. 27). Von Rad does not linger to consider the oddity of his proposal that the poem initially concluded with a "magnificent, negative result," that is, God's establishing wisdom but keeping it to Himself. The general theological logic of portrayals of beginning and end, of creation and eschaton, is that they have strong existential and ethical implications for the here and now: they are constitutive in that they specify basic aspects of what it should mean to live appropriately as a creature in God's creation. One expects that which is constituted at creation to be communicated to the created order. So one would expect this account of the divine establishing of wisdom at creation to be followed by a divine address to humanity (ʾādām). In other words, one expects a scenario comparable in its logic to that of Genesis 1:28, where creation is followed by communication.

Finally, it is surely an appreciation of the contextual resonance between this poem and the opening narrative that should prevent the interpreter from finding the conclusion of the poem disappointingly trite or platitudinous. Of course, it is easy to imagine numerous contexts in which an axiom such as "piety is wisdom" can sound disappointing, unsuited to "real life" beyond the nursery or Sunday school. But when we read the conclusion of the poem with its constitutive principle that "the fear of the Lord is wisdom" in the light of Job's displaying and maintaining fear of God and departing from evil amid utter dereliction, then things look different. However easily wisdom can be reduced to banality, the poem depicts impossible wisdom made possible.

---

47. This also appears to be the force of the well-known parallel in 2 Chron. 19:6–7, where Jehoshaphat commissions judges: "Now let the fear of the LORD be upon you; take care what you do, for there is no perversion of justice with the LORD our God, or partiality, or taking of bribes." Here the "fear of God," which is to characterize the judges, surely has less to do with fearing God more than humans, than it does with replicating the divine qualities that the text enumerates. Compare also the discussion of how best to read Isa. 5:16 in chap. 5 above.

Conclusion

The contested nature of biblical interpretation, always an issue, is perhaps particularly an issue in the book of Job, where readings both of the whole and of the parts vary so enormously. Although I have presented my reading of Job 1:1–2:10 and 28:1–28 in relation to alternative construals, there is still much more that could be said, not least if I were to attempt to relate the reading offered here to a reading of the book as a whole. For, in brief, if wisdom demonstrated through maintenance of the fear of God is *an* answer to Job's problem, it is not *the* answer, or at least not the sole answer, within the book as a whole.[48]

By way of conclusion I will touch on two issues in which the understanding and possible appropriation of the content of the biblical text relate to the way in which one reads it.

Wisdom and Scientific Knowledge

A reading of Job 28 depends on the decision one takes about the meaning of "wisdom" in the refrain and the conclusion. I have argued for the importance of taking "wisdom" in a familiar Old Testament sense of "a form of knowledge that enables one to live well," in a context-specific way with reference to the problem posed by the narrative of Job: how one is to know how to live well in situations of incomprehensible affliction.

What, however, is the epistemic content of such wisdom? In particular, how does it relate to the kinds of knowledge of the world and the human condition that humans have produced over the centuries, and especially in recent times through the astonishing development of the natural sciences and all that they have made possible? To put it sharply, does Job 28 advocate, or at least encourage, anti-intellectualism? This issue is raised by Edwin Good in his commentary on Job 28:28:

> Wisdom, as the god defines and conveys it to humans, has nothing to do with knowledge as we habitually think about it. Our culture takes as an unambiguous good, our model of and precondition for wisdom, the scientific or technological knowledge exhibited by the first part of this poem. The culture that produced the Book of Job looked on that kind of knowledge with contempt. Our research universities and laboratories and government grants would have been unthinkable in that culture, where wisdom came not from the acquisition

48. Since I am generally unpersuaded by proposals that readings of Job as a whole entail ironic reconstruals of its constituent elements, I do not think that a reading of the whole would significantly alter the reading of the part offered here, even though there is a real question about the role it would play within the whole.

of knowledge but from religion and morality. To be wise was to fear the god and avoid evil.[49]

Good's critique is curious, despite the undoubted fact that the modern West has seen an increase in scientific and technological knowledge and capability unimaginable to anyone who lived in ancient Israel. What firm evidence is there for the "contempt" toward scientific/technological knowledge on the part of "the culture that produced the Book of Job"? The tone of Job 28:1–11 is itself in no way contemptuous, nor is the portrayal of Solomon's wide-ranging (for his time) knowledge (1 Kings 4:29–34 [MT 5:9–14]). It may be that Good is retrojecting into the ancient context of Job his dislike of religiously inspired dismissiveness toward scientific achievement in a contemporary context.

Further, when Good says that our culture considers scientific and technological knowledge to be "our model of and precondition for wisdom," I am puzzled to know what he means. For it is hardly controversial to distinguish between wisdom and scientific knowledge with its applications, and to suggest that the latter does not entail the former. (Are top scientists not just cleverer but also wiser than others? Does access to technology enable attainment of deep understanding of life?) Not a few people observe that the massive increase in Western society's scientific knowledge and technological ability has not brought with it a commensurate increase in the art of living well. Clearly, much depends on how one defines "wisdom."

A possible analogy for appreciating what is at stake here might be to develop the difference between what is accessible via a third-person perspective (objective, external) and a first-person perspective (subjective, internal). The third-person perspective includes everything that can be described and analyzed by the natural sciences, which study what is "out there" and are in principle accessible to anyone. The first-person perspective includes everything that is only accessible via human consciousness—moral and aesthetic realities, such as faith, hope, love, trust, goodness, beauty, and not least wisdom—in other words, realities that feature prominently in religious faith and in the humanities more generally, realities that have an inescapable "subjective" element, inaccessible in certain ways to others. Of course, the social sciences, especially psychology and sociology, can give extensive third-person accounts of what is important in religious faith and the humanities by considering their human and public embodiments; also neuroscience can extensively analyze the conditions of the brain that enable consciousness and first-person realities to function.

49. Edwin M. Good, *In Turns of Tempest: A Reading of Job, with a Translation* (Stanford, CA: Stanford University Press, 1990), 292.

Nonetheless, the first-person realities are not reducible to the third-person analyses. Moreover, the ways in which investigators themselves partake of the first-person dimension of the realities they investigate makes enormous difference to the conceptual frames of reference they adopt, to their decisions as to what deserves attention, to the ways in which they understand and evaluate, and to the kinds of explanatory reductions that they do and do not endorse.

A deservedly acclaimed discussion of the philosophical issues here is Thomas Nagel's *The View from Nowhere*. Nagel discusses "how to combine the perspective of a particular person inside the world with an objective view of that same world, the person and his viewpoint included." He argues for the irreducibility of subjective perspectives, especially in relation to "those powerful reductionist dogmas which seem to be part of the intellectual atmosphere we breathe." Nagel also contends for the necessary existential complementarity of objective and subjective perspectives: "One must arrange somehow to see the world both from nowhere and from here, and to live accordingly." Yet he also admits the impossibility of eliminating all conflicts between subjective perspectives and objective detachment. His bottom line is that we lack the appropriate conceptuality to give a good account of the problem.[50]

These issues have also been constructively addressed, from a theological angle, by Roger Scruton in the 2010 Gifford Lectures. Scruton suggests that the reality and presence of God should be thought of by analogy with the reality and presence of the self and first-person consciousness. Both represent "subjects" whose reality cannot be scientifically established as "objects"—but which are no less real for that reason.[51]

Thus one might, for example, rhetorically emphasize the way in which the things that humanly matter most are inaccessible to scientific knowledge and discovery, and that one could search the whole universe, with its innumerable galaxies and light-years, and never find hope or love "out there" in space and time. The point would not be to deny the reality of hope and love, but to underline (perhaps polemically and anti-reductively) that it is a category mistake to suppose that they yield their reality to human scientific endeavor, whatever the astonishing range of scientific achievements.

In terms of Job 28, one might suggest that wisdom represents a first-person perspective as distinct from the kinds of knowledge and achievement that are attainable via a third-person perspective. In other words, the concern of the rhetoric in Job 28 can readily be read as intrinsically *methodological*: how can one attain wisdom? Such a first-person reality can only be attained by first-person means.

Thus the poem is not making a restrictive claim that the only wisdom worth having is religious knowledge, as Good seems to think. Nor is it making a different restrictive claim, as Clines seems to think, when he says that

50. Thomas Nagel, *The View from Nowhere* (New York and Oxford: Oxford University Press, 1986), esp. 3, 81, 86.

51. Roger Scruton, *The Face of God*, Gifford Lectures (London and New York: Continuum, 2012). For example, Scruton says: "The question of God's presence often looks insoluble. Rightly understood, however, it resembles the question of your and my presence. And we must try to answer them both together" (52).

the point of 28:28 is that wisdom "can only be acquired by the devout and the righteous"[52]—at least if the implication is that there is some antecedent group of the righteous who in this poem are limiting wisdom to their in-group. Rather, the point is that among the many kinds of knowledge that are available to humans, the supremely valuable knowledge of how to live well, especially when faced with affliction or tragedy, is available to anyone who will meet the requirement of living resolutely with faith and integrity.

What Kind of Prescription for Life Does the Text Present?

One of the keys to my reading has been attentiveness to literary context, the relationship between the fear of God that Job displays in the opening narrative and the fear of God that is defined as wisdom. Many interpreters either do not notice the linkage or leave its interpretive potential more or less unexploited. Yet even a recognition of its substantive significance does not necessarily lead to the reading offered here. David Robertson, who thinks that attempts to read Job in its received form are generative of irony, comments on 28:28: "This is precisely the wisdom Job has followed all his life (chapters 1–2) and where has it got him: the ash-heap. Some wisdom!"[53] Comparably, David Clines comments: "It is hard not to see the relation between these sentences [28:28 and 1:1] as ironic. If fearing God and turning aside from evil is what has got Job into this unhappy condition (and that is the thrust of the prologue), the value of this prescription for life is seriously undermined."[54] These seem to be instructive examples of non-attuned readings, which in effect score a point at the expense of taking the text seriously.[55] On the one hand, the thrust of the prologue is *not* that Job's fear of God and turning from evil brought him into misery. If he had not had these qualities, there could have been no question of testing their authenticity; but if there had been no test, there would have been no misery. His qualities were not the problem, and there is no implication whatever in the text that fear of God in itself engenders an "unhappy condition."

On the other hand, the implicit assumptions in the way that Robertson and Clines formulate their critiques are surely open to question. Despite the narrative's rejection of the suspicion that Job's piety may be essentially instrumental

---

52. Clines, "Job 28:28," 77.
53. Robertson, *Literary Critic*, 33–34, 46.
54. Clines, "Job 28:28," 84.
55. Contemporary biblical scholarship affords all-too-regular occasion to ponder the sentiment succinctly expressed by Robert Alter: "The language of criticism now often reflects an emotional alienation from the imaginative life of the text under discussion" (*The Pleasures of Reading in an Ideological Age* [New York: Simon & Schuster, 1989], 15).

in relation to God, there remain various ways in which piety may have consequences that need not be problematic. The proposition that to live with faith and integrity should lead to a good life, and that that is a legitimate reason for living with faith and integrity, should be uncontroversial, at least for any (would-be) believer—although of course the notion of a "good life" needs considerable discussion as to what it means and does not mean. The problem arises if one construes faith and integrity in instrumental terms, such that if they do not lead to the attainment of a "good life," then it is pointless to maintain them. It is the difference between faith and integrity having intrinsic value with some expectation of certain consequences, and their having solely or predominantly instrumental value. Suspicion that the latter may be the case prompts the satan to speak up.

To generalize the issue somewhat, the priorities that are surely present within the Job texts we have looked at are shared widely within the biblical canon. Elsewhere within the Old Testament, Habakkuk famously depicts the righteous person, in a context of affliction and puzzlement and scorn, as living by "faithfulness [*ĕmūnāh*]" (Hab. 2:4); and he ends with a personal testimony of comparable faithfulness in time of overwhelming disaster (3:17–19). Within the book of Isaiah, an unnamed voice asks a searching question about how people are to respond to the servant of Yhwh, whose repeated afflictions have just been recounted (Isa. 50:4–9):

> Who among you fears the Lord
>   and obeys the voice of his servant,
> who walks in darkness
>   and has no light,
> yet trusts in the name of the Lord
>   and relies upon his God? (50:10)

Within the New Testament it is supremely Jesus in his passion who displays comparable qualities. Whatever his own hopes and preferences, his deepest concern is to be faithful to his Father: "My Father, if it is possible, let this cup pass from me; yet not what I want but what you want" (Matt. 26:39). Faith is about faithfulness, not an easy life.

If I may venture a summary generalization, my reading of the literature on Job 1–2 and 28 has left me with a sense that the interpretive thesis for which I am arguing here—that the maintenance of faith and integrity, especially *in extremis*, is wisdom—gets little, if any, hearing for one reason above all others: it is considered dull, shallow, simplistic, boring. It represents "conventional piety," and (by implication) the conventionally pious lead predictably dull and intellectually unstimulating lives, all of which is (by implication) generative of no more than boredom or perhaps suspicion.[56] How different from the Job of the speeches, who is interesting precisely because he abandons the conventions of piety and speaks with unrestrained passion.

Admittedly, piety can be dull and dim. But need it be so? People who bear great hardship with faithful patience and courage are deeply admirable if one has the privilege, usually a humbling privilege, of knowing them. Perhaps to some extent the issue is the age-old problem of how to make goodness appear imaginatively interesting.[57] But the problem is also surely to some degree one of perspective: the extent and nature of one's comfort or affliction may make a marked difference to one's evaluations of moral and spiritual stability in both self and others. Interpretation and appropriation of major existential issues in the biblical text are ultimately inseparable from an interpreter's assumptions and circumstances.

56. David Penchansky comments that the "legendary Job" [i.e., the Job of the narrative, who is commended by 28:28] functions to "confirm the easy piety of the superficially religious, reaffirming the control of the religious establishment" (*The Betrayal of God: Ideological Conflict in Job* [Louisville: Westminster John Knox, 1990], 32).

57. This ranges from, e.g., medieval murals of heaven and hell, in which the angels and saints regularly seem less interesting than the demons and the damned, to contemporary cinema, where goodness is usually "complexified" to make it interesting. For example, in Peter Jackson's rendering of J. R. R. Tolkien's *The Lord of the Rings*, Aragorn displays self-doubt, Faramir wavers, and Elrond inclines to despair of Middle-Earth and pressures Arwen to break faith with Aragorn (with which she goes along for a while). Presumably this was considered cinematically more interesting than the unwavering integrity and resolve to resist faithlessness and Sauron to the end, come what may, that Aragorn, Faramir, Elrond, and Arwen display in Tolkien's own (consistently engaging) portrayal in the book.

Epilogue

Many more studies of Old Testament passages, additional to those in the preceding eight chapters, could be offered. My present purpose, however, is solely to offer representative readings, so as to try to convey some flavor of the Old Testament as a whole. Perhaps my leaving such large gaps may encourage others to continue.

At this point, rather than just stopping, I hope it will be more helpful to conclude by drawing together some threads and trying to clarify aspects of the journey that the reader (who has read the whole) has undertaken.

The Theological Content and Shape of the Book

First, why have I discussed these particular Old Testament texts and not others? In a sense the selection is somewhat arbitrary, as it could so easily, and without loss, have been different; there is so much of interest in the Old Testament that has not been considered here. One honest justification must be that these happen to be passages on which I have worked and about which I have thought for a long time. I was drawn to them both by their theological and existential import and by the interpretive challenges they pose. Nonetheless, I think that there is shape, development, and coherence to the eight studies.

I start with the Shema, which on any reckoning is a key text and which focuses on "A Love Supreme." It directs us (readers of this book) to fundamental questions of God and what it might mean to be oriented toward God in terms of allegiance and priorities in daily living. Among other things I try to show how the concerns of the biblical text can help us begin to escape the undue intellectualization of religious faith. This intellectualization characterizes many contemporary conceptions of theology, popular as well as academic, and thereby narrows our conception of what it might mean to take God seriously. A core affirmation about God and related symbolic practices combine to form an identity and frame patterns of daily living.

Election is likewise a core Old Testament concern, and its articulation in Deuteronomy is not only one of its best-known formulations but also complementary to the Shema. In "A Chosen People" I try to capture the distinctive thought of the deuteronomic text, that the logic of the particularity of election is in essence the logic of love. This locates election within the wonder of grace and offers resources for tackling recurrent objections to election, when particularity in relation to the one God is conceived as a problem. The accompanying discussion of election in relation to ḥērem and issues of violence does not, of course, do more than scratch the surface of the problems. But if a metaphorical reading of ḥērem is on the right track, it reminds us of some of the enduring practical responsibilities that are intrinsic to maintaining loving faithfulness, both then and now.

The reading of the narrative of the manna as "Daily Bread" tries to disclose the discipline of daily living in the light of grace that is to characterize Israel as God's people. Although the primary focus is the narrative in Exodus 16, there is also a recapitulation of the meaning of the manna in Deuteronomy 8. A consequence of this is that the basic concerns and sequence within Moses's exposition of the nature of Israel as the covenant people of YHWH in Deuteronomy 6–8 are retained in my first three chapters. The use of the manna motif in the New Testament and Christian tradition also indicates further metaphorical moves (analogous to those suggested in chapter 2) that highlight the range of ways in which the disciplines of daily living can be realized.

In "Does God Change?" I try to show how a well-known puzzle in the Old Testament portrayal of God—that God "does repent" and that God "does not repent"—is best understood by recognizing that two distinct issues are at stake. However, these two issues, if taken together, can be seen as a paradox that leads us into a deeper appreciation of further foundational aspects of the biblical understanding of God and of religious language. On the one hand, Jeremiah 18 axiomatically sets out prophetic speech on behalf of God as response-seeking, revolving around the dynamics of warning and invitation; moreover, the God who seeks response is Himself responsive. On the other hand, the sovereign will of God for His people remains prior to, and not dependent on, their ability or willingness to respond. In important ways this re-expresses some of the key concerns of the first two chapters, that God's will for those whom He chooses, and their responses, are to be understood in terms of the dynamics of true relationship, that is, the logic of love.

The fifth chapter, "Isaiah and Jesus," is my attempt to offer a selective reading of a major prophetic book in a way that articulates further core elements of the Old Testament vision of God and humanity. What is said of God and what is said of humanity are seen to be intrinsically related, and human greatness is re-envisaged, over against common understandings, in terms of appropriating and displaying the moral qualities of God Himself. The paradoxical principle that "all who exalt themselves will be humbled, but all who humble themselves will be exalted" shows, here as elsewhere, strong resonance between Old and New Testament understandings of God and of faith.

The first five chapters thus seek to articulate theological and moral understandings that might all reasonably, I think, be regarded as "doctrinally foundational" for the vision of God and of human life with God (even if many other elements might also be so considered), at least when Israel's scriptures are read as the Christian Old Testament. God is the focus for identity and allegiance on the part of those who know themselves loved and called to faithfulness, who are to live by the disciplines of grace, responsive to fresh summons to loyalty and trust in God, and learning to realize their humanity through a self-dispossessing integrity that practices justice.

The remaining three chapters have a slightly different orientation (a different location within a spectrum). They are primarily to do with perennially problematic dimensions within human response to God. In chapter 6, "Educating Jonah," I take Jonah as the paradigm of the person who knows religious truth, and can, as it were, cite chapter and verse, without genuinely understanding it for what it is—which is why the religious truth that confronts him generates annoyance and anger, rather than joy. Religious language can be harder to understand and appropriate than it may initially appear to be. Compassion can be a demanding reality, and to learn it is more than a cerebral exercise. The fact that Jonah's resentment toward God is focused on key theological passages, Exodus 34:6–7 and Jeremiah 18:7–8, both of which feature in my discussions elsewhere, conveniently links this chapter with other content in the book.

The problem explored in Psalms 44 and 89 under the heading "Faith and Perplexity" is one that I take to be basic and recurrent in a life of faith. The problem is the disparity between the expectations of faith and the disappointing and brutal realities that may be encountered in practice. It is a striking testimony to the depth and honesty of the Old Testament that the problem should be formulated as starkly and unreservedly as it is in these psalms. Jews and Christians, in their comparable but distinct ways, have a long history of engaging with this problem, and some consideration of their engagements helps elucidate what a theological rationality that is attuned to Scripture should, and should not, entail.

Finally, in "Where Is Wisdom?" we see another important facet of a biblical understanding of life with God. The wisdom that is in focus in Job is not, I argue, the wisdom for getting on well in life generally, such as is articulated in Proverbs. Rather, it is the wisdom that arises when a person, like Job, has to walk uncomprehendingly through devastation and darkness. This wisdom, although it has an intellectual component, is primarily a matter of integrity and faithfulness, for Job (unlike the reader) never comes to understand the reason for his affliction. This discussion of Job 1–2 and 28 complements the discussion of Psalms 44 and 89.

In the final three chapters there is a focus upon certain challenging dimensions of life with God. There is the struggle for genuine understanding that can overcome selfish complacency, the need to maintain faithfulness in the midst of anguish and perplexity, and the learning of wisdom through resisting easy theological rationalizations. The vision of God enriches humanity because it is demanding and creates what it seeks, that is, growth and depth.

Overall, the theological content of the Old Testament is presented representatively, in such a way as to try to include subject matter that is on any reckoning important both for understanding the Old Testament in itself and for appropriating it within Christian faith. In terms of thinking about the nature of theological interpretation of Scripture as a practice, there are at least two consistent concerns. One is the way in which an understanding of God is never a speculative or abstract issue but is always inseparable from an understanding of what human life is meant—and can be enabled—to be. The other is that detailed readings of specific texts, rather than the more familiar practice of thematic collating of texts and topics, is a fully appropriate vehicle for "Old Testament Theology."

Hermeneutical Approaches and Assumptions

It will be obvious, both from the selection of biblical passages and from the manner of their discussion, that this is a distinctively Christian reading of Israel's scriptures, which is what the book's subtitle specifies. I hope that it will be equally obvious that this Christian reading seeks to be attentive to the specific voices and the distinctive nuances of the ancient Hebrew text in a philologically and conceptually alert way. There is more than one frame of reference and more than one goal for reading Israel's scriptures. But this in no way means that "anything goes," for good reading will be alert to, and responsibly constrained by, the text in relation to its various contexts. In this section it may be helpful to try to summarize what I understand to be at least some of the characteristic and recurrent moves that I make in seeking to do justice to Israel's scriptures as Christian Scripture.

An Overall Stance for Reading the Hebrew Text

One way of posing the issue could be this: Is the approach adopted here historical? Much would depend on the definition of "historical." If "historical" means a concern for the nature and development of Israel's religious thought and practice, both in itself and in relation to its ancient Near Eastern context of origin—an enterprise that has been basic to modern biblical scholarship, and where there has often not been much difference whether it is designated "history of Israelite religion" or "Old Testament theology"—then the answer is no. That is not what I have done, though I hope that some of the analyses of the texts could in some way contribute to such discussions, just as I have in numerous ways benefitted from such scholarly work. But if "historical" means a disciplined philological engagement with the meaning of the ancient Hebrew texts that seeks to do justice to their intrinsic idioms and conventions, and that seeks to reveal something of the subject matter that was a concern to the biblical writers, then the answer is yes.

It might help to pose the issue differently. In my discussions I have made use of the conceptuality of the world within, the world behind, and the world in front of the text. Almost all interpreters are interested, in one way or another, in the world within the text. The question becomes how one contextualizes this world within the text, which relates also to the nature of the imaginative moves that are brought to bear upon it. The dominant move in modern biblical scholarship has been to relate the world within the text to the world behind the text—to look backward, as it were, from the Old Testament to the world that gave rise to it, the immediate world of Israel and also the wider world of the ancient Near East. This means, for the most part, a focus on times and places before ever there was an Old Testament, when at most there were incipient collections and compilations of material that only over time became Israel's scriptures. My approach, by contrast, has been to focus primarily upon the world within the text in relation to the world in front of the text—to look forward from Israel's scriptures toward those enduring faiths, both Jewish and Christian, that appropriate this material as Scripture and understand themselves in relation to it. For this approach, Israel's scriptures as an authoritative collection are a given from the outset (and issues to do with these scriptures being received in Greek as well as Hebrew, and with disagreements over the boundaries of the canon, make no significant difference to this basic stance).

In drawing this basic distinction of approach, there is no need to polarize unnecessarily. Many scholars whose primary interest is the world behind the text are still interested in facets of the world in front of the text. And in my readings, although the world behind the text has been subordinated, it has not been ignored; judgments about the nature and genre of the text and how best to read it are informed by judgments about likely context and date of origin (despite the great difficulties in being confident about such matters, given the paucity of firm evidence). This is most obvious, perhaps, in the discussion of *ḥērem* in chapter 2, but also, in differing ways, in, say, the manna narrative and the book of Jonah.

Specific Assumptions (1): The Significance of the Canon and Its Theological Grammar

To take Israel's scriptures as a given leads fairly directly, I think, to certain interpretive assumptions and priorities. For example, my interest is in the meaning and implications of these documents rather than in the nature of the religious history that gave rise to them. On this approach there is a clear distinction between "Old Testament theology," the moral and religious meaning of these texts, and a "history of Israelite religion." As is often pointed out, the voices that are significant within the canonical collection of Israel's scriptures may not have been representative or initially influential within Israel's religion—as is sometimes conjectured for Deuteronomy and as is self-attested for the prophet Jeremiah (just as the life and ministry of Jesus hardly met with general acceptance at the time). The recognition of certain documents as in some sense normative implies moral and theological value judgments on the part of the communities that make the recognition. The documents come to be seen as the mature fruit and enduring wisdom of the complex religious history that gave rise to them. Their continuing use as a canonical collection implies the acceptance of certain critical judgments and norms—a "grammar"—with regard to what henceforth constitutes right language about, and faithful relationship with, the living God. However much the right understanding and implementation of that grammar may be contested by Jews and Christians, both among themselves and between each other, the continuing challenge to engage with and realize that grammar, amid countless recontextualizations, becomes essential for Jewish and Christian faiths respectively. A concern with this grammar is perhaps most obvious in the discussions of what it means to say that Yhwh is "one" (*'eḥād*), and that He does and does not "repent" (*niḥam*). However, in one way or another, the concern is present within every chapter.

Specific Assumptions (2): Canonical and Literary Context for Imaginative Reading

Another corollary of this approach is that the canonical collection itself becomes the primary context for interpretation. Of course, the formative influence of the contexts of origin is sometimes discernible within the texts and as such remains significant. Nonetheless, a location within the canonical collection itself represents a recontextualization of the documents, which is of high interpretive importance for the reading of them as Scripture. In general terms, two streams in recent scholarship converge and flow strongly: on the one hand, the "literary turn" of much recent scholarship, not least with its interest in the phenomenon of intertextuality, and on the other hand a "canonical approach" with its concern for the theological grammar of the biblical text. Together these enable contemporary interpreters to re-enter conversation in significant ways with premodern interpreters, who moved around freely and imaginatively within the world of the text.

For example, constructive imaginative and theological use can be made of intertextual resonances, regardless of whether the authors of the texts in question were aware of such resonances—we do not need to know what we cannot in fact be sure of anyway. I perhaps most explicitly make use of this principle in the discussion of Psalms 44 and 89, but it is implicit throughout. Alternatively, I seek to enter the world of the text with full imaginative seriousness, as in the reading of the story of the manna, in a way that is generally more characteristic of premodern than of modern interpreters. Of course, there are questions that I have not sought to resolve about how best to inform and discipline the imagination, so that constructive engagement does not degenerate into fancy or fantasy. It is appropriate that a contemporary imagination may make moves that some premoderns might not have made—as in resisting certain historicizing rationalizations in relation to the size and resources of Israel in the manna story because of an awareness of the genre of the text. Yet again, a recognition that moral and theological issues may be explored in narrative form, as in the story of Job, directs the interpreter to an imaginative attentiveness to the world of the text, where sensitivity to the narrative conventions and the nature of the subject matter makes far more difference to interpretation than conjectures about how the text may relate to one or other place and time in Israelite history.

*Specific Assumptions (3): The Relationship between Text
and Reader, and Theological Interplay between the World
of the Reader and the World of the Text*

In a closely related way, the present approach seeks to take seriously the shift
of perspective within much recent biblical scholarship from object to subject,
a move toward recognizing the importance of the reader in the processes of
interpretation. An interest in the world of the text in relation to the world
in front of the text can be aligned with renewed interest in the relationship
between text and reader, although they are not identical.

In this context it is appropriate to draw attention to the way in which I have
drawn on resources from post-biblical Jewish and Christian faiths (the world in
front of the text) in order to engage more fully the biblical subject matter (the
world of the text). It is perhaps a curious feature of biblical study that while
scholars generally feel free to draw on their contemporary understanding of
society, politics, ideology, psychology, and so on, for interpreting the biblical
text—for there is a necessary interplay between understanding subject matter now and understanding it in the past—they are often much more hesitant
when it comes to drawing on historical and contemporary understandings of
theology, ethics, and spirituality.

This is presumably because of the lingering influence of weighty factors in the history of biblical
study as a modern academic discipline. Too often in the eighteenth and nineteenth centuries,
when fresh philologically and historically informed understandings of the likely origin and
meaning of particular texts differed from the way in which those texts had come to be understood
in post-biblical faith, there was a sadly common ecclesial tendency to try to use the historic
post-biblical understanding to disallow or disqualify the new philological understanding. As a
result, the debates often came to be characterized in shorthand as a conflict between reason and
faith, or between history and dogma. There was a strong, and not unjustified, sense that it was
only by disentangling the Bible from the theological formulations of the Church that its true
meaning could be understood and appreciated in its own right. As so often, major debates at
formative moments tend to leave a legacy of thinking in their terms and categories even when
situations have changed. On the one hand, the disappearance of the dominant institutional
role that the churches used to have in most Western societies changes the socio-political and
cultural assumptions within which biblical study is now undertaken (though there continue
to be sufficient examples of bad practice in certain educational contexts to give continuing
vigor to the old paradigm). On the other hand, the flourishing of literary and hermeneutical
research, together with renewed theological thinking, makes available a wide range of conceptual options in interpretation that simply were not available in the formative eighteenth- and
nineteenth-century debates.

It seems to me that there is no good reason not to draw on classic and
contemporary understandings of theology, ethics, and spirituality in the interpretation of Israel's scriptures. If Christian faith is genuinely rooted in, and
in significant ways continuous with, the content of the Old Testament, then
some of its perspectives and practices ought to be drawing out the intrinsic

implications of the biblical text. Of course, it is vital that such perspectives should be utilized in a disciplined and appropriate way, that is heuristically, to illuminate rather than prejudge, and with openness to the heuristic value of other understandings. In particular, I am aware of my indebtedness to many Jewish readings of their scriptures, and I have tried to acknowledge Jewish insights at various points along the way.

An approach to the text that utilizes the resources of a Christian reader can take many forms. For example, in chapter one I suggested that an understanding of idolatry that is articulated in the New Testament and classic Christian tradition may perhaps be utilized to further a re-reading and deepening understanding of idolatry that is already incipiently present within the Old Testament. Rather differently, when considering the possible implications of *ḥērem* as a metaphor, I suggested that strong disengagement from certain practices should still be a mark of faithful discipleship. Nonetheless, I resisted finding any simple equivalent to the destruction of religious images, as though there were any one thing whose rejection would constitute faithfulness; for in the diversity of contemporary life, those things that are not intrinsically evil but that may become obstacles to faithfulness vary greatly. Thus the discernment of legitimate diversity of practice, rather than a blanket approach, is surely appropriate.

It may be, however, that the most succinct way of making the point at issue here is that I read the Old Testament as both a philologist and a theologian.

Conclusion

A recurrent note that has been sounded in recent hermeneutical discussions is that the interpretation of the biblical text can be in significant ways analogous to the interpretation of the text of a play or a musical score. Numerous kinds of scholarly activity can usefully be carried out on such texts and scores. For many a scholar the establishment of, say, a good critical edition of a dramatic text, or an illuminating contextualization of a musical score within the oeuvre of its composer, can be a satisfying end in itself. However, the more the text or score is classic and resonant and loved, the more there is a widespread sense that the crowning achievement of extensive scholarly activity is when it takes on a kind of behind-the-scenes role whereby actors and musicians, that is, practitioners, are enabled to put on a fresh performance—a performance that brings the drama or the music to life and communicates its content in a fresh way, such that eyes and ears, even if already familiar with the content, are newly opened.

So too I would argue that the crowning achievement of a theological interpretation of Scripture should be performance, that is ways of living, on the part of believers and those sympathetically interested, who are enabled to realize more fully that wholeness of life to which God calls. I hope that the content has intellectual interest and coherence for those who may have no desire to perform it. Nonetheless, performance is the ultimate goal of this study of the Hebrew Bible as Christian Scripture.

Bibliography

Albertz, Rainer. *A History of Israelite Religion in the Old Testament Period*. Translated by John Bowden. 2 vols. Old Testament Library. London: SCM, 1994.

Allen, Leslie C. *The Books of Joel, Obadiah, Jonah, and Micah*. New International Commentary on the Old Testament. Grand Rapids: Eerdmans, 1976.

Alter, Robert. *The Five Books of Moses*. New York: W. W. Norton, 2004.

———. *The Pleasures of Reading in an Ideological Age*. New York: Simon & Schuster, 1989.

———. *The Wisdom Books*. New York: W. W. Norton, 2010.

Amit, Yairah. "'The Glory of Israel Does Not Deceive or Change His Mind': On the Reliability of Narrator and Speakers in Biblical Narrative." *Prooftexts* 12 (1992): 201–12.

Anderson, Arnold Albert. *Psalms (1–72)*. New Century Bible. London: Marshall, Morgan & Scott, 1972.

———. *Psalms (73–150)*. New Century Bible. London: Marshall, Morgan & Scott, 1972.

Augustine. *Confessions*. Translated by Henry Chadwick. World Classics. Oxford and New York: Oxford University Press, 1991.

Barth, Karl. *Church Dogmatics*. Edited by G. W. Bromiley and T. F. Torrance. Translated by G. W. Bromiley et al. Edinburgh: T&T Clark, 1936–69. Translation of *Die kirchliche Dogmatik*. Zurich: Theologischer Verlag Zurich, 1932–67.

Barton, John. "'The Work of Human Hands' (Ps 115:4): Idolatry in the Old Testament." *Ex Auditu* 15 (1999): 63–72. Reprinted in *The Ten Commandments*, edited by William P. Brown, 194–203. Louisville: Westminster John Knox, 2004.

Bash, Anthony. *Forgiveness and Christian Ethics*. New Studies in Christian Ethics. Cambridge: Cambridge University Press, 2007.

Bell, Rob. *Velvet Elvis: Repainting the Christian Faith*. Grand Rapids: Zondervan, 2005.

Berlin, Adele, and Marc Zvi Brettler, eds. "Jonah." In *The Jewish Study Bible*, 1198–1204. Oxford: Oxford University Press, 2004.

The Bible and Culture Collective. *The Postmodern Bible.* New Haven and London: Yale University Press, 1995.

Biblia Sacra iuxta vulgatam versionem. 2nd ed. 2 vols. Stuttgart: Deutsche Bibelgesellschaft, 1983.

Bickerman, Elias. "Jonah *or* The Unfulfilled Prophecy." In *Four Strange Books of the Bible,* 1–49. New York: Schocken Books, 1967.

Birch, Bruce, Walter Brueggemann, Terence Fretheim, and David Petersen. *A Theological Introduction to the Old Testament.* Nashville: Abingdon, 1999.

Block, Daniel I. "The Privilege of Calling: The Mosaic Paradigm for Missions (Deut 26:16–19)." In *How I Love Your Torah, O LORD! Studies in the Book of Deuteronomy,* 140–61. Eugene, OR: Cascade Books, 2011.

Bord, Lucien-Jean, and David Hamidović. "Écoute Israël (Deut. VI 4)." *Vetus Testamentum* 52/1 (2002): 13–29.

Borgen, Peder. *Bread from Heaven: An Exegetical Study of the Concept of Manna in the Gospel of John and the Writings of Philo.* Supplements to Novum Testamentum. Leiden: Brill, 1965.

Bosworth, David. "Revisiting Karl Barth's Exegesis of 1 Kings 13." *Biblical Interpretation* 10/4 (2002): 360–83.

Bradley, Ian, ed. *The Penguin Book of Hymns.* London: Penguin, 1990.

Braulik, Richard. "Deuteronomy and the Birth of Monotheism." In *The Theology of Deuteronomy,* translated by Ulrika Lindblad, 99–130. North Richland Hills, TX: BIBAL, 1994.

Brenner, Athalya. "Job the Pious? The Characterization of Job in the Narrative Framework of the Book." *Journal for the Study of the Old Testament* 43 (1989): 37–52.

Briggs, Charles Augustus. *Psalms.* 2 vols. International Critical Commentary. Edinburgh: T&T Clark, 1907.

Briggs, Richard S. "Biblical Hermeneutics and Scriptural Responsibility." In *The Future of Biblical Interpretation: Responsible Plurality in Biblical Hermeneutics,* edited by Stanley E. Porter and Matthew R. Malcolm. Milton Keynes: Paternoster, 2013.

———. *The Virtuous Reader: Old Testament Narrative and Interpretive Virtue.* Studies in Theological Interpretation. Grand Rapids: Baker Academic, 2010.

Brown, Dan. *The Da Vinci Code.* New York: Doubleday, 2003.

Brown, Francis, Samuel Rolles Driver, and Charles Augustus Briggs. *A Hebrew and English Lexicon of the Old Testament.* Oxford: Clarendon, 1907.

Brueggemann, Walter. "The Book of Exodus." In *The New Interpreter's Bible,* edited by Leander E. Keck et al., 1:675–981. Nashville: Abingdon, 1994.

———. *Genesis.* Interpretation: A Biblical Commentary for Teaching and Preaching. Atlanta: John Knox, 1982.

———. *Theology of the Old Testament: Testimony, Dispute, Advocacy.* Minneapolis: Fortress, 1997.

Brueggemann, Walter, with Carolyn J. Sharp. *Living Countertestimony: Conversations with Walter Brueggemann.* Louisville: Westminster John Knox, 2012.

Buckley, Michael. *At the Origins of Modern Atheism*. New Haven and London: Yale University Press, 1987.

Burrows, Ruth, OCD. *Love Unknown*. London and New York: Continuum, 2011.

Calvin, John. *Commentary on the Book of Psalms*. Translated by James Anderson. 5 vols. In *Calvin's Commentaries*. Edinburgh: Calvin Translation Society, 1845–49. Reprint, Grand Rapids: Baker Books, 2005.

———. *Commentaries on the Four Last Books of Moses: Arranged in the Form of a Harmony*. Translated by Charles William Bingham. 4 vols. In *Calvin's Commentaries*. Edinburgh: Calvin Translation Society, 1852–55. Reprint, Grand Rapids: Baker Books, 2005.

———. *Commentaries on the Twelve Minor Prophets*. Translated by John Owen. 5 vols. In *Calvin's Commentaries*. Edinburgh: Calvin Translation Society, 1846–49. Reprint, Grand Rapids: Baker Books, 2005.

Campbell, Antony, and Mark O'Brien. *Sources of the Pentateuch: Texts, Introductions, Annotations*. Minneapolis: Fortress, 1993.

Carasik, Michael. *The Commentators' Bible: The JPS Miqra'ot Gedolot*. Vol. 2, *Exodus/Shemot*. Philadelphia: Jewish Publication Society of America, 2005.

Carroll, Robert P. *Jeremiah*. Old Testament Library. London: SCM, 1986.

———. *Wolf in the Sheepfold: The Bible as a Problem for Christianity*. London: SPCK, 1991.

Cassuto, Umberto. *A Commentary on the Book of Exodus*. Translated by Israel Abrahams. Jerusalem: Magnes, 1967.

Cavanaugh, William. *Migrations of the Holy: God, State, and the Political Meaning of the Church*. Grand Rapids: Eerdmans, 2011.

Chabot, Jean-Baptiste, Charles Simon Clermont-Ganneau, et al., eds. *Répertoire d'épigraphie sémitique*. Académie des inscriptions et belles-lettres (France). Commission du Corpus inscriptionum semiticarum. Paris: Imprimerie nationale, 1900–1968.

Chapman, Stephen B. "Martial Memory, Peaceable Vision: Divine War in the Old Testament." In *Holy War in the Bible: Christian Morality and an Old Testament Problem*, edited by Heath A. Thomas, Jeremy Evans, and Paul Copan, 47–67. Downers Grove, IL: IVP Academic, 2013.

———. "Perpetual War: The Case of Amalek." Paper presented in Cheltenham (UK) on May 31, 2012, at an International Symposium on the Bible and Spirituality, sponsored by the University of Gloucestershire and the British Bible Society. Publication forthcoming.

Cheyne, Thomas Kelly. *The Book of Psalms*. 2 vols. 3rd ed. London: Kegan Paul, Trench, Trübner, 1904.

Childs, Brevard S. *Biblical Theology of the Old and New Testaments*. London: SCM, 1992.

———. "Does the Old Testament Witness to Jesus Christ?" In *Evangelium, Schriftauslegung, Kirche: Festschrift für Peter Stuhlmacher zum 65. Geburtstag*, edited by Jostein Ådna, Scott J. Hafemann, and Otfried Hofius, 57–64. Göttingen: Vandenhoeck & Ruprecht, 1997.

———. *Exodus*. Old Testament Library. London: SCM, 1974.

———. *Introduction to the Old Testament as Scripture*. London: SCM, 1979.

————. *Isaiah*. Old Testament Library. Louisville: Westminster John Knox, 2001.

————. *Old Testament Theology in a Canonical Context*. London: SCM, 1985.

————. *The Struggle to Understand Isaiah as Christian Scripture*. Grand Rapids: Eerdmans, 2004.

Church of England. *The Book of Common Prayer*. Cambridge: Cambridge University Press, 1662.

Claassens, L. Juliana. "Isaiah." In *Theological Bible Commentary*, edited by Gail R. O'Day and David L. Petersen, 209–22. Louisville: Westminster John Knox, 2009.

Clements, Ronald E. *Old Testament Theology: A Fresh Approach*. Marshall's Theological Library. Basingstoke: Marshall, Morgan & Scott, 1978.

Clifford, Richard J. "Psalm 89: A Lament over the Davidic Ruler's Continued Failure." *Harvard Theological Review* 73 (1980): 35–47.

Clines, David J. A. *The Bible and the Modern World*. Biblical Seminar 51. Sheffield: Sheffield Academic Press, 1997.

————, ed. *The Dictionary of Classical Hebrew*. 8 vols. Sheffield: Sheffield Academic / Phoenix Press, 1993–2011.

————. "'The Fear of the Lord Is Wisdom' (Job 28:28): A Semantic and Contextual Study." In *Job 28: Cognition in Context*, edited by Ellen van Wolde, 57–92. Leiden: Brill, 2003.

————. *Job 1–20*. Word Biblical Commentary 17. Dallas: Word, 1989.

————. *Job 21–37*. Word Biblical Commentary 18A. Nashville: Nelson, 2006.

————. "Psalm 2 and the MLF (Moabite Liberation Front)." In *Interested Parties: The Ideology of Writers and Readers of the Hebrew Bible*, 244–75. Journal for the Study of the Old Testament: Supplement Series 205. Sheffield: Sheffield Academic Press, 1995.

Coetzee, John Maxwell. *Disgrace*. London: Vintage, 2000.

Cole, R. Alan. *Exodus*. Tyndale Old Testament Commentaries. London: Tyndale, 1973.

Colenso, John. *The Pentateuch and the Book of Joshua Critically Examined*. London: Longman & Green, 1862.

Cook, John Granger. *The Interpretation of the Old Testament in Greco-Roman Paganism*. Studien und Texte zu Antike und Christentum 23. Tübingen: Mohr Siebeck, 2004.

Cooper, Alan. "In Praise of Divine Caprice: The Significance of the Book of Jonah." In *Among the Prophets: Language, Image and Structure in the Prophetic Writings*, edited by Philip R. Davies and David J. A. Clines, 144–63. Journal for the Study of the Old Testament: Supplement Series 144. Sheffield: JSOT Press, 1993.

Cross, Frank Moore. "The Themes of the Book of Kings and the Structure of the Deuteronomistic History." In *Canaanite Myth and Hebrew Epic: Essays in the History of the Religion of Israel*, 274–89. Cambridge, MA: Harvard University Press, 1973.

Dahl, Nils Alstrup. "Contradictions in Scripture." In *Studies in Paul: Theology for Early Christian Mission*, 159–77. Minneapolis: Augsburg, 1977.

Davidson, Andrew Bruce. *The Book of Job*. Cambridge Bible for Schools and Colleges. Cambridge: Cambridge University Press, 1895.

Davidson, Robert. *The Vitality of Worship: A Commentary on the Book of Psalms.* Grand Rapids and Cambridge: Eerdmans, 1998.

Davies, William David, and Dale C. Allison. *The Gospel according to Saint Matthew.* 3 vols. International Critical Commentary. Edinburgh: T&T Clark, 1988.

Davis, Ellen. "Job and Jacob: The Integrity of Faith." In *The Whirlwind: Essays on Job, Hermeneutics and Theology in Memory of Jane Morse,* edited by Stephen Cook, Corinne L. Patton, and James W. Watts, 100–120. Journal for the Study of the Old Testament: Supplement Series 336. London: Sheffield Academic Press, 2001.

———. "The Poetics of Generosity." In *The Word Leaps the Gap: Essays on Scripture and Theology in Honor of Richard Hays,* edited by J. Ross Wagner, C. Kavin Rowe, and A. Katherine Grieb, 626–45. Grand Rapids: Eerdmans, 2008.

———. *Scripture, Culture, and Agriculture: An Agrarian Reading of the Bible.* Cambridge: Cambridge University Press, 2009.

Dawkins, Richard. *The God Delusion.* London: Bantam, 2006.

Dentan, Robert C. *The Knowledge of God in Ancient Israel.* New York: Seabury, 1968.

Dhorme, E. *A Commentary on the Book of Job.* Translated by Harold Knight. London: Nelson, 1967.

Dorival, Giles, ed. and trans. *La Bible d'Alexandrie: Les Nombres.* Paris: Cerf, 1994.

Dozeman, Thomas B. *Exodus.* Eerdmans Critical Commentary. Grand Rapids: Eerdmans, 2009.

———. "Inner-Biblical Interpretation of Yahweh's Gracious and Compassionate Character." *Journal of Biblical Literature* 108 (1989): 207–23.

Driver, Samuel Rolles. *The Book of Daniel.* Cambridge Bible for Schools and Colleges. Cambridge: Cambridge University Press, 1905.

———. *The Book of Exodus.* Cambridge Bible for Schools and Colleges. Cambridge: Cambridge University Press, 1918.

———. *An Introduction to the Literature of the Old Testament.* 6th ed. International Theological Library. Edinburgh: T&T Clark, 1897.

———. *A Treatise on the Use of the Tenses in Hebrew and Some Other Syntactical Questions.* Edited by W. Randall Garr. Reprinted 3rd ed. 1892. Biblical Resources Series. Grand Rapids: Eerdmans, 1998.

Driver, Samuel Rolles, and George Buchanan Gray. *The Book of Job.* International Critical Commentary. Edinburgh: T&T Clark, 1921.

Drosnin, Michael. *The Bible Code.* London: Weidenfeld & Nicholson; New York: Simon & Schuster, 1997.

———. *The Bible Code 2: The Countdown.* London: Weidenfeld & Nicholson; New York: Simon & Schuster, 2002.

———. *The Bible Code: Saving the World.* London: Weidenfeld & Nicholson; New York: Simon & Schuster, 2010.

Eadmer of Canterbury. *The Life of Saint Anselm.* Edited and translated by R. W. Southern. Oxford Medieval Texts. Oxford: Clarendon, 1972.

Earl, Douglas S. *The Joshua Delusion? Rethinking Genocide in the Bible.* Eugene, OR: Cascade Books, 2010.

———. *Reading Joshua as Christian Scripture.* Journal of Theological Interpretation Supplements 2. Winona Lake, IN: Eisenbrauns, 2010.

Eaton, John H. *Kingship and the Psalms.* Studies in Biblical Theology 2nd series, 32. London: SCM, 1976.

———. *The Psalms: A Historical and Spiritual Commentary with an Introduction and New Translation.* London and New York: T&T Clark, 2003.

Ego, Beate. "The Repentance of Nineveh in the Story of Jonah and Nahum's Prophecy of the City's Destruction—A Coherent Reading of the Book of the Twelve as Reflected in the Aggada." In *Thematic Threads in the Book of the Twelve,* edited by Paul L. Redditt and Aaron Schart, 155–64. Beihefte zur Zeitschrift für die alttestamentliche Wissenschaft 325. Berlin and New York: de Gruyter, 2003.

Eichrodt, Walther. *Theology of the Old Testament.* Translated by J. A. Baker. 2 vols. Old Testament Library. London: SCM, 1961–67. Translation of *Theologie des Alten Testaments.* 2 vols. 5th ed. Berlin: Evangelische Verlagsanstalt, 1957.

Epstein, Isidore, ed. and trans. *The Babylonian Talmud: Seder Moʿed.* Vol. 4. London: Soncino, 1938.

———, ed. *The Babylonian Talmud: Seder Nezikin.* Vol. 2. Translated by Maurice Simon. London: Soncino, 1935.

Erasmus, Desiderius. *Collected Works of Erasmus.* Vol. 63, *Expositions of the Psalms.* Edited by Dominic Baker-Smith. Translated by Michael J. Heath. Toronto: University of Toronto Press, 1997.

Feldmeier, Reinhard, and Hermann Spieckermann. *God of the Living: A Biblical Theology.* Translated by Mark E. Biddle. Waco: Baylor University Press, 2011.

Ferreiro, Alberto, ed. *The Twelve Prophets.* Ancient Christian Commentary Series: Old Testament 14. Downers Grove, IL: InterVarsity, 2003.

Fishbane, Michael. *Biblical Interpretation in Ancient Israel.* Oxford: Clarendon, 1985.

———. *Sacred Attunement: A Jewish Theology.* Chicago and London: University of Chicago Press, 2008.

Foster, Paul. "Why Did Matthew Get the *Shema* Wrong? A Study of Matthew 22:37." *Journal of Biblical Literature* 122/2 (2003): 309–33.

Fox, Michael V. *Proverbs 1–9.* Anchor Bible 18A. New York: Doubleday, 2000.

———. "Reading the Tale of Job." In *A Critical Engagement: Essays on the Hebrew Bible in Honour of J. Cheryl Exum,* edited by David J. A. Clines and Ellen van Wolde, 145–62. Hebrew Bible Monographs 38. Sheffield: Sheffield Phoenix, 2011.

Fox, Robin Lane. *The Unauthorized Version: Truth and Fiction in the Bible.* London: Viking, 1991.

Frankl, Viktor E. *Man's Search for Meaning.* Translated by Ilse Lasch. New York: Pocket Books, 1984. Translation of *Ein Psychologe erlebt das Konzentrationslager.* Vienna: Jugend & Volk, 1946.

Fretheim, Terence E. *Exodus*. Interpretation: A Bible Commentary for Teaching and Preaching. Louisville: John Knox, 1991.

———. *The Message of Jonah: A Theological Commentary*. Minneapolis: Augsburg, 1977.

Freud, Sigmund. *Moses and Monotheism*. Translated by Katherine Jones. London: Hogarth, 1939. Translation of *Der Mann Moses und die monotheistische Religion: Drei Abhandlungen*. Amsterdam: Allert de Lange, 1939.

Geller, Stephen. "Manna and Sabbath: A Literary-Theological Reading of Exodus 16." *Interpretation* 59 (2005): 5–16.

Gerstenberger, Erhard S. *Theologies in the Old Testament*. Translated by John Bowden. Minneapolis: Fortress, 2002.

Ginzberg, Louis. *Legends of the Jews*. Translated by Henrietta Szold and Paul Radin. JPS Classic Resources. 2nd ed. 2 vols. Philadelphia: Jewish Publication Society, 2003.

Goldingay, John. *Old Testament Theology*. Vol. 1, *Israel's Gospel*. Downers Grove, IL: InterVarsity, 2003.

———. *Old Testament Theology*. Vol. 3, *Israel's Life*. Downers Grove, IL: IVP Academic, 2009.

———. *Psalms*. Vol. 2, *Psalms 42–89*. Baker Commentary on the Old Testament Wisdom and Psalms. Grand Rapids: Baker Academic, 2007.

———. *Theological Diversity and the Authority of the Old Testament*. Grand Rapids: Eerdmans, 1987.

———. "The Theology of Isaiah." In *Interpreting Isaiah: Issues and Approaches*, edited by David G. Firth and H. G. M. Williamson, 168–90. Downers Grove, IL: IVP Academic, 2009.

Good, Edwin M. *In Turns of Tempest: A Reading of Job, with a Translation*. Stanford, CA: Stanford University Press, 1990.

Gordon, Ernest. *Miracle on the River Kwai*. London and Glasgow: Collins, 1963. Reprint, London: Fount, 1995.

Gordon, Robert P. *1 and 2 Samuel*. Exeter: Paternoster, 1986.

Gottwald, Norman K. *The Hebrew Bible: A Socio-Literary Introduction*. Philadelphia: Fortress, 1985.

Grabbe, Lester L. "*Adde Praeputium Praeputio Magnus Acervus Erit*: If the Exodus and Conquest Had Really Happened." *Biblical Interpretation* 8, no. 1/2 (2000): 23–32.

———. Review of Jörg Jeremias, *Die Reue Gottes: Aspekte alttestamentlicher Gottesvorstellung*. BibS(N) 65. Neukirchen-Vluyn: Neukirchener Verlag, 1975.

Grayson, A. Kirk. "Nineveh." In *Anchor Bible Dictionary*, edited by David Noel Freeman, 4:1118–19. 6 vols. New Haven: Yale University Press, 1992.

Green, Garrett. *Imagining God: Theology and the Religious Imagination*. San Francisco: Harper & Row, 1989.

Greenberg, Moshe. "Job." In *The Literary Guide to the Bible*, edited by Robert Alter and Frank Kermode, 283–304. London: Fontana, 1989.

————. "On the Political Use of the Bible in Modern Israel: An Engaged Critique." In *Pomegranates and Golden Bells: Studies in Biblical, Jewish, and Near Eastern Ritual, Law and Literature in Honor of Jacob Milgrom*, edited by David P. Wright, David Noel Freedman, and Abi Hurvitz, 461–71. Winona Lake, IN: Eisenbrauns, 1995.

Gunn, David M., and Danna Nolan Fewell. *Narrative in the Hebrew Bible.* Oxford Bible Studies. Oxford: Oxford University Press, 1993.

Gunton, Colin. *The One, the Three and the Many: God, Creation and the Culture of Modernity.* Cambridge: Cambridge University Press, 1993.

Habel, Norman C. *The Book of Job.* Old Testament Library. London: SCM, 1985.

Halpern, Baruch. "'Brisker Pipes than Poetry': The Development of Israelite Monotheism." In *From Gods to God*, 13–56. Forschungen zum Alten Testament 63. Tübingen: Mohr Siebeck, 2009.

————. *David's Secret Demons: Messiah, Murderer, Traitor, King.* Grand Rapids: Eerdmans, 2001.

Halpin, Tony. "Cries of 'Shame' as Pussy Riot Jailed over Anti-Putin Stunt." In *The Times* [London], August 18, 2012.

Hamling, Tara. *Decorating the "Godly" Household: Religious Art in Post-Reformation Britain.* New Haven: Yale University Press, 2010.

Hardy, Thomas. *The Mayor of Casterbridge.* London: Smith, Elder, 1886.

Hazony, Yoram. *The Philosophy of Hebrew Scripture.* Cambridge: Cambridge University Press, 2012.

Hengel, Martin. *Property and Riches in the Early Church: Aspects of a Social History of Early Christianity.* Translated by John Bowden. London: SCM, 1974.

Hilary of Poitiers. *The Trinity.* Translated by Stephen McKenna, CSsR. Fathers of the Church 25. New York: Fathers of the Church, 1954.

Hinchliff, Peter. *John William Colenso, Bishop of Natal.* Leaders of Religion. London and Edinburgh: Nelson, 1964.

Hoffman, Yair. "The Deuteronomistic Concept of the Ḥerem." *Zeitschrift für die alttestamentliche Wissenschaft* 111 (1999): 196–210.

Horbury, William. "Extirpation and Excommunication." *Vetus Testamentum* 35/1 (1985): 13–38.

Hume, David. *Dialogues concerning Natural Religion; and, The Natural History of Religion.* Edited by J. C. A. Gaskin. Oxford World's Classics. Oxford: Oxford University Press, 1993.

Humphreys, Colin. *The Miracles of Exodus: A Scientist's Discovery of the Extraordinary Natural Causes of the Biblical Stories.* London and New York: Continuum, 2003.

Jackson, Kent P. "The Language of the Mesha Inscription." In *Studies in the Mesha Inscription and Moab*, edited by J. Andrew Dearman, 93–95. ASOR/SBL Archaeology and Biblical Studies 2. Atlanta: Scholars Press, 1989.

Jackson, Kent P., and J. Andrew Dearman. "The Text of the Mesha Inscription." In *Studies in the Mesha Inscription and Moab*, edited by J. Andrew Dearman, 96–130. ASOR/SBL Archaeology and Biblical Studies 2. Atlanta: Scholars Press, 1989.

Jacob, Benno. *The Second Book of the Bible: Exodus*. Translated by Walter Jacob. Hoboken, NJ: Ktav, 1992.

Jacobs, Alan. *A Theology of Reading: The Hermeneutics of Love*. Boulder, CO: Westview, 2001.

Jasper, David. *A Short Introduction to Hermeneutics*. Louisville: Westminster John Knox, 2004.

Jenson, Philip. *Obadiah, Jonah, Micah: A Theological Commentary*. Library of Hebrew Bible / Old Testament Studies 496. New York and London: T&T Clark, 2008.

Jeremias, Jörg. *Die Reue Gottes: Aspekte alttestamentlicher Gottesvorstellung*. Biblische Studien 65. Neukirchen-Vluyn: Neukirchener Verlag, 1975.

John Chrysostom. *St. John Chrysostom: Commentary on the Psalms*. Vol. 1. Translated by Robert Charles Hill. Brookline, MA: Holy Cross Orthodox Press, 1998.

Jones, Douglas Rawlinson. *Jeremiah*. New Century Bible. Grand Rapids: Eerdmans, 1992.

Jones, Scott. *Rumors of Wisdom: Job 28 as Poetry*. Beihefte zur Zeitschrift für die alttestamentliche Wissenschaft 398. Berlin and New York: de Gruyter, 2009.

Josephus. Translated by H. St. J. Thackeray et al. 10 vols. Loeb Classical Library. Cambridge, MA: Harvard University Press, 1926–65.

Joüon, Paul, and Takamitsu Muraoka. *A Grammar of Biblical Hebrew*. 2 vols. Subsidia biblica 14. Rome: Pontifical Biblical Institute, 1991. Reprinted as one vol. Subsidia biblica 27. Rome: Pontifical Biblical Institute, 2006.

Jung, Carl G. *Answer to Job*. Translated by R. F. C. Hull. Cleveland and New York: Meridian, 1970.

Kähler, Martin. *Der sogennante historische Jesus und der geschichtliche, biblische Christus*. Leipzig: A. Deichert, 1896. Reprint, Munich: Chr. Kaiser, 1956. Translated by Carl E. Braaten as *The So-Called Historical Jesus and the Historic Biblical Christ*. Philadelphia: Fortress, 1964.

Kaiser, Walter C., Jr. *The Messiah in the Old Testament*. Studies in Old Testament Biblical Theology. Grand Rapids: Zondervan, 1995.

———. *Toward an Old Testament Theology*. Grand Rapids: Zondervan, 1991.

Kaminsky, Joel S. "Wrestling with Israel's Election: A Jewish Reaction to Rolf Knierim's Biblical Theology." In *Reading the Bible for a New Millennium: Form, Concept, and Theological Perspective*, vol. 1, *Theological and Hermeneutical Studies*, edited by Wonil Kim, Deborah Ellens, Michael Floyd, and Marvin A. Sweeney, 252–62. Studies in Antiquity and Christianity. Harrisburg, PA: Trinity Press International, 2000.

———. *Yet I Loved Jacob: Reclaiming the Biblical Concept of Election*. Nashville: Abingdon, 2007.

Kaufmann, Yehezkel. *The Religion of Israel*. Translated and abridged by Moshe Greenberg. New York: Schocken Books, 1972.

Kautzsch, Emil, ed. *Gesenius' Hebrew Grammar*. Translated by A. E. Cowley. Oxford: Clarendon, 1910.

Keel, Othmar. "Zeichen der Verbundenheit: Zur Vorgeschichte und Bedeutung der Forderungen von Deuteronomium 6,8f. und Par." In *Mélanges Dominique Barthélemy: Études bibliques offertes à l'occasion de son 60e anniversaire*, edited by Pierre Casetti et al., 159–240. Orbis biblicus et orientalis 38. Fribourg: Éditions universitaires; Göttingen: Vandenhoeck & Ruprecht, 1981.

Keil, Carl F., and Franz Delitzsch. *Commentary on the Old Testament*. Vol. 5, *Psalms*. Translated by Francis Bolton. Edinburgh: T&T Clark, 1866–91. Reprint, Peabody, MA: Hendrickson, 2006.

Kidner, Derek. *Psalms 1–72*. Tyndale Old Testament Commentaries. London: Inter-Varsity, 1973.

Kim, Hyun Chul Paul. "Jonah Read Intertextually." *Journal of Biblical Literature* 126/3 (2007): 497–528.

Knierim, Rolf P. *The Task of Old Testament Theology: Method and Cases*. Grand Rapids: Eerdmans, 1995.

Lane, Nathan C. *The Compassionate but Punishing God: A Canonical Analysis of Exodus 34:6–7*. Eugene, OR: Pickwick Publications, 2010.

Larsen, Timothy. "Bishop Colenso and His Critics: The Strange Emergence of Biblical Criticism in Victorian Britain." In *The Eye of the Storm: Bishop John William Colenso and the Crisis of Biblical Interpretation*, edited by Jonathan A. Draper, 42–63. Journal for the Study of the Old Testament: Supplement Series 386. London and New York: T&T Clark, 2003.

Lash, Nicholas. "Amongst Strangers and Friends: Thinking of God in our Current Confusion." In *Theology for Pilgrims*, 36–51. London: Darton, Longman & Todd, 2008.

———. *The Beginning and the End of "Religion."* Cambridge: Cambridge University Press, 1996.

Leavis, Frank Raymond. *The Great Tradition: George Eliot, Henry James, Joseph Conrad*. Harmondsworth: Penguin/Pelican, 1972. Reprint of London: Chatto & Windus, 1948.

Leithart, Peter J. *Deep Exegesis: The Mystery of Reading Scripture*. Waco: Baylor University Press, 2009.

Levenson, Jon D. *The Death and Resurrection of the Beloved Son: The Transformation of Child Sacrifice in Judaism and Christianity*. New Haven and London: Yale University Press, 1993.

———. "The Eighth Principle of Judaism and the Literary Simultaneity of Scripture." In *The Hebrew Bible, the Old Testament, and Historical Criticism*, 62–81. Louisville: Westminster John Knox, 1993.

———. *Inheriting Abraham: The Legacy of the Patriarch in Judaism, Christianity, and Islam*. Library of Jewish Ideas. Princeton: Princeton University Press, 2012.

———. Review of Rolf P. Knierim, *The Task of Old Testament Theology: Method and Cases*. *Religious Studies Review* 24 (1998): 39–42.

———. "Theological Consensus or Historicist Evasion? Jews and Christians in Biblical Studies." In *The Hebrew Bible, the Old Testament, and Historical Criticism*, 82–105. Louisville: Westminster John Knox, 1993.

———. "The Universal Horizon of Biblical Particularism." In *Ethnicity and the Bible*, edited by Mark G. Brett, 143–69. Biblical Interpretation Series 19. Leiden: Brill, 1996.

Levine, Herbert J. *Sing unto God a New Song: A Contemporary Reading of the Psalms.* Indiana Studies in Biblical Literature. Bloomington and Indianapolis: Indiana University Press, 1995.

Lewis, C. S. *Collected Letters.* Vol. 3, *Narnia, Cambridge, and Joy, 1950–1963.* Edited by Walter Hooper. London: HarperCollins, 2006.

Lienhard, Joseph T., SJ, ed., with Ronnie J. Rombs. *Exodus, Leviticus, Numbers, Deuteronomy.* Ancient Christian Commentary on Scripture: Old Testament 3. General editor, Thomas C. Oden. Downers Grove, IL: InterVarsity, 2001.

Lohfink, Gerhard. *Does God Need the Church? Toward a Theology of the People of God.* Translated by Linda M. Maloney. Collegeville, MN: Liturgical Press, 1999.

Lohfink, Norbert. "*Ḥāram; Ḥērem.*" In *Theological Dictionary of the Old Testament,* 5:180–99. Edited by G. Johannes Botterweck, Helmer Ringgren, and Heinz-Josef Fabry. 15 vols. Grand Rapids: Eerdmans, 1974–2006.

Lohr, Joel N. *Chosen and Unchosen: Conceptions of Election in the Pentateuch and Jewish-Christian Interpretation.* Siphrut 2. Winona Lake, IN: Eisenbrauns, 2009.

Lubac, Henri de. *The Mystery of the Supernatural: Milestones in Catholic Theology.* New York: Crossroad, 1998.

Lüdemann, Gerd. *The Unholy in Holy Scripture: The Dark Side of the Bible.* Translated by John Bowden. London: SCM, 1997.

Luther, Martin. "Large Catechism." Translated by F. Bente and W. H. T. Dau. In *Triglot Concordia: The Symbolical Books of the Evangelical Lutheran Church, German-Latin-English,* 565–773. St. Louis: Concordia Publishing House, 1921. www.gutenberg.org/ebooks/1722.

Luz, Ulrich. *Matthew 1–7: A Continental Commentary.* Translated by Wilhelm C. Linss. Minneapolis: Fortress, 1989.

MacDonald, Nathan. *Deuteronomy and the Meaning of "Monotheism."* Forschungen zum Alten Testament 2/1. Tübingen: Mohr Siebeck, 2003.

———. "Monotheism and Isaiah." In *Interpreting Isaiah: Issues and Approaches,* edited by David G. Firth and H. G. M. Williamson, 43–61. Downers Grove, IL: IVP Academic, 2009.

———. "The Origin of 'Monotheism.'" In *Early Jewish and Christian Monotheism,* edited by Loren T. Stuckenbruck and Wendy E. S. North, 204–15. Journal for the Study of the New Testament: Supplement Series 263. London: T&T Clark, 2004.

Magonet, Jonathan. *Form and Meaning: Studies in Literary Techniques in the Book of Jonah.* Bible and Literature Series 8. Sheffield: Almond, 1983.

———. "Jonah, Book of." In *Anchor Bible Dictionary,* edited by David Noel Freeman, 3:936–42. 6 vols. New Haven: Yale University Press, 1992.

Maimonides, Moses. *The Guide for the Perplexed.* Translated by Michael Friedländer. New York: Dover, 1956.

Malory, Sir Thomas. *Le morte d'Arthur.* Edited by John Rhys. 2 vols. Everyman's Library. London: Dent, 1906.

Mann, Thomas W. *The Book of the Torah: The Narrative Integrity of the Pentateuch.* Atlanta: John Knox, 1988.

Mason, Rex. *Propaganda and Subversion in the Old Testament.* London: SPCK, 1997.

Mayes, Andrew David Hastings. *Deuteronomy.* New Century Bible. Grand Rapids: Eerdmans, 1979.

McCann, J. Clinton, Jr. "The Book of Isaiah—Theses and Hypotheses." *Biblical Theology Bulletin* 33/3 (2003): 88–94.

McKane, William. *Jeremiah.* 2 vols. International Critical Commentary. Edinburgh: T&T Clark, 1986.

Melville, Herman. *Moby Dick.* New York: Harper & Brothers, 1851.

Miller, Patrick D. "The Psalter as a Book of Theology." In *Psalms in Community: Jewish and Christian Textual, Liturgical, and Artistic Traditions,* edited by Harold W. Attridge and Margot E. Fassler, 87–98. Society of Biblical Literature Symposium Series 25. Atlanta: Society of Biblical Literature, 2003.

Mishnah, The. Translated by Herbert Danby. Oxford: Clarendon, 1933.

Moberly, R. W. L. *The Bible, Theology, and Faith: A Study of Abraham and Jesus.* Cambridge Studies in Christian Doctrine. Cambridge: Cambridge University Press, 2000.

———. "Biblical Criticism and Religious Belief." *Journal of Theological Interpretation* 2 (2008): 71–100.

———. "Biblical Hermeneutics and Ecclesial Responsibility." In *The Future of Biblical Interpretation: Responsible Plurality in Biblical Hermeneutics,* edited by Stanley E. Porter and Matthew R. Malcolm, 105–25. Milton Keynes: Paternoster, 2013.

———. "Christ in All the Scriptures? The Challenge of Reading the Old Testament as Christian Scripture." *Journal of Theological Interpretation* 1/1 (2007): 79–100.

———. "Election and the Transformation of Ḥerem." In *The Call of Abraham: Essays on the Election of Israel in Honor of Jon Levenson,* edited by Gary Anderson and Joel Kaminsky, 67–89. Notre Dame, IN: University of Notre Dame Press, 2013.

———. "'God Is Not a Human That He Should Repent' (Numbers 23:19 and 1 Samuel 15:29)." In *God in the Fray: A Tribute to Walter Brueggemann,* edited by Tod Linafelt and Timothy K. Beal, 112–23. Minneapolis: Fortress, 1998.

———. "How Appropriate is 'Monotheism' as a Category for Biblical Interpretation?" In *Early Jewish and Christian Monotheism,* edited by Loren T. Stuckenbruck and Wendy E. S. North, 216–34. Journal for the Study of the New Testament: Supplement Series 263. London and New York: T&T Clark, 2004.

———. "How Can We Know the Truth? A Study of John 7:14–18." In *The Art of Reading Scripture,* edited by Ellen F. Davis and Richard B. Hays, 239–57. Grand Rapids: Eerdmans, 2003.

———. "How May We Speak of God? A Reconsideration of the Nature of Biblical Theology." *TynBul* 53/2 (2002): 177–202.

———. "'Interpret the Bible Like Any Other Book?' Requiem for an Axiom." *Journal of Theological Interpretation* 4 (2010): 91–110.

———. "Isaiah and Jesus: How Might the Old Testament Inform Contemporary Christology?" In *Seeking the Identity of Jesus: A Pilgrimage,* edited by Beverly Gaventa and Richard Hays, 232–48. Grand Rapids: Eerdmans, 2008.

———. "Is Election Bad for You?" In *The Centre and the Periphery: A European Tribute to Walter Brueggemann*, edited by Jill Middlemas, David J. A. Clines, and Else K. Holt, 95–111. Hebrew Bible Monographs. Sheffield: Sheffield Phoenix, 2010.

———. "Is Monotheism Bad for You? Some Reflections on God, the Bible, and Life in the Light of Regina Schwartz's *The Curse of Cain*." In *The God of Israel*, edited by Robert P. Gordon, 94–112. University of Cambridge Oriental Publications 64. Cambridge: Cambridge University Press, 2007.

———. "Jonah, God's Objectionable Mercy, and the Way of Wisdom." In *Reading Texts, Seeking Wisdom*, edited by David F. Ford and Graham Stanton, 154–68. London: SCM, 2003. Also issued in *Journal of Scriptural Reasoning* 3/1 (2003), http://etext.virginia.edu/journals/ssr/issues/volume3/number1.

———. "Miracle in the Hebrew Bible." In *The Cambridge Companion to Miracles*, edited by Graham Twelftree, 57–74. Cambridge: Cambridge University Press, 2010.

———. *The Old Testament of the Old Testament*. Overtures to Biblical Theology. Minneapolis: Fortress, 1992. Reprint, Eugene, OR: Wipf & Stock, 2001.

———. "On Learning Spiritual Disciplines: A Reading of Exodus 16." In *Reading the Law: Studies in Honour of Gordon J. Wenham*, edited by J. G. McConville and Karl Möller, 213–27. Library of Hebrew Bible / Old Testament Studies 461. New York: T&T Clark, 2007.

———. "Pentateuch." In *The New Interpreter's Dictionary of the Bible: Me–R*, vol. 4. Edited by Katharine Doob Sakenfeld, 430–38. Nashville: Abingdon, 2009.

———. "Preaching Christ from the Old Testament." In *"He Began with Moses . . .": Preaching the Old Testament Today*, edited by Grenville J. R. Kent, Paul J. Kissling, and Laurence A. Turner, 233–50. Nottingham: Inter-Varsity, 2010.

———. "Preaching for a Response? Jonah's Message to the Ninevites Reconsidered." *Vetus Testamentum* 53/2 (2003): 156–68.

———. *Prophecy and Discernment*. Cambridge Studies in Christian Doctrine. Cambridge: Cambridge University Press, 2006.

———. "*Qyn*/Lament." In *New International Dictionary of Old Testament Theology and Exegesis*, edited by William A. VanGemeren, 4:880–82. 5 vols. Carlisle: Paternoster: 1997.

———. "Solomon and Job: Divine Wisdom in Human Life." In *Where Shall Wisdom Be Found?*, edited by Stephen C. Barton, 3–17. Edinburgh: T&T Clark, 1999.

———. "Theological Interpretation, Presuppositions, and the Role of the Church: Bultmann and Augustine Revisited." *Journal of Theological Interpretation* 6 (2012): 1–22.

———. *The Theology of the Book of Genesis*. Old Testament Theology. New York and Cambridge: Cambridge University Press, 2009.

———. "Toward an Interpretation of the Shema." In *Theological Exegesis: Essays in Honor of Brevard S. Childs*, edited by Christopher R. Seitz and Kathryn Greene-McCreight, 124–44. Grand Rapids: Eerdmans, 1999.

———. "What Is Theological Commentary? An Old Testament Perspective." In *Theological Commentary: Evangelical Perspectives*, edited by R. Michael Allen, 172–86. London and New York: T&T Clark, 2011.

———. "'Who Is Jesus Christ for Us Today?' Peter's Confession (Matthew 16:13–28) Reconsidered." In *Christology and Scripture: Interdisciplinary Perspectives*, edited by Andrew T. Lincoln and Angus Paddison, 7–21. Library of New Testament Studies 348. London and New York: T&T Clark, 2007.

———. "Whose Justice? Which Righteousness? The Interpretation of Isaiah V 16." *Vetus Testamentum* 51/1 (2001): 55–68.

———. "'Yahweh Is One': The Translation of the Shema." In *Studies in the Pentateuch*, edited by J. A. Emerton, 209–15. Vetus Testamentum: Supplement Series 41. Leiden: Brill, 1990. Reprinted in *From Eden to Golgotha: Essays in Biblical Theology*, by R. W. L. Moberly, 75–81. South Florida Studies in the History of Judaism 52. Atlanta: Scholars, 1992.

Monroe, Lauren A. S. "Israelite, Moabite and Sabaean War-*Ḥērem* Traditions and the Forging of National Identity: Reconsidering the Sabaean Text *RES* 3945 in Light of Biblical and Moabite Evidence." *Vetus Testamentum* 57 (2007): 318–41.

Moran, William L. "The Ancient Near Eastern Background of the Love of God in Deuteronomy." *Catholic Biblical Quarterly* 25 (1963): 77–87.

Motyer, J. Alec. *The Prophecy of Isaiah*. Leicester: Inter-Varsity, 1993.

———. "Three in One or One in Three: A Dipstick into the Isaianic Literature." *Churchman* 108/1 (1994): 22–36.

Murray, Gilbert. *Aeschylus: The Creator of Tragedy*. Oxford: Clarendon, 1940.

Nagel, Thomas. *The View from Nowhere*. New York and Oxford: Oxford University Press, 1986.

Newsom, Carol. "The Book of Job." In *The New Interpreter's Bible*, edited by Leander E. Keck et al., 4:317–637. Nashville: Abingdon, 1996.

Niditch, Susan. *War in the Hebrew Bible: A Study in the Ethics of Violence*. New York and Oxford: Oxford University Press, 1993.

Nielsen, K. "*sātan*," *TDOT* 14:73–78.

Nogalski, James D. *The Book of the Twelve: Hosea–Jonah*. Smyth & Helwys Bible Commentary. Macon, GA: Smyth & Helwys, 2011.

———. "Recurring Themes in the Book of the Twelve: Creating Points of Contact for a Theological Reading." *Interpretation* 61/2 (2007): 125–36.

Noth, Martin. *Exodus*. Translated by John Bowden. Old Testament Library. London: SCM, 1962.

Oden, Robert. *The Bible without Theology: The Theological Tradition and Alternatives to It*. San Francisco: Harper & Row, 1987.

Oden, Thomas C., general ed. Ancient Christian Commentary on Scripture: Old Testament [series]. Downers Grove, IL: InterVarsity, 2001–.

Ollenburger, Ben C. "Gerhard von Rad's Theory of Holy War." Introduction to Gerhard von Rad's *Holy War in Ancient Israel*, edited and translated by Marva J. Dawn, 1–33. Grand Rapids: Eerdmans, 1991.

Origen. *Contra Celsum*. Translated with introduction and notes by Henry Chadwick. Cambridge: Cambridge University Press, 1965.

———. "Homily XXVII on Numbers." In *Origen: An Exhortation to Martyrdom, Prayer, and Selected Writings*, 245–69. Translated and introduced by Rowan A. Greer. Classics of Western Spirituality. London: SPCK, 1979.

———. *Origen: Homilies on Genesis and Exodus*. Translated by Ronald Heine. Fathers of the Church 71. Washington, DC: Catholic University of America Press, 1982.

Oswalt, John N. *The Book of Isaiah, Chapters 1–39*. New International Commentary on the Old Testament. Grand Rapids: Eerdmans, 1986.

Paine, Thomas. "Concerning God, and the Lights Cast on His Existence and Attributes by the Bible." In *The Age of Reason: Part I*. London: printed by Barrois, 1794. Reprinted in *Thomas Paine Collection: Common Sense, Rights of Man, Age of Reason, An Essay on Dream, Biblical Blasphemy, Examination of the Prophecies*. Charleston, SC: Forgotten Books, 2007.

———. "The Old Testament." In *The Age of Reason: Part II*. London: H. D. Symonds, 1795. Reprinted in *Thomas Paine Collection: Common Sense, Rights of Man, Age of Reason, An Essay on Dream, Biblical Blasphemy, Examination of the Prophecies*. Charleston, SC: Forgotten Books: 2007.

Pelikan, Jaroslav. *Christianity and Classical Culture: The Metamorphosis of Natural Theology in the Christian Encounter with Hellenism*. Gifford Lectures. New Haven and London: Yale University Press, 1993.

———. *Credo: Historical and Theological Guide to Creeds and Confessions of Faith in the Christian Tradition*. Vol. 4 of *Creeds and Confessions of Faith in the Christian Tradition*. Edited by Jaroslav Pelikan and Valerie Hotchkiss. New Haven: Yale University Press, 2003.

———. *Interpreting the Bible and the Constitution*. New Haven and London: Yale University Press, 2004.

Penchansky, David. *The Betrayal of God: Ideological Conflict in Job*. Louisville: Westminster John Knox, 1990.

Pfeiffer, Robert H. *Introduction to the Old Testament*. London: A&C Black, 1948.

Philo Judaeus. *Philo*. Translated by F. H. Colson, G. H. Whitaker, and R. Marcus. 12 vols. Loeb Classical Library. Cambridge, MA: Harvard University Press, 1929–62.

Plaut, W. Gunther. *The Torah: A Modern Commentary*. New York: Union of American Hebrew Congregations, 1981.

Polzin, Robert. *Moses and the Deuteronomist: A Literary Study of the Deuteronomic History*. New York: Seabury, 1980.

Powell, Marvin A. "Weights and Measures." In *Anchor Bible Dictionary*, edited by David Noel Freeman, 6:897–908. 6 vols. New Haven: Yale University Press, 1992.

Preuss, Horst Dietrich. *Old Testament Theology*. Translated by Leo G. Perdue. 2 vols. Old Testament Library. Edinburgh: T&T Clark, 1995–96.

Pritchard, James B., ed. *Ancient Near Eastern Texts Relating to the Old Testament*. 3rd ed. Princeton: Princeton University Press, 1969.

Propp, William H. C. *Exodus 1–18*. Anchor Bible 2. New York: Doubleday, 1999.

Pullman, Philip. "Heat and Dust." *Third Way* 25/2 (April 2002): 22–26. Reprinted in *Church Times* (April 5, 2002): 14–15.

Pusey, Edward Bouverie. *The Minor Prophets*. Vol. 5, *Jonah and Nahum*. London: James Nisbet, 1907.

Rad, Gerhard von. "The Deuteronomistic Theology of History in the Book of Kings." In Gerhard von Rad's *Studies in Deuteronomy*, translated by David Stalker, 74–91. Studies in Biblical Theology 9. London: SCM, 1953. Translated from *Deuteronomium-Studien*. Forschungen zur Religion und Literatur des Alten und Neuen Testaments 40. Göttingen: Vandenhoeck & Ruprecht, 1948.

———. *Deuteronomy*. Translated by Dorothea Barton. Old Testament Library. London: SCM, 1966.

———. *Genesis*. Translated by John Marks. Old Testament Library. Rev. ed. London: SCM, 1972.

———. *Moses*. Edited by K. C. Hanson. Translated by Stephen Neill. 2nd ed. Cambridge: James Clarke, 2012. Translation of *Mose*. Wege im die Bibel 3. Göttingen: Vandenhoeck & Ruprecht, 1940.

———. "The Prophet Jonah." In *God at Work in Israel*, translated by John Marks, 58–70. Nashville: Abingdon, 1980.

———. *Old Testament Theology*. Translated by D. M. G. Stalker. 2 Vols. Old Testament Library. London: SCM, 1965–75.

———. *Wisdom in Israel*. Translated by James D. Martin. London: SCM, 1972. Translation of *Weisheit in Israel*. Neukirchen-Vluyn: Neukirchener Verlag, 1970.

Rendtorff, Rolf. *The Canonical Hebrew Bible: A Theology of the Old Testament*. Translated by David Orton. Tools for Biblical Study. Leiden: Deo, 2005.

———. "Isaiah 56:1 as a Key to the Formation of the Book of Isaiah." In *Canon and Theology: Overtures to an Old Testament Theology*, 181–89. Translated by Margaret Kohl. Overtures in Biblical Theology. Minneapolis: Fortress, 1993.

Reventlow, Henning Graf. *The Authority of the Bible and the Rise of the Modern World*. Translated by John Bowden. London: SCM, 1984.

Robertson, David. *The Old Testament and the Literary Critic*. Guides to Biblical Scholarship: Old Testament. Philadelphia: Fortress, 1977.

Robinson, Marilynne. *Gilead*. New York: Picador, 2004.

Rogerson, John W. *A Theology of the Old Testament: Cultural Memory, Communication and Being Human*. London: SPCK, 2009.

Sacks, Jonathan. "Credo." *The Times* [London], April 20, 2002.

Salters, Robin B. *Jonah and Lamentations*. Old Testament Guides. Sheffield: JSOT Press, 1994.

Sarna, Nahum. "Psalm 89: A Study in Inner Biblical Exegesis." In *Studies in Biblical Interpretation*, 377–94. Philadelphia: Jewish Publication Society, 2000.

Sasson, Jack M. *Jonah*. Anchor Bible 24B. New York: Doubleday, 1990.

Sawyer, John F. A. *Prophecy and the Prophets of the Old Testament*. Oxford Bible Studies. Oxford: Oxford University Press, 1987.

Schäfer-Lichtenberger, Christa. "JHWH, Israel und die Völker aus der Perspektive von Dtn 7." *Biblische Zeitschrift* 40 (1996): 194–218.

Schart, Aaron. "The Jonah Narrative within the Book of the Twelve." In *Perspectives on the Formation of the Book of the Twelve*, edited by Rainer Albertz, James D. Nogalski, and Jakob Wöhrle, 109–28. Beihefte zur Zeitschrift für die alttestamentliche Wissenschaft 433. Berlin and New York: de Gruyter, 2012.

Scheindlin, Raymond. *The Book of Job: Translation, Introduction, and Notes.* New York and London: W. W. Norton, 1998.

Schwartz, Regina M. *The Curse of Cain: The Violent Legacy of Monotheism.* Chicago: University of Chicago Press, 1997.

Scruton, Roger. *The Face of God.* Gifford Lectures. London and New York: Continuum, 2012.

Seibert, Eric A. *Disturbing Divine Behavior: Troubling Old Testament Images of God.* Minneapolis: Fortress, 2009.

Seitz, Christopher R. *The Goodly Fellowship of the Prophets: The Achievement of Association in Canon Formation.* Acadia Studies in Bible and Theology. Grand Rapids: Baker Academic, 2009.

———. "Of Mortal Appearance: Earthly Jesus and Isaiah as a Type of Christian Scripture." In *Figured Out: Typology and Providence in Christian Scripture*, 103–16. Louisville: Westminster John Knox, 2001.

———. *Prophecy and Hermeneutics: Toward a New Introduction to the Prophets.* Studies in Theological Interpretation. Grand Rapids: Baker Academic, 2007.

Sharp, Carolyn J. "'Are You for Us, or for Our Adversaries?' A Feminist and Postcolonial Interrogation of Joshua 2–12 for the Contemporary Church." *Interpretation* 66/2 (2012): 141–52.

Sherwood, Yvonne. *A Biblical Text and Its Afterlives: The Survival of Jonah in Western Culture.* Cambridge: Cambridge University Press, 2000.

Short, J. Randall. *The Surprising Election and Confirmation of King David.* Harvard Theological Studies 63. Cambridge, MA: Harvard University Press, 2010.

Simon, Uriel. *Jonah.* Jewish Publication Society Bible Commentary. Philadelphia: Jewish Publication Society, 1999.

Skinner, John. *Prophecy and Religion: Studies in the Life of Jeremiah.* Cambridge: Cambridge University Press, 1930.

Sommer, Benjamin D. "Appendix: Monotheism and Polytheism in Ancient Israel." In *The Bodies of God and the World of Ancient Israel*, 145–74. New York: Cambridge University Press, 2009.

———. "Dialogical Biblical Theology: A Jewish Approach to Reading Scripture Theologically." In *Biblical Theology: Introducing the Conversation*, by Leo G. Perdue, Robert Morgan, and Benjamin D. Sommer, 1–53. Library of Biblical Theology. Nashville: Abingdon, 2009.

Stafford, William. *The Way It Is: New and Selected Poems.* Minneapolis: Graywolf, 1998.

Steinbeck, John. *East of Eden.* New York: Viking, 1952.

Steinmetz, David. "Uncovering a Second Narrative: Detective Fiction and the Construction of Historical Method." In *The Art of Reading Scripture*, edited by Ellen F. Davis and Richard B. Hays, 54–65. Grand Rapids: Eerdmans, 2003.

Stern, Philip D. *The Biblical Ḥerem: A Window on Israel's Religious Experience*. Brown Judaic Studies 211. Atlanta: Scholars Press, 1991.

Sugirtharajah, R. S. *Exploring Postcolonial Biblical Criticism: History, Method, Practice* Chichester: Wiley-Blackwell, 2012.

Sweeney, Marvin. "Jonah." In *The Twelve Prophets*, 1:301–34. 2 vols. Berit Olam. Collegeville, MN: Liturgical Press, 2000.

Tate, Marvin E. *Psalms 51–100*. Word Biblical Commentary 20. Dallas: Word, 1990.

Terrien, Samuel. *The Psalms: Strophic Structure and Theological Commentary*. Eerdmans Critical Commentary. Grand Rapids: Eerdmans, 2003.

Tertullian. *La chair du Christ*. Edited, translated, and annotated by J.-P. Mahé. 2 vols. Sources chrétiennes 216–17. Paris: Cerf, 1975.

Theodoret of Cyrus. *Commentary on the Psalms: Psalms 1–72*. Translated by Robert Charles Hill. Fathers of the Church 101. Washington, DC: Catholic University of America Press, 2000.

Thompson, John A. *Deuteronomy*. Tyndale Old Testament Commentaries. London: InterVarsity, 1974.

Tigay, Jeffrey. *The JPS Torah Commentary: Deuteronomy*. Philadelphia and Jerusalem: Jewish Publication Society, 1996.

Tolkien, J. R. R. *The Letters of J. R. R. Tolkien*. Edited by Humphrey Carpenter. London: George Allen & Unwin, 1981.

———. *The Return of the King*. London: George Allen & Unwin, 1965.

Trible, Phyllis. "Divine Incongruities in the Book of Jonah." In *God in the Fray: A Tribute to Walter Brueggemann*, edited by Tod Linafelt and Timothy K. Beal, 198–208. Minneapolis: Fortress, 1998.

Vallely, Paul. "A Protest Founded on the Gospels." *Church Times* [Anglican, UK], August 24, 2012.

Vanhoozer, Kevin J. "On Scripture." In *The Cambridge Companion to C. S. Lewis*, edited by Robert MacSwain and Michael Ward, 75–88. Cambridge: Cambridge University Press, 2010.

Veijola, Timo. "Höre Israel! Der Sinn und Hintergrund von Deuteronomium VI 4–9." *Vetus Testamentum* 42 (1992): 528–41.

———. "The Witness in the Clouds: Ps 89:38." *Journal of Biblical Literature* 107 (1988): 413–17.

Verbin, Nehama. *Divinely Abused: A Philosophical Perspective on Job and His Kin*. London and New York: Continuum, 2011.

Volf, Miroslav. "Christianity and Violence." In *War in the Bible and Terrorism in the Twenty-First Century*, edited by Richard S. Hess and Elmer A. Martens, 1–17. Bulletin for Biblical Research Supplements 2. Winona Lake, IN: Eisenbrauns, 2008.

Wagner, Siegfried. "*Chûs.*" In *Theological Dictionary of the Old Testament*, 4:271–77. Edited by G. Johannes Botterweck, Helmer Ringgren, and Heinz-Josef Fabry. 15 vols. Grand Rapids: Eerdmans, 1974–2006.

Waltke, Bruce K., with Charles Yu. *An Old Testament Theology: An Exegetical, Canonical, and Thematic Approach.* Grand Rapids: Zondervan, 2007.

Ward, James M. "The Literary Form and Liturgical Background of Psalm LXXXIX." *Vetus Testamentum* 11 (1961): 321–39.

Warrior, Robert Allen. "Canaanites, Cowboys, and Indians: Deliverance, Conquest, and Liberation Theology Today." In *The Postmodern Bible Reader*, edited by David Jobling, Tina Pippin, and Ronald Schleifer, 188–94. Oxford: Blackwell, 2001.

Weeks, Stuart. *An Introduction to the Study of Wisdom Literature.* London and New York: T&T Clark, 2010.

Weinfeld, Moshe. "The Ban on the Canaanites in the Biblical Codes and Its Historical Development." In *History and Traditions of Early Israel: Studies Presented to Eduard Nielsen*, edited by André Lemaire and Benedikt Otzen, 142–60. Vetus Testamentum: Supplement Series 50. Leiden: Brill, 1993.

———. *Deuteronomy and the Deuteronomic School.* Oxford: Clarendon, 1972.

———. *Deuteronomy 1–11.* Anchor Bible 5. New York: Doubleday, 1991.

———. "Expulsion, Dispossession, and Extermination of the Pre-Israelite Population in the Biblical Sources." In *The Promise of the Land: The Inheritance of the Land of Canaan by the Israelites*, 76–98. Taubman Lectures in Jewish Studies 3. Berkeley: University of California Press, 1993.

Weiser, Artur. *The Psalms.* Translated by Herbert Hartwell. Old Testament Library. London: SCM, 1962. Translation of *Die Psalmen.* 5th ed. Das Alte Testament Deutsch 14–15. Göttingen: Vandenhoeck & Ruprecht, 1959.

Wellhausen, Julius. *The Book of Psalms.* Translation by Horace Howard Furness and John Taylor. Sacred Books of the Old and New Testaments: A New English Translation. New York: Dodd, Mead, 1898.

Whybray, R. Norman. *Job.* Readings: A New Biblical Commentary. Sheffield: Sheffield Academic Press, 1998.

———. "'Shall Not the Judge of All the Earth Do What Is Just?' God's Oppression of the Innocent in the Old Testament." In *Shall Not the Judge of All the Earth Do What Is Just? Studies on the Nature of God in Tribute to James L. Crenshaw*, edited by David Penchansky and Paul L. Redditt, 1–19. Winona Lake, IN: Eisenbrauns, 2000.

Wiesel, Elie. *One Generation After.* Translated by Lily Edelman and the author. New York: Random House, 1970.

Wiesenthal, Simon. *The Sunflower: On the Possibilities and Limits of Forgiveness.* 2nd ed. New York: Schocken Books, 1997.

Williams, Rowan. *Faith in the Public Square.* London: Bloomsbury, 2012.

———. "Remorse." In *Lost Icons: Reflections on Cultural Bereavement*, 95–138. Edinburgh: T&T Clark, 2000.

Williamson, H. G. M. *The Book Called Isaiah.* Oxford: Clarendon, 1994.

————. *Isaiah 1–5*. International Critical Commentary. London and New York: T&T Clark, 2006.

Wilson, Gerald H. *The Editing of the Hebrew Psalter*. Society of Biblical Literature Dissertation Series 76. Chico, CA: Scholars Press, 1985.

————. *Psalms*. Vol. 1. The NIV Application Commentary. Grand Rapids: Zondervan, 2002.

Wolde, Ellen van. *Mr and Mrs Job*. London: SCM, 1997.

Wolff, Hans Walter. *Obadiah and Jonah: A Commentary*. Translated by Margaret Kohl. Minneapolis: Augsburg, 1986. Translation of *Dodekapropheton*. Vol. 3, *Obadja und Jona*. Biblischer Kommentar Altes Testament. Neukirchen-Vluyn: Neukirchener Verlag, 1977.

Wright, N. T. "Monotheism, Christology and Ethics: 1 Corinthians 8." In *The Climax of the Covenant*, 120–36. Edinburgh: T&T Clark, 1991.

Wyschogrod, Michael. *The Body of Faith: God in the People Israel*. Northvale, NJ: Jason Aronson, 1996.

Younger, K. Lawson. "Some Recent Discussion on the Ḥerem." In *Far from Minimal: Celebrating the Work and Influence of Philip R. Davies*, edited by Duncan Burns and John W. Rogerson, 505–22. Library of Hebrew Bible / Old Testament Studies 484. London: T&T Clark, 2012.

Zimmerli, Walther. *Old Testament Theology in Outline*. Translated by David E. Green. Edinburgh: T&T Clark, 1978.

Zvi, Ehud Ben. "Infinite but Limited Diversity: A Heuristic, Theoretical Framework for Analyzing Different Interpretations of the Book of Jonah." In *Signs of Jonah: Reading and Rereading in Ancient Yehud*, 129–54. Journal for the Study of the Old Testament: Supplement Series 367. London: Sheffield Academic Press, 2003.

————. "Jonah." In *The Jewish Study Bible*, edited by Adele Berlin and Marc Zvi Brettler, 1198–1204. Oxford and New York: Oxford University Press, 2004.

Zvi, Ehud Ben, and James D. Nogalski. *Two Sides of a Coin: Juxtaposing Views on Interpreting the Book of the Twelve/the Twelve Prophetic Books*. AG 201. Piscataway, NJ: Gorgias, 2009.

Author Index

Subject Index

abasement, 164–79
Abraham, 43
    as archetypal embodiment of Israel, 44
    election of, 46
    as focus of Yhwh's delight, 45
    promise to, 213
    testing of, 245
Abishag, 19n27
abuse, ascribed to God, 258
Achan, 71
action movie, conventions in, 260–61
Advent, 151
affliction, 101, 276
'aḥat, 20, 226–27
Ahaz, 128n41, 150–51, 172
'āhēv, 21–24, 43
Ahijah, 147
'almāh, 19n27
altar, 16
    beyond Jordan, 71
Amalek, 134
Ambrose (of Milan), 149
America/American
    civil religion, 40
    constitution, analogy with biblical
        interpretation, 161–62
    prophetic interest in, 154
    Puritans in, 53
Ames, John, 181
anachronisms, 160–61
'ānāw, 96–98
ancient Near East, 57–58, 283
    ethics of, 57–58
ancient world, 18
anointed, 234, 237

Anselm (of Canterbury), 102, 240n59
anthropomorphism, 108, 129–30
Antiochus Epiphanes, 149, 219
anxiety
    ideological, 2
    modern Western, 57, 72
    of selective appropriation, 30
apocalyptic literature, 148–49
    distinction from prophecy, 148
apologetic argument, 187
apostasy, 38
apostolic era, 13
appropriation, 32, 72, 283–84
    history of, 23
    use of imagination in, 72–73
    logic of, 30
    of Old Testament, 30, 42, 49, 157–58
    of pain and perplexity, 233
archaeology/archaeological, 14, 69
Arianism, 12
Aristotle, 113
ark, the, 84
Assyria/Assyrian, 58n55, 150, 168, 185, 199–
        200, 207, 230, 236
astrology, 154–55
atheism, 40
Augustine (of Hippo), 115, 149–50, 183–84,
        187, 197, 240n59
Auschwitz, 238
Austen, Jane, 158–59
'ayin, 34

Baal, prophets of, 218
Babylon, Babylonian, 33, 168
    king, 173

313

Scripture Index